ISBN 978-1-330-35018-8
PIBN 10036807

Similar Books Are Available from
www.forgottenbooks.com

1 MONTH OF
FREE
READING

at
www.ForgottenBooks.com

By purchasing this book you are eligible for one month membership to ForgottenBooks.com, giving you unlimited access to our entire collection of over 700,000 titles via our web site and mobile apps.

To claim your free month visit:
www.forgottenbooks.com/free36807

ELEMENTARY BOOK-KEEPING

A TEXT-BOOK FOR BEGINNERS

BY

L. CUTHBERT CROPPER

*Fellow of the Institute of Chartered Accountants in England and Wales;
Senior Examiner in Book-keeping to the London Chamber of
Commerce; an Examiner to the Royal Society of Arts,
and formerly a Lecturer to the Chartered
Accountant Students' Society of
London
Author of "Book-keeping and Accounts," a text-book for Intermediate
and Advanced Students of Book-keeping*

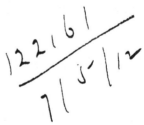

LONDON

MACDONALD AND EVANS

4 ADAM STREET, ADELPHI, W.C.

1911

Printed by
BALLANTYNE & COMPANY LTD.
Tavistock Street Covent Garden
London

PREFACE

In a former work, *Book-keeping and Accounts*, written for students of the "Intermediate" and "Advanced" grades, the author remarked that there is now no lack of competent teaching of Book-keeping on practical and modern lines for students of these grades.

It is a matter of regret that the same commendation cannot be accorded to the teaching, as a whole, in the "Elementary" grades.

Much of the Elementary examination work of the present day shows that methods and phraseology long since obsolete in the commercial world are still widely taught.

This defect probably explains the humiliating fact that many business men, when engaging lads for counting-house work, express a preference for such as "have not been taught Book-keeping at school." A scrutiny of some of the text-books still widely used sufficiently proves that this preference is not an altogether unfounded prejudice. For, in many of these books, the student is instructed in the use of "Waste Books," "Balance Accounts," and "Goods Accounts," and is taught to journalise every item, *including Cash*—methods which had been discarded in the commercial world before the author commenced his professional experience more than twenty years ago!

The author recognises that some of these methods permit the theory of Book-keeping to be presented in an apparently simple way, easy to teach by text-book and in class, when compared with the direct introduction of the beginner to modern counting-house usages. In the opinion of the author, however, it is unfair that the young student should be handicapped by the inculcation of methods and principles which he must painfully unlearn as soon as he comes to close grip with actual business practice, when he could be introduced, at the

v

outset, to modern methods and be given a really useful intro-duction to his life's work.

Again, some of the elementary text-books in current use present the student with such a bare skeleton of even the preliminary stages of double-entry Book-keeping that, when he has mastered the lessons put before him, he has acquired no knowledge, even of the elements of Book-keeping, that is of any practical value.

These serious shortcomings have been in constant evidence in the many thousands of examination papers which have passed through the author's hands.

The experience thus gained has been kept constantly in mind in the preparation of this little treatise, and earnest endeavour has been made to ensure:

(a) That the student shall have nothing whatever to *unlearn* when faced by actual counting-house work.

(b) That, while presenting the theory of Book-keeping by double entry in as simple a manner as the natural difficulty of the subject will permit, each progressive step has been made with a view to carrying the student to the conclusion which must be reached if instruction is to be practically useful.

(c) That the instruction shall be based upon modern commercial usage, and fulfil throughout the require-ments of the principal bodies who examine in the subject.

The author has gratefully to acknowledge the valuable assistance rendered by his former pupil, Mr. Stanley G. Smith, A.C.A., "Final" Prizeman, Institute of Chartered Accountants.

L. C. C.

16 FINSBURY CIRCUS,
LONDON, E.C,

CONTENTS

ELEMENTARY BOOK-KEEPING

CHAPTER I

ELEMENTARY COMMERCIAL TERMS

BEFORE I attempt to explain to you how a business man "writes up" or "keeps" his books of account, it will be better, I think, if I explain a few elementary commercial matters which are of daily occurrence in the business life of a trader.

If you will carefully read and remember the explanations which follow, you will have much less trouble in grasping the detailed instructions which are given in the remainder of the book. These explanations and definitions will also serve the purpose of giving you some idea of the nature of the dealings which a merchant has to record in his business books.

BOOK-KEEPING is the art of recording in a suitable form a person's business dealings, so that, at any time, their nature and effect may be clearly seen.

A trader should be able to ascertain from his books clearly and readily how he stands, and what is the result of his various transactions.

The test of good book-keeping is that it should supply the greatest amount of necessary information with the least possible trouble.

Many students commence their study of this subject with the idea that book-keeping begins and ends with the record of all moneys received and paid.

As you will soon learn, however, there are a great many transactions in which no money passes at all.

AN ACCOUNT is a statement of a particular matter, or series of dealings expressed, according to book-keeping form, in words and figures.

The matters and figures set forth in an "Account" are usually arranged together so that the result of them may be readily seen.

The simplest form of Account is the ordinary tradesman's bill with which nearly everybody is familiar.

In such a "Bill," or "Account," the cost prices of the various goods supplied by the tradesman to his customer are entered

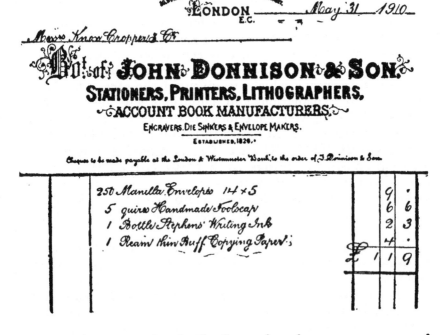

underneath one another in the form of a column or a compound addition sum. When the entries are complete, this column is added up in order to show the total amount which the customer owes to the tradesman.

In business a statement of goods supplied by a trader to his customer is called an Invoice. A specimen form of an Invoice is given above.

The *invoice* given on this page shows only one set of money columns and a single total representing the value of the goods sold by the trader to his customer.

Very little thought will show you, however, that for the trader's own book-keeping purposes an account of this kind is incomplete. Something more must be added to the above figures in order that the trader's dealings with any particular customer may be clearly shown.

It is not enough for the trader to show what he has sold to his customer. He must also show in his books what his customer has paid to him. If the trader did not do this, he might ask his customer to pay his bill twice over!

In order to show clearly how matters stand as between the trader and his customers, the trader's books are ruled with every page divided into two halves by means of a vertical line ruled down the centre of each page. On that part of the page which stands to the left of this vertical line, all the goods supplied by the trader to his customer are set out and arranged one under another. On the other part of the page all the sums of money received by the trader from his customer are entered in a similar manner. If the customer duly pays to the trader all that he owes him, the figures on the left-hand side of the page, for the goods supplied, will total up to the same amount as the figures on the right-hand side of the page, for money received from the customer. This agreement of the two totals shows that, at the end of these various dealings, neither party owes anything to the other.

The total of the specimen Invoice given on p. 2 has been set out below on the left hand of a two-sided account, together with the amounts of four other invoices for goods bought previously. It has been assumed that Messrs. Knox, Cropper and Co. have paid for the goods in instalments, viz., 15s. 6d., 6s. 3d. and £1 1s. 9d. respectively. These sums are duly set out on the right-hand side of the account. You will notice that each side of the account totals up to £2 3s. 6d., and this agreement shows that everything has been settled between the parties.

Knox, Cropper & Co.

1910.		S.B.	£	s.	d.	1910.		C.B.	£	s.	d.
May 11	To Goods	139		9	0	May 17	By Cash	91		15	6
„ 16	„ „	„		6	6			C.B.			
„ 18	„ „	„		2	3	„ 22	„ „	99		^	3
„ 21	„ „	„		4	0			C.B.			
„ 31	„ „	140	1	1	9	„ 31	„ „	140	1	1	9
		£	2	3	6			£	2	3	6

The form of the two-sided account given above is that known as a **Ledger Account.** The Ledger is the principal book of account kept by a trader, and in it are recorded for future reference the various "accounts" showing his dealings with his customers and his creditors. The ordinary form of Ledger Account, as will be made clear later in this treatise, can be used to contain information as to other important matters relating to the trader's every day dealings. The form of ruling used for a Ledger Account kept for a *person* can be used equally well to record the trader's dealing in *things—e.g.* "Cash" and "Goods." A Ledger Account can also be framed so as to contain a variety of other information which a trader needs. These various matters will be explained in a subsequent chapter.

At this stage it will suffice to say that if you were engaged in business your Ledger, if properly kept, would contain the following different kinds of accounts, viz.:

1. **Personal Accounts**—*i.e.* accounts showing your dealings with **persons.**

2. **Real Accounts**—*i.e.* accounts showing your dealings in **things,** *e.g.* Cash, Horses, Buildings, Furniture, Goods, &c.

3. **Nominal Accounts**—*i.e.* accounts giving you particular information about your business, other than the matters shown by the two classes of accounts mentioned above. Nominal Accounts are usually either (*a*) accounts showing profits you have made; (*b*) accounts showing losses you have sustained; or (*c*) an account showing what you are worth after allowing for all your debts.

The difference between the total of the entries made on the debit side of a given Ledger Account, when compared with the total of the entries on the credit side, is called the **balance of** the account.

The following procedure is necessary to "Balance" a Ledger Account:

(*a*) In order to make the two sides, debit and credit, add up to the same total, the *difference* between the two sides of the account must be inserted on whichever side is the smaller of the two

(*b*) After the "Balance" has been inserted, the two sides of the account must be added and "ruled off."

(*c*) The "Balance" of the account must be entered a second time, below the "ruling off," upon the *opposite* side to that on which it was entered before the account was ruled off. The second entry of the "Balance" forms the starting balance of the account for the ensuing period, and frees the account from unwieldy totals.

An example of a "balanced" account is given below. It is the account of Messrs. J. Francis & Co., as it would appear in your Ledger, assuming that you were a coffee merchant who had sold them parcels of coffee from time to time, and received various sums of Cash from them at different dates. When the account has been "balanced" Messrs. J. Francis and Co. are shown as owing you £292 10s. 0d.

Dr.*			£	s.	d.				£	s.	d.
1910 Mar. 1	To 30 bags of coffee	S.	65	10	0	1910. Mar. 22	By Cash	C.	65	10	0
„ 12	„ 100 bags of coffee	S.	292	10	0	„ 23	„ „	C.	15	10	0
„ 22	„ 30 bags of coffee	S.	65	10	0	„ 23	„ „	C.	50	0	0
						„ 31	„ Balance carried forward	✓	292	10	0
		£	423	10	0			£	423	10	0
1910. Mar. 31	To Balance brought down .	✓	292	10	0						

J. FRANCIS & Co. Cr.*

* For the explanation of these headings see under "Debtor" and "Creditor."

DEBTOR: a person who owes you something.

CREDITOR: a person to whom you owe something.

"**DR.**" is a contraction of "Debtor"; "**CR.**" is a contraction of "Creditor."

The left-hand side of a Ledger account is known as the **Debit** (or **Dr.**) side. The right-hand side of the account is known as the **Credit** (or **Cr.**) side. If the debit side of an account is greater than the credit side, the *difference* between the two sides is called a **Debit Balance**. If the credit side is the greater of the two the necessary "Balance" is called a **Credit Balance**. The entry of an item on the debit side of a Ledger account is often referred to as "*Debiting*" that item to the particular Ledger account.

The verb "*To Credit*" is similarly used to express the making of entries on the credit side of an account.

POSTING is the book-keeping term applied to the making of entries in the Ledger. When you have entered a transaction in the Ledger you are said to have "posted" it. All entries transferred, or " posted," from the subsidiary books to the Ledger bear page references.

A " folio " column is provided in all books of account, and the page of the Ledger to which the item has been " posted " is entered in that column. The corresponding column in the Ledger bears the page of the subsidiary book from which the item has been " posted."

TRANSACTIONS is the term applied to a business man's dealings in money or goods, or with persons.

In other words, any event which needs to be recorded in a trader's books is termed a " Transaction."

A business man's transactions usually consist chiefly of :

1. Paying and receiving money.
2. Buying and selling goods.

The object of a business man is to make profits by means of his transactions.

The usual manner in which a business man makes profits is by purchasing, or making, certain kinds of saleable articles, and by selling them for more than they have cost him. If the business man *makes* the goods which he sells he is called a **Manufacturer**; if, on the other hand, he *buys* the goods ready for immediate sale from a manufacturer, he is called a **Merchant**.

PROFIT.—The difference between the price at which a business man sells his goods and the price which he has paid for them, if he is a merchant, or what they have cost him to make, if he is a manufacturer, is called **Gross Profit**. Gross profit is the difference between the cost price and the selling price, and does not include any allowance for the business man's " office " and other trading expenses.

If the trader's office expenses, and all the other necessary expenses incurred in carrying on his business, are deducted from the " Gross Profit," the amount of profit then remaining is called the " Net Profit."

The " Net Profit " made by a business man represents the actual profit which he has made after paying all expenses. In other words, the " Net Profit " represents the actual income which the trader has derived from his business.

ASSETS (French, *assez* = enough).—The whole of a trader's possessions at any particular date are, in book-keeping, termed his " Assets." The word is also used in the singular number (Asset) to represent a particular piece of property.

LIABILITIES (French, *lier* = to bind).—The total amount owing by a trader to his creditors at any particular date is, in book-keeping, termed his "Liabilities." "Liability," in the singular number, represents a debt owing by a trader, or a claim which can be made upon him by any one else.

CAPITAL.—The amount by which a trader's assets exceed his liabilities at any particular date is, in book-keeping, termed his "Capital." The term "Capital" represents the trader's estimated real or "net worth" at that date—*i.e.* the amount of money which he might be expected to have left after paying all his liabilities, if he were to sell the whole of his possessions for cash.

SOLVENCY.—If a trader's assets equal, or exceed, his liabilities he is obviously able to pay all his debts. He is then said to be "Solvent" (Latin, *solvere* = to pay). If a trader's liabilities exceed his assets it will be obvious that he cannot pay *all* his debts, and he is therefore said to be "Insolvent."

An insolvent person is liable to be made "Bankrupt" by his creditors. On "Bankruptcy" occurring, a trader's assets are taken from him by law, and are divided among his creditors in proportion to their claims.

BANKS AND BANKING.—In olden times, traders used to keep all their cash locked in strong boxes at their places of business. At the present time business men rarely keep much cash in their possession, but leave the greater part of their money with their Bankers.

A **Banker** is a person whose business it is to take charge of money for other people. The largest Bank in the United Kingdom is the Post Office Savings Bank, conducted by the Government, which holds over £160,000,000 of depositors' money. This Bank, however, is one which was formed in order to enable people to save money, and differs considerably from the ordinary Commercial Bank—one important difference being that a Savings Bank usually requires a short period of notice before repaying money deposited with it.

The ordinary Commercial Bank holds the money left with it by its customers on the understanding that it must immediately repay the whole, or any part of it, whenever the customer requires it to do so. A Banker makes these repayments to the person who brings him a written order, signed by his customer, directing payment out of that customer's balance of a specified sum of money. These written orders are known as **Cheques.** Cheques must be written, according to a certain

8 ELEMENTARY BOOK-KEEPING
legal form, and require to bear a penny stamp (either an
The system of Banking explained above has become very

PETTY CASH.—The sums of cash kept by a business man
in his cash-box for the purpose of making small payments are,
business it is necessary to make trifling purchases, or to incur

SALES.—A business man usually sells his goods to his
standing that the customer shall pay for them at the end of

Sales effected for immediate payment are known as "**Sales

Sales effected upon the understanding that they shall be paid
for at some future date are known as "**Sales on Credit**" or
"**Credit Sales.**"

"Cash Sales" are, generally speaking, less frequent than
"Credit Sales." It is usually to the advantage of a trader to
them in order to re-sell them gradually, and in smaller quan-

Special varieties of sales are also to be met with. For example,
sales are made "**on sale or return,**" and on the "**hire-purchase**"
system. In the former case the goods are despatched by a
standing that the latter is to sell them if possible. If the goods
remain unsold they may be returned to the sender. In cases
of this kind the shopkeeper does not become personally liable to

"**Hire-purchase**" sales are those effected upon the understanding that payment for the goods is to be made by the buyer
in instalments spread over a number of months or years. Until
the last instalment has been paid, the goods remain the legal
property of the seller ; and until the purchase has been completed, the purchaser is, in a legal sense, only a "hirer" of the

DISCOUNT.—If a trader has sold goods to a customer "on

count" if the latter pays for the goods before the day agreed upon. This kind of discount is an allowance made from the customer's debt to encourage prompt payment, and is called a **"Cash Discount."**

Another kind of " Discount " is frequently met with, and you must be careful not to confuse the two.

Merchants often issue printed price lists and catalogues, in which the goods they deal in are offered for sale at fixed prices. From these fixed, or " list," prices they frequently make deductions varying with the standing of the proposed buyer, or with the rise and fall in value of similar goods in the market.   These deductions from the " list " price of the particular goods are called **"Trade Discounts."** In a merchant's books " Trade Discounts " are entered as a deduction from the " list " price of the goods bought; the buyer is only shown as owing the official list price *minus* the " Trade Discount."

Example.—Ten bicycles are sold by you " on credit " to A. Brown on January 1, 1910, at £10 each, subject to a " Trade Discount " of 10 per cent. A. Brown is not obliged to pay for these bicycles until three months after buying them, but if he pays within one month after buying them from you, he is to be entitled to a " Cash Discount " of, say, 5 per cent.

Answer.—A. Brown must be treated by you in your books as owing you, not £100, but £100 less 10 per cent. " Trade Discount "—*i.e.* £90.

If A. Brown prefers to do so, he can wait until the end of March 1910, and he must then pay you the £90. On the other hand, should he elect to discharge his debt to you not later than the end of January 1910, he is entitled to pay you £85 10s. only—*i.e.* £90, less 5 per cent. " Cash Discount "— in full settlement of all that he owes you.

You must take particular notice that in this example the " Cash Discount " is calculated on the amount of cash actually due from A. Brown (£90), and not upon the " list " price of the bicycles (£100).   In cases where you find a " Trade Discount " and a " Cash Discount " appearing in connection with the same transaction, you must always calculate the " Cash Discount " upon the amount due *after* deducting the " Trade Discount."

BILLS OF EXCHANGE.—When a trader sells goods to a customer " on credit," it is frequently found that the person who buys them prefers to wait until the end of the agreed period of credit before he pays for the goods. This experience is common notwithstanding any cash discount which the seller may offer in order to induce his customer to pay him promptly. On the other hand, a trader who has sold goods to a customer "on credit" would frequently prefer to have them paid for before the end of the stated time agreed upon. The trader himself has his own creditors to pay, and his own business to carry on, and he naturally prefers to have ready money for his goods.

In order to combine the desire of the average debtor not to pay his debt until the appointed time with the desire of the average creditor for speedy payment, documents known as "Bills of Exchange" are made use of.

A **Bill of Exchange** is a short written document signed by a debtor, whereby he promises to pay his creditor a certain sum of money on a stated day. The sum of money referred to in the Bill is payable not only to the creditor to whom the Bill was originally given, but alternatively to any person who may acquire the Bill.

The usefulness of a Bill of Exchange to the creditor who receives it arises mainly out of the fact that, if the debtor who has signed it is reputed to be solvent and is well thought of locally, the creditor will have no difficulty in turning the "Bill" into ready money, although it may not yet be due for payment. Banks and other institutions are always willing to purchase, at a "Discount," that is to say, for something less than their face value, Bills of Exchange bearing the signatures of traders who are well regarded commercially. Bankers buy Bills of Exchange as temporary investments for their funds.

Payment of a Bill of Exchange which is expressed to be payable at any given date, or after the expiration of any particular period of time, cannot be enforced legally until the expiration of three days beyond the stated date or time : *e.g.* a Bill which is dated January 1, 1910, and is stated as being payable one month * after the date it bears, falls due for payment, not on February 1, 1910, but on February 4, 1910. These additional days are called **"Days of Grace,"** and must always be taken into account in ascertaining when a Bill of Exchange will fall due for payment.

The "Discount" deducted by Bankers when buying a Bill of Exchange is arrived at as follows :

The interest, at a given rate per cent. per annum, upon the face value of the Bill is calculated from the day upon

* *Note.*—If a period of time is mentioned in months, calendar months are to be understood.

which the Bill was "discounted" until the day upon which (after allowing for the three "Days of Grace") it will fall due for payment. The amount of interest calculated in this manner represents the amount of the "Discount" which will be charged by the Banker who buys the Bill.

Example.—If a Bill for £100, dated January 1, 1910, payable "one month after date"—*i.e.* February 4, 1910—is "discounted" on January 1, 1910, at 4 per cent. per annum, the amount of the "Discount" is the interest on £100 for 34 days at 4 per cent. per annum—*i.e.* 7s. 5d. The seller of the Bill consequently receives only £99 12s. 7d. for it, the Bank receiving the whole £100 at its due date. The 7s. 5d. represents the Bank's remuneration for parting with £99 12s. 7d. of its funds for the 34 days.

In actual form a Bill of Exchange takes the shape of a letter written by the creditor to his debtor, requesting the latter to pay a certain sum of money on a certain date, either to the creditor himself or to his "Order." The debtor signifies his assent to this request, and binds himself to comply with it, by writing his signature across the written request itself, adding sometimes the word "Accepted," and usually indicating a place where the money will be paid. Further remarks concerning the technicalities of Bills of Exchange will be found in Chapter XII.

Bills of Exchange received by a man from his debtors whereby the latter promise to pay him certain sums of money are called, in his books, **Bills Receivable.**

Bills of Exchange given by a man to his creditors whereby he promises to pay them certain sums of money are called, in his books, **Bills Payable.**

Every Bill of Exchange is thus a "Bill Receivable" from the point of view of the person who receives it, and a "Bill Payable" from the point of view of the person who gives it.

RETURNS.—When a trader makes purchases of goods it sometimes happens that the goods delivered are not the particular goods which were ordered. They may be of a different quality to that which was stipulated for, or of a poorer quality than the "Sample" which was originally shown, or they may be faulty or damaged. Again, more goods may have been sent than were ordered.

In these and similar cases the trader will send back the goods with which he is dissatisfied, to the person from whom he bought them. At the same time he will claim that whatever he has been charged for the unsatisfactory goods shall be refunded to him, or deducted from the invoice. The seller, in such cases, usually makes the allowance claimed.

Goods so sent back by a person to whom they have been sold or delivered are known as "Goods Returned," or "Returns"; they are called **Returns Outwards** by the person who sends them back, and **Returns Inwards** by the person who receives them back.

A **TRIAL BALANCE** is a list of the balances of the accounts appearing in a trader's ledger. When extracting such a list the debit balances are always separated from the credit balances.

A **BALANCE SHEET** is a statement showing the assets and liabilities of a trader, company, or firm. In other words, a Balance Sheet is a statement which shows the financial position of the business to which it relates.

A **CONSIGNMENT** is a parcel of goods sent by one merchant, the **Consignor**, to another, the **Consignee**, the latter being instructed to sell the goods and to send the proceeds to the consignor. The consignee is usually paid for his trouble by being allowed to keep a small percentage of the money which he obtains for the consignment. This percentage is called "**Commission.**"

A **SOLE TRADER** is a person who trades alone—*i.e.* without partners.

A **FIRM**, or a **PARTNERSHIP**, is a business owned jointly by a number of persons. Partnership is legally defined as "the relation which subsists between persons carrying on a business in common with a view to profit."

A **COMPANY** is an association of persons for trading or other purposes. Certain legal formalities must be complied with before such an association can be formed. A Company exists by itself, as if it were a legal person, and is, in theory, perpetual. It is not affected by the death of its members, as is the case with a partnership.

A **LIMITED LIABILITY COMPANY** is a company the members of which cannot be called upon for more than a stated sum of money, however deeply involved in debt the company may become. The sum for which any individual member is liable is limited to the amount of stock, or the number of shares, which he has agreed to purchase.

An **UNLIMITED COMPANY** is a company the members of which are each and all liable for the whole of the company's debts without restriction. Very few of such companies now exist. The members of a partnership are also subject to unlimited liability as regards the debts of the partnership.

BAD DEBTS are debts due to you but which, so far as you can judge, will never be paid. **DOUBTFUL DEBTS** are debts that are due to you but which you think will probably not be paid in full.

DRAWINGS are the sums periodically taken, or "Drawn," by a business man out of his business for his private purposes. They are really sums drawn by the trader in anticipation of the profits which he estimates that he is making.

STOCK or **STOCK-IN-TRADE** is the term used to denote the total amount of goods held for future sale in any given business at any particular date.

EXERCISES.

1A.

1. What is meant by the term "Book-keeping"?
2. What information should a trader's books provide him with? What test must be applied to decide whether a given system of book-keeping is a good one or not?
3. Define and explain an "Account."
4. From the following particulars prepare a form of Invoice to be rendered by A. Robinson & Co. to R. May :- March 2, 1910, A. Robinson & Co. sold to R. May on credit ½ gross hair-pin boxes @ 80s. per gross, 4 dozen glove boxes @ 20s. per dozen, 4 dozen collar boxes @ 16s. per dozen, and ¼ gross fancy trinket boxes @ £7 10s. 0d. per gross.
5. Arrange the transactions set forth in Question 4, together with the following additional information, in the form of an account kept by A. Robinson & Co. in order to show their dealings with R. May, viz. : Cash received by A. Robinson & Co. from R. May March 21, 1910, £2 15s. 0d. ; March 29, 1910, £1 17s. 6d. ; April, 2, 1910, £6 9s. 0d.
6. What is a "Ledger"?

1B.

1. How many different classes of accounts are usually to be found in a Ledger? State the characteristic features of each class of account.
2. What is meant by the process of "balancing" a Ledger Account?
3. Explain the following terms : Debtor, Creditor, Dr. side of a Ledger Account, Cr. balance of a Ledger Account.
4. What is meant by "Posting" a ledger?
5. Explain the terms "Transactions," "Folio."
6. Explain the term "Profits"? How does a business man usually make profits?

1C.

1. What are (a) Gross Profits, (b) Net Profits? Explain the difference between the two terms.
2. What are (a) Assets, (b) Liabilities?

3. What name is given to the difference between a trader's Assets and his Liabilities? What does this difference represent?

4. Explain the terms (1) Solvent, (2) Insolvent, (3) Bankrupt.

5. What is the function of a Banker? Explain briefly the principles upon which he carries on his business.

6. What is the "Petty Cash"? Explain its uses.

1D.

1. What is a cheque?

2. Explain "Cash" sales, and sales "on Credit," stating in what respects they differ. Which class of sale is more usual in business?

3. What are sales made "on sale or return," and "on hire-purchase."

4. What are (1) "Cash Discounts," and (2) "Trade Discounts"? Compare these two kinds of discount. Under what circumstances does a "Trade Discount" arise?

5. You purchase on March 2, 1910, from the Swiftsure Cycle Co., Ltd., ten "Velox" bicycles listed in their catalogue at £7 10s. 0d. each. You are allowed a "Trade Discount" of 10 per cent. from the list price, because you are buying the bicycles for export, and you are offered a "Cash Discount" of 2½ per cent. for payment within 14 days of delivery in London. Assuming that you pay for the bicycles on March 10, 1910, what will be the amount of the cheque which you will send to the Cycle Company?

6. You sell to R. Jones on March 3, 1910, 50 pairs of 12 button length ladies' Chamois gloves at the "list" price of 2s. per pair, subject to 5 per cent. "Trade Discount," and 4 ladies' hats, Paris models, at £6 10s. 0d. for the four. How much does R. Jones owe you for these various goods?

1E.

1. What is a Bill of Exchange? Why is it largely used in commerce?

2. One of your debtors hands you a Bill of Exchange whereby he promises to pay you £100 three months hence. Can you convert the Bill of Exchange into ready money now, or must you wait until it becomes due?

3. What are "Days of Grace"?

4. One of your debtors hands you, on July 1, 1910, a Bill of Exchange for £100, accepted by him, payable "one month after date": the Bill is dated July 1, 1910. What amount of money will you receive if you discount the Bill with your Bankers on July 8, 1910, at 4½ per cent. per annum?

5. When do the following Bills of Exchange fall due for payment?

(a) A Bill dated February 4, 1910, for £500, payable "three months after date."

(b) A Bill dated March 3, 1910, for £700, payable "60 days after date."

6. Calculate the discount on each of the Bills mentioned in Question 5; Bill (a) being discounted on February 19, 1910, at 3½ per cent. per annum, and Bill (b) being discounted on March 26, 1910, at 2¾ per cent. per annum.

1F.

1. What are (a) "Returns Inwards," (b) "Returns Outwards," and what is the difference between them?

2 Explain the expressions "Trial Balance," "Balance Sheet," and "Consignment."

3. What is the difference between the following : (a) "Sole Trader." (b) a "Partnership," (c) a "Company," and (d) a "Limited Liability Company"?

4. What is an "Unlimited Company"?

5. Explain the terms "Bad Debts" and "Doubtful Debts."

6. I sold 12 pairs of gloves to Robert Henderson on June 3, 1910, at 2s. per pair, less 5 per cent. trade discount, and I agreed that, if Henderson paid me before July 1, 1910, I would allow him a further 2½ per cent. discount. What is the difference, if any, between these two allowances?

1G.

1. What is the meaning of the abbreviations "Dr." and "Cr."

2. Are the uses of book-keeping confined to the record of cash receipts and payments?

3. Name two transactions which do not involve the payment or receipt of cash, but could be recorded in a trader's books.

4. A trader sells a parcel of goods at a profit. Would you rather have a sum equal to the "Gross" Profit or to the "Net" Profit on the transaction?

5. Write an invoice containing six transactions.

6. Is there any difference in the form of a "Personal" Account and a "Real" Account?

1H.

1. Compare the kind of transaction you would expect to find in a "Nominal" Account with those which would appear in a "Personal" Account.

2. If John Smith purchased goods of the value of £50 from you on May 2, 1910, and paid you £30 on account on May 12, 1910, on which side of his account in your Ledger would the balance of this account appear on May 31, 1910?

3. Prepare a fresh account for Messrs. J. Francis & Co. (given on p. 5) on the assumption that the coffee sold to them on March 12, 1910, was invoiced at £250 9s. 0d., and that they paid a further sum of cash on account amounting to £25 on March 25, 1910.

4. State whether the balance of the account as amended above is a "Credit" or a "Debit" Balance.

5. Does a cheque require a stamp?

6. If a trader sent you to purchase some postage stamps (5s.), and you had to take a tram (2d.) in order to get to the nearest post office, what term should you use to express the nature of these payments?

CHAPTER II

THE CASH BOOK

THE **Cash Book** is the book in which a person writes, or "enters," the sums of money received and paid by him.

If properly kept, a Cash Book has the following advantages:

1. It shows the owner of it how much money he has received, and how much he has paid away.
2. It shows the owner how much money there should be left, at any given time, in his cash-box.
3. It relieves its owner of the necessity of counting his money whenever he wishes to know how much he has in hand.

A person who keeps a Cash Book must, of course, occasionally count his money in order to be sure that it agrees with the amount shown by his Cash Book as being in hand. It is possible that the keeper of a Cash Book may forget to set down some receipt or payment. If carelessness of this kind has occurred the Cash Book "Balance" will, of course, be incorrect. Any mistakes which may have been made will, however, disclose themselves when the cash itself is counted and compared with the Cash Book "Balance."

In order to prepare a Cash Account, in its simplest form, all that is necessary is a sheet of paper divided into halves by means of a thick vertical line ruled down the middle.

The left-hand half of the page is for the record of moneys *received*, the right-hand half of the page is for moneys *paid away*.

The sums of money *received* are entered underneath one another on the left-hand side of the page in the form of a compound addition sum.

The sums of money *paid away* are similarly entered on the right-hand side of the page in the form of a compound addition sum.

All that is absolutely necessary in the ruling of a Cash Account is the thick vertical line previously referred to, which divides the page into two halves. In actual practice, however, each half of the page is ruled with certain additional lines, which form columns, and serve to keep the various items ranged in orderly form underneath one another.

For instance, lines are ruled vertically on each half of the page to provide spaces wherein the number of pounds, shillings, and pence received or paid can be entered methodically underneath one another. It would be difficult to add up the payments if they were scattered, without any method whatever, over the right-hand half of the page. The ruling of money columns to contain the receipts and payments prevents confusion and renders addition easy.

Thin vertical lines are likewise ruled on either side of the page to record the dates on which the various receipts and payments took place. Other vertical lines are ruled in order to arrange together, one under another, the names of the persons to whom, or from whom, money has been paid or received.

You must not be bewildered or discouraged if, either in this present book or in a more advanced one, you are presented with account forms made up of many lines. The multiplication of ruled lines is introduced in accounts for the purpose of dividing the pages into sections and sub-sections for the sake of clearness and analysis.

Such rulings do not in any way affect the simple principles upon which the Cash Account is constructed.

The following is the form in which a simple Cash Book, or Cash Account, is ruled:

Dr.   CASH BOOK (Simple form).   *Cr.*

	RECEIPTS.*						PAYMENTS.*				
Date.	Particulars.	Ledger folio.	£	s.	d	Date.	Particulars.	Ledger folio.	£	s.	d.
A	B	C	D	E	F	G	H	I	J	K	L

* NOTE.—In practice the words "Receipts" and "Payments" do not appear; they are included here solely for the sake of clearness.

B

The left-hand side of the page is designed for the record of all sums of money *received* by the owner of the Cash Book. The right-hand side serves a similar purpose for all sums of money paid away.   In other words, all money that "*comes in*" is entered on the *left hand* (or "*Debit*") side, and all money that "*goes out*" is entered on the *right hand* (or "*Credit*") side. Both receipts and payments must be entered carefully one under another, in order that, in due course, the additions of the two money columns may be readily made.

The "Date" column A on the "Receipts" side must contain the date on which the particular sum of money recorded came in.

The "Particulars" column B on the "Receipts" side must contain the name of the person from whom the sum of money was received.   The reason why he paid the money to the owner of the Cash Book is usually also briefly stated, *e.g.* "repayment of loan."

The "Ledger folio" column C must contain a memorandum of the page in another book, called the Ledger, which will be explained later, where further information as to the receipt in question will be found.

The money columns D, E, and F, on the "Receipts" side, are designed to contain the number of pounds, shillings and pence, respectively, of which each sum of money received is made up.

Columns G to L on the right-hand side of the account are ruled to contain similar information concerning the sums of money *paid away* by the owner of the Cash Book.

When a person commences to keep a Cash Book for the first time, he must, of course, count his money in order to find how much he has in hand at the date on which he commences, or "opens" his Cash Book.   The amount thus found to be in hand must be entered in the Cash Book as if it were a receipt —*i.e.* as if it had just "come in."   As a matter of fact, this money did, of course, actually "come in" some time or other.

The foregoing explanations should enable you to understand the lines upon which a Cash Account is constructed, and an example may now be given.

EXAMPLE.—*I started to keep a Cash Book on February* 1, 1910.

1. On February 1, 1910, I had in my cash-box £3 2s. 9d.
2. On February 2, I received £5 from William Jones for a table which I sold to him.

3. On February 3, I paid £3 13s. 0d. to H. Wilson, my tailor, for a suit of clothes which he had made for me.

4. On February 3, I lent L. Cunningham £2

5. On February 4, I paid to Morris and Company, for various new books which I bought from them, £1 10s. 0d.

6. On February 5, L. Cunningham repaid me the £2 which I lent to him on February 3.

7. On February 8, I paid M. Hubert, for a pair of new boots, £1 1s.

Prepare my Cash Account, and show how much I had in hand on February 8, 1910.

Having ruled my Cash Account in accordance with the form given on p. 17, I must proceed as follows

Item No. 1.—On February 1, I had in my cash-box £3 2s. 9d.

This money must be entered on the left-hand, *i.e.* " Debit," side of the Cash Account, as if it were a receipt. You must remember that the Cash Account I am going to keep is, literally, a history of the money which goes into and comes out of my cash-box. This being so, the " Balance " of cash with which I start must be treated as having " come in," in other words, it is a receipt for the purpose of being recorded in my Cash Account. The date, February 1, must be entered in the " Date " column, and the words " To balance " must be entered in the " Particulars " column. The sum of £3 2s. 9d. must bo entered in the money columns.

The words " To balance," when used in a Cash Book, are meant to indicate the amount of money in hand which was brought forward from a previous date.

In this case there was in hand on February 1 an amount, or " balance," of money brought forward from previous days of £3 2s. 9d.

It is customary to put the word " To " at the beginning of each entry in the " Particulars " column, as has been done in the case of the words " To balance " given above. The addition of the word " To " is, perhaps, not very useful, but custom has rendered its adoption practically universal in this country. You must remember not to omit it.

Item No. 2. February 2. Received £5 from W. Jones for a table sold to him.

This item represents a receipt. The money having " come in," it must be entered on the " Receipts," *i.e,* the " Debit " side of the account.

· The date, "February 2," must be entered in the "Date" column. "To W. Jones for a table sold to him," must be written in the "Particulars" column, and £5 0s. 0d. must be entered in the money columns.

When the word "To" has once been written against an entry on the debit side of the Cash Book it is sufficient to put a "ditto" sign (,,) to represent a repetition of the word "To" at the beginning of each entry that follows on the same page. No part of the remainder of the entries must be allowed to intrude into this space.

For example :

		£	s.	d.
1910.				
Feb. 1.	To balance	3	2	9
„ 2.	„ W. Jones for a table sold to him	5	0	0

Item No. 3. February 3. Paid £3 13s. 0d. to H. Wilson, my Tailor, for a suit.

This being a payment, the cash having "gone out," it must be entered on the "payments," *i.e.* the right-hand, or "Credit," side of the account.

The date, "February 3," must be entered in the "Date" column "By H. Wilson, amount owing to him for suit," must be written in the "Particulars" column, and £3 13s. 0d. must be placed in the money columns.

It is customary to prefix the word "By" to all entries on the "Credit" side of the account in the same way in which the word "To" is used in the case of entries on the "Debit" side. The custom is again perhaps a little unnecessary, but it has become practically universal, and should be followed.

Item No. 4. February 3. Paid L. Cunningham £2.

This again is a payment, the cash having "gone out"; it must therefore be entered on the "Credit" side of the account as under :

February 3.   By L. Cunningham .   .   £2   0   0
                amount lent to him.

Item No. 5. February 4. Paid Morris & Co. for new books £1 10s.

This is a payment, the cash having "gone out," it must therefore be entered on the "Credit" side of the account as under :

February 4.   By Morris & Co.   .   .   £1 10 0
amount owing to them
for sundry new books.

*Item No 6.   February 5.   L. Cunningham repaid the £2
lent to him on February 3.*

This is a receipt, the cash having "come in," it must consequently be entered on the "Debit" side of the account as under:

February 5.   To L. Cunningham .   ,   £2   0   0
loan repaid by him.

*Item No. 7.   February 8.   Paid M. Hubert for a pair
of new boots £1 1s.*

This being a payment, the cash having "gone out," it must be entered on the "Credit" side of the account as under:

February 8.   By M. Hubert .   .   .   £1   1   0
Cost of 1 pair of boots.

My Cash Book, prepared on the above lines, would appear as under:

Dr.		CASH BOOK.			Cr.	

1910.		£	s.	d.	1910.		£	d.
Feb. 1	To Balance .	3	2	9	Feb. 3	By *H. Wilson*— Amount owing to him for a suit .	3	13	0
„ 2	„ *W. Jones*— For a table sold to him	5	0	0	„ 3	„ *L. Cunningham*— Amount lent to him	2		0
, 5	„ *L. Cunningham*— Loan repaid by him	2	0	0	„ 4	„ *Morris & Co.*— Amount owing to them for sundry new books .	1	10	0
					„ 8	„ *M. Hubert*— Cost of 1 pair of boots .	1	1	0
	Note.—Total of debit side £10 2s. 9d.					*Note.*—Total of credit side £8 4s. 0d.			

You will notice that a memorandum appears at the foot of each side of the account stating the totals of the entries made on either side, as under:

Total of the Debit side	*Total of the Credit side*
£10 2s. 9d.	£8 4s. 0d.

In actual practice these totals are made in the first instance *in pencil* in the money columns, and are rubbed out after the account has been completed.

Upon examining my Cash Book you will notice that I have received £10 2s. 9d. in all, and that I have paid away £8 4s. 0d. I ought therefore to have £1 18s. 9d. in my cash-box at the close of the transactions given above. This £1 18s. 9d. is called my "balance of cash in hand."

Let us suppose now that, having written up my Cash Book as far as is shown in the above illustration, I wish to close it and to start afresh—in other words, suppose that I wish to "balance and rule off my Cash Book" as on February 8.

My procedure will be as follows:

1. I must enter the balance left in hand (£1 18s. 9d.) in the "Credit" column of the Cash Book, just as if I had paid it away.

2. Thereupon I must add up both sides of the Cash Book; they will each now amount to the same total, viz., £10 2s. 9d. I must rule across the money columns the horizontal lines always used in the case of ordinary compound addition sums.

3. I must enter afresh the balance in hand (£1 18s. 9d.), placing it this time on the "Debit" side of the account, just as if it were a fresh receipt. If you will think a little you will see that the new period, which I am about to commence, does actually receive the "balance of cash in hand" from the old period.

Having made the entry, I shall have a fresh balance to start with on February 8, and the money columns of my Cash Book will be no longer encumbered with information as to receipts or payments which have occurred before that date.

My Cash Book will now appear as under, after "balancing" it upon the lines set forth above.

CASH BOOK.

Dr.   Cr.

1910.		F1	£	s.	d.	1910.		F2	£		d.
Feb. 1	To Balance .	√	3	2	9	Feb. 3	By *H. Wilson*— Amount owing to him for a suit . .		3	13	0
„ 2	„ *W. Jones*— For a table sold to him		5	0	0	„ 3	„ *L. Cunningham*— Amount lent to him		2		0
„ 5	„ *L. Cunningham*— Loan repaid by him					„ 4	„ *Morris & Co.*— Amount owing to them for sundry new books		1	10	0
						„ 8	„ *M. Hubert*— Cost of 1 pair of boots .		1		0
						„ 8	„ Balance carried forward .	√	1	18	9
			£ 10	2	9				£ 10	2	9
1910. Feb. 9	To Balance brought forward .	√	1	18	9						

You should note the following points arising out of this account :

1. The Balance which is written *above* the totals bears the date of the *last* day of the period under consideration, viz., February 8.

2. The balance which is "brought down" bears the date of the *first* day of the following period, *i.e.* February 9.

This custom is generally applied to the balancing, not only of Cash Books, but of all accounts.

3. The "folio" columns (marked F1 and F2) are not used in the Cash Book as shown here, because it is given as a separate illustration apart from any other books. In practice, however, every amount on either side, except the "balances," would have its appropriate folio reference attached, to show where

further details as to the items in question may be found in the other books of account which we shall consider at a later stage.

All Accounts are "balanced" in a similar manner to that which has been employed in the Cash Account given above. In the account already given the entries on the debit side amounted to more than those on the credit side; hence the balance was first of all inserted on the credit side above the ruling in order to make the totals of the two sides equal in amount, and was then "brought down" on the debit side. This is an example of a "Debit Balance."

If the total of the credit items in an account exceeds the total of the debit items, the "balance" is inserted first of all on the debit side, and is subsequently "brought down" on the credit side. In such a case the balance would be called a "Credit Balance."

An example of an account (not a Cash account, but a Ledger account) in which the balance is brought down on the credit side will be found on p. 78.

It has already been stated (p. 7) that very few business people keep much of their cash in their own hands, but leave the greater part of it with their bankers.

Some traders keep no money at all in hand. They pay all the money they receive into their banking account at once, and make all their payments by means of cheques. In such cases the banker practically becomes the trader's cashier.

If a trader follows this course he can keep his Cash Account, or Cash Book, upon exactly the same lines as the one illustrated on p. 17. He can enter all his receipts, every one of which he pays into his bank, on the debit side of the account, and he can enter all the cheques he draws and pays away on the credit side of the account. The balance with which he starts his banking account will be entered as the first item, at the top of the debit side, just as the starting balance of money in hand was entered in the example given. His closing balance with his banker will be treated in exactly the same way as the closing balance of money in hand was treated.

In fact, the trader who adopts the plan of keeping all his money with his banker keeps his Cash Book exactly as if the money entrusted to his bankers were actually money in his own hands. This is, of course, quite the usual way of looking at matters, and is common in business. Money left with a banker on current account is repayable "on demand": it is quite reasonable and usual, therefore, to regard it as the exact equivalent of money in hand. The existing banking system of this country is a very strong one, and the trader has little need to doubt the safety of the money left in the hands of his banker.

An example of the Cash account of a trader who keeps no cash in hand, and uses his bank account for all receipts and payments is here given.

Example :

Arthur Robinson is a trader who pays all the money he receives into his account with the London Joint Stock Bank, Ltd., and makes all his payments by means of cheques drawn upon them.

From the following particulars write up Robinson's Cash Book and "balance" it as on February 7, 1910.

		£	s.	d.
1910.				
Feb. 1.	Balance standing at this date to the credit of A. Robinson with his Bankers	149	2	10
„ 2.	Received from O. Vivian in cash and banked the same	5	0	0
„ „	Received from the Newchurch Brickworks their cheque and banked the same	10	19	8
„ 3.	Paid the following, by cheques drawn upon the London Joint Stock Bank :			
	The Eastborough Gas Company, Gas bill for quarter to December 31, 1909	4	2	9
	Messrs. Praed Brothers, cash on account	15	0	0
	H. Lewis (A. Robinson's book-keeper) for one month's salary to February 3, 1910.	10	10	0
„ 4.	Received from Abel Morris £10 in bank-notes, £2 in gold, and his cheque for £5 10s. 9d. Banked these various remittances. Total	17	10	9
„ „	Paid Robert Lowe, by cheque on account	3	2	6
„ 5.	Paid The Proprietor of the *Morning Herald*, by cheque, for standing advertisement for one month . . .	12	10	0
„ 7.	Received cheque from West & Sons in payment for work done for them, and banked the same	109	3	9

A. ROBINSON.   CASH BOOK

Dr.   (containing Bank transactions only).   *Cr.*

1910.			£	s.	d.	1910.			£	s.	d.
Feb. 1	To Balance brought forward .	√	149	2	10	Feb. 3	By *East-borough Gas Co.*— Gas bill for quarter ended Dec. 31, 1909 .				9
„ 2	„ *O. Vivian*— Cash .		5	0	0						
„ „	„ *The New-church Brick-works*— cheque		10	19	8	„ „	„ *Praed Bros.*— On account		15	0	0
„ 4	„ *Abel Mor-ris*— Cash from him: Bank-notes £10, gold £2, cheque £5 10s. 9d.		17	10	9	„ „	„ *Salaries*— H. Lewis, for month ended Feb. 3, 1910 .		10	10	0
„ 7	„ *West & Sons*— Payment for work done cheque		109	3	2	„ 4	„ *R. Lowe* . On account		3	2	6
						„ 5	„ *Proprie-tors of the Morning Herald*— Standing advertise-ment for one month		12	10	0
						„ 7	„ Balance carried forward .	√	246	11	2
		£	291	16	5			£	291	16	5
1910. Feb. 8	To Balance brought forward .	√	246	11	2						

* The wording in relation to this item is thus set forth owing to the practice (to be explained later) of keeping one "Salaries" account in the Ledger for all salaries paid.

I have now shown you how to prepare the Cash Account of a trader who keeps *all* his money in his cash-box, and also that of a trader who keeps *all* his money with his bankers.

I must now explain to you how the Cash Account is prepared in cases where the trader keeps *part* of his money with his bankers, and *part* of it in hand.

Many traders keep the greater part of their money with their bankers for the sake of convenience and safety, and at tho same time always keep a certain amount of coin in their office cash-boxes. It often happens that some of a trader's receipts come to him in the shape of coin and notes, and that he keeps this money in hand for the purpose of making certain kinds of payments. It will be obvious, for instance, that workmen's wages cannot be paid by cheque; for payments of this nature therefore coin is indispensable.

If a trader keeps a certain sum of money in his cash-box for such purposes, he may, from time to time, take out of his cash-box any sums of money which he thinks will not be wanted for immediate payments, and he may pay these sums into his banking account. Again, if his cash-box balance runs down very low he may replenish it by drawing a sum of money from his banking account and putting it into his cash-box.

A trader who keeps his cash in the way just described may, should he choose to do so, keep two Cash Accounts, or Cash Books, upon the lines previously explained. He could keep one Cash Account, or Cash Book, for his *Bank* transactions, and another for his *Cash* transactions. In such a case he would enter all payments made by cheque in his "Bank" Cash Book, and all payments made in cash in his "Cash" Cash Book. His receipts would be treated similarly.

If the trader took money out of his cash-box and paid it into his banking account he would treat it as having been paid away in his "Cash" cash account, and as having been received in his "Bank" Cash Book. Conversely, if he drew money from his bank account and placed it in his cash-box he would enter it as a payment in his "Bank" Cash Book, and as a receipt in his "Cash-Box" Cash Book.

To keep two separate Cash Books, one for "cash" and the other for the "bank account," would, however, be troublesome. It is obviously better to keep only one book for the two kinds of receipts and payments if it can be managed.

By using what is known as a "Double Column" **Cash Book** a trader can enter his "cash" and "bank" transactions side by side, and can keep them running together on the same page. By entering both kinds of transactions together on the same page the trader can see the *whole* of his cash position, and both "cash-box" and "bank" balances, at a glance. This is an obvious advantage.

A "double column" Cash Book is so called because it contains *two* money columns on the debit side, and *two* money columns on the credit side, in the place of the *one* money column upon each side shown in the simple form of Cash Book already given.

One of the debit money columns and one of the credit money columns are kept for " cash-box " transactions, the other pair of money columns, debit and credit, being used for " bank " transactions.

A form of "Double Column" Cash Book is given on p. 33, wherein the money columns are lettered as set out below for the purpose of reference in the descriptions which follow :

Debit " Cash " column	. . . .	D 1.
Debit " Bank " column	. . . .	D 2
Credit " Cash " column	. . . .	C 1.
Credit " Bank " column	. . . .	C 2.

The rules for entering up this Cash Book are as follow :

All the money that " *comes in* " is entered on the *debit* side, in the " Cash " or " Bank " columns respectively, according as the money goes into the " cash-box " or to the " bank account."

In like manner all cash that "*goes out*" is entered on the *credit* side, in the " Cash " or " Bank " columns respectively, according as the money goes out of the cash-box or the bank account.

These rules may be explained in fuller detail as follows ·

1. **Starting balances in hand.**—The " Cash " and " Bank " balances are entered in the debit " Cash " column (D 1) and debit " Bank " column (D 2) respectively, on the same horizontal line. The words "To Balances" are entered in the " Particulars " column.

2. **Receipts.**—All the " cash " that is received and placed directly in the office cash-box is entered on the debit side of the Cash Book, the amount being placed in the debit " Cash " column (D 1).

All the money that is paid into the bank is entered on the debit side of the Cash Book ; the amounts being placed in the debit " Bank " column (D 2).

3. **Payments.**—Everything paid in cash taken out of the office cash-box is entered on the credit side of the Cash Book, the amount being placed in the credit " Cash " column (C 1).

All money drawn from the bank account is entered on the credit side of the Cash Book, the amount of the cheque being placed in the credit " Bank " column (C 2).

4. **Closing balances.**—At the end of the period taken, the Cash Book is " balanced " and ruled off. Balancing is effected

exactly upon the same lines as those already explained as governing the balancing of the simple form of Cash Book, except that there are *two* balances to carry forward.

The two "Cash" columns are added, and their balance is entered and carried forward in the debit "Cash" column in the ordinary way. The "Bank" columns are similarly treated. The balance shown by them is entered, both above and below the ruling-off, on the same line as that on which the "Cash" balance has already been entered. The two balances are thus carried forward side by side.

After the balances have been entered, the two "Cash" columns will add up to the same total, and that total will be entered in ink between the ordinary horizontal lines which rule off the columns. The two "Bank" columns will, in like manner, add up to the same total.

An example may, perhaps, make matters clearer.

Example

William Smith is a trader who keeps part of his money in his cash-box and the remainder with his bankers.

His transactions for the first four days of March 1910 were as shown below. They are to be entered in his Double Column Cash Book, which is to be balanced as on March 5, 1910.

1910.

March 1. Balance of office cash in hand £70; bank balance £120 19s. 3d.

„ 2. Received in cash from J. Brown £25, and from H. Pratt £10. These sums were placed in the office cash-box.

„ 4. Received from Wilson & Co., their cheque for £5, and paid the same into the bank.

„ 5. Paid wages from the office cash-box £12 10s.
Paid from the office cash-box into the bank £70.
Drew cheque in favour of the Guardian Assurance Company for £5 9s. 6d., being one year's fire insurance premium upon office and warehouse.

The form of Double Column Cash Book in which these transactions are set forth is given on p. 33. It should be carefully studied in conjunction with the following explanations:

· 1910.

March 1. Balance of office cash in hand £70, Bank balance £120 19s. 3d.

These items signify that Mr. William Smith had, as on March 1, 1910, £70 in his cash-box, and £120 19s. 3d. in his bank account.

These facts must be recorded in his Cash Book by making an entry at the top of the debit (or left-hand) side, under date March 1, 1910, as follows :

1910.   "Cash" column.   "Bank" column.

March 1.   To Balances   £70 0 0   £120 19 3

The £70 is entered in the "Cash" column, and the £120 19s. 3d. in the "Bank" column, both on the same line of the page. They form the first entries in each of these columns.

March 2.   Received in cash from J. Brown £25, and from H. Pratt, £10, both these sums being placed in the office cash-box.

Both these items are receipts. In each case cash has "come in," and must be entered on the **debit** side of the Cash Book. These items are both receipts in money and are both placed in the office cash-box; they must both consequently be entered in the "Cash" column.

The necessary entries are as under:

                "Cash" column.   "Bank" column.

March 2. To J. Brown   £25 0 0

    "   "   " H. Pratt   £10 0 0

March 4.   Received from Wilson & Co. their cheque for £5 and paid the same into the Bank.

In this case Wilson & Co. have given Mr. William Smith a cheque upon their bankers for £5. Mr. Smith does not take this cheque himself to Wilson & Co.'s bankers upon whom it is drawn; he prefers the easier course of paying it into his account with his own bankers for them to collect for him. When his bankers have collected the £5 in question, they will add it to the £120 19s. 3d. they already hold for Mr. Smith.

The cheque for £5 has been received first by Mr. Smith and then by his bankers; it must therefore be entered on the debit side of the Cash Book. It has been paid into the bank, consequently it must appear in the "Bank" column, as follows :

                "Cash" column.   "Bank" column.

March 4. To Wilson & Co.   £5 0 0

March 5.   Paid wages from the office cash-box £12 10s.

This item shows that £12 10s. has been paid; it must consequently be entered on the credit side of the Cash Book. It is the office cash-box which has parted with the money, consequently it is in the "Cash" column that the payment must be recorded.

The entry thus appears as follows:

	"Cash" column.	"Bank" column.
March 5. By wages	£12 10	

March 5. Paid from the office cash-box into the bank £70.

This kind of entry very often confuses the student, who frequently fails to understand the real nature of the transaction which has taken place.

This is a very common entry in an actual business Cash Book, and you must make sure that you learn how to deal properly with it.

The item quoted above means, as far as Mr. Smith's Cash Book is concerned, that *two* transactions have taken place, and not *one* only, as some students seem to imagine.

First, the office cash-box has parted with £70.
Secondly, the bank has received £70.

It is quite clear, consequently, that we must record both these transactions.

The first transaction, viz., the fact that the office cash-box has parted with £70, must be entered on the **credit** side of the Cash Book, because the cash has been paid away. It must be entered in the "Cash" column, because it is the office cash-box which has parted with the money.

The necessary entry is therefore as follows ·

	"Cash" column.	"Bank" column.
March 5. By cash paid to Bank . .	£70 0 0	

The other transaction, viz., the fact that the bank has received £70, must be entered on the **debit** side of the Cash Book, because it is a receipt from the bank's standpoint. It is entered in the "Bank" column because it is into the bank that the money has been paid.

The necessary entry is as follows:

	"Cash" column.	"Bank" column.
To cash received from office cash-box .		£70 0 0

The remaining transaction is as follows :

March 5. Drew cheque in favour of the Guardian Assurance Company, being £5 9s. 6d. for one year's fire insurance premium upon offices and warehouse.

This item is a payment made by the bank on behalf of Mr. W. Smith. It must, consequently, be entered on the credit side of the Cash Book. It is out of the bank account that the money has been paid ; it is, therefore, in the " Bank " column that the amount of £5 9s. 6d. must be entered as follows ·

	" Cash " column.	" Bank " column.
March 4. By Insurance (Guardian Assurance Company). . .		£5 9 6

When all these transactions have been entered in Mr. Smith's Cash Book according to the instructions given above, you must find what is the total of the amounts entered in each of the four columns. These totals are usually entered, in the first instance, *in pencil*, in the columns themselves, and are rubbed out afterwards when the account has been ruled off.

You will find that the totals in the case of the Cash Book given on p.33, are as follows :

Debit side.	Credit side.
" Cash " column.	" Cash " column.
£105 0 0	£82 10 0
" Bank " column.	" Bank " column.
£195 19 3	£5 9 6

From these figures the balances which it is necessary to enter in the two columns on March 5 are arrived at as follows :

"Cash" columns. Balance = £105 0 0 − £82 10 0
i.e. £22 10 0.

"Bank" columns. Balance = £195 19 3 − £5 9 6
i.e. £190 9 9.

These balances must be entered respectively in the " Cash " and " Bank " credit columns, and all the four money columns must then be added up. You will find that the two " Cash " columns add, in each case, to £105. The " Bank " columns, in each case, add to £195 19s. 3d. The columns are then " ruled off " in the usual way.

Dr.

Date	Details	Ledger folio	Cash (D 1) £	s.	d.	Bank (D 2) £	s.	d.
1910. Mrch 1	To Balances brought forward.	* v	70	0	0	120	19	3
,, 2	,, J. Ben	35	25	0	0			
,, ,,	,, H. Pratt	36				5	0	0
,, 4	,, Wilson & Co.	37	10	0	0	70	0	0
,, 5	,, C sh	C						
	Totals { "Cash." £105 0s. 0d. "Bank." £195 19s. 3d. }		£105	0	0	£195	19	3
1910. March 6	To Balances brought fwd	v	22	10	0	190	9	9

Cr. (C 2)

Date	Details	Ledger folio	Cash (C 1) £	s.	d.	Bank (C 2) £	s.	d.
1910. March 5	By Wages	*	12	10	0			
,, ,,	,, Bank	42 C	70	0	0			
,, ,,	,, Insuran e. (Guardian Assurance Co. 1 year's Fire Insurance premium)	43				5	9	6
	Totals { "Cash." 82 0s. 0d. "Bank." £5 9s. 6d. }							
,, ,,	By Balances carried ord	v	22	10	0	190	9	9
		£	105	0	0	£195	19	3

* The figures used in the ' ' (' folio" columns are imaginary and for illustration purposes only. They would, in practice, be the numbers of the pages in the "Ledger," whereon the various entries appearing in the Cash Book are again written, or "posted." Transfers from "Cash" to "Bank," and vice versa, are recorded only in the Cash Book, hence in these cases a ' or 'C' (indicating the word 'Contra' is used instead of a Ledger folio, to show that the entry in question appears also on the opposite side of the page.

The balances, as on March 5, are then re-entered on the debit side of the Cash Book, underneath the ruling-off lines.

As previously explained these balances form the starting balances for the next period.

As I have already explained to you, it is usual in many businesses for the trader both to allow and to receive small discounts, known as "Cash Discounts," when his debtors pay their debts to him, or when he himself pays his own creditors. (See p. 9.)

Such allowances act as an inducement to a debtor to pay his debts before they are due.

In some businesses almost every receipt or payment of a debt is accompanied by a "Discount" allowance. For the sake of convenience, an additional pair of money columns is ruled in the Cash Book for the record of discounts received and allowed.

It is necessary that I should make a short digression at this point in order to sketch briefly the history of an entry after it has been made in the Cash Book. Except for the footnote given in the form on p. 33, no detailed mention has been made of a very important book called the "Ledger." I have purposely adopted this course in order not to confuse you at the beginning of your study of the subject. At this point it is difficult, however, to proceed further without mentioning the Ledger; I will now, therefore, explain briefly the uses of this book.

The Ledger is the most important book in double-entry book-keeping. It contains the whole of the trader's transactions concisely classified in sections called "Accounts." These accounts are ruled exactly in the same way as the Cash Account given on p. 17, and a further and more detailed description of them will be found in Chapter VII. The Cash Book itself is the largest Ledger account. It has been taken out of the Ledger and bound separately because of its bulk. As will be explained more fully later, you must always remember that the Cash Book is really a part of the Ledger. In olden days it used to be part of the Ledger itself, but is now always bound as a separate book for greater convenience in handling. The cardinal principle of double-entry book-keeping, as will be explained in detail at a later stage, is that every transaction must be entered in some form or other in *two* Ledger accounts, on the *debit* side in the one account, and on the *credit* side in the other. At this stage of your studies I do not wish you to attempt to follow out this principle in full detail. All that you need fix in your mind is that *the entries which you have seen made in the Cash Book are, at a later stage, written again, in some account or other, in a book called the "Ledger."*

In due course I shall explain the Ledger more fully, and show you how it is written up.

Going back now to the point where I made this digression, it is possible to explain *why* cash discounts are taken note of in the Cash Book.

Every sum of money paid by a trader to a creditor—in addition to being entered in the Cash Book—is entered in the Ledger in an account headed with the creditor's name. Every amount of discount allowed by the creditor to the trader must also be entered in the same Ledger account.

If the majority of cash payments made to creditors are accompanied by discount allowances it will obviously save time if we can make one entry only in the creditor's Ledger account for the two items—cash and discount, instead of having to make a separate entry for each of them.

In order to be able to make one entry only for both cash and "cash discount" in the creditor's Ledger account, the trader uses a Cash Book possessing an additional money column on the payments side. In this additional money column, which is called the "discount" column, the trader makes a note of all the cash discounts allowed to him when making payments to his creditors, and he notes each allowance of discount against its relative cash payment. He is then enabled to enter (*i.e.* to "post") in the creditor's account in his Ledger the total cash paid and discount received in one item.

As with the cash discounts received from creditors so in the case of cash discounts allowed to debtors, an extra "Memorandum" column is ruled on the debit side of the Cash Book.

Whenever a discount allowance is made to a debtor upon payment of his account, the allowance is entered in the "Discount" column on the debit side of the Cash Book, against the entry referring to the money received from him. The total of the Cash received from the debtor and the discount allowed to him is entered ("posted") on the credit side of the debtor's account in the Ledger, thus avoiding the posting of two separate entries.

An example of a "**Three Column Cash Book**" containing Discount columns appears on the next page, the following transactions having been entered in it.

Example:

1910. April 1, Cash Balance, £40, Bank Balance, £75; April 2, Received from J. Brown £20 in cash, and allowed him discount, £2; Paid £50 to the bank from office cash; April 4, Drew cheque in favour of W. Wright for £62 10s., discount received, £3; April 5, Received cheque from J. Jones & Co., £30, allowed them discount £3, and banked the cheque.

You will notice (1) that the £2 allowed to J. Brown on April 2 is entered in the debit "Discount" column against the £20 received from him, (2) that the £3 discount received from W. Wright on April 5 is entered in the credit "Discount" column against the £62 10s. paid to him by cheque on that date, and (3) that the £3 allowed to J. Jones & Co. on April 5 is entered in the debit "Discount" column against the £30 received from them on that date.

I shall explain to you, in a subsequent chapter, how the totals of the "Discount" columns are dealt with.

I have already mentioned that a Cash Book, or a Cash Account, shows how much cash the owner of it has, or should have, in hand at any particular date, and that it shows its owner this information without putting him to the trouble of counting his money. This statement needs to be considered in further detail. In cases where a two or three column Cash Book is used, the cash columns, taken together, show the owner of the book how much money should be in his cash-box at the date to which the Cash Book has been written up. The obvious way for him to check the accuracy of his Cash Book, as regards "cash in hand," is, of course, to count the money which actually remains in his cash-box. If the contents of his cash-box tally exactly with the balance shown by the "cash" columns of the Cash Book, the trader can assume that the items in the book have been correctly entered.

The "Bank" columns of the Cash Book show how much money the owner of the Cash Book has with his banker, and how much he may draw out in case of need, but, for the reasons to be explained hereafter, the balance shown by the Cash Book will not always tally exactly with the balance appearing in the "Bank Book" in which the banker records his transactions with the trader.

If you, being a trader, pay cheques, postal orders, or other

THREE COLUMN CASH BOOK.

Dr.

Date.	Particulars.	Ledger folio.	Discount (allowed). £ s. d.	Cash (received). £ s. d.	Bank (paid in). £ s. d.
1910. April 1	To Balances .	*			
,, 2	,, J. Brown .	v 37	2 0 0	40 0 0	75 0 0
,,	,, Cash .	C		20 0 0	50 0 0
,, 5	,, J. Jones & Co. .	74	3 0 0		30 0 0
			£5 0 0 (1.22)	£60 0 0	£155 0 0
1910. April 6	To Balances brought down	v		10 0 0	92 10 0

Cr.

Date.	Particulars.	Ledger folio.	Discount (received). £ s. d.	Cash (paid). £ s. d.	Bank (drawn out). £ s. d.
1910. April 2	By Bank	*		50 0 0	62 10 0
,, 4	,, W. Wright	C 77	3 0 0		
,, 5	,, Balances carried down	v		10 0 0	92 10 0
			£3 0 0 (1.22)	£60 0 0	£155 0 0

* The figures inserted in the folio columns are imaginary, and for illustration purposes only. See note to Cash Book on p. 33.

forms of money which take time to collect, into your banking account, your banker will, in most cases, postpone entering them in your Bank Book until he has actually collected the cash for them ; you, however, will have debited them in the "bank" column of your Cash Book directly you have paid them into your bank.

Similarly, if you draw cheques upon your banker and send them by post to various persons to whom you owe money, those persons, or their bankers, will not claim the money from your banker for perhaps a day or two after you have forwarded the cheques to them. It will be obvious that your banker will not enter the amount of a cheque to your debit in your bank book until he has actually paid it, although you will naturally enter all the cheques drawn by you in the "Bank" column of your Cash Book directly you have sent the cheques away.

Items of these two kinds may cause your bank book to show a larger or a smaller balance than is shown by the "Bank" columns of your Cash Book, and in order to reconcile the two balances a short sum has to be worked out. This sum is called a "Reconciliation Statement." You must always remember that it is your Cash Book which shows your *true* bank balance.

If you think for a moment you will see that the bank balance shown by your Cash Book is the *actual balance* which will remain in your banking account when all the outstanding and uncollected cheques have been paid or credited, as the case may be.

An example is given below showing how this "reconciliation" of the Cash Book with the bank book is effected.

Example:

On the evening of December 31, 1909, the Cash Book of Messrs. Harris Bros., of London, showed a balance of £172 16s. 4d. as being in their Banker's hands. The bank book, however, showed a balance of only £64 12s. 3d. in their favour. The difference was accounted for as follows: (1) a cheque drawn upon the Bank of Ireland, Dublin, by a debtor for £125 had been paid to the banker on the afternoon of December 31, and this cheque would not be credited to Messrs. Harris Bros. in their bank book until three days later, as it would take three days for the banker to collect it. (2) A cheque for £16 15s. 11d. had been sent on December 30, 1909, to a creditor living at Edinburgh, and insufficient time had elapsed for the presentation of this cheque to Messrs. Harris Bros.' banker for payment by him.

These differences are set out in the following statement:

BANK RECONCILIATION STATEMENT,
December 31, 1909.

	£	s.	d.
Balance as per Cash Book	172	16	4
Deduct. Cheque on the Bank of Ireland, Dublin, paid into Bank Account on the afternoon of December 31, 1909, but not yet collected	125	0	0
	47	16	4
Add. Cheque drawn December 30, 1909, and sent to Edinburgh, but not yet presented to bankers for payment .	16	15	11
Balance as per Bank Book	£64	12	3

A Bank Book is given by a Banker to each customer, when the latter opens his banking account. The bank book is periodically left by the customer with his banker in order that it may be written up to date.

Owing to the fact that the bank book is thus frequently passing between the banker and his customer, it is known as the "Bank Pass-book," or, more briefly, the "Pass-book." It is ruled in the form of a Cash Book; all sums paid into the bank by the customer are placed on the one side, and all the cheques paid by the banker on the customer's behalf are placed on the other side.

PETTY CASH BOOK

I have already explained to you that, even in a business in which all the Cash receipts are paid immediately into the bank, and, where possible, all payments are made by cheque, it is usually found necessary to keep small sums of money in the office. Such small payments as are necessary for postages, telegrams, and office sundries, occur in every business and cannot be paid in any other way than in coin.

To the small sums so kept in hand the name of "Petty Cash" is given. The clerk who is entrusted with the keeping of the Petty Cash is known as the Petty Cashier.

The book in which these payments are recorded is known as the **Petty Cash Book.** It consists, first, of the ordinary form of Cash Account, as given on p. 17, coupled, secondly, with a number of "memorandum" columns for the purpose of separating the expenditure into different classes.

A form of Petty Cash Book is given on the next page. You must not be confused by its many columns; no new principle is involved, the columns being merely for the purpose of analysis. For the convenience of reference in the explanations which follow, each of the money columns is lettered at its foot.

All the sums received by the Petty Cashier are entered on the *debit* side of the Petty Cash Book, the amounts being placed in column T 1.

All sums paid away are entered on the *credit* side of the Petty Cash Book, the amounts expended being placed in column T 2.

As far as the whole of the columns to the left of, and including, column T 2 are concerned, the Petty Cash Book in no wise differs from the simple form of Cash Account given on p. 17.

The columns to the right of column T 2 are used to classify the payments appearing in column T 2.

It will be seen that columns A to H are headed with the names of various kinds of expenditure, viz., Telegrams, Postage, Printing and Stationery, Cleaning, Fuel, Gas and Electric Light, and Sundries; but any other suitable headings can, of course, be used instead of, or in addition to, those given in the example.

If any given item of expenditure appearing in column T 2 comes within any of the headings given above, it is copied in the column bearing that heading, *e.g.* the first item in the example is the payment of 3*s*. 6*d*. for Postage. This 3*s*. 6*d*. consequently appears first in the Total column (T 2), and secondly in the "Postage" column (B). Every other item of expenditure which can be placed in columns A to H is similarly treated, and the columns A to H are kept continuously added and carried forward.

The object of using columns A to H, and of going through this process of repeating in them the various payments is to ensure that a clear view may be kept of the total spent up to a fixed date in each classified form of expense. You will see from the example given that, during the month of January

Cr.

Date	Details	Total (£ s. d.)	Telegrams (A) (£ s. d.)	Postage (B) (£ s. d.)	Printing and Stationery (C) (£ s. d.)	Cleaning (D) (£ s. d.)	Fuel (E) (£ s. d.)	Gas and Electric Light (F) (£ s. d.)	Telephone Charges (G) (£ s. d.)	Sundries (H) (£ s. d.)	Ledger Account	Ledger Amount (£ s. d.)	Folio	Total (£ s. d.)
1910. Jan. 1	Postage	0 3 6		0 3 6										30 0 0
„ 3	Brown & Co.	1 4 9			1 4 9									
„ 6	Housekeeper, cleaning, and sundries	2 9 4				2 6 4				0 3 0				
„ 8	H. Rose extra discount paid him	0 10 9									H. Rose	0 10 9	396	
„ 18	Housekeeper	6 0 2				5 4 2	0 12 0			0 4 0				
„ 22	Telegrams	0 5 6	0 5 6											
„ 26	Postage	1 10 0		1 10 0										
„ 29	Gas Co. to 31/12/08.	4 2 5						4 2 5						
„ 31	Trunk calls for month	0 7 9							0 7 9					
„ 31	Sundry stationery	0 1 4			0 1 4									
	Forward £	16 15 6	£0 5 6	£1 13 6	£1 6 1	£7 10 6	£0 12 0	£4 2 5	£0 7 9	£0 7 0		£0 10 9		£30 0 0

1910, 5s. 6d. in all was spent in Telegrams, £1 13s. 6d. for Postages, £1 6s. 1d. for Printing and Stationery, and so forth. In this way the owner of the business can keep a watch upon the expenditure of the Petty Cashier.

If the Petty Cashier makes any payment which cannot be classified under any of the headings of columns A to H (or whatever other columns there may be), he must enter the amount in column I, known as the "Ledger" column. Looking at the example given, you will see that the Petty Cashier paid 10s. 9d. on January 8 to a customer named H. Rose. Now, there is no heading styled "H. Rose" among the headings of the columns A to H, consequently the 10s. 9d. is placed in column I with "H. Rose" inserted against it as a description.

The totals of columns A to I, if added across the page, should equal the total of column T 2. This is obvious, seeing that everything that is entered in column T 2 is repeated in one or another of columns A to I.

Columns T 1 and T 2 can be "balanced" at any given date in exactly the same way as the simple form of Cash Book is balanced. Whenever these columns are balanced, the whole of columns A to I are added and ruled off.

I shall explain to you in a subsequent chapter how the totals of the analysis columns in the Petty Cash Book are dealt with in the Ledger.

The best way of keeping the Petty Cash is that known as the **Imprest System.** The principle of this system is that the Cashier is given a fixed round sum of money, say £5, £10, £20, or so on, to start with. At stated periods the exact amount that he has spent is refunded to him, so that he commences at every succeeding period with the same fixed round sum. The following example of this system relates to the Petty Cash Book given on p. 41.

A Petty Cashier is started on January 1, 1910, with a fixed balance of £30 for Petty Cash. His cash is to be made up monthly. By the end of January he has spent £16 15s. 6d., and therefore he has only £13 4s. 6d. left in hand. On February 1 he would be given a fresh cheque for the exact amount of his expenditure during January, viz., £16 15s. 6d., which, with his balance in hand of £13 4s. 6d., would restore his starting balance for February to its fixed figure of £30. This process is repeated on the first day of every month.

If the original sum given to the Petty Cashier be afterwards found to be too large or too small, it can, of course, be decreased or increased at convenience.

EXERCISE 2A.

1. What is a Cash Book?
2. How is a Cash Book "balanced" at the end of any given period?
3. Is it the more usual practice of traders to keep all their money in their own possession, or with their Bankers? What are the advantages of the latter plan?
4. George Borrow keeps a small amount of cash for current purposes in his office cash-box. On May 2, 1910, finding that he had more cash in hand than he required, he paid £30 into the bank. Show how this payment would be entered in G. Borrow's Cash Book.
5. What is a "three column" Cash Book? Rule a form of such a Cash Book, and enter three payments and three receipts therein.
6. What is the "Imprest" system of keeping Petty Cash? Rule a form of Petty Cash Book suitable for use in a business where payments under the following headings were frequent : Postages, Cables, Travelling Expenses, Housekeeper, Trade Expenses.

EXERCISE 2B.

The following are the cash transactions of Hubert Dales for the month of April 1910. Prepare his Cash Book, and balance it as on April 30, 1910 :

1910. April 1, Balance of cash in hand at this date, £5 2s. 10d. ; April 3, Bought two hats for £1 1s. ; April 5, Received from Robert Hart in repayment of money lent to him, £10 ; April 10, Bought suit of clothes, £5 10s. ; April 13, Received from James Smith for bicycle sold to him, £8 ; April 18, Bought cricket bat, £1 1s. ; April 21, Received for old clothes sold, 15s. ; April 29, Paid travelling expenses, 18s. 2d.

EXERCISE 2C.

From the following particulars write up the Cash Book of W. Johnston and balance it as at the end of February 1910 :

1910. Feb. 1, Balance of cash in hand brought forward from last month, £17 16s. 4d. ; Feb. 3, Received from W. R. Johnston, amount owing by him, £2 9s. 1d. ; Feb. 7, Received from V. Laughlin and Bros., amount owing by them, £1 4s. 9d. ; Feb. 9, Paid Mr. W. Lepper, on account, for stationery supplied, £3 2s. 9d. ; Feb. 10, Received from J. Mercier amount owing by him, £3 1s. 4d. ; Feb. 12, Received from Mitchell Bros. amount owing by them, 5s. 9d. ; Feb. 14, Paid W. B. Montgomery & Co., amount owing to them, £1 9s. 8d. ; Feb. 15, Paid Moore and Sons, Ltd., for goods supplied, £6 9s. 3d. ; Feb. 17, Received from Mallen & Murray, amount owing by them, £5 2s. 6d. ; Feb. 18, Paid Pease O'Neill for repairs to premises, £1 3s. 4d. ; Feb. 23, Paid R. Reade & Co. amount owing to them, 3s. 6d. ; Feb. 26, Lent O. Musgrave £2 ; Feb. 26, Received from Nicholls & Co. on account, £5 ; Feb. 28, O. Musgrave repaid the sum lent him on the 26th, £2 ; Paid Waring & Co. for goods supplied, £1 2s. 9d ; Received from Vaughan Bros. on account, £4.

EXERCISE 2D.

E. Rankine is a trader who keeps no cash at his office, but pays all moneys received into his banking account, and makes all his payments by cheque. From the following particulars write up his Cash Book, balancing it as on February 28, 1910.

1910. Feb. 1, Balance at the Bank as on this date, £362 14s. 9d. ; Feb. 3, Received from Bourne Bros. cheque for £124 13s. 9d. ; Feb. 4, Paid Hotchkiss & Cording, Ltd., by cheque, £79 14s. 2d. ; Feb. 7, Received from Lloyd & Co. cash and paid same into bank, £5 10s. 4d. ; Feb. 8, Paid W. Bentall by cheque on account, £117 14s. 9d. ; Feb. 10, Paid by cheque for goods bought at auction, £109 10s. 6d. ; Feb. 11, Received from O. Capper cheque for goods sold by auction, £32 9s. 4d. ; Feb. 12, Paid Twiss & Co. by cheque, £14 3s. ; Feb. 14, Lent Horace Evans by cheque, £7 ; Feb. 16, Received from C. Lees in postal orders, and paid same into bank, 14s. 9d. ; Feb. 17, Received from Mason & Co. cheque and paid the same into bank, £192 14s. 6d ; Feb. 18, Paid Semon & Co. by cheque on account, £204 12s. 6d. ; Feb. 21, Received from R. Dickie cheque for £5 and postal orders for £2, and paid the same into bank, £7 ; Feb. 23, Paid Lenzie Bros. by cheque, £17 2s. 9d. ; Feb. 24, Received from O. C. Deverellin bank-notes, and paid the same into bank, £15 ; Feb. 25, Paid King & Warby by cheque, £3 2s. 9d. ; Feb. 28, Horace Evans repaid by cheque the £7 lent to him on Feb. 14 ; Paid by cheque salaries for February, £15.

EXERCISE 2E.

W. Rutherford is a trader who keeps the whole of his cash with his Bankers, the Union of London and Smiths Bank, Ltd. He pays all his receipts into his banking account, and makes all his payments by cheque. The following are his transactions for the month of February 1910. Write up his Cash Book, and balance it as on February 28, 1910.

1910. Feb. 1, Balance at the bank at this date, £104 13s. 2d. ; Feb. 3, Received from M. Strain cash, £4 10s. 9d. ; Feb. 5, Received from Shaw & Co. cheque, £32 6s. 4d. ; Feb. 8, Paid by cheque to W. B. Shields, £19 2s. 11d. ; Feb. 10, Received from Stratton Bros., cash £2 and postal order 3s. 6d., £2 3s. 6d. ; Feb. 11, Drew cheque in favour of M. Shillington, £4 9s. ; Drew cheque for gas bill to 31.12.09, Westchurch Gas Company, £3 17s. 11d. ; Feb. 14, Received from the Eastern Supply Stores, Ltd., their cheque, £62 19s. 8d. ; Feb. 17, Paid by cheque to J. Webb, £21 3s. 6d. ; Feb. 19, Received from the Great Eastern Railway Co. their cheque for compensation for goods damaged in transit, £4 9s. 6d. ; Feb. 23, Received from McKeown & McAusland by cheque, £17 14s. 2d. ; Drew cheque in favour of V. Turtle, collector of rates, £8 0s. 4d. ; Lent M. Meacher by cheque, £5 ; Feb. 26, Received from William Sloan cash £4 10s. 9d. and cheque £10, £14 10s. 9d. ; Feb. 28, Paid by cheque M. Wilson, collector of taxes, for income-tax, £6 19s. 3d. ; M. Meacher repaid to me in cash, £5 ; Received from J. W. Reade, money order £1 10s. 9d. and bank-note £5, £6 10s. 9d. ; Paid by cheque salaries for February, £10 5s.

EXERCISE 2F.

C. Ashford is a trader who keeps the greater part of his cash with his Bankers, but he also keeps a small balance of cash in his office cash-box. From the following particulars write up C. Ashford's Cash Book in "double column" form, and balance it as on February 28, 1910.

1910. Feb. 1, Balances at this date cash in hand £5 10s. 9d., and at bank, £283 15s. 6d. ; Feb. 2, Drew from bank for office cash, £25 ; Feb. 3, Received from R. Mason in cash (placed in cash-box), £10 5s. 6d. ; Feb. 4, Received from Fotherick & Co. cheque, and banked the same, £129 14s. 10d. ; Feb. 5, Paid to North-Eastern Railway Co. by cheque, £3 9s. 2d. ; Feb. 8, Paid from office cash for repairs to safe, 15s. ; Feb. 9, Received from Grey & Gough in cash (placed in cash-box), £11 10s. ; Paid by cheque to Foley Bros. on account, £32 16s. 3d. ; Feb. 11, Received from the Deep Vale Tanning Company, Ltd., by cheque, and banked the same, £117 14s. 9d. ; Feb. 14, Received from Brown Bros. in cash (placed in cash-box), £3 4s. 6d. ; Feb. 16, Paid by cheque electric lighting bill to Dec. 31, 1909, £8 11s. 4d. ; Feb. 17, Paid by cheque to L. D. Evans, £14 6s. ; Feb. 18, Paid from office cash for goods purchased at auction to-day, £13 10s. 5d. ; Feb. 21, Received from Liscombe Bros. by cheque and banked same, £26 0s. 11d. ; Feb. 22, Received from Blandy & Co. in cash (placed in cash-box), £1 4s. 6d. ; Feb. 23, Paid from office cash into the bank, £20 ; Feb. 25, Received cash (placed in cash-box) for sundry goods sold "for cash," £1 17s. 5d. ; Feb. 26, Paid from office cash wages to date, £9 4s. 6d. ; Feb. 28, Paid by cheque clerk's salary to date, £6 5s.

EXERCISE 2G.

M. Priestman is a trader who keeps part of his cash at his Bankers and part in his office cash-box. From the following particulars write up his Cash Book in "three column" form, balancing it at the end of the month.

1910. Feb. 1, Balances at this date : cash in hand, £45 2s. 9d., balance at bank, £179 16s. 5d. ; Feb. 2, Paid E. Gibbs from office cash, £15 2s. 9d., being allowed discount, 17s. 3d. ; Feb. 3, Received from T. Howell & Co. cheque for £52 10s. (paid same into bank), allowed them discount, £2 10s. ; Feb. 4, Paid from office cash for repairs to office desks, £1 3s. 5d. ; Feb. 5, Drew from bank for office cash, £20 ; Feb. 8, Received from J. Friend cash (placed in office cash), £17 6s. 2d. ; allowed him discount, £1 13s. 10d. ; Feb. 9, Paid by cheque, £32 6s. 9d. to Houghton & Co., being allowed discount, £3 2s. 6d. ; Paid for goods purchased at auction (by cheque), £25 3s. 6d. ; Feb. 11, Paid J. Morris in cash £30, being allowed discount, £1 10s. ; Feb. 14, Received from W. Lewis £5 cash (placed in office cash) and cheque for £16 3s. 4d. (paid same to bank) ; Feb. 16, Paid by cheque property tax for year 1909–10, £6 4s. 9d. ; Feb. 17, Paid by cheque to the Hampstead Tube Co., Ltd., £10, being allowed discount, 2s. 6d. ; Feb. 18, Paid from office cash gas bill, £1 14s. 3d., and fire insurance premium, 7s. 9d. ; Feb. 21, Received from J. Jones £10 in cash (placed in office cash) ; Feb. 22, Lent R. Keene (from office cash), £2 ; Feb. 24, Paid from office cash into the bank, £30 ; Feb. 25, Received from W. Little cheque and paid the same to bank for £13 4s. 2d., allowed him discount, £1 2s. ; Feb. 28, Paid from office cash salaries for month, £10 5s.; Received from M. Wemyss cheque (and paid the same to bank), £32 4s. 9d., and cash (placed in office cash), £14 6s. 2d., allowing him discount, £1 17s. 10d.

EXERCISE 2H.

From the following particulars prepare the Petty Cash Book of S. Fry, including analyses columns for the following classes of expenditure, viz., (1) Postage, (2) Telegrams and Cables, (3) Housekeeping and Cleaning, (4) Stationery, (5) Electric Light, including bulbs, (6) Advertisements, Donations and Subscriptions, (7) Travelling Expenses, (8) Repairs, (9) Sundries, and (10) a "Ledger" column. Balance the Petty Cash Book as on February 16, 1910.

1910. Feb. 1, Drew from the bank for petty cash purposes, £30 ; Feb. 2, Paid postage 1s. 10d., and telegrams 3s. 6d. ; Feb. 3, Paid fares 1s. 2d., postage 1s. 6d., and telegrams 6d. ; Feb. 4, Paid postage 3s. 6d. ; Feb. 5, Paid postage 10d., and housekeeper and cleaning £1 2s. 9d. ; Feb. 7, Paid postage 1s. 2d., and electric light bulbs 6s. 2d. ; Feb. 8, Paid telegrams 1s. 5d., repairs to electric bells 6s. 9d., postage 2s. 3d., and ink 6d. ; Feb. 9, Paid cost of new coal-scuttle 8s. 9d. (debit furniture account in "Ledger" column), and postages 1s.; Feb. 10, Paid postages 2s. 4d., stationery 6s. 9d., and fares to Woolwich 3s. 4d., cost of advertisement in "Post Office London Directory," £1 10s., cost of standing advertisement in "Feathered World," £4 10s. ; Feb. 11, Paid telegrams 1s. 4d., and postage 3s. 9d. ; cost of repainting name on office door, 10s. 6d., fares to Ludgate Circus, 4d., and cost of two dozen boxes for samples, 4s. 2d. ; Feb. 12, Paid postage 1s. 9d., and telegrams 2s. 9d., cost of cable message to Fry & Lewisohn, New York, £1 2s. ; Feb. 14, Paid donation to the Central Trade Protection Association, 5s., and postage 1s. 9d., housekeeper's book and cleaning to Feb. 12, £1 7s. 3d., cost of new electric light bulbs, 4s. 2d. ; Feb. 16, Paid telegrams 1s. 3d., postage 3s. 6d., and cost of cable message to Fry & Lewisohn, £1 3s., fares to Chiswick, 2s. 4d.

CHAPTER III

PURCHASES BOOK, PURCHASES RETURNS BOOK

PURCHASES BOOK

I HAVE already explained to you, in Chapter I., that when a trader buys goods he usually buys them "on credit," *i.e.* upon the understanding that a stated period of time is to be allowed to elapse before he will be called upon to pay for them.

If a trader buys goods, and pays cash for them immediately, the transaction appears in the first instance in the Cash Book; cash "goes out" to pay for the goods, and this necessitates an entry on the "payments" side of the Cash Book, in the manner already explained in Chapter II. Purchases for "prompt cash" are not, as I have already told you, so common in actual business as those which are made "on credit."

In order that a trader may know at any time what goods he has bought on credit a special book, known as a "**Purchases Book,**" or "Purchases Journal," is kept by him.

A Purchases Book, in its simplest form, is merely a list of the goods bought on credit from time to time by the owner of the book. Each purchase is set out with its principal details, the entry being headed with the name of the person from whom the goods have been bought.

The ordinary ruling of a Purchases Book is as follows:

PURCHASES BOOK.

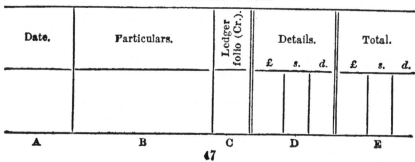

Date.	Particulars.	Ledger folio (Cr.).	Details.			Total.		
			£	s.	d.	£	s.	d.
A	B	C	D			E		

The columns given in the above form are used as follows:

Column A is designed to record the *date* on which each purchase of goods was made by the owner of the book.

Column B is designed to record the *particulars* of the purchase, that is to say, (*a*) the name of the person from whom the goods were bought, followed by (*b*) a description of the goods themselves, their number or quantity, price, &c.

Column C is designed to contain the "*Ledger folio*," *i.e.* the number of the page in the trader's Ledger in which the purchase is afterwards re-entered or "posted." The Ledger account in which the "posting" is made is headed with the name of the seller of the goods.

Column D is designed to contain the *prices*, in pounds, shillings and pence, of each individual piece or parcel of goods bought, in cases where several pieces or parcels of goods are bought at the same time from one particular person.

Column E is designed to contain the *total* amount, in pounds, shillings and pence, of the purchase made.

In the case of goods bought subject to a "Trade" discount, the gross, or "list," price of the goods bought is entered in column D, the trade discount is then deducted in the same column, and the net amount of the purchase is carried out into column E.

All purchases made "on credit" are entered in the Purchases Book one after another in the order in which they have taken place. The amounts placed in Column E are added at the foot of the page, and the total of each page is carried forward to the top of the next page until the end of a month, or any other agreed period, has been reached. When the end of the month, or other fixed period, has been reached, the additions cease with the total then shown, and Column E is ruled off. A fresh total commences to be built up in similar manner with the beginning of the next month or other period.

Column D is not added at its foot, it is only an explanatory column.

An example of a Purchases Book is given on p. 50, and the following transactions have been entered in it.

1910.

Feb. 7.   Bought of Dickens & Co. on credit a suite of Sheraton dining-room furniture, mahogany, for £50. Bought of Brown & Co. on credit, 4 mahogany occasional chairs at £1 5s. each, *i.e.* £5 in all.

Feb. 8. Bought of Robert Riches, on credit, a suite of fumed oak bedroom furniture for £34 10s. and two oval inlaid mirrors at £1 10s. each.

„ 9. Bought of Oliver Archer, on credit, four mahogany 4' 6" bedsteads at £6 10s. each, and one chest of drawers, walnut, at £5.

„ 10. Bought of Merryweather & Co., on credit, twenty library chairs, oak, at £1 each, and a suite of inlaid mahogany bedroom furniture at £30 ; *both these purchases being subject to a " Trade" discount of 5 per cent.*

The procedure necessary in order to record the above purchases in the Purchases Book is as follows ·

Feb. 7. Bought of Dickens & Co., on credit, a suite of Sheraton dining-room furniture, mahogany, for £50.

In order to record this item " Feb. 7 " is written in the " Date" column, and *Dickens & Co.*, followed by a description of the goods, in the " Particulars" column. The amount of £50 is placed in the " Total" money column. Only one parcel of goods has been bought, so there is nothing to enter in the " Details" column (Column D).

Feb. 7. Bought of Brown & Co., on credit, four mahogany occasional chairs at £1 5s. each, i.e. £5 in all.

This item is similar to the one preceding it, and is entered in the Purchases Book in the same way.

Feb. 8. Bought of Robert Riches, on credit, a suite of fumed oak bedroom furniture for £34 10s., and two inlaid oval mirrors at £1 10s. each.

In this case two parcels of goods were bought at the same time, and the " Details" column therefore comes into use.

The date and the name of the seller are entered in the ordinary way, as also are the particulars of the goods bought.

The cost of the suite of furniture (£34 10s.) is entered in the " Details" column, and the cost of the two oval mirrors (£3) is entered in the same column on the next line.

The total of these two items taken together (£37 10s.) is then placed in the " Total" money column.

Feb. 9. Bought of Oliver Archer, on credit, four mahogany 4' 6" bedsteads at £6 10s. each, and one chest of drawers, walnut, at £5.

D

These two transactions resemble the transactions of the preceding day, and are treated in a similar manner.

Feb. 10. *Bought of Merryweather & Co., on credit, twenty library chairs, oak, at £1 each, and a suite of inlaid mahogany bedroom furniture at £30, both these purchases being subject to a trade discount of 5 per cent.*

This is an example of a purchase on the amount of which the seller makes a special deduction of 5 per cent. from the nominal, or "list," price.

The two parcels of goods bought (the twenty chairs, £20, and the suite of furniture, £30) are entered in the Purchases

PURCHASES BOOK.

Date.	Particulars.	Ledger folio (Cr.).	Detail.			Total.		
			£	s.	d.	£		d.
1910. Feb. 7	*Dickens & Co.—* Suite of Sheraton dining-room furniture, mahogany　.　.	124				50		0
„ 7	*Brown & Co.—* 4 mahogany occasional chairs at £1 5s. 0d. each　.　.　.	127				5		0
, 8	*Robert Riches—* Suite of fumed oak bedroom furniture　.　.　.　. 2 oval inlaid mirrors at £1 10s. 0d. each　.　.　.　.　.	131	34 3	10 0	0 0	37	10	0
„ 9	*Oliver Archer—* 4 mahogany 4' 6" bedsteads at £6 10s. 0d. each　.　.　. 1 chest of drawers (walnut)　.	76	26 5	0 0	0 0	31	0	0
„ 10	*Merryweather & Co.* 20 library chairs (oak) at £1 each Suite of inlaid mahogany bedroom furniture　.　.　.		20 30 50	0 0 0	0 0 0			
	Less 5 per cent. Trade discount	109	2	10	0	47	10	0
	Carried forward to the next page of the Purchases Book　.					£171	0	0

Book, just as the double purchases of Feb. 8 and 9 were entered. The total, £50, is not, however, placed forthwith in the "Total" column; it is entered in the "Details" column. From this total of £50 in the "Details" column the £2 10s. trade discount allowed is deducted—the same column being utilised for the purpose—and the real cost of the purchase (£47 10s.) is then, and not until then, placed in the "Total" column. The reason for treating the "Trade" discount in this manner is that £47 10s.—i.e. the "list" price less the "Trade" discount—is the real cost of the goods to the owner of the Purchases Book, and not the nominal figure of £50.

After all these transactions have been entered in the Purchases Book, as explained above, the "Total" column is added, and carried forward to the top of the next page.

At the end of a stated time, usually monthly, the addition of the "Total" column ceases; the column is ruled off, and a fresh total is then commenced to be built up for the following period.

In a subsequent chapter I will explain how the purchases that appear in the Purchases Book are recorded in the Ledger.

PURCHASES RETURNS BOOK

(RETURNS OUTWARDS BOOK).

As I have already explained, it very often happens that a trader returns to the person from whom he bought them various parcels of goods which are found to be unsatisfactory. When he returns goods in this way the trader claims, and usually obtains, an allowance from the seller of the goods. This allowance is based upon the original invoice price of the goods.

For example, if a trader, A.B., buys on credit 10 bales of fancy goods from C.D. at £5 per bale, and afterwards returns two of the bales as unsatisfactory, C.D. will probably "allow" to A.B. the cost of 2 bales at the original price of £5 per bale.

When a purchaser returns to the seller the whole or part of a purchase, the "allowance" made by the latter to the former is not deducted directly from the amount of the original invoice.

The original purchase of the goods is, for book-keeping purposes, allowed to stand unaltered, and the "return" made is treated as though the goods "returned" had been re-sold by the dissatisfied buyer to the person from whom he had originally bought them.

For example, in the case of the "return" set out above, the transaction would be treated in the books as follows:

1. As though A.B. had bought from C.D. 10 bales of goods at £5 per bale, *i.e.* £50.
2. As though A.B. had subsequently re-sold to C.D. the 2 unsatisfactory bales of goods at the same price of £5 per bale, *i.e.* £10. The result of these entries would be that the £10 owing by C.D. to A.B. would, in the Ledger Account kept by A.B. for C.D., be set off against the £50 owing by A.B. to C.D. and only the difference (£40) would be paid by A.B. to C.D.

This procedure is much simpler for book-keeping purposes than any attempt to alter the original invoice of £50. When a figure has once been entered in the books, it is generally better not to alter it, even though it be incorrect. The more scientific way is to pass such fresh entries through the books as will adjust, or correct, the original entry of the transaction.

Moreover, it is simpler for the trader's office staff if returns can be treated as "re-sales" in this manner. As soon as the invoice for each purchase is received, it can be at once entered in the Purchases Book ; and if any of the goods are afterwards found to be unsuitable, the matter can be rectified, by means of the Returns Book, as a separate transaction at a later date. An obvious reason for adopting this method is that the fact of the unsatisfactory condition of some of the goods is not always discovered at the time of their delivery. It sometimes happens that their unsuitability is only disclosed when they commence to be manufactured or sold.

The Returns Outwards Book is ruled in exactly the same form as the Purchases Book, and it is written up in an almost identical manner. A specimen form is given below.

RETURNS OUTWARD BOOK.

Date of Return.	Particulars.	Ledger folio (Dr.).	Details.			Total.		
			£	s.	d.	£	s.	d.
A	B	C	D			E		

The columns given in the above form are used as follows :

Column **A** is to record the *date* on which the goods returned were sent back to the person from whom they were originally bought.

Column **B** is to record the *particulars* of the goods sent back, *i.e.* (*a*) the name of the person to whom they were returned, (*b*) a description of the goods themselves, their number, or quantity, price, and the reason why they were sent back.

Column **C** is designed to contain the "*Ledger folio*," *i.e.* the number of the page in the trader's Ledger in which the fact that the return has been made, and its particulars, are afterwards entered in the "Ledger account" of the person to whom the goods were returned.

Column **D** is designed to contain the *price*, in pounds, shillings and pence, of each individual parcel or quantity of goods returned in cases where several pieces or quantities of goods are sent back at the same time to the original seller.

Column **E** is to contain the *total* amount, in pounds, shillings and pence, of the "return" made, *i.e.* the amount of the allowance to be claimed from the original seller.

In cases where a "Trade" discount has been allowed off the original cost of the goods returned it is only the net price, *i.e.*, the price after allowing for the deduction of the "Trade" discount, that the dissatisfied purchaser can claim from the seller to whom he "returns" the goods. In this case the nominal or "list" price of the goods returned is written in Column D, and from it the "Trade" discount is deducted in the same column; the real amount of the allowance claimed in respect of the "return" is the net figure thus arrived at, and it is then carried into the "Total" column (column E).

All returns made by the trader are entered in the Returns Outwards Book, one after another, in the order in which they have taken place.

As was explained in the case of, the Purchases Book, the Returns Outwards Book is added at the foot of each page, and the total of each page is carried forward to the head of the following page. When the end of a month—or other fixed period of time—has been reached, the total of the Returns Outwards to that date ceases, and the column is ruled off. A fresh total is then commenced to be built up for the ensuing period.

In a subsequent chapter I will explain to you how "returns" are dealt with in the trader's Ledger.

An example of a Returns Outwards Book is given on p. 56, in which the following transactions have been entered:

1910.

Feb. 14.   Returned to Cunningham Bros., Leeds, 4 bales of woollen shirtings, damaged in transit, and received an allowance therefor at the invoice price, £15 per bale.

  „   15.   Returned to Hubert and Co., Manchester, the following goods, " Not equal to sample ":
            3 pieces of fancy coloured silk velvet, bought at £4 10s. per piece.
            4 pieces of Japanese silk, bought at £2 5s. per piece, being allowed full invoice price therefor.

  „   16.   Returned to Gremaud et Cie., Lyons, 4 pieces of grey silk, bought at £5 per piece less 10 per cent. trade discount, and was allowed full net price therefor, the colour of the goods not being that which was ordered.

The necessary procedure in order to record the above returns in the Returns Outwards Book is as follows :

Feb. 14, 1910.   Returned to Cunningham Bros., 4 bales woollen shirtings, damaged in transit, at £15 per bale, i.e. £60.

In this case 4 bales of woollen goods originally bought at £15 per bale arrived in a damaged condition, and were forthwith returned to the sellers (Cunningham Bros.).

The date of the return (Feb. 14, 1910) is entered in the "Date" column (column A), while the name of the original sellers (Cunningham Bros.), to whom the goods were returned, is entered upon the same line in the "Particulars" column (column B).

In the "Particulars" column, under the name of the persons to whom the goods were returned, the details of the goods sent back are entered, together with a memorandum of the reason for returning them.

The total amount claimed from Messrs. Cunningham Bros. is entered in the "Total" column (column E). There is nothing to be entered in column D, as only a single parcel of goods was returned. Upon this "return" being posted in Cunningham Bros.' Ledger account, a memorandum of the page of the Ledger on which their account appears is entered in column C (the " Ledger folio " column), serving the double purpose of a reference page number, and an indication that the amount has been duly posted in the Ledger.

> *Feb. 15. Returned to Hubert and Co. the following goods, not equal to sample, viz.:*
>
> 3 *pieces of fancy coloured silk velvet, at £4 10s. per piece (£13).*
>
> 4 *pieces of Japanese silk, at £2 5s. per piece (£9).*

This is a transaction wherein the return of two different parcels of goods must be dealt with. This fact necessitates the use of column D. In all other respects the requisite entry is made in the Returns Outwards Book upon exactly similar lines to those explained in the case of the previous transaction.

To record this transaction, " Feb. 15 " is entered in the " Date " column (column A), while " Hubert and Co." is entered in the same line in the " Particulars " column (column B).

In the " Particulars " column on the next two lines the two parcels of goods returned are set out, the one under the other, while the allowance claimed for each parcel is entered in column D in the same two lines. The total of the allowance claimed (£22 10s.) is entered in the " Total " column (column E), and is afterwards included in the additions of the total of that column.

> *Feb. 16. Returned to Gremaud et Cie., Lyons, 4 pieces of grey silk, bought at £5 per piece, less 10 per cent. trade discount, the colour not being as ordered, i.e. :*
>
> 4 *pieces at £5 = £20, less 10 per cent. trade discount, £2 = £18.*

This transaction resembles the transaction of February 14, except for the fact that it relates to the return of certain pieces of silk upon which a " Trade " discount of 10 per cent. was allowed at the time when they were originally bought.

The purchaser, when he bought these particular goods, was only charged with 90 per cent. of their nominal or " list " price; he can, therefore, only claim an allowance of 90 per cent. of the "list" price upon such of the goods as he returns to the seller.

Column D is used for the purpose of deducting the "Trade" discount. The "list" price of the goods, viz., £20, is first written in column D against the corresponding entries for the details of the return recorded in columns A and B.

From the £20 entered in column D, the £2 "Trade" discount is deducted, and the net figure, £18, being all that can be claimed for the goods returned, is extended into column E.

The Returns Outwards Book is added at the foot of the page, and the total, £100 10s., is shown as being carried forward to the next page.

RETURNS OUTWARDS BOOK
(or Purchases Returns Book).

Date.	Particulars.	Ledger folio (Dr.).	Details.			Total.		
			£	s.	d.	£	s.	d.
1910. Feb. 14	*Cunningham Bros.*, Leeds— 4 bales woollen shirtings at £15 0s. 0d. per bale, damaged in transit	146				60		
„ 15	*Hubert & Co.*, Manchester— 3 pieces fancy coloured silk velvet at £4 10s 0d. per piece 4 pieces Japanese silk at £2 5s. 0d. per piece, not equal to sample	192	13 9	10 0	0 0	22	10	0
„ 16	*Gremaud et Cie.*, Lyons— 4 pieces of grey silk at £5 0s. 0d. per piece, colour not as ordered . . . . *less* 10 per cent. trade discount	326	20 2	0 0	0 0	18		
	Carried forward to the next page of the Returns Outwards Book . . .					£100	10	0

EXERCISE 3A.

1. For what purpose does a trader keep a Purchases Book? 2. Rule a form suitable for a Purchases Book, and enter therein six transactions. 3. How many kinds of Returns Books are there? Rule a form of each kind, and enter therein six transactions. 4. On June 1, 1910, I bought, on credit, from Maples Bros., 6 "Barnes" cricket bats @ 19s. 6d.

each, and 1 dozen best "match" cricket balls @ 38s. per dozen, and
was allowed a trade discount of 10 per cent. on the total cost of the
goods. Enter these purchases in my Purchases Book. 5. On June 4,
1910, I returned to Maples Bros. 1 "Barnes" cricket bat, the handle
of which was faulty, and ¼ dozen "match" cricket balls, the stitching
of which was defective. Enter these returns in my "Returns Outwards
Book." 6. For what reasons do you prefer to enter the returns mentioned in the previous question in the "Returns Outwards Book,"
rather than alter the figures which were entered in the books to record
the original purchase of the goods?

EXERCISE 3B.

Enter the following particulars in my Purchases Book :

1910. June 1, Bought from J. Fry & Co., 3 "Special Club" tennis
rackets @ 16s. 6d. each ; June 3, Bought of R. Hawke, 1 dozen canvas
tennis racket covers @ 18s. per dozen ; June 5, Bought of B. Ayres,
12 dozen "Wimbledon" tennis balls @ 10s. per dozen ; June 7,
Bought of T. Haywood. 6 "College" hockey sticks @ 7s. 6d. each ;
June 9, Bought of R. Duke, 2 dozen best composition hockey balls
@ 8s. 6d. per dozen ; June 12, Bought of B. Ayres, 1 dozen pairs shin
guards @ 18s. 6d. per dozen pairs.

EXERCISE 3C.

From the following particulars make out the Purchases Book of
Robert Wilson & Co., photographic dealers ·

1910. March 1, Bought of the Optimax Optical Co., 4 "Vrela" ¼ plate
hand cameras, R.R. lens. @ 18s. each, £3 12s. ; 1 "Optimax" ¼ plate
hand camera, fitted with "Brugex" best anastigmatic lens and
shutter, @ £4 15s.; March 1, Bought of Kendall & Young, 10 guinea
"Amorphic" ¼ plate hand cameras at 15s., £7 10s. ; 5 folding
"Antesta" ¼ plate hand cameras with metal slides @ 30s., £7 10s. ;
March 2, Bought of Dufour et Cie., 1 "Tirailleur" folding hand
camera, post-card size, fitted with "Helion" No. 9 F6-8 lens and
"Sola" shutter (pneumatic release) @ £8 10s. ; 1 case for ditto,
solid leather, @ 15s. 6d. ; 1 adjustable aluminium tripod for ditto
@ £1 5s. ; March 3, Bought of Whitley & Co., 1 "Linstrat" enlarger, 10 in. condenser, with "M" series lens with Waterhouse
diaphragm, @ £9 8s. ; 1 "Kensington" enlarger, 5½ in. condenser,
achromatic objective, Iris diaphragm, @ £2 15s. ; March 4, Bought
of Fowler Bros. & Agnew, 20 "Preste" watch cameras, @ 7s. 6d.,
£7 10s. ; 20 outfits for ditto, @ 2s., £2 ; Bought of C. Weil, 2
special "M.V.W." ¼ plate camera sets, polished mahogany, triple-
extension camera, 2 double dark slides, "Metron" R.R. lens, F8,
three-fold tripod, @ 55s. per set, £5 10s. ; 6 "Claspa" diaphragmatic
shutters, ¼ plate, @ 21s. £6 6s. ; 1 "Claspa" pneumatic release, @
£1 2s.

EXERCISE 3D.

From the following particulars write up the Purchases Book of
Magnus Bros., furniture dealers :

1910. March 1, Bought of Gilchrist & Co., 3 mahogany revolving
bookstands, 18½ in. by 18½ in. top, height 2 ft. 6 in., @ £3 15s. each,

£11 5s.; March 2, Bought of R. Usher, 3 Chippendale mahogany occasional tables, 1 ft. 9 in. by 1 ft. 9 in., @ at 21s. each, £3 3s. ; March 2, Bought of W. Eadie, 6 mahogany overmantels, 4 ft. high by 4 ft. wide, @ £1 15s. each, £10 10s. ; March 3, Bought of Ballard & Aitchison, 1 Sheraton inlaid mahogany overmantel, 5 ft. wide by 2 ft. 9 in. high, @ £2 ; 1 fumed oak bedroom suite (C 927) complete, @ £6 10s. ; 1 5-ft. satin-walnut wardrobe (made in four parts), at £7 5s. ; March 5, Bought of Baines Bros., 3 box ottomans with fixed scroll, fitted with special hinges opening both sides, upholstered, buttoned in cretonne, part hair, @ £1 15s. each, £5 5s. ; 3 ditto, all hair, superior quality, @ £3 10s. each, £10 10s. ; 1 6 ft. adjustable end Chesterfield settee in tapestry, upholstered fibre and wool, @ £3 10s. ; March 7, Bought of Pfeiffer and Ebhardt, 20 Austrian bent wood arm-chairs, No. 327W, @ 10s. each, £10 ; 10 ditto chairs, No. 328W, @ 5s. each, £2 10s. ; Bought of M. Lamb & Sons, 5 "Kindergarten" nursery chairs, pattern J, @ 12s. each, £3, less 10 per cent. trade discount, 6s., £2 14s. ; March 8, Bought of R. Unwin, 4 sets of tea tables (4 in set), plain polished top, @ 22s. per set, £4 8s. ; 1 invalid's carrying-chair, @ £1 12s. 6d.

EXERCISE 3E.

From the following particulars make out the Purchases Book of Robert Bird, silversmith.

1910. May 2, Bought of Rice Bros., 5 electro-plated crumb scoops @ 17s. each. May 6, Bought of the Everwear Plate and Cutlery Co., Birmingham, 5 egg frames, plated, 6 cups, @ 32s. each ; 3 egg frames, plated, 4 cups @ 26s. each. May 14, Bought of Wearman Bros., 1 silver-mounted claret jug @ £2 15s. ; 1 plated mounted claret jug @ £1 7s. 6d. ; 3 silver-mounted cut glass biscuit boxes @ £3 2s. 6d. each ; 1 E.P.N.S. 8-inch waiter (engraved) @ 23s. 6d. May 21, Bought of Rice Bros., 1 presentation silver tea-set (to order) engraved, Order C 295, £16 3s. 6d. ; May 28, Bought of S. W. Murphy, 1 E.P.N.S. chafing-dish @ £2 12s. 9d. ; 1 plated egg-steamer, plain, @ 16s. 6d. ; 1 plated muffin dish @ 19s. 6d. ; May 31, Bought of R. Holmes, 1 set of 4 entrée dishes, plated, chased edges, second quality, @ £5 17s. 6d. per set.

EXERCISE 3F.

From the following particulars write up the Purchases Book of the International Fur Association, Ltd.

1910. March 7, Bought of Strelski and Zoitoff, St. Petersburg, 6 Astrachan muffs @ £1 10s. each, and 3 Fox muffs @ £3 5s. each ; Bought of Lewis Charles & Co. 2 dyed Musquash coats @ £12 each, less 5 per cent. trade discount ; March 8, Bought of Harrison Bros., 6 Mink stoles @ £5 each ; March 10, Bought of Jacobsen & Weil, 12 Marmot muffs @ £1 2s. each, less 5 per cent. trade discount ; 12 Moleskin muffs @ £2 each, less 5 per cent. trade discount ; 12 Bear muffs @ £2 5s. each, less 5 per cent. trade discount ; March 15, Bought of Hearst & Co., 3 Grey Squirrel ties @ 42s. each, and 3 Grey Squirrel muffs @ 45s. each ; March 16, Bought of R. Lewisohn, 2 fur-lined tweed coats @ £5 each ; 2 fur-lined cloth coats @ £7 5s. each. March 23, Bought of Rosoff and Meer 1 Bear stole @ 45s., and 1 Bear muff @ £2 ; March 29, Bought of Méricourt Frères, Paris, 1 Sable stole @ £15 and 1 Sable muff @ £10, both subject to 5 per cent. trade discount; March 31, Bought of Bielski, Drammen & Co., Moscow, 3 Caracul coats @ £7 5s. each ; 1 Moleskin tie @ 22s. ; Bought of Gebruder Strohl, 1 Astrachan muff @ 32s., and 1 Skunk stole @ £2.

EXERCISE 3G.

From the following particulars prepare the Returns Outwards Book of V. Lake, optical dealer.

1910.   April 1, Returned to Evans & Co. 1 nickel case pedometer C 119, invoiced at 7s. 3d., mechanism faulty.   April 16, Returned to W. Lord & Sons, 1 watch aneroid with revolving altitude scale, 20,000 ft., "received damaged," invoiced at £1 15s., 1 surveying aneroid, in case, "not as ordered," invoiced at £2 10s.   April 23, Returned to R. Benn & Sons, 1 pair "Adjutant" Field-glasses, "one lens cracked," invoiced at £2 3s. ; 1 altitude meter, M 79, "scale incorrect," invoiced at £1 3s. 9d.   April 30, Returned to J. Milnes & Sons, Ltd., 1 mercurial pediment barometer, oak frame, "faulty," invoiced at £2 1s.

EXERCISE 3H.

From the following particulars prepare the Purchases Returns Book of Hubert Smith.

1910. March 21, Returned to Pannell Bros. 2 tables, top 20 in. sq., "not as ordered," invoiced at 15s. each, £1 10s.   March 22, Returned to Hare & Co. 1 office arm-chair, invoiced at 12s., "one leg broken," 12s. ; 1 small table, invoiced at 8s., "top badly scratched," 8s.   March 24, Returned to Mr. Chase 1 lady's rocking chair, cane, invoiced @ 12s., ordered "upholstered plush," 12s.   March 29, Returned to Wharton & Co. 1 bath-chair, wicker, invoiced at £1 15s., medium size ordered, small size received.   March 31, Returned to Hare & Co. 1 japanned and decorated dressing-chest, "glass cracked," invoiced at £1 2s. ; 1 mahogany occasional table, "top cracked," invoiced at 19s. 6d. ; 1 cretonne-covered sofa, "cretonne wrong pattern," invoiced at £1 15s.

CHAPTER IV

SALES BOOK. SALES RETURNS BOOK

SALES BOOKS

I HAVE explained to you in the previous chapter how a trader keeps his Purchases Book and his Purchases Returns Book. I must now explain to you how he keeps his " Sales **Book**," or " Sales Journal," and his " Sales Returns Book," both of which follow upon much the same lines as the books which record his purchases.

As is the case with a trader's purchases, his sales are also mainly " on credit."   Cash purchases and Cash sales find their first place of record in the trader's Cash Book; but purchases and sales on credit demand the use of special books to contain their original record.

The form of Purchases Book given on p. 50 could be used for a Sales Book with one trifling alteration, viz., the heading of column C (the " Ledger folio " column), which would have to be altered from " Ledger folio *Cr.*" to " Ledger folio *Dr.*" The necessity for this alteration is due to the fact that sales *to* a person are " posted " to his *debit* in the Ledger account kept to record the dealings with him, whereas purchases *from* a person are " posted " to his *credit* in the same account.

A form of Sales Book, prepared by effecting this alteration in the form of the " Purchases Book," is given on p. 61.   The columns of this book are designed to contain information upon the same lines of classification as were adopted in the case of the " Purchases Book."

Column **A** is designed to contain the *date* of the sale.
Column **B** is for the record of the *particulars* of the sale, viz., the name of the person to whom the goods have been sold, together with the quantities supplied, descriptions, qualities, and prices of the various articles.

60

Column **C** is the "*Ledger folio*" column, *i.e.* the column which gives the page, or folio, of the Ledger wherein the trader records his transactions with the particular customer to whom he has sold the goods.

Column **D** is designed to contain the *prices*, in pounds, shillings and pence, of each individual piece, or parcel, of goods sold, in cases where several parcels or pieces are sold to a customer at the same time.

Column **E** is provided for the *total* amount of the sale in pounds, shillings and pence.

SALES BOOK.

Date.	Particulars.	Ledger Föi o (Dr.).	Details.			Total.		
			£	s.	d.	£	s.	d.
A	B	C	D			E		

In cases where goods are sold by the trader subject to a special "Trade" discount, the gross or "List" price of the goods sold is entered in column D. The amount of the "Trade" discount is then deducted in the same column, and the net amount of the sale—*i.e.* the net price which the purchaser will have to pay—is carried into column E.

All sales made "on credit" are entered in the Sales Book, one after another, in the order in which they take place. The amounts placed in column E are added at the foot of the page, and the total of each page is carried forward to the top of the next page until the end of a month, or other period of time, is reached.

When the end of the month or other period is reached the total of column E is written in ink, and the column is ruled off in the ordinary way. A fresh total is commenced to be built up at the beginning of the next month, or other period.

I shall explain to you in due course how a trader records his sales in the Ledger.

A form of Sales Book is given on p. 63, in which the following transactions have been entered·

1910.

		£	s.	d.
Feb. 14.	Sold on credit to Venables & Co.			
	1 Empire tea service at .	10	0	0
	1 set of etched table glass at .	4	16	0
„ „	Sold on credit to Martin Bros.			
	10 dozen ivory-handled table knives at 25s. per dozen .	12	10	0
Feb. 15.	Sold on credit to W. Mead, subject to trade discount of 5 per cent.			
	20 dozen dessert knives at 25s. per dozen	25	0	0
	An assortment of china and glass goods at	12	10	0

The procedure necessary in order to record the above sales in the Sales Book is as follows

		£	s.	d.
Feb. 14.	*Sold on credit to Venables & Co.*			
	1 Empire tea service at . . .	10	0	0
	1 set of etched table glass at . .	4	16	0
		£14	16	0

To record this transaction " Feb. 14 " is entered in the " Date " column, and the name of the customer, " Venables and Co.," followed by the details of the articles sold, is entered in the " Particulars " column. The two money sums, viz., £10 10s. 0d. and £4 16s. 0d. respectively, are entered in column D, against the particulars given concerning them, their total, £14 16s. 0d., being carried into column E.

Feb. 14.	*Sold on credit to Martin Bros.*	
	10 dozen ivory-handled table knives	
	at 25s. per dozen . .	£12 10s. 0d.

To record this transaction, " Feb. 14 " is entered in the " Date " column, and the name of the customers, " Martin Bros.," followed by the details of the articles sold to them, is entered in the " Particulars " column.

The amount of the sale, £12 10s. 0d., is entered directly in the "Total" column (column E), there being no need to make use of column D, inasmuch as only one parcel of goods was sold.

Feb. 15. *Sold on credit to W. Mead, subject to 5 per cent. trade discount.*

	£	s.	d.
20 *dozen dessert knives at* 25s. *per dozen*	25	0	0
An assortment of china and glass goods	12	10	0
	£37	10	0

In this case a "Trade" discount was allowed, the amount of which must be deducted from the total of the sale in column D, just as was the case with the "Trade" discount deducted from the purchase given on p. 50.

To record this transaction "Feb. 15" is entered in the "Date" column, and the name of the purchaser, "W. Mead,"

SALES BOOK (Sales Day Book).

Date.	Particulars.	Ledger folio (Dr.).	Details.			Total.		
			£	s.	d.	£	s.	d.
1910. Feb. 14	*Venables & Co.*—							
	1 Empire tea service		10	0	0			
	1 set of etched table glass	39	4	16	0	14	16	0
" "	*Martin Bros.*—							
	10 dozen ivory-handled table knives @ 25s. per dozen	92				12	10	0
" 15	*W. Mead*—							
	20 dozen dessert knives @ 25s. per dozen		25	0				
	Assortment of china and glass goods as per carbon copy of invoice		12	10	0			
			37	10	0			
	Less 5 per cent. trade discount	99	1	17	6	35	12	6
	Total carried forward to the next page of the Sales Book					£62	18	6

is placed in the " Particulars " column, followed by the details of the goods sold. The " List " prices of the goods (£25 and £12 10s. 0d. respectively) are placed in the " Details " money column (column D), and a total is made of them, £37 10s. 0d., still in the same column.

From this total, £37 10s. 0d., the "Trade" discount of 5 per cent., £1 17s. 6d., is deducted, and the net total, £35 12s. 6d., is then extended into the "Total" column (column E).

The total of the transactions, £62 18s. 6d., is shown as being carried forward to the next page.

SALES RETURNS BOOK

(Returns Inwards Book).

A trader is frequently obliged to agree to take back goods which he has sold to his customers. Just as, in his turn, a trader often returns unsatisfactory goods to the persons from whom he bought them, so, for identical reasons, his customers frequently claim the right of returning unsatisfactory goods to him.

The reasons for the return of goods to a trader may be many and various, e.g. "goods not equal to sample," "goods not as ordered," "goods delivered in a faulty condition," "goods damaged in transit," &c. Whatever the reason for their return may be, the trader usually agrees to take back goods with which his customers are dissatisfied, and allows them either the full price at which the goods were originally sold, or some other price arranged by compromise.

Goods returned to a trader are styled in his books "Returns Inwards"; the goods which he returns to other people are called, as was stated in the previous chapter, "Returns Outwards."

I explained to you in Chapter III. that when a trader returned unsatisfactory goods to the person from whom he bought them, the transaction was treated, for book-keeping purposes, as a re-sale by the original buyer of the unsatisfactory goods to the original seller, and that the entry recording the original purchase was left unaltered in the trader's books, notwithstanding the fact that part of the goods have been subsequently sent back.

Similarly, if a trader sells goods to a customer, and is afterwards obliged to take some of them back, the original sale is recorded in the books and is allowed to remain unaltered. The goods taken back by the trader are recorded in his books as a re-purchase of them by him from his customer.

This may appear at first sight to be a roundabout method of procedure. A little actual experience, however, will soon show you that, from a book-keeper's standpoint, the principle adopted is the only practical one.

I have already explained to you that, with the exception of one trifling alteration, the form of Purchases Book given in Chapter III. can be employed equally well as a Sales Book. In a similar way the form of Purchases Returns (Returns Outwards) Book given in Chapter III., needs only one trifling alteration in order that it may be employed as a Sales Returns (Returns Inwards) Book.

All that is necessary to convert the form of Returns Outwards Book given upon p. 52 into a Returns Inwards Book is the alteration of the words " Ledger folio *Dr.*" in the " Ledger folio " column, into " Ledger folio *Cr.*"

A form of Returns Inwards Book is given below:

SALES RETURNS BOOK (Returns Inwards Book).

Date.	Particulars.	Ledger folio (Cr.).	Details.			Total.		
			£	s.	d.	£	s.	d.
A	B	C	D			E		

Column **A** is designed to contain the *date* when the goods were received back by the trader.

Column **B** is designed to contain the *particulars* of the " Return," beginning with the name of the customer who has returned the goods, and continuing with the detailed particulars of the goods sent back.

Column C is the "*Ledger folio*" column, *i.e.* it is designed to contain the folio upon which the return inwards is posted to the credit of the customer's Ledger account.

Column D is designed to contain the *price* of each individual parcel of goods returned in cases where several parcels of goods are returned at the same time to the trader.

Column E is designed to contain, in pounds, shillings and pence, the *total* amount allowed to the customer for the goods returned by him.

In cases where a "Trade" discount has been allowed to the customer at the time when the goods were originally sold to him, a similar "Trade" discount must be deducted (in column D) from the "List" prices of the goods taken back.

A form of Returns Inwards Book is given on p. 68, in which the following transactions have been entered:

		£	s.	d.
1910.				
Feb. 14.	Received from Holmes & Co., 5 pieces of unbleached cotton sheeting, returned by them as inferior in quality to sample	5	7	6
„ 15.	Received from Furness & Son, 2 cases of fancy goods, returned by them as not being delivered in reasonable time	7	10	0
	1 package assorted Austrian skins, returned owing to poor colour	32	6	9
„ 16.	Received from C. Leslie, 5 pieces of silk voile returned by him as being damaged in transit. The invoice price of these goods was £11, less 5 per cent. trade discount, viz.	10	9	0

The necessary procedure for the record of the above "Returns" in the Returns Inwards Book is as follows:

		£	s.	d.
1910.				
Feb. 14.	*Received from Holmes & Co., 5 pieces of unbleached cotton sheeting, returned by them as being inferior in quality to sample*	5	7	6

The date, Feb. 14, is entered in the "Date" column (column A), and the name of the dissatisfied customers, Holmes & Co., is entered on the same line in the "Particulars" column (column B). The detailed description of the unsatisfactory goods is given in column B immediately after the name of the customer, and the amount allowed, £5 7s. 6d., is entered opposite to these details in the "Total" column (column E).

<table>
<tr><td>1910.</td><td></td><td>£</td><td>s.</td><td>d.</td></tr>
<tr><td>Feb. 15.</td><td>Received from Furness & Son, 2 cases of fancy goods, returned by them as not being delivered in reasonable time . . .</td><td>7</td><td>10</td><td>0</td></tr>
<tr><td></td><td>1 package of assorted Austrian skins, returned owing to poor colour . . .</td><td>32 .</td><td>6</td><td>9</td></tr>
</table>

The date, Feb. 15, is entered in the "Date" column, and the name of the customers, Furness & Son, is entered on the same line in the "Particulars" column.

The two parcels of goods are entered in the "Particulars" column, one under the other, and the sums allowed for each parcel respectively (£7 10s. 0d. and £32 6s. 9d.) are entered in the "Details" column (column D). The total allowance made, £39 16s. 9d., is entered in the "Total" column (column E).

<table>
<tr><td>1910.</td><td></td><td>£</td><td>s.</td><td>d.</td></tr>
<tr><td>Feb. 16.</td><td>Received from C. Leslie, 5 pieces of silk voile returned by him as being damaged in transit. The invoice price of these goods was £11 0s. 0d., less 5 per cent. trade discount, viz. . . . . .</td><td>10</td><td>9</td><td>0</td></tr>
</table>

The date, Feb. 16, is entered in the "Date" column and the name of the customer, C. Leslie, is entered on the same line in the "Particulars" column (column B).

The details of the goods returned are placed in the "Particulars" column underneath the name of the customer, and the "List" price of the goods, £11 0s. 0d., is placed in column D.

The Trade discount (11s.) is deducted from the £11 0s. 0d. in column D, and the net amount allowed to C. Leslie is then carried into column E.

The Returns Inwards Book is added at the foot of each page, and the totals are carried forward from page to page until the end of a month, or other fixed period. A fresh total of Returns for the following month, or other period, then begins to be built up.

I shall explain to you in due course how Returns Inwards are posted in the trader's Ledger.

In the example given, the total of the Returns Inwards Book is shown as being carried forward to the next page.

SALES RETURNS BOOK (Returns Inwards Book).

Date.	Particulars.	Ledger folio (Cr.).	Details.			Total.		
			£	s.	d.	£	s.	d.
1910. Feb. 14	Holmes & Co.— 5 pieces of unbleached cotton sheeting returned as inferior in quality to sample . .	95				5	7	6
„ 15	Furness & Son— 2 cases of fancy goods not delivered within reasonable time		7	10	0			
„ 16	. 1 package assorted Austrian skins returned as being of poor colour	88	32	0	9	39	16	9
„ „	C. Leslie— 5 pieces of silk voile damaged in transit . . . . Less 5% trade discount . .	32	11	0 11	0 0	10	9	0
(	Carried forward to the next page of the Sales Returns Book					£55	13	3

EXERCISE 4A.

1. For what purpose is a Sales Book kept? 2. Rule a form of Sales Book and enter six transactions therein. 3. Enter the following transactions in my Sales Book: 1910, June 3, Sold to Hamilton & Co. 20 pairs 12-button length chamois gloves @ 2s. per pair. June 6, Sold to H. Winter 2 dozen ladies' blouses assorted silk @ 7s. 6d. each. June 7, Sold to R. Boots & Co. 1 dozen fancy "Pyrenees" wool capes @ 16s. each. 4. On June 10, 1910, H. Winter returned 2 of the blouses sold to him as "faded." I agree to allow him the original price paid by him for them. How would you enter this return of goods in my books? 5. On June 15 I sold to C. Summershouse 10 bags of coffee @ 80s. per bag, less 10 % trade discount. Enter this transaction in my Sales Book. 6. Mention some of the usual reasons for which traders return goods, and state the terms upon which such goods are usually allowed to be returned.

EXERCISE 4B.

Enter the following sales in my Sales Book:

1910. June 1, Sold to S. Boorman & Co. 2 dozen table knives @ 25s. per dozen; June 3, Sold to A. Barrow 12 gold bracelets @ 26s. each;

June 6, Sold to J. Steward 3 clocks @ 80s. each ; June 7, Sold to B. Bashall 10 watches @ 36s. each ; June 8, Sold to R. Olney 20 alarm clocks @ 3s. 9d. each ; June 9, Sold to H. Hope & Co. 10 dozen dessert knives @ 50s. per dozen.

EXERCISE 4C.

From the following particulars make out the Sales Book of Robert Cranstoun, miller and flour merchant ; all the undermentioned sales are " on credit " ·

1910. April 18, Sold O. Littlebury 10 barrels finest American flour @ 24s. per barrel (barrel included), £12.   April 19, Sold C. Bromwich 7 bags (7-lb.) Vertax wholemeal @ 1s. per bag, 7s. ; 20 bags Egyptian lentils @ 1s. per 4-lb. bag, £1.   April 20, Sold M. Darton 100 bags (6-lb.) "Suprema" self-raising flour @ 1s. per bag, £5 ; 50 bags "Hawthorn" flour @ 1s. 1d. per bag, £2 14s. 2d. ; 100 7-lb. bags "Nutra" wholemeal flour @ 1s. 2d. per bag, £5 16s. 8d.   April 20, Sold Weir & Watson 50 140-lb. bags Canadian flour @ 15s. per bag, £37 10s.; 10 4-lb. bags Egyptian lentil flour @ 1s. per bag, 10s.   April 21, Sold E. R. Smith & Co. 4 280-lb. sacks of brown meal @ 28s. per sack, £5 12s. ; 2 140-lb. sacks of finest Hungarian flour @ 16s. 6d. per sack, £1 13s. ; 10 7-lb. bags "Vertax" wholemeal, finely ground, @ 1s., 10s. ; 100 3½-lb. bags "Bananina" @ 6d. per bag, £2 10s. ; 50 5-lb. bags "O.K." snow-white pastry flour @ 10d. per bag, £2 1s. 8d. ; 2 280-lb. sacks stone-ground flour @ 27s. per sack, £2 14s. ; 3 dozen tins peaflour @ 6s. 6d. per dozen tins, 19s. 6d.   April 21, Sold Scott Bros. 50 7-lb. bags "Splendax" wholemeal, finely ground, @ 1s. per bag, £2 10s.

EXERCISE 4D.

From the following particulars write up the Sales Book of Messrs. Meister & Co., musical instrument dealers :

1910. April 1, Sold Hope & Co. 3 violins, superior quality, by Rousselet et Cie., full size, @ 63s., £9 9s. ; Sold Siegfried Bros. 2 violin beginner's sets, ½ size, @ 15s. per set, £1 10s.   April 2, Sold to J. and M. Wagner, 1 violincello, superior quality, by Rousselet et Cie. (Paris), oil varnish, @ £5 12s. ; 1 violincello bow, superior quality, silver mounted, @ 18s. ; 1 waterproof fancy tweed violincello cover, @ 11s.   April 4, Sold W. Carruthers, 3 Zither banjos, 5 string, walnut shell and handle, @ 37s. 6d., £5 12s. 6d. ; 1 Zither banjo, "Professional," 10¼ in., walnut shell, mahogany handle, @ £3 2s. ; 1 lady's banjo, German silver hoop, white pegs, @ 23s. 6d.   April 4, Sold the Eagleshill String Band (William Jones, Hon. Secretary) 1 mandoline, French make, 8 strings, @ 25s. ; 2 mandolines, Italian make, 8 strings, @ 31s., £3 2s. ; 2 dozen mandoline plectrums, shell, @ 2s. per dozen, 4s.   April 5, Sold R. Fry, 4 tambourines, 11 inch, with 6 pairs jingles, @ 1s. 9d., 7s.; 2 tambourines, 10 inch, with 3 pairs jingles, @ 8d., 1s. 4d. ; 1 piccolo, English cocoa, pillar key, @ 10s. 6d.; 1 conductor's baton, ebony with three silver mounts, @ 5s. ; 2 triangles with beaters, @ 2s., 4s. ; 1 metronome, walnut, with bell (French make) @ 5s. 8d. ; April 7, Sold Vermeer & Woelft 1 Renaissance style new model upright grand pianoforte, 7 octaves, oblique scaling, iron frame, under-damper check repeater action, 4 ft. 2 in., @ £26 10s.

EXERCISE 4E.

From the following particulars make out the Sales Book of H. Fox & Co., grain dealers :

1910. March 21, Sold Hudson & Brown 5 sacks of barley (No. 32) @ 17s. 6d. per sack ; Sold Mrs. C. A. Williams 6 sacks torrefied barley @ 16s. 3d. per sack, and 4 bushels split beans @ 4s. 3d. per bushel ; Sold E. Wallace 10 cwt. chaff @ 8s. 5d. per cwt., and 10 cwt. bran @ 7s. 4d. per cwt. ; Sold Suttley & Sturrock 2 sacks of linseed @ 33s. 6d. per sack, 1 bushel best flat maize at 4s. 3d., and 2 cwt. crushed maize @ 8s. 7d. per cwt. March 22, Sold Priestley & Co., Ltd , 2 sacks of poultry mixture @ 13s. 8d. per sack, 1 sack of tares @ 26s. 3d. per sack, and 1 cwt. ground Sussex oats @ 18s. 11d. per cwt. ; Sold The Easthorpe Farms. Ltd., 4 cwt. of cattle cakes @ 8s. 6d. per cwt., and 3 cwt. rice meal @ 7s. 4d. per cwt. ; March 23, Sold R. A. Skinner 1 bushel of dari @ 4s. 9d. per bushel, and ½ cwt. of best white groats @ 8s. 11d. per ½ cwt.

EXERCISE 4F.

Enter the following transactions in the Sales Book of the Californian Preserved Fruit Supply Co. Ltd. :

1910. March 7, Sold Haysome & Co. 50 cases of preserved apricots in tins, "Gloria" brand, @ 11s. per case, and 10 cases of preserved Bartlett pears, "Luxtra" brand, @ 15s. per case ; Sold J. W. Howarth 40 cases of lemon cling peaches in tins, "Aura" brand, @ 14s. per case, and 20 cases apricots (peeled) in tins, "Superba" brand, @ 21s. per case ; both less 5 per cent. trade discount. March 8, Sold Collins & Colman 50 cases assorted preserved fruits in tins (each case containing 1 dozen tins apricots, ½ dozen tins pears, and ½ dozen tins peaches) @ 22s. per case, less 5 per cent. trade discount ; and 1 sample case of pineapple (chunks) @ 17s. 6d. per case. March 10, Sold Klenck's Stores, Ltd., 5 dozen bottles French cherries in syrup @ 10s. 3d. per dozen bottles, 10 dozen bottles English strawberries in syrup @ 6s. 6d. per dozen bottles, and 10 dozen bottles (large) raspberries in syrup @ 22s. per dozen bottles. March 11, Sold Elston, Sons & Co. 5 cases extra quality apricots in tins @ 24s. 6d. per case, and 1 dozen bottles English plums @ 8s. per dozen bottles. March 12, Sold W. Kimber 3 cases of peeled apricots in tins, "Capitada" brand, @ 25s. per case, less 2½ per cent. trade discount, and 12 cases lemon cling peaches, sliced, @ 24s. 6d. per case, less 5 per cent. trade discount.

EXERCISE 4G.

From the following particulars make out the Returns Inwards Book kept by Messrs. Merrison & Co., lace and fancy goods merchants :

1909. May 2, Messrs. Hope & Co., Bristol, returned 3 lace scarves, 90 ins. by 20 ins., invoiced to them @ 2s. 6d., "wrong pattern," 7s. 6d. Received from J. Mear, Lincoln, 1 lace plastron with collar attached, "torn," invoiced @ 3s. 6d. May 3, Received from C. Wye, Bristol, 3 Brussels lace handkerchiefs, "sent in excess of number ordered," invoiced @ 24s. each, £3 12s. May 5, Received from Hudson Bros., Tulse Hill, 1 coloured silk shawl, "colour not as ordered," invoiced @ 7s. Received from Mme. Levarque, 347 Regent

Street, W., 1 Irish point lace collar, invoiced @ 15s., "inferior quality." May 7, Received from the Eastern Counties Fancy Goods Stores, Dereham, 1 dozen initial linen hemstitch handkerchiefs, "wrong initial letter," invoiced @ 8s. per dozen ; 3 dozen drawn thread handkerchiefs, invoiced @ 5s. per dozen, "not as ordered," 15s. ; 3 pieces coloured Sarsenet ribbon, "wrong colours," invoiced @ 2s. per piece of 36 yards, 6s. May 9, Received from Mme. Françoise, 127 Pont Street, W., 1 piece 3½ ins. wide coloured sarsenet ribbon, "wrong colour," invoiced @ 17s. 6d. per piece ; ½ piece black silk faille corded ribbon (3½ ins.) "not ordered," invoiced @ 12s. 9d.

EXERCISE 4H.

From the following particulars write up the Sales Returns Book of the Euston Carpet Supply Co.:

1910. May 17, Received from J. Brown, 2 seamless Axminster carpet squares, 12 ft. × 10 ft. 6 in., "wrong size," invoiced @ £4 each, £8. May 18, Received from D. Mackenzie 10 Brussels squares 12 ft. × 9 ft., assorted colours, "inferior quality to those ordered," invoiced @ £2 15s. each, less 10 per cent. trade discount ; 10 squares @ £2 15s. £27 10s., less 10 per cent. trade discount £2 15s. £24 15s. May 19, Received from O'Connor & Long 1 heavy Roman bordered bedroom art carpet, 12 ft. × 15 ft., "wrong colour," invoiced @ £3 2s. 6d. ; 2 Corona bordered bedroom art carpets, 9 ft. × 15 ft., "wrong pattern," invoiced @ £2 ; 1 hearth-rug, 72 in. × 36 in., W.C. 992, "stained with grease," invoiced @ 9s. 6d. May 24, Received from G. Lloyd & Cecil, Ltd., 2 Axminster corridor rugs, 9 ft. × 3 ft., "wrong size," invoiced at 16s. each, £1 12s. ; 1 Goat-skin hearth-rug, grey, invoiced @ 18s. 9d., "skin faulty." May 26, Received from the Streatham Stores Co., Ltd., 1 mottled hearth-rug, 64 in. × 27 in., "stained," invoiced @ 3s.

CHAPTER V

THE THEORY OF DOUBLE-ENTRY

On several occasions brief reference has been made in the preceding pages to the "Double-Entry" system of book-keeping. It has now become necessary to explain what this expression means.

In the first place I must mention that there are methods of keeping books other than that known as the double-entry system. "Double-entry" book-keeping has, however, stood the test of four hundred years' continuous use, and it may be safely claimed for it that it is the only system worthy of adoption by the practical business man.

Before explaining the double-entry method in detail, I will recount a few of the special advantages which it affords.

Book-keeping by Double-Entry :

1. Provides the trader with a complete history of all his transactions.
2. Is, to a very great extent, self-checking as regards arithmetical accuracy. In other words it prevents and discloses mistakes.
3. Shows at any given date what the trader possesses, how much he owes to his creditors, and how much his debtors owe to him.
4. Shows what the trader has made or lost during any given period, and how he has incurred the loss, or made the profit.
5. Shows the trader at any given date exactly what his financial position really is.

These are weighty recommendations.

The advantages set out above are rendered possible by, and are the direct result of, the most important principle of the system, namely, that *every transaction must be entered twice.* This important principle is peculiar to the double-entry system of book-keeping.

At first sight it may appear to you that this principle must involve a large amount of unnecessary work.

The additional work entailed in entering every transaction twice over is not, however, so heavy as might be imagined. Successive generations of accountants have devised many ingenious ways of lessening the labour involved.

Before I explain in detail how transactions are framed in double-entry form for record in the books, it is necessary that I should describe the various kinds of accounts which the book called the **Ledger** contains.

I have already mentioned that the most important book kept by a trader is known as the " Ledger." The Ledger is the book in which the entries recording a trader's transactions are " laid up," or stored, for future reference. A trader's Ledger is practically a summary of every transaction which has taken place in his business.

A Ledger consists of a number of pages ruled in a special way. These pages are designed to contain a number of sections which are called **Ledger** Accounts.

There are three kinds of Ledger Accounts, viz. :

(1) **Real** Accounts, which are kept for "*things*" owned by the trader.

(2) **Personal** Accounts, which are kept for *persons* dealt with by the trader, and

(3) **Nominal or Impersonal** Accounts, which are accounts showing (a) *profits*, (b) *losses*, or (c) the trader's "*net worth.*"

I have already explained to you that the Cash Book is a section of the Ledger ; it is nothing more nor less than one of the Ledger accounts, *i.e.*, the " Cash " account, bound separately because it has, owing to its size, became too unwieldy to be included in the Ledger itself.

A specimen Cash account is given below, prepared according to the form given on p. 23, and containing the following cash transactions :

1910.			£	s.	d.
Feb.	1.	Balance of cash in hand	60	0	0
„	2.	Lent C. Hubert in cash	30	0	0
„	3.	„ „ „	25	0	0
„	10.	C. Hubert repaid me in cash	50	0	0
„	18.	Lent C. Hubert in cash	15	0	0
„	22.	C. Hubert repaid me in cash	10	0	0

Dr. CASH ACCOUNT. *Cr.*

1910.			£	s.	d.	1910.				£	s.	d
Feb. 1	To Balance . .	√	60	0	0	Feb. 2	By C. Hubert (Loan account) Loan		37*	30	0	0
„ 10	„ C. Hubert, Loan account (re-payment) .	37*	50	0	0	„ 3	„ „ „		37*	25	0	0
„ 22	„ „ „	37*	10	0	0	„ 18	„ „ „		37*	15	0	0
						„ 22	„ Balance carried down . .		√	50	0	0
		£	120	0	0				£	120	0	
1910.												
Feb. 23	To Balance brought down . .	√	50	0	0							

* The folio numbers (37) inserted above refer to the distinctive number of the foli on which C. Hubert's Account appears. Folio numbers are always entered in thi way in order to facilitate easy reference to the Accounts in which the entries reappea See C. Hubert's Account on p. 77.

Let us deal first of all with the rules which apply when we are constructing **Real Accounts**.

If you will carefully study the Cash account given above you will find that the following rules have been observed in its construction, viz. :

1. All the cash which has been received, or which has "come in," has been entered on the debit, or left-hand, side *Examples* of which are the two receipts of £50 and £10 from C. Hubert.

2. All the cash which has been parted with, or which has "gone out," has been entered on the credit, or right-hand, side : *Examples* of this kind are the three sums lent to C. Hubert, £30, £25, and £15 respectively.

These simple rules must be followed in making out, not only the Cash account, but every other "Real" account. In other words, everything *received* must be entered on the *debit* side of the account kept to record the trader's dealings in that particular "thing," and everything *parted with* must be entered on the *credit* side of the same account.

If, for example, the account which we are constructing is the trader's "Horses" account, the cost of every horse that he purchases must be entered on the debit side of the "Horses" account, and the selling price of every horse that he sells must be entered on the credit side of the account. The same rules also apply if the account represents any kind of property whatever, *e.g.*, land, buildings, carts, harness, money, furniture, or machinery.

This rule may be stated shortly as follows, for the purpose of being committed to memory, viz. :

Debit everything that " comes in," credit everything that " goes out."

This is the rule for preparing an account relating to "things."

I have already explained to you that the great bulk of a trader's transactions take place " on credit " terms.   It will be obvious to you, therefore, that the trader must keep accurate accounts of all his dealings with the persons with whom he deals on credit.

I must now explain to you how to prepare these Personal Accounts. You will readily understand how necessary it is that a trader should be able to ascertain easily, at any time, from the accounts he keeps for the persons with whom he deals, (a) How much he owes to them, and (b) How much they owe to him.

In order that this necessary information shall be readily available, the following rules must be observed in the construction of Personal accounts :

1. The ruling used must be the same as that of the Cash account already given.

2. The account must be headed with the name of the person with whom the trader is dealing.   For example, if the trader deals with C. Hubert, he will open an account in his Ledger ruled and headed as illustrated below.

FORM OF A PERSONAL ACCOUNT.

Dr.   C. Hubert (Loan Account).   *Cr.*

Date.	Details.	Folio.	£	s.	d.	Date.	Details.	Folio.	£	s.	d.

3. Everything paid or delivered by the trader to the person with whom he has dealt is entered on the *debit*, or left-hand, side of the account kept by him for this person.

4. Everything received by the trader from the person with whom he has dealt is entered on the *credit*, or right-hand, side of the account kept by him for this person.

It is now possible to make out, by way of illustration, the Personal account of C. Hubert relating to the example previously used in this chapter.

The transactions are as follow:

	1910.		£	*s.*	*d.*
(1)	*Feb.* 2.	*Lent C. Hubert in cash* . .	30	0	0
(2)	„ 3.	„ „ „ . .	5	0	0
(3)	„ 10.	*C. Hubert repaid me in cash* .	50	0	0
(4)	„ 18.	*Lent C. Hubert in cash* . .	15	0	0
(5)	„ 22.	*C. Hubert repaid me in cash* .	10	0	0

The first transaction is a loan of £30 from the trader to C. Hubert. In other words, £30 has been *paid* or delivered by the trader to C. Hubert. According to the rules set out above this entry must therefore be made on the *debit*, or left-hand, side as follows:

1910.
Feb. 2. *To cash lent* £30 0 0

The second transaction is a similar loan to C. Hubert of £25, it must, therefore, be similarly entered on the *debit* side as follows:

Feb. 3. *To cash lent* £25 0 0

The account, as it stands after these two transactions have been entered in it, shows a balance of £55 owing from C. Hubert to the trader whose books are being constructed.

The third transaction is a repayment by C. Hubert to the trader of £50 on account of the foregoing borrowings.

In this case £50 has been *received* by the trader from C. Hubert. This sum must therefore be entered on the *credit* side of C. Hubert's account, according to the rule given on p. 75. It will be obvious that, as the money which was lent to C. Hubert has been placed on the left-hand side of his account, the money received from him in repayment of the loan cannot be placed anywhere else than on the opposite, *i.e.,* the right-hand, side of the same account.

The necessary entry is made on the credit side as follows:

Feb. 10. *By cash repaid* .   .   . £50 0 0

If, after these three transactions have been entered, both sides of the account are compared, it will be seen that £30 and £25 (£55 in all) have been entered on the debit side, and £50 has been entered on the credit side. The debit entries thus exceed the credit entries by £5; this means that £5 more has been lent to C. Hubert than he has repaid; in other words, he is a *debtor* to the trader for £5.

The fourth transaction is a loan of £15 to C. Hubert. Since £15 has been *paid* to C. Hubert this sum must be *debited* to his account as follows:

Feb. 18. *To cash lent* £15   0   0

The fifth transaction is another repayment by C. Hubert; £10 having been *received* from C. Hubert it must be entered on the *credit* side of his account as follows:

Feb. 22. *By cash repaid* £10   0   0

If both sides of C. Hubert's account are now added, the total of the entries appearing on the debit side will be found to amount to £70, and the total of the entries appearing on the credit side will be found to be £60. The debit entries thus exceed the credit entries by £10. The meaning of this is, that C. Hubert still owes £10 to the trader or, in other words, that he is the trader's *debtor* for £10. The account is ruled off in the ordinary way, the balance of £10 owing by C. Hubert being brought down upon the debit side. The completed account then appears as follows:

37   C. HUBERT (Loan Account).   37

Dr.   *Cr.*

1910.		*	£	s.	d.	1910.			£	s.	d.
Feb. 2	To cash, loan .	C	30	0	0	Feb. 10	By Cash, repay- ment . .	C	50	0	0
„ 3	„ „ .	C	25	0	0	„ 22	„ „ „ .	C	10	0	0
„ 18	„ „ .	C	15	0	0	„ „	„ Balance car- ried down .	✓	10	0	0
		£	70	0	0			£	70	0	0
1910.											
Feb. 23	To Balance brought down . .	✓	10	0							

* The references marked "C" inserted in this column refer to the Cash Book, in which the various entries given above in C. Hubert's account originally appear. See the Cash Account   p. 74.

The following rules apply to all Personal accounts kept by a trader :

(a) If the total of the items on the debit side of the account exceeds the total of the items on the credit side, the person whose name is at the head of the account *owes to the trader* the amount of the " balance," *i.e.* the difference in amount between the two totals.   In these circumstances the account is said to show a debit balance.

(b) If the total of the items on the credit side of the account exceeds the total of the items on the debit side, the *trader owes* the amount of the difference, or " balance," to the person whose name is at the head of the account.

The account, in these circumstances, is said to show a credit balance.

You will readily understand that the balance of a Personal account kept by a trader for a party with whom he has dealings may sometimes show a debit balance and at other times a credit balance, as between the parties.

For example, if a trader whose books you are keeping sells on May 2, 1910, £100 worth of goods to John Brown, and, on May 3, a further £50 worth of goods to the same person, John Brown's account will, on May 3, 1910, show a *debit* balance of £150.   If, on May 4, 1910, the trader himself buys £200 worth of goods from John Brown the account will thereupon show a *credit* balance of £50, *i.e.* £200 *minus* £150.

These transactions are set forth in the following example.

Dr.						JOHN BROWN.					Cr.	
				£	s.	d.				£	s.	d.
1910.							1910.					
May 2	To Goods sold .	39		100	0	0	May 4	By Goods purchased	73	200	0	0
„ 3	„ „ .	40		50	0	0						
„ 4	„ Balance carried down . .	✓		50	0	0						
		£		200	0	0				£ 200	0	0
							1910.					
							May 5	By Balance brought down . .	✓	50	0	0

In the earlier part of this chapter I have shown you how to make out a " Real " account, and the example used as an illustration consisted of a list of the cash transactions of a trader with a person named C. Hubert. The trader paid to and received from C. Hubert certain sums of money, and from these transactions we constructed the trader's Cash account.

In this chapter I have also explained how to prepare a "Personal" account, and the example used as an illustration was the Personal account of the same C. Hubert, as it would appear in the trader's Ledger.

Both the trader's Cash account and the Personal account which he keeps for C. Hubert thus relate to the same series of transactions between the two persons.

Below I print a list of the transactions, and then I reprint (1) The trader's Cash account, and (2) the account which he keeps for C. Hubert.

I have numbered the transactions from 1 to 6, and these numbers are followed in the two accounts.

TRANSACTIONS.

	1910.		£	s.	d.
(1)	Feb. 1	Balance of cash in hand	60	0	0
(2)	„ 2	Lent C. Hubert in cash	30	0	0
(3)	„ 3	„ „ „	25	0	0
(4)	„ 10	C. Hubert repaid me in cash	50	0	0
(5)	„ 18	Lent C. Hubert in cash	15	0	0
(6)	„ 22	C. Hubert repaid me in cash	10	0	0

Dr.   CASH ACCOUNT.   **Cr.**

1910.				£	s.	d.	1910.				£	s.	d.
Feb. 1	To Balance (1)	.	✓	60	0	0	Feb. 2	By C. Hubert—					
10	„ C. Hubert—							Loan Account(2)	37	30	0	0
	Loan Account (4)	37	50	0	0	„ 3	„ „ „ (3)	37	25	0	0
„ 22	„ „ „ (6)	37	10	0	0	„ 18	„ „ „ (5)	37	15	0	0
							„ 22	„ Balance carried down . .	✓	50	0	0
			£	120	0	0				£	120	0	0
1910.													
Feb. 23	To Balance brought down . .	✓	50	0	0							

Dr.   C. HUBERT (Loan Account).   **Cr.**

1910.				£	s.	d.	1910.				£	s.	d.
Feb. 2	To Cash (loan) (2)	C	30	0	0	Feb. 10	By Cash (4) .	.	C	50	0	0	
„ 3	„ (3)	C	25	0	0	„ 22	„ „ (6) .	.	C	10	0	0	
„ 18	(5)	C	15	0	0	„ 23	„ Balance carried down . .	✓	10	0	0		
		£	70	0	0				70	0	0		
1910.													
Feb. 23	To Balance brought down . .	✓	10	0	0							

If you study the two foregoing accounts very carefully, and trace transactions 1 to 6 in each of them, you will discover the following important facts:

(1) That each of the transactions Nos. 1 to 6 appears in the *Cash account.*

The reason for this is that they are all either receipts or payments of *cash.*

(2) That each of the transactions Nos. 1 to 6 also appears in *C. Hubert's account.*

The reason for this is that they all related to either receipts from, or payments to, *C. Hubert.*

(3) That every transaction appearing on the *debit* side of the Cash account appears again on the *credit, i.e.* the opposite, side of C. Hubert's account; and

(4) That every transaction appearing on the *credit* side of the Cash account appears again on the *debit, i.e.* the opposite, side of C. Hubert's account.

The fact that every transaction in the one account appears on the opposite side in the other account is not merely a coincidence; *it is the direct result of the principal rule of double-entry book-keeping:*

The one cardinal rule upon which book-keeping by double-entry is based is this:

That every transaction, whatever its nature, can and must be entered in two accounts, on the debit side in one of them, and on the credit side in the other.

This principle is repeated more briefly in the following statement, viz.: **That every debit entry requires its credit entry, and every credit entry requires its debit entry.**

You must commit this rule to memory. The principle it embodies underlies every account book, and every account throughout the whole system of double-entry book-keeping, whether the books be those of a small trader or of a great company. In double-entry book-keeping every transaction of every kind must be framed in the form of "a debit entry in one account and a credit entry in another account," the two entries being equal in amount. It may not always be easy, at first sight, to divide a complicated transaction in this way, but it is always possible, as you will comprehend as we proceed.

You may perhaps think that I am dwelling with too much emphasis upon this rule, but I find that many students experience great difficulty in grasping the fact that the same transaction can bear both a debit and a credit aspect. If you will think carefully, however, you will understand: (1) that there must be two parties to every transaction, and (2) that each of the parties necessarily regards the transaction from a different point of view.

For example, say I have bought on credit a ton of coal for 28*s*. from John Cave. I have *received* the coal and John Cave has *parted with* it. I must recognise these two facts when I enter the transactions in my books. John Cave having *parted with* goods of the value of 28*s*. is my *creditor* for that amount. I must therefore *credit* his account with 28*s*. I have *received* the goods and I must therefore *debit* my "Coal account" with the 28*s*. as I am John Cave's *debtor* for that amount.

In these facts we have a simple illustration of the most important rule of double-entry book-keeping.

I have already told you what are the rules for preparing "Real" and "Personal" accounts. They supply part of the rules necessary when dividing and arranging transactions in debit and credit entries.

You have learned, for instance, that accounts of "things" ("Real" accounts) are debited with all the "things" received, and are credited with all the "things" parted with.

Consequently, a transaction which embraces the parting with one piece of property in exchange for another piece of property is easily recorded.

For example, the parting with a sum of money in exchange for a parcel of goods.

The property received is *debited* in the account kept for that particular kind of property, and the property parted with is *credited* in the account kept for that particular kind of property.

For example, if cash to the amount of £30 is expended in the purchase of a horse, the "Cash" account is *credited* with the money paid away (£30), and the "Horses" account is *debited* with the same sum as representing the value of the horse purchased.

From this procedure we get the following rule: *Where "things" are exchanged for "things," debit the "things" received and credit the "things" parted with.*

You have also learned that when money or property is parted with, the money, or property, account is *credited*, and furthermore, that when money or property is paid or delivered to some *person*, that the account of that person is *debited*.

F

For example, the payment of £30 cash to C. Hubert on February 2, 1910 (p. 76) was *credited* in the " Cash " account (p. 79) and *debited* in C. Hubert's Personal account (p. 79).

This gives us another rule for use when dividing transactions into debit and credit.

When " things " are paid away, or delivered to, a person, debit the Personal account of the party who receives them, and credit the account kept for the " things " parted with.

For example, if £20 in cash, or a horse worth £20, is parted with to C. Brown, whether to discharge a debt owing to him, or for any other purpose, *credit* " Cash " account, or " Horses " account, with £20 and *debit* C. Brown's Personal account with the same sum.

If money, or other property, is received from any *person*, the rule for separating this transaction into debit and credit is the exact opposite of the rule stated immediately above; the nature of the transaction is the exact opposite of the payment or delivery of " things " to a person, and the rule is necessarily the exact opposite also. It is as follows :

When " things " are received from a person, debit the " things " received to an account kept for them, and credit the Personal account kept for the person from whom they have been received.

For example, if W. Jones pays you £30 in cash, or sells you on credit a horse worth £30, you must *debit* £30 to the account kept for the particular " things " in question, *i.e.* you must debit £30 to " Cash " account or to " Horses " account, and you must *credit* £30 to W. Jones's Personal account.

Every book-keeping transaction must be arranged in " double-entry " form entirely upon its own merits, and without the slightest reference to any transaction of any kind which has gone before.

Some students find it difficult at first to grasp this essential rule. If you will think carefully, however, you will understand that when you are entering transactions from day to day in a set of books, you must take each transaction as it comes, and deal with it as a separate item. You cannot balance accounts every time a fresh transaction has to be entered. And, even supposing such a proceeding were possible, it would be unnecessary because, when you so desire, you can at any time balance any account, by the rules I have given you, and find how the trader stands with reference to the particular "person" or "thing" represented by the account.

You have seen the rule referred to above illustrated in the case of the cash payment of £20 to C. Brown mentioned on p. 82. In that case the £20 was credited to "Cash" account, and debited to C. Brown's Personal account. It makes no difference whatever whether the £20 was the first transaction that took place between the trader and C. Brown, or the last. It makes no difference whether, at the time when this transaction took place, C. Brown owed money to the trader, or whether the trader owed money to C. Brown; all that needed to be considered was the fact that the trader had parted with £20 in cash to C. Brown. Considered separately on its own merits—as every entry must be—this transaction involved a *debit* to C. Brown's account, and a *credit* to the trader's "Cash" account.

If a trader pays money to another person, the reason for which he makes the payment makes no difference to the necessity for stating the transaction in double-entry form. It may be that the money has been paid by the trader to the other person as a loan, or it may have been paid to that person in settlement of a debt owed to him by the trader. Of course these facts are matters which affect the "balance" of the Personal account kept by the trader for the party with whom he has dealt, but they do not affect the form of the double-entry necessary to record the individual transaction. All cash payments made by a trader to another person must be *credited* in the trader's Cash account, and *debited* in the Personal account of the other party, quite irrespective of the state of the "balance" of the account then running between them.

Similarly, if a trader receives money, or other property, from another person he must *credit* the Personal account of the party from whom he has received it, and he must *debit* the account kept for the particular "thing" received, entirely irrespective of any previous happenings or dealings between them.

Each person with whom you deal is, in book-keeping, treated as being your *debtor* for everything that you have paid or delivered to him, and as being your *creditor* for everything that he has paid or sent to you. The things paid or delivered by you must be entered by you on the left-hand, or "*debit*," side of the account kept by you for the person with whom you have dealt; the things paid or sent to you by the person with whom you have dealt must be entered by you on the right-hand, or *credit*, side of the account kept by you for that person. If the items for which the other party is your debtor, *i.e.* the items on the *debit* side of the Personal account kept by you in his name, exceed in amount the items for which he is your creditor, *i.e.* the items on the *credit* side of the same account, the other party is, on balance, your debtor for the difference. If matters are the other way round the other party is, on balance, your creditor for the difference between the two sides of the account.

I have now instructed you how to prepare a " Personal " account and a " Real " account, and how to frame, in the form of a " double-entry," any transaction which involves Personal accounts and Real accounts.

There remains one class of accounts which I have not yet explained, viz., Nominal accounts.

Nominal Accounts are accounts which are kept for the sole purpose of enabling transactions which involve " profits " and " losses " to be stated in proper double-entry form.

It will be obvious to you that a trader cannot carry on his business without incurring " losses " and expenses.

To begin with the simplest possible illustration : If a person (who is assumed to keep a proper Cash account) were to lose a shilling from his cash-box, he would be unable, if Nominal accounts had not been invented, to record this loss in the form of a double entry.

The shilling having been parted with, an entry for it would be made on the credit side of the Cash account. This having been done, the matter would seem to be complete. There would be no account to which the shilling could be debited. Nothing would have been received in exchange for it, hence there would be no " Real " account which could be debited.

To meet difficulties of this kind, " Nominal " accounts are opened in the trader's Ledger.

In the case of " losses," separate Ledger accounts are opened for each particular kind of " loss," and all payments for " losses " are *debited* in these accounts, each in its appropriate account.

In the case of the shilling lost from the cash-box referred to above, the *credit* entry would appear, as has already been explained, in the " Cash " account. A Ledger account headed " Sundry losses," or some other suitable title, would be opened and a *debit* entry for one shilling would be made in that account.

In this way the entry for the "loss" sustained is thrown into the form of a double-entry, and the requirements of the " double-entry " system are properly complied with

These " Nominal" accounts are sometimes called **Fictitious Accounts**—the payments made for " losses " and expenses being looked upon as payments made to an imaginary person, whose account is debited with them. If you can, by a stretch of imagination, conceive that the shilling lost in the example referred to was not lost, but was paid away to a person named " Sundry Losses," the reason why the amount is debited to " Sundry Losses Account " will become clear.

The illustration of the lost shilling was chosen for its simplicity, but the principle is just the same when the " losses" and expenses which actually occur in most businesses are being dealt with. For further illustration: A trader must pay salaries to the clerks who work for him, he must pay rent and rates and for the gas and water and other necessaries he uses. The money expended in these directions does not yield the trader any result in the shape of cash or other property, but is an expense or "loss" incurred in carrying on his business.

The rule for the correct double-entry of money or other property paid away by the trader in the shape of "losses" or expenses can now be stated as follows:

Credit the property parted with in the Property ("Real") account and debit a Nominal account opened for the particular kind of "loss" or expense incurred.

For example, if the trader, whose books are being kept, pays away on March 1, 1910, £10 for a clerk's salary for one month, and £5 for a trade advertisement in a newspaper, he must *credit* the £10 and the £5 in his " Cash " account; he must *debit* the £10 to a Nominal account, entitled " Salaries," and the £5 to a Nominal account entitled " Advertising," thus completing the double-entry.

The trader's " Salaries " account referred to in the foregoing paragraph is illustrated below.

Dr. SALARIES ACCOUNT. *Cr.*

1910. March 1	To Cash— J. Brown, Salary for February . C	£ 10	s. 0	d. 0			

Just as the trader may incur a "loss," or part with property for which he receives no lasting value, so he may become possessed of property without doing or giving anything for it— *i.e.* he may make a profit.

The entries necessary in order to record the profits made by the trader are framed upon precisely the same principle as that already explained in the case of his "losses." That is to say, suitable Nominal accounts are opened to record them. The only difference being that their *effect* as "profits" is, of course, exactly the opposite of that of the "losses" previously explained.

If we assume that the trader whose books are being kept has received a sum of money, say £5, from an anonymous donor. as a gift, it is only by employing a "Nominal" account that the necessary double-entry can be effected for this transaction. The £5 must, as has already been explained, be *debited* in the trader's "Cash" account, and it must be *credited* in some other account, but the proper account for the credit entry is a matter requiring consideration. It is impossible to credit the £5 to any "Personal" account, because the name of the donor is not known; it is equally impossible to credit it to any "Real" account, for nothing has been parted with in exchange for it. It is only by opening a "Nominal" account under the heading of "Sundry Profits," or some other suitable title, and by crediting the £5 in it, that the "double-entry" can be effected at all.

In this case, again, the illustration is not one which is likely to occur in practical business, but the same principle, of course, applies to the many instances of "profits," or "gains," which are common in most businesses. For example, in cases where the trader pays prompt cash for goods he is purchasing he will probably be allowed "discount"; he will also receive "interest" upon any money he may have on deposit with his bankers, or he may earn "commission" for selling goods for other people, and so on.

The rule for the proper recording of money or property received by the trader in the shape of "profits"—*i.e.* without any property being parted with—may now be stated as follows:

Debit the property acquired to the proper "Real" account, and credit a "Nominal" account opened for the particular kind of profit made.

For example, if, on March 1, 1910, the trader receives £10 as compensation for allowing a telephone company to place one of their telephone poles in his courtyard, the £10 received must be *debited* to "Cash" account, and it must be *credited* to a "Nominal" account entitled "Sundry Profits," or some other suitable title. Similarly, if the trader receives £20 for allowing the wall of one of his warehouses to be used as an advertising station for posters, the £20 must be *debited* to "Cash" account, and *credited* to "Rent of Advertising Stations," or some other suitable "Nominal" account.

The trader's "Sundry Profits" account referred to in a previous paragraph is illustrated below.

Dr.	SUNDRY PROFITS ACCOUNT.				Cr.
				£	s.	d.
	1910.
Mar. 1	By Cash from National Telephone Co. Compensation for allowing erection of telephone pole in my courtyard .	C	10	0	0

There is one other kind of "Nominal" account which I must explain to you, and, with this explanation, my preliminary sketch of "double-entry" book-keeping principles may end. The account to which I refer is known as the trader's **Capital Account.** As I explained to you in the case of the accounts kept for "profits" and "losses," so the "Capital" account is also one which has been devised solely in order that the needs of the theory of "double-entry" book-keeping may be satisfied.

If a trader starts in business with a certain amount of money and other property, and owing nothing to any creditors, his real, or "net worth," at the beginning of his venture is the amount of the money and other property owned by him. This "net worth" is, in book-keeping, known as his "Capital." If he starts in business owning a certain amount of money and other property, but owing certain liabilities, his Capital, *i.e.* his real or "net" worth, at the date of commencing business is the amount of his total possessions, *minus* the total amount of his liabilities.

For example, if W. Parry starts in business on March 1, 1910, possessing cash £200, and premises worth £500, but owing £300 to Robert Hughes, W. Parry's "Capital" is £200 + £500 − £300, *i.e.* £400.

I have already explained to you, in the preceding portion of this chapter, that when we proceed to open the books of a trader upon "double-entry" principles we must—

(1) *Debit* everything he possesses in suitable "Real" accounts;

(2) *Debit* everything owed to him by other persons in "Personal" accounts headed with their respective names; and

(3) *Credit* everything owed by the trader to other persons in "Personal" accounts headed with their respective names.

All this must be done, but, in order to satisfy the essential rule of "double-entry" book-keeping, something more than this must be done.

Except in the very rare event of the trader owning exactly the same total amount of property, including cash and debts due to him, as he owes to other persons, the total of the entries representing Assets, made, as described above, in the various accounts upon the *debit* side, will not be exactly equal in amount to the total of the entries, representing Liabilities, made in the various accounts on the *credit* side.

You are already aware that the principal rule of "double-entry" book-keeping is that all entries made in a Ledger on the one side must be balanced by entries similar in amount on the other side of the Ledger. This rule applies with just as much force to the entries made by the trader when he first opens his books, as it does to the entries made by him at any subsequent time.

It was for the purpose of ensuring that the trader's opening entries should harmonise with this rule that the "Capital account" was devised.

The rules regarding the opening of the trader's Capital account are as follow:

A. *If the trader's total Assets exceed his total Liabilities, the difference between the two totals must be entered on the credit side in a "Nominal" account, entitled the "Capital" account.*

B. *If the trader's total Liabilities should exceed his total Assets, the difference between the two totals must be entered on the debit side in a "Nominal" account, entitled the "Capital" account.*

Case A is the rule which applies to the great majority of traders. Case B only comes into use if the trader owes more than he owns, *i.e.* when he is "insolvent."

The making of the entry in the trader's Capital account, according to Case A or Case B, as may be necessary, has the effect of causing the total opening entries made by the trader upon the *debit* side of his Ledger to be equal to the total of the similar entries made by him on the *credit* side of his Ledger. The essential double-entry rule is thus complied with, and the trader starts operations with books which "agree," *i.e.* which contain entries on each side totalling up to the same amount.

An example may serve to make these rules clearer :

Example.—Taking again the facts already referred to on p. 87, in the case of W. Parry, it is stated that he commenced business on March 1, 1910, possessing Cash £200, and premises worth £500, but owing £300 to Robert Hughes. His "net worth," or "Capital," is, as you have already seen, the difference between his total Assets and his total Liabilities, *i.e.* £200 *plus* £500 *minus* £300, viz., £400.

The entries which must be made by W. Parry in order to open his Books properly are as follow :

Dr.	*Cr.*
1. £200 must be *debited* to the " Cash " account.	
2. £500 must be *debited* to the " Premises " account.	
3. Robert Hughes' Personal account must be *credited* with	£300
4. W. Parry's " Capital " account must be *credited* with the difference between the Assets and the Liabilities set forth above, viz.	£400
£700	£700

You will see that the above process results in entries to the total of £700 being made on each side of the Ledger, a result which conforms to the primary rule of double-entry book-keeping.

W. Parry's Capital account is illustrated below.

			1910.				£	s.	d.
			Mar. 1	By Excess of Assets over Liabilities at this date .	J		400	0	0

Dr.   W. PARRY—CAPITAL ACCOUNT.   *Cr.*

* The letter "J" placed in this column is an abbreviation of the word "Journal." The Journal is a book used to classify entries, and is fully explained in Chapter VI.

EXERCISE 5A.

1. What are the advantages of double-entry book-keeping compared with other systems? 2. How many kinds of Ledger Accounts are there? Enumerate them, and explain how they differ from each other. 3. What are the rules for preparing (*a*) a " Personal Account," (*b*) a " Real Account"? 4. What are " Nominal Accounts "? For what reason are they kept? 5. Explain what is meant by the trader's " Capital Account"; what is the meaning of a balance on this account, if it appears (*a*) on the credit side (*b*) on the debit side? 6. Explain briefly the following rule: " Every debit requires its credit, and *vice versa*." 7. Give a specimen ruling of a " Personal Account," and enter three transactions in it on each side, and bring down the balance at their conclusion.

EXERCISE 5B.

From the following particulars prepare W. Morrison's Account as shown in my books, balancing it as on June 30, 1910:

1910. June 1, W. Morrison owed me £30 14s. 9d ; June 3, Sold 10 chests of tea to W. Morrison on credit, £30 ; June 4, Received cheque from W. Morrison, £5 14s. 9d. ; June 6, Sold to W. Morrison on credit, 30 bags of coffee, £75 ; June 7, Bought from W. Morrison on credit, 2 bags of cocoa, £3 4s. 9d. ; June 11, Received cash from W. Morrison, £100 ; June 13, Sold to W. Morrison on credit, 5 bags of coffee, £12 15s , 10 chests of tea, £27 10s. ; June 14, Sold to W. Morrison on credit, 10 bags of coffee, £28, 1 bag of cocoa, £1 10s. 6d. ; June 14, Bought from W. Morrison on credit, 3 bags of coffee, £9 7s. 6d. ; June 18, W. Morrison returned 2 bags of coffee, sold to him on the 14th inst. as unsuitable, £5 12s. ; June 20, Received cheque from W. Morrison, £15 3s. 6d. ; June 25, Returned to W. Morrison 1 bag of coffee, damaged by damp, £3 2s. 6d. ; June 30, Received cash from W. Morrison, £15 10s. ; Paid for 1 typewriter bought at W. Morrison's request and forwarded to him £12 16s. 6d. ; Paid, on W. Morrison's Account, railway charges on typewriter, 3s. 6d.

EXERCISE 5C.

Explain the double-entries which are necessary in order to record the following transactions :

1. £30 cash spent in buying a horse. 2. The purchase, on credit, of 2 horses from J. Brown for £15 each. 3. The repayment of £30 to J. Brown. 4. The receipt of a cheque (paid to bank) for £25 from W. Harris, who owes the trader that sum. 5. The payment of £2 10s. from office cash for advertising in a trade paper. 6. The sale of 2 horses for £22 10s. by auction for cash. 7. The exchange by the trader of a cart worth £35 for 7 sheep worth £5 each. 8. The accidental loss of a sovereign from the office cash-box. 9. The withdrawal of £20 from the trader's bank account in order to replenish his office cash-box. 10. The payment of £10 by cheque as compensation for injuries sustained by one of the trader's workmen in the ordinary course of his occupation. 11. The payment from petty cash of 2s. 6d. for telegrams sent. 12. The purchase for cash (paid from office cash) of £3 worth of stationery. 13. The lending (by cheque) of £5 to M. Weeks.

14. The receipt from Michael & Co. of a cheque (paid to bank) for £25 and bank-notes (placed in office cash-box) for £15 on account of a debt they owe to the trader. 15. The sale of a piece of freehold land owned by the trader for £500, paid to the trader by cheque (banked). 16. The payment by cheque of £35 for repainting the trader's warehouse. 17. The payment of £25 from the office cash-box into the trader's banking account. 18. Sold to R. Verney on credit 3 horses @ £15 each.

EXERCISE 5D.

Explain the double-entry which is necessary to record each of the following transactions :

1910. June 2, Bought a piece of land for £300 at an auction, paying the money at once by cheque to the auctioneer ; Drew from bank to replenish the office cash-box, £20 ; Paid by cheque for repairs to type-writer, £1 2s. 10d. ; June 3, Bought, on credit, a horse from O. Wilson for £20 ; June 4, Paid O. Wilson by cheque on account, £10 ; June 6, Received from R. Cunningham cheque (banked) for £100 lent him a year ago, together with cash (placed in office cash-box) £4 10s. for 1 year's interest on the loan ; Paid to H. Edwards in cash £5 that I owed him ; Received from A. Horner £5 5s. cheque (paid to bank) for my commission for disposing of his motor-car for him ; June 7, Paid O. Wilson in cash further on account, £5 ; Exchanged a quantity of old iron rails from my stock, valued at £155, for a second-hand motor-car ; June 8, Paid by cheque to W. Manners for repairs to motor-car, £3 6s. 6d. ; June 9, Paid for a pair of spare motor tyres and a duplicate set of accessories for future use, £12 5s. ; Received from C. Huggins cheque for £30 on account of the money he owes me, paid same into bank ; Bought from C. Williams a quantity of stationery for office use, to be paid for next month, £10 12s. 6d. ; June 10, Sold one horse by auction for £25 in cash (paid to bank) ; June 11, Paid for an office writing table, by cheque, £4 10s.

EXERCISE 5E.

From the following particulars prepare : 1. My Cash Account. 2. My Horses Account. 3. Charles Wilson's Account as shown in my Ledger. 4. My Expenses Account. Bring down the balances of these accounts on June 30, 1910.

1910. June 1, Balance of cash in hand, £25 9s. 6d. ; June 3, Bought of Charles Wilson, on credit, 2 horses @ £15 each, £30 ; June 4, Paid Charles Wilson on account, in cash, £10 ; June 6, Sold 1 horse for cash by auction, £18 6s. ; June 7, Paid Charles Wilson further on account, in cash, £5 ; June 9, Bought of Charles Wilson, on credit, 2 horses @ £18 each, £36 ; June 13, Paid Charles Wilson on account, cash, £10 ; June 14, Sold 3 horses for cash by auction, £54 10s. ; June 15, Bought of Charles Wilson on credit 2 horses at £16 each, £32 ; June 18, Paid Charles Wilson on account, cash, £30 ; June 21, Paid cash for travelling expenses, 12s. 9d. ; Sold 1 horse for cash by auction, £17 3s. 9d. ; June 23, Paid in cash railway charges on horses sold, £1 4s. 6d. ; June 27, Paid Charles Wilson on account, cash, £10 ; June 29, Paid cash for stationery supplied and used, 3s. 6d. ; June 30, Paid in cash veterinary surgeon's fee for examining a horse, 10s. 6d. ; Paid in cash subscription to "The Horse" for six months, 13s.

EXERCISE 5F.

From the following particulars prepare: 1. My Cash Account including "Bank" and "Cash" columns. 2. The personal accounts of R. Bradbury and C. Wright in my Ledger. 3. My Trade Expenses Account. 4. My Freehold Premises (134 Friday Street) Account. 5. My Purchases Book. Balance Nos. 1-4 as on June 11, 1910.

1910. June 1, Balance at bank £1685 10s. 9d. ; Drew from bank for office cash, £25 ; Bought of R. Bradbury, on credit, 20 chests of Ceylon tea @ £3 per chest, £60 ; June 2, Paid by cheque telephone subscription for one year, £15 15s. ; June 3, Paid from office cash for clerks' salaries, £4 5s. ; June 4, Bought of C. Wright, on credit, 125 chests of tea @ £2 10s. per chest, £312 10s. ; Paid R. Bradbury by cheque, £50 ; June 6, Paid from office cash to R. Bradbury, £10 ; Bought of R. Bradbury on credit 10 chests of tea @ 55s. per chest, £27 10s. ; June 7, Paid for freehold premises (134 Friday Street), bought to-day at auction (by cheque) £1000 ; Paid by cheque lawyer's fees for deeds relating to purchase of 134 Friday Street (debit to Premises account), £5 5s. 6d. ; June 8, Paid by cheque to C. Wright on account, £100 ; Drew from bank for office cash £60 ; June 9, Paid from office cash to R. Bradbury, £27 10s. ; paid by cheque builder's account for structural alterations at 134 Friday Street (debit to Premises account), £10 3s. 9d. ; Bought from R. Bradbury on credit 5 chests of tea @ 56s. 6d. per chest, £14 2s. 6d. ; June 10, Paid from office cash clerks' salaries, £4 5s. ; June 11, Paid from office cash into bank, £15.

EXERCISE 5G.

1. A. Fletcher commenced to keep his books by double-entry on January 1, 1910. His position at that date was as follows : Trade creditors: R. Brown, £360 9s. 2d. ; V. Robinson, £172 16s. 5d. ; B. Jones, £36 1s. 3d. ; stock of goods in hand, £36 35s. 10d. ; freehold shop, value £520 ; owing to M. Verity for balance of purchase price of shop, £100 ; cash at bank, £36 2s. 5d. ; cash in cash-box, £1 2s. 9d. ; owing to Messrs. Deedes & Co., solicitors, for their charges for defending a law-suit, £10 10s. State in what accounts the foregoing balances are to be entered, and upon which side, and give the amount of A. Fletcher's Capital account on January 1, 1910. 2. C. Jones started business on February 1, 1910. His position was then as follows: Cash at bank, £300 14s. 6d. ; Stock of tea in hand, 340 chests No. 1, valued at 52s. per chest ; 25 chests No. 2 valued @ 51s. 6d. per chest ; 15 chests No. 3, valued @ 48s. 6d. per chest ; 62 chests No. 4, valued @ 46s. 9d. per chest ; Debtors—A. Brown, £111 1s. 11d. ; B. Child, £1101 11s. 1d. ; C. Higgins, £110 1s. 10d. ; D. Walsh, £110 11s. 10d. ; M. Harvey, £11 11s. 10d. ; D. Ryan, £1 1s. 11d. Creditors—B. Fitch, £30 3s. 10d. ; C. Drew, £33 13s. 1d. ; R. Miles, £301 3s. 11d. ; W. Rees, £313 10s. 3d. ; L. Leon, £331 1s. 3d. What was the amount of C. Jones's capital when he commenced business? 3. Classify the following Ledger accounts as among (a) "Real," (b) "Personal," and (c) "Nominal" accounts, viz., Machinery account, Telegrams and Postages account, J. Wilson & Co.'s account, Wages account, Buildings account, Discounts Received account, R. Brown (Loan) account, Premises account, Cash account.

EXERCISE 5H.

1. Robert Hedges commenced to keep his books by double-entry on June 1, 1910. On that date his position was as follows : He possessed machinery valued at £1000, his stock-in-trade was valued at £800, he had cash in hand £10, and at the bank £250, and debts were due to him from J. Ball £210, and R. Warner £56. He owed debts to F. Ford £620, and B. Bosham £110. What was the amount of Robert Hedge's capital as on June 1, 1910? 2. What are the rules for preparing "Nominal" accounts? Open Nominal accounts under suitable headings for the following :

1910. June 1, Received £5 interest from J. Dickinson upon my loan to him ; June 3, Received £10 as discount from the Ceylon Planters Co. on paying them their account for tea purchased ; June 4, Allowed H. Evans £15 on his complaining that coffee supplied to him was short weight ; June 5, Paid £3 to a clerk who was dismissed without notice ; June 6, Received £3 from the Midland Railway on my claim for goods damaged in transit.

CHAPTER VI

THE JOURNAL

I EXPLAINED to you in the previous chapter that every transaction must be recorded in the form of a double entry—in other words, in order that every transaction may be recorded properly, some Ledger account must be *debited*, and some other Ledger account must be *credited*, with the same amount.

I must now, however, qualify this rule by explaining to you that it is not necessary that the whole of the entry, representing any particular transaction, should be made in *one* Ledger account. Should the circumstances of the case require it, parts of the entry may be debited or credited in two or more accounts, provided always that the total of the separate debit entries equals in amount the amount of the corresponding credit entry, and *vice versa*.

Example.—Suppose that you buy, on credit, from J. Jones, a horse for £20, together with a set of harness for £5, *i.e.* a total purchase of £25, the following entries will be necessary

Dr.   Cr.

£20 will be *debited* to " Horses Account " for
    the value of the horse purchased ;

£ 5 will be *debited* to " Harness Account " for
    the value of the harness purchased ;
               and

    J. Jones's Personal account will be *credited*
    with the total value of the property received
    from him, viz. £25

£25 Debit Total.   Credit Total £25

From the above illustration you will see that *two debit* entries have been made amounting to £25 in all, and that these entries exactly equal the total of the *single credit* entry made (£25).

In a similar manner, you may make one entry on the *debit* side of an account in your Ledger, and balance, or "offset," it by making two or more entries in various accounts on the *credit* side.

Example.—Suppose that you had sold, on credit, to D. Smith a horse for £15, a cart for £10, and a set of harness for £5, a total sale to D. Smith of £30. In these circumstances the necessary entries would be as follow·

Dr.   Cr.

You would *credit* "Horses Account" with £15 for the horse sold to D. Smith;

You would *credit* "Carts Account" with £10 for the cart sold to D. Smith;

You would *credit* "Harness Account" with £5 for the harness sold to D. Smith;

and

£30 would be *debited* to D. Smith's Personal account for the total value of the horse, cart, and harness sold to him.

£30 Debit Total.   Credit Total £30

In the above illustration, *one* entry for £30 on the *debit* side is balanced, or "offset," by *three* entries amounting to £30 in all on the *credit* side.

In order that transactions of a complicated nature may be properly recorded, it is sometimes necessary to make several entries on the debit side of the Ledger, and to balance them by several credit entries.

This complication is, however, more apparent than real. No new principle is involved. The only necessary rule to remember is that the total of the *debit* entries must be exactly equal in amount to the total of the *credit* entries, in order that the chief rule of double-entry book-keeping may be satisfied.

Example.—Let us suppose that you are the owner of a horse worth £25 and a set of harness worth £5, and that you have exchanged them with somebody who gives you a motor-bicycle worth £20 and a bookcase worth £10 for them.

In order to record this exchange of property the following entries are necessary;

Dr.   Cr.

You must *credit* "Horses Account" with £25 being the value of the horse exchanged;

You must *credit* "Harness Account" with £ 5 being the value of the harness exchanged;

and

£20 must be *debited* to "Motor Bicycle Account," being the value of the motor-bicycle acquired.

£10 must be *debited* to "Furniture Account," being the value of the bookcase acquired.

£30 Debit Total.   Credit Total £30

The above illustration will, I think, make it clear to you that, provided the total of the debit entries and the total of the credit entries equal one another, as many fractional entries may be made on either side of the Ledger as may be necessary in order properly to record a given transaction. The number of fractional entries made is, in fact, quite immaterial; but it is *absolutely necessary* that the totals on the two sides must equal one another in amount.

The Sales Book, Purchases Book, Returns Inwards and Returns Outwards Books, which you have already become familiar with in Chapters III. and IV., are based upon the principle of balancing, or "offsetting," a number of debit entries by a single credit entry, or *vice versa*. I promised, when I described the form of these books to you, that at a later stage of this treatise I would explain to you more fully how they are used. The principle of double-entry which I have just explained governs their construction, *although you may not have realised the fact*.

At first sight these various methods of carrying out the double-entry rule may appear to be difficult to understand. If you will give the matter a little close thought and attention, however, you will be surprised how soon all the difficulties will disappear.

Each of the four books in which the "Sales," "Purchases," and "Returns" are recorded is known in book-keeping as a "Journal." A Journal is a book in which a trader records his transactions in proper double-entry form soon after they have occurred. The literal meaning of the word "Journal" is a "daily record" (Latin, *diurnus* = daily). A Journal has been compared to a sieve. The comparison is a happy one, because all entries recorded in the Journal are "sifted" into their respective debit and credit places.

As I shall explain to you later, other forms of Journals exist besides the four books mentioned above. In a Journal, whatever its particular use or form may be, transactions are analysed, or "sifted," in double-entry form: that is to say, the particular Ledger accounts which are to be debited and credited are clearly shown. From these Journals the necessary entries in the Ledger can be readily made whenever the book-keeper has leisure to make them.

For different classes of transactions different forms of Journals are used, all suitably ruled for the purpose of saving labour as far as possible when posting the Ledger.

In modern practical business, two kinds of Journal are employed, viz.:

(1) Journals kept for special classes of transactions, *e.g.* "Sales Journals," "Purchases Journals," &c.

(2) A Journal, known simply as the "Journal," or the "Journal Proper." In this book the trader analyses in double-entry form all those transactions which cannot be suitably recorded either in the "special" Journals referred to in paragraph (1), or in any other book.

I have already explained to you, in Chapters III. and IV., some of the uses of the "special" Journals, viz., the "Sales Journal," the "Purchases Journal," and the "Returns Inwards" and "Returns Outwards" Journals. In those chapters I described the form of the above books to you, but, for various reasons, I did not, at that stage, explain their use completely. I will now conclude my explanation of these four "special" Journals before I discuss the "Journal Proper"—the latter book being entirely new to you.

The Sales Book, or Sales Journal, is a journal employed for the purpose of offsetting a number of debit entries in the Ledger by one credit entry equal in amount to the total of the various debits. This plan obviously saves labour as compared with the tedious process of making a separate credit entry for every individual debit entry.

Every sale made by a trader on credit must, in accordance with the principles laid down in the previous chapter, be debited in the Personal Ledger account of the purchaser of the goods. It must also—and this is new to you—be *credited* in

G

a ledger account entitled "Sales." In another chapter I shall explain more fully the meaning and uses of a "Sales" account.

You will readily understand that a great deal of clerical labour would be required if every sale had to be credited separately in the "Sales" account. It is in order to avoid this unnecessary labour that the Sales Journal is employed.

All sales made on credit are entered in the Sales Journal, as they take place. From the Sales Journal the Ledger accounts of the various purchasers are *debited* with the value of the goods sold to them. At stated periods (usually monthly) the Sales Journal is added, and the *total* of the sales to that date is *credited*, in one amount, in the "Sales" account.

Example.—If you refer to p. 63 you will find a form of "Sales Journal." In this form the total of the Sales entered amounts to £62 18s. 6d. This total is shown as having been carried forward to the next page. If, however, there were no further sales during the month of February, the total, £62 18s. 6d., instead of being carried forward would be posted to the *credit* of the "Sales" account in the Ledger. The *credit* entry thus made for £62 18s. 6d. would equal, and offset, the three *debit* entries for £14 16s. 0d., £12 10s. 0d., and £35 12s. 6d. respectively, made from the Sales book in the Personal accounts of the various persons to whom goods had been sold.

The Sales Journal thus serves a twofold purpose.

First, it is useful to the trader because it supplies him with a list, in order of date, of all the sales made by him to his customers on credit. He could not do without such a list, whether he kept his books by double-entry methods or not.

Secondly, by showing a total of the sales for any given period, it allows the necessary double-entry to be made with the least possible trouble.

The Purchases Book, or Purchases Journal, is constructed upon exactly similar lines, except for the fact that all the necessary entries are made on the *opposite* side of the Ledger, and in different accounts. I have already explained in Chapter III. that every purchase that is made is entered in the Purchases book as it occurs, and is posted to the *credit* of the Ledger account of the person from whom the goods have been purchased. At periodical intervals (usually monthly) the entries in the Purchases book are added together, and the total of the Purchases to that date is posted to the *debit* of a Ledger account, entitled "Purchases" account.

Example.—In the case of the Purchases book illustrated on p. 50, if no further purchases had been made during the month of February, the total, £171 0s. 0d., would not be shown as having been carried forward to the next page, but would be shown as having been posted to the *debit* of the "Purchases" account. This debit of £171 0s. 0d. would equal, and offset, the entries of £50 0s. 0d., £5 0s. 0d., £37 10s. 0d., £31 0s. 0d., and £47 10s. 0d. respectively, made to the *credit* of the Personal accounts of the various persons from whom the goods had been purchased.

The Returns Books (Inwards and Outwards) are based upon the same principle. That is to say, a *number* of entries on one side or the other in the Ledger are offset by *one* entry of an amount equal to their total, on the opposite side, in order to save labour in posting.

Every return made to the trader by a dissatisfied purchaser, *i.e.* every "Return Inwards," is entered by the trader in his "Returns Inwards" book, as has already been explained to you in Chapter IV. The value of each parcel of goods thus returned is entered, or "posted," by the trader on the *credit* side of the Personal Ledger account of the dissatisfied buyer. You will remember that Returns received from a person are entered to the credit of his account because they have been "received" from him.

In order that the rule of double-entry book-keeping may be satisfied, it is necessary that all these *credit* entries shall be "balanced" by a *debit* entry or entries of an amount equal to the total of the various credits. In order that this may be done with the least possible trouble, the trader periodically makes the additions of the Returns Inwards book, and posts the total arrived at to the *debit* of a Ledger account, entitled "Returns Inwards." This single *debit* to the Returns Inwards account equalises and offsets all the separate *credit* entries previously made in the Personal accounts of the dissatisfied customers.

Example.—In the case of the Returns Inwards Book given on p. 68, if no further Returns Inwards had been received during the month of February, the total, £55 13s. 3d., would have been posted to the debit of the "Returns Inwards Account." This *debit* of £55 13s. 3d. would thus have equalled, and offset, the entries of £5 7s. 6d., £39 16s. 9d., and £10 9s. 0d. respectively, made to the *credit* of the Personal accounts of the dissatisfied customers.

The Returns Outwards Book is constructed upon lines exactly similar to those employed in the Returns Inwards Book, the only differences being those which naturally arise out of the opposite nature of the transactions.

Goods returned by a trader to persons from whom they have been bought are entered by the trader in his Returns Outwards Book, as has been explained in Chapter III.

Every return made by the trader is posted to the *debit* of the Personal Ledger account kept for the person from whom the goods were received. At periodical intervals the entries in the Returns Outwards Book are added together, and the total of the Returns for the period is posted to the *credit* of an account entitled " Returns Outwards." This *credit* entry of the total of the Returns equals, and balances, the various *debit* entries previously made in the accounts of the persons to whom the goods were returned.

Example.—If, in the case of the Returns Outwards Book given on p. 56, no further Returns Outwards had taken place during the month of February, the total, £100 10s. 0d., would have been posted to the credit of the " Returns Outwards Account." This *credit* of £100 10s. 0d. would thus have equalled, and offset, the entries of £60 0s. 0d., £22 10s. 0d., and £18 0s. 0d. respectively, previously made to the *debit* of the persons to whom the goods were returned.

I may now briefly repeat the rules governing the use of the four " special " Journals which I have explained above, in order that you may learn them in summarised form.

1. The Sales Book, Day Book, Sales Day Book, or Sales Journal.

All Sales made on credit are entered in the Sales Journal as they occur, and are posted separately to the *debit* of the Personal accounts of the purchasers in the Ledger. The monthly, or other periodical, totals of the Sales Journal are posted to the *credit* of the " Sales Account."

2. The Purchases Book, Invoice Book, Bought Book, Purchases, or Bought, Journal.

All Purchases made on credit are entered in the Purchases Journal as they occur, and are posted separately in the Ledger.

to the *credit* of the Personal accounts of the sellers. The monthly, or other periodical, totals in this book are posted to the *debit* of the " Purchases Account."

3. The Returns Inwards or Sales Returns Book.

All goods returned to the trader by dissatisfied purchasers are entered in this book as they are received, and are posted separately to the *credit* of the dissatisfied customer. The monthly, or other periodical, totals in this book are posted to the *debit* of the " Returns Inwards Account."

4. The Returns Outwards or Purchases Returns Book.

All goods returned by the trader to the persons from whom he has purchased them are entered in this book as and when they are returned, and are posted to the *debit* of the persons to whom they are returned.

The monthly, or other periodical, totals in this book are posted to the *credit* of the " Returns Outwards Account."

In some business houses other special Journals exist in addition to the four books explained above. I do not propose to deal with them here. It will be sufficient to say that if in practice you find any particular kind of transactions constantly recurring in the books of a business, it is usually more convenient to prepare them for entry in the Ledger by means of a special Journal kept solely for that particular class of transaction. The principles involved are precisely the same as those already explained. They merely need suitable application to the needs of each individual case.

The transactions of a trader as a whole may be divided into two classes, viz. :

    (1) Cash transactions, *i.e.* those transactions which are recorded in the Cash Book, or the Petty Cash Book.
    (2) Transactions which are *not* cash transactions.

Cash transactions are entered, immediately upon their occurrence, in the Cash Book, on the debit side if they are receipts, and on the credit side if they are payments. Petty Cash payments are entered on the payments (credit) side of the Petty Cash Book.

The entry of cash transactions in the Cash Book, or the Petty Cash Book, affords a sufficient indication as to the particular Ledger accounts in which such items should be posted,

In other words, entries in these two books need no further preparation before they are posted in the Ledger.

I have already told you that the Cash Book is a Ledger account bound separately, and, in accordance with the double-entry rule, it therefore follows that every item debited in it must be entered on the credit side of some other Ledger account, and *vice versa.* All cash transactions are entered as they occur on one side or the other of the Cash Book, and the book-keeper can, at a later date, complete the double-entry by " posting " the Cash Book entries in the proper Ledger accounts under the following rules :

(*a*) That all items entered on the *debit* side of the Cash Book must be entered, or " posted," on the *credit* side of some Ledger account.

(*b*) That all items entered on the *credit* side of the Cash Book must be entered, or " posted," on the *debit* side of some Ledger account.

The above explanations will help you to understand the following important rules, which you must make a point of remembering, viz. :

(1) *The process of entering cash transactions in the Cash Book prepares or " sifts " them at the same time in the proper form for entry in the Ledger. They do not need, therefore, to be entered in any Journal,* nor is any further process of preparation or analysis necessary before they are posted in the Ledger.*

(2) *Transactions which are not cash transactions must, on the other hand, be marshalled or arranged in double-entry form by means of some "Journal" before they can be posted in the Ledger.*

The urgent necessity of providing some book, or books, in which to arrange non-cash transactions will be clear to you if you consider the following reasons :

(*a*) Their very varied nature.

(*b*) The fact that transactions of this kind are not grouped together in the same manner in which cash transactions are collected in one account.

* A "Journal" is, as you will learn later on, a book in which *any* kind of transaction can be marshalled, or prepared in double-entry form. In some old-fashioned text-books students are taught to enter all cash transactions in the Journal in addition to recording them in the Cash Book. This is a wholly needless waste of labour, and never occurs in actual business.

(c) The necessity for making a clear record of every transaction as and when it occurs.

(d) The great convenience of being able to "post" the various items at leisure, instead of being obliged to enter every transaction in the Ledger as soon as it occurs.

All non-cash transactions are arranged in books called "Journals."

Each particular kind of non-cash transaction that occurs constantly is arranged, as far as possible, in a Journal kept for that special purpose, *e.g.* the "Sales Journal," the "Purchases Journal," &c. I have referred to Journals of this class earlier in the present chapter.

In addition to these constantly occurring transactions, other kinds of non-cash transactions arise in every business which cannot be suitably entered in any of the "special" Journals.

In order to provide for transactions of this nature a book called the **Journal**, or the Journal Proper, is used. In this Journal all those transactions which cannot be suitably recorded in any other book are prepared in proper double-entry form before they are posted in the Ledger.

Before I proceed to explain the Journal Proper in detail, I think it will be useful if I give you a list of the books we have already dealt with, as they now form a complete list of what are known as the "Books of original entry," that is to say, the books in which the transactions are entered immediately upon their occurrence, and from which the necessary Ledger postings are afterwards made.

BOOKS OF ORIGINAL ENTRY

(1) **The Cash Book** (p. 16) for the record of cash transactions, and (1a) **The Petty Cash Book** (p. 39) for the record of petty cash transactions.

(2) **The Journals**, for non-cash transactions, divided into

(1) **The "Special" Journals** for special classes of non-cash transactions :

e.g. {
The Purchases Journal (p. 47).
The Sales Journal (p. 60).
The Returns Inwards Journal (p. 64).
The Returns Outwards Journal (p. 51).
}

(2) **The Journal,** or **Journal Proper** (p. 94), for all non-cash transactions which are not provided for by the "Special" Journals.

In connection with the above books you must remember the following important rules:

(1) The Cash Book and the Petty Cash Book are themselves Ledger accounts bound separately, and the entries in them are portions of double-entries, the other portions being posted elsewhere in various Ledger accounts.

(2) The Journals are not Ledger accounts in any sense; they are merely memorandum books, ruled in various ways, in which transactions are "sifted," or arranged, in double-entry form for subsequent entry in the two or more Ledger accounts concerned.

THE JOURNAL PROPER

It is how necessary to explain the "Journal Proper" and its uses.

I have already told you that the "Journal" is the book in which all those non-cash transactions which cannot be suitably entered in any other book of original entry are arranged in proper double-entry form.

The form of the Journal is very simple; it contains a couple of sets of money columns placed side by side on the right-hand side of the page. One of these sets of money columns is designed to contain the *debit* portion of the double-entry, while the other is to contain the *credit* portion. Columns are provided on the extreme left-hand side of the page to contain the date of each transaction, and a "folio" column is also provided, in which are inserted the "folios," *i.e.* the pages, in the Ledger. whereon the debit and credit sides of the entry are posted.

The actual form of the Journal is as follows:

A	B	C	D	E

Column A, the "Date" column, is designed to contain the date of the transaction.

Column B, the "Particulars" column, is designed to contain the titles of the various accounts which are to be debited or credited in relation to each transaction journalised. Those accounts which are to be debited in relation to any given transaction are placed underneath each other, and they are followed by the account or accounts to be credited, similarly ranged.

At the conclusion of every Journal entry a small space is left, and a line is drawn across the page, as shown in the accompanying example, in order that the entry may not be confused with the one immediately following it.

Column C is the "Folio" column. It contains the numbers of the folios, *i.e.* pages, whereon the entries set forth in the Journal are posted in the Ledger.

Column D is the "Debit" money column. In it the amounts to be debited to the various accounts concerned are entered, each against the name of the account to which it is to be posted, as explained above (column B).

Column E is the "Credit" money column. In it the amounts to be credited to the various accounts concerned are entered, each against the name of the account to which it is to be credited.

You will understand these rules more clearly if you carefully follow the example given below :

Example.—Let us assume that you purchase on credit on April 16, 1910, from J. Jones, for use in your business, a second-hand boiler, and an assortment of second-hand plant and machinery, at an inclusive price of £60.

This transaction makes the following entries necessary :

1. A *debit* of £60 to "Plant and Machinery Account," because plant and machinery worth £60 has been acquired.

2. A *credit* of £60 to J. Jones's "Personal Account," because property of the value of £60 has been received from him.

The transaction must be journalised as follows :

1. The date, April 16, 1910, is entered in the "Date" column.

2. On the same line as that on which the date has been recorded in the "Date" column, the name of the account to be debited—"Plant and Machinery Account"—is entered in the "Particulars" column, followed by the abbreviation "Dr."

for "Debtor." The name of the account to be debited is always entered as far as possible to the left of the "Particulars" column.

3. The amount to be debited to the "Plant and Machinery Account," £60, is entered on the same line in the debit set of money columns against the name of the account ("Plant and Machinery Account") already appearing there.

4. On the following line the name of the account to be credited, "J. Jones," is entered in the "Particulars" column, underneath the name of the account debited, but a little more to the right-hand side. The word "To" is prefixed to the name of the account to be credited.

5. The amount to be credited to J. Jones's account, £60, is entered upon the same line as the words "J. Jones," but in the *credit* set of money columns.

6. A note of the general nature of the transaction is written in the "Particulars" column, on the line, or the next few lines, immediately following that on which the credit entry appears. This description of the transaction is called the Narration, and it should be as brief, and as clear as possible. In the case I have just mentioned, the Narration, "for second-hand plant and machinery purchased," would be sufficient.

The transaction given above would appear in the Journal as follows :

JOURNAL.

1910.			£	s.	d.	£	s.	d.
April 16	Plant and Machinery Account, Dr.	131	60	0	0			
	To J. Jones	189				60	0	0
	For second-hand plant and machinery purchased.							

From the transactions we have just journalised the necessary entries would be made in the Ledger as follows

1. The "Plant and Machinery Account" would be *debited* with £60. The Ledger folio of the "Plant and Machinery Account" has been taken to be 131, and this folio number has been entered in the "Folio" column.

2. £60 would be *credited* to the "Personal Account" of J. Jones. The Ledger folio of this account has been taken to be 189, and this folio has been inserted in the "Folio" column.

The transaction shown by way of an example in the specimen form of Journal given above is of a simple nature, there being only one account to be debited with a certain sum of money, and another account to be credited with a like amount.

More complicated transactions, however, frequently occur wherein, for example, a single debit entry for a certain sum is to be equalised by two or more credit entries for different portions of this sum—the total credit entries equalling in amount the debit entry—or *vice versa*.

For example, the trader may exchange a horse worth £50, receiving for it a cart worth £30, and hay worth £20. To record this transaction properly the trader must, in accordance with the rules previously given to you, credit his "Horses Account" with £50, and must debit "Cart Account" with £30, and "Fodder Account" with £20. The Journal entry will therefore appear as follows:

JOURNAL.

1910. March 2				£	s.	d.	£	s.	d.
	Sundries, viz.—								
	Cart Account . . . Dr.	37		30	0	0			
	Fodder Account . . Dr.	38		20	0	0			
	To Horses Account . .	40					50	0	0
	For goods exchanged this day.								

Other compound entries must be treated according to their requirements in a similar manner. The word "Sundries" must be prefixed to the accounts to be debited or credited if there is more than one account on either side.

A further illustration may be given in which more than one entry is required on each side of the Journal.

For example, let us assume that the trader parts with a horse worth £50 and harness worth £10, receiving in exchange a cart worth £30 and fodder to the value of £30. The entry for this transaction will be as follows:

JOURNAL.

1910. April 7				£	s.	d.	£	s.	d.
	Sundries— Dr.								
	To Sundries, viz.—								
	Cart Account . . .	45		30	0	0			
	Fodder Account . . .	46		30	0	0			
	Horses Account. . .	47					50	0	0
	Harness Account . .	48					10	0	0
	For goods exchanged this day.								

I have already explained to you that the entries which are passed through the Journal are those which cannot be suitably entered in any other book of original entry. In actual practice, they are mainly confined to "transfers" or "adjustments" of amounts between any two or more Ledger accounts, together with the entries which it is necessary to make at the beginning and at the end of a trading period.

Transfers between two or more Ledger accounts are usually of a simple nature, and do not require explanation in detail. They may, of course, vary greatly in character, but their arrangement in the form of a Journal entry is not often difficult.

The following examples of transfers between different Ledger accounts may serve to make the respective Journal entries which are necessary to record them more clear to you.

Examples.—Make the Journal entries necessary to adjust the following matters, dating them, in each case, March 2, 1910:

1. £10 received from Henry Brown in settlement of a debt owed by him has been posted from the Cash Book in error, to the credit of Arthur Brown's account instead of to the credit of Henry Brown.

2. £50 has been paid to a solicitor in connection with a law-suit. It was, however, posted to the debit of the "General Expenses Account," the ledger-keeper forgetting that it should have been posted to the separate account kept for "Legal expenses."

3. £10 15s. was paid to Norris Bros., who are manufacturers of office furniture. The ledger-keeper assumed that the money was paid for office furniture, and therefore posted the amount to the debit of the "Office Furniture Account." In reality, however, the money was paid for repairs to the existing office furniture, no new furniture having been acquired. The item should therefore have been posted to the "Repairs Account."

4. £65 was paid to an auctioneer who conducted a sale of horses and sheep. The ledger-keeper assumed that the £65 represented the cost price of two horses, and posted the whole of the amount from the Cash Book to the debit of the "Horses Account."

He afterwards discovered that the £65 was made up as follows:

Cost of 2 horses at £25 each · · · ·	£50
Cost of 3 sheep at £5 each · · · ·	£15
	£65

In order to adjust the above errors the following entries are necessary :

1. The £10 must be *credited* to Henry Brown, and *debited* to Arthur Brown, to whose account it was improperly credited in the first place.

2. The £50 must be *debited* to the " Legal Expenses Account," and *credited* to the " General Expenses Account," to which account it was improperly debited in the first place.

3. The £10 15s. must be *debited* to the " Repairs Account," and *credited* to the " Office Furniture Account," to which account it was improperly debited in the first place.

4. Of the £65 already debited to " Horses Account," £50 must be allowed to remain ; the balance of £15 must be *credited* to " Horses Account," and *debited* to " Sheep Account." The credit entry of £15 in the " Horses Account " has the effect of cancelling £15 of the original debit of £65, and leaves a net debit of £50 in the account as representing the cost of the two horses purchased.

These adjustments are arranged in the Journal as follows

JOURNAL.

1910.		£	s.	d.	£	s.	d.
March 2	Arthur Brown . . . Dr. To Henry Brown— For amount received from the latter, but incorrectly posted to the credit of the former and now transferred.	10	0	0	10	0	
" "	Legal Expenses Account . Dr. To General Expenses Account— For legal expenses posted in error to General Expenses Account and now transferred.	50	0	0	50		
" "	Repairs Account . . Dr. To Office Furniture Account— For amount posted in error to the debit of Office Furniture Account and now transferred.	10	15	0	10	1	
" "	Sheep Account . . . Dr. To Horses Account— For amount debited in error to Horses Account and now transferred.	15	0	0	15		

In addition to providing a record of any transfers which may be necessary between different Ledger accounts there are two other important occasions upon which the Journal is of use to the book-keeper. They are as follow ·

1. When a person begins to keep a set of books by double-entry the Assets and Liabilities with which he commences business, together with the amount of his " Capital," are set out in the Journal in the form of one comprehensive double-entry. This record is valuable for future reference, and in addition, the " starting balances " are posted in the Ledger from the entry.

2. At the end of each year, it is customary for a trader to prepare his annual accounts in order to ascertain what profit, or what loss, he has made during that period. In order to effect this purpose transfers of various amounts from one Ledger account to another are necessary. These transfers are made by means of Journal entries and furnish a permanent record for future reference.

The former class of Journal entry (1) needs explanation at this stage. I think, however, that it is better that I should defer the explanation of the latter class (2) until I show how the annual accounts of a trader are prepared. You will therefore find the second class of Journal entry referred to above explained in due course in Chapters IX. and X.

Starting Balances.

When a person begins to keep a set of books according to the double-entry system, it is necessary that he shall enter in his books full particulars of his financial position at the date on which he commences business.

It is also necessary, as I have already explained, that any entries made by him when opening his books shall conform to the principal rule of double-entry book-keeping, *i.e.*, that all *debit* entries made by him must be equalised by *credit* entries for an equal amount, and *vice versa*.

When a trader wishes to start book-keeping by double-entry he usually finds that his position is as follows :

(1) He owns certain possessions, called, in book-keeping terms, " Assets," *e.g.* Cash, Book-Debts, Stock, Machinery, &c.

(2) He owes certain Liabilities, *e.g.* amounts due to trade creditors, loans, &c.

The trader very rarely finds that the total value of his

Assets exactly equals the total amount of his Liabilities. He usually finds either (*a*) that the total of his Assets exceeds the total of his Liabilities, in which case he is "worth" the difference in value between them, or (*b*) that the total of his Liabilities exceeds the total of his Assets, in which case he is "insolvent" to the extent of the difference between them.

This being the case, it will not be sufficient for the trader, on commencing to keep books by double-entry, to—

(1) Debit each Asset owned by him to an Asset Account headed with its descriptive title.

(2) And to credit each Liability in its proper Ledger Account.

He must make these entries, it is true, but he must, in addition, make a further entry in order that the totals of the entries on each side of his Ledger may be equal in amount.

In order, therefore, to complete the double-entry in such cases, a Nominal Account, entitled the trader's **Capital Account**, is opened in his Ledger. To this account is *credited* the amount by which the trader's Assets exceed his Liabilities. On the other hand, should the trader be "insolvent," the amount by which his Liabilities exceed his Assets is *debited* to the Capital Account.

By these means, the Capital account shows, as on the date on which the trader commences to keep his books by double-entry, how much he was then "worth," or the extent to which he was "insolvent."

In actual practice the details of the assets, liabilities, and capital with which the trader commences double-entry book-keeping are stated in the form of one comprehensive Journal entry. This Journal entry is made before any other entries in the books have been attempted, and it furnishes a record of his original financial position.

The opening Journal entry necessary when commencing to keep a set of books by double-entry is made as follows:

(1) Enter in the "Date" column of the Journal the date on which the entry is made, followed, in the "Particulars" column, by the wording "Sundries: Dr. To Sundries."

(2) Enter in the "Particulars" column the names of all the "Asset" accounts (*i.e.* "Real" or "Personal" accounts) to be opened for the various items of property possessed. These names must follow one another, each occupying one line. The

amounts (in pounds, shillings, and pence) of the Assets possessed must be entered in the *debit* set of money columns, each against its proper heading.

(3) All the Liabilities must be entered in a similar manner.

Note.—The Liabilities must be arranged a little more to the right-hand side of the page than the Assets.

(4) Enter the heading "Capital Account" immediately after the entry of the last liability.

(5) Enter against the heading "Capital Account" the amount of the difference between the trader's Assets and Liabilities. Enter this difference (*a*) in the *credit* set of money columns if the trader possesses more than he owes, or (*b*) in the *debit* set of money columns if the trader owes more than he possesses.

(6) The two sides of the Journal entry will now equal one another. The additions of both the cash columns can be entered in ink in order to show clearly that the debit and credit totals agree. The totals so arrived at may then be ruled off.

(7) At the conclusion of the entry insert the following "narration," viz., "for assets, liabilities and capital as on this date."

The heading "Sundries: Dr. To Sundries" indicates that more than one Ledger account must be debited in relation to the Journal entry, and that more than one Ledger account must be credited. If there was only one Ledger account to be debited or credited on either side the word "Sundries" could be omitted as regards that particular side.

In actual practice the balance of "Cash in hand" when the trader commences business forms part of his "opening" Journal entry. From this Journal entry the "starting cash balance" is inserted in the Cash Book. This is the one exception to the general rule that no cash transactions need be passed through the Journal.

The reason for including the cash in hand in an "opening" Journal entry is the obvious necessity of preparing a record in a complete form of the whole of the trader's Assets, *including, of course, his cash,* as well as his Liabilities. If the cash in hand was omitted from the entry it would be clear to you that the difference between the debit and credit items, that is to say, the "Capital," would not be correctly stated.

An example will serve to make the foregoing explanation clearer to you.

Example.—On March 2, 1910, Hubert Smith commenced to keep a set of books by double-entry. He possessed on that date, cash £100, a freehold warehouse valued at £500, and a debt of £50 due to him from Robert Riches. On the other hand, he owed to W. Hooper £150, and to H. Wood £75.

Prepare the Journal entry necessary in order to open Hubert Smith's books.

H. Smith possesses Assets worth £100 + £500 + £50—*i.e.* £650 in all, and he owes to other persons £150 + £75, *i.e.* £225 in all. His Capital, or "net worth," is therefore £650 − £225, *i.e.* £425. The Journal entry necessary to "open" his books is as follows:

JOURNAL.

1910. March 2		£	s.	d.	£	s.	d.
	Sundries: Dr.						
	To Sundries—						
	Cash	100	0	0			
	Freehold Warehouse	500	0	0			
	Robert Riches	50	0	0			
	W. Hooper				150	0	0
	W. Wood				75	0	0
	Hubert Smith Capital Account				425	0	0
	For assets, liabilities, and capital as on this date.						
		£650	0	0	£650	0	0

In modern business houses the uses of the Journal are strictly confined to the record of:

(*a*) "Opening" entries.
(*b*) Transfers and adjustments which may be necessary between various Ledger accounts during a trading period, and such other items as cannot, owing to their nature, be suitably recorded in any other book.
(*c*) "Closing" entries, that is to say, transfers between Ledger accounts at the close of a trading period.

In olden times *every* transaction was passed through the Journal, and it was only after the experience of many years that accountants devised the several "special" Journals, the uses of which I have explained to you, in order to obviate the excessive labour involved by the old-fashioned and cumbersome methods.

It is an unfortunate fact that some text-books still teach the student to journalise all transactions in the Journal Proper before passing them into the Ledger. Many candidates endeavour to follow this laborious course when working examination exercises with the inevitable result that they are unable to complete their papers in the time allowed.

That this process of journalising every entry would be impossible in a large business house will be clear to you, I think, because you will readily understand how soon such a system would break down in a business where it would be impossible for one clerk to cope with the proper record of every transaction in a single book.

The special books for the record of sales, purchases, returns, &c., which I have explained to you, were devised in order to meet the urgent need for a subdivision of the counting-house work, and to cope with the vast increase of detail which has arisen in modern business transactions.

I want you clearly to understand that when you enter actual commercial life, you will find that the uses of the Journal are *strictly confined* to the three headings (*a*), (*b*), (*c*), which I have given you above. In some counting-houses, indeed, no Journal at all is used, the necessary entries being made from one Ledger Account to another. This, however, is a course which I do not advise you to adopt.

You must be particularly careful to remember these facts. Remember also, when you are answering examination questions, that it is only necessary to make use of the Journal for entries such as those I have described, unless, of course, you are specially asked to journalise a given transaction or series of transactions.

Now that I have given you this plain warning, I may tell you that the form of the Journal is such that *any* transaction, whatever its nature may be, can be arranged in the form of a Journal entry.

Indeed, in my opinion, it will form a very useful book-keeping exercise for you to gain as much practice as possible in journalising transactions of every kind. I give you this advice because, in my opinion, every student ought to acquire the habit of *thinking in Journal entries*. In other words, you should acquire the habit of arranging transactions in proper double-entry form by means of Journal entries. This habit will often help you to deal with transactions which may otherwise appear to be very difficult. Be careful, however, to remember that I give you this advice as a *book-keeping exercise only*, because you will not find that the Journal is used for such purposes in actual business life.

It may possibly help you to acquire practice in the preparation of Journal entries if I conclude this chapter with a brief recapitulation of the rules which govern the construction of Journal entries. They are, of course, merely the rules which govern the construction of every double-entry, but are of sufficient importance to bear repetition.

1. All Assets acquired must be *debited* to their respective asset accounts.

2. All Liabilities incurred must be *credited* to their respective liability accounts.

3. Persons to whom you give or deliver property must be *debited* with the value of the property.

4. Persons from whom you receive property must be *credited* with the value of the property

5. Everything that "comes in" must be *debited* to its proper Real account.

6. Everything that "goes out" must be *credited* to its proper Real account.

7. "Losses" and expenses must be *debited* to the relative "Loss" or Expense account.

8. Profits made must be *credited* to the relative "Profit" account.

9. You must regard every transaction, whether with a person or in a thing, as though it was the first of its kind. When preparing the necessary entry in double-entry form, you must ignore all previous transactions with the same person, or in the same thing.

10. Finally, and perhaps the most important rule of all, "every debit requires its credit, and every credit requires its debit," consequently, "the total of the debit entries must equal the total of the credit entries."

EXERCISE 6A.

1. What is a "Journal?" 2. What are "Special" Journals? Mention four examples. 3. What is the "Journal Proper," and what are its uses? 4. What are the "Books of Original Entry"? What are their uses in double-entry book-keeping? 5. Is the Cash Book a Journal? Is it necessary to journalise Cash transactions? 6. Explain the use of the "discount" columns in a Cash Book; to what account, and on which side of it are (1) the "debit discount" column, (2) the "credit discount" column, posted? 7. State the rule which governs the preparation, or classification, of entries before they are posted in the Ledger. 8. Rule a form of Journal proper, and enter therein six transactions. 9. Explain how to prepare the Journal entry which is necessary in order to open a set of books by double-entry.

EXERCISE 6B.

Prepare Journal entries for the following transactions, dating them March 22, 1910 ·

Bought on credit from C. Brown & Co. 2 horses @ £15 each, and a set of harness for £7 10s. Sold on credit to W. Morrison 3 sheep @ £4 10s. each, 1 pig @ £5, and a set of harness for £5 15s. Exchanged 1 horse worth £15 and a mahogany table worth £10 with J. Brown, who gave me for them a motor-bicycle worth £20 and a rifle worth £5. I am the owner of 500 £1 shares in the Velox Motor Manufacturing Co. Ltd., which cost me £500. The Company has been taken over by the Muswell Motor Manufacturing Co., Ltd. Received £500 4 per cent. Second Debentures of the latter Company in exchange for my shares in the former Company. I am also the owner of 200 £5 Ordinary Shares of the Muswell Motor Manufacturing Co., Ltd., which cost me £1000. I surrendered my share certificate to the Company, receiving in exchange 90 £5 First Preference Shares of the Company (worth £450) and 110 £5 Second Preference Shares of the Company (worth £550).

EXERCISE 6C.

Journalise the following transactions, ruling the necessary forms :

R. Long commenced business as a Coal Merchant on June 1, 1910, with the following assets : Cash at Bank, £200 ; plant and fixtures £60 ; and horse and cart, £30. He paid all cash received into his Bank. During June the following transactions took place : June 3, Purchased coal from the X.Y. Colliery Co., Ltd., £160 ; June 8, Sold coal to T. Philipps, £20 ; June 11, Sold coal to J. Hall, £110 ; June 15, Purchased coal from the X.Y. Colliery Co., Ltd., £360 ; June 16, Received cash from T. Philipps, £20 ; June 17, Received cash from J. Hall (on account), £80 ; June 24, Paid cheque to the X.Y. Colliery Co., Ltd., £200.

EXERCISE 6D.

Journalise the following transactions, ruling the necessary forms :

1. On March 1, 1910, J. Brown commenced business with £700 to the credit of his account at the Union Bank ; his transactions were : March 1, Bought goods from H. J. Miles, £158 10s. 6d. March 2, Paid for advertisements by cheque, £5 10s. ; Drew cheque for petty cashier, £10 ; Received from Rowe & Sons a horse and harness worth £35 in exchange for goods worth that amount. March 4, Sold goods to Goldy & Co., £153 16s. 8d. March 5, Drew cheque for warehouse furniture, £120 ; Bought goods from Rowe & Sons, £326 19s. March 7, Paid by cheque for travelling expenses, £8 10s. ; Received from Goldy & Co., cash (paid to Bank) £52. March 9, Paid wages by cheque, £12 10s. March 11, Bought goods from H. J. Miles, £36 14s. 9d. March 12, Paid Rowe & Sons by cheque £320, Discount £6 19s. ; Bought goods for cash (paid by cheque), £85 ; Drew out of Bank for office cash, £70. March 14, Sold goods for cash (paid to Bank), £24 15s. 8d. ; Paid for telephone rental by cheque, £4 5s. March 16, Paid wages by cheque, £16. March 18, Paid to Bank from office cash, £60. March 19, Paid for warehouse cleaning from office cash, £4 15s.

Note.—All receipts are paid into the Bank immediately upon their receipt unless otherwise stated, all payments are made by cheque unless otherwise stated.

EXERCISE 6E.

Journalise the following transactions, ruling the necessary forms. Date the entries March 15, 1910.

Exchanged two horses worth £25 each for a carriage worth £50; Exchanged a motor-bicycle worth £25 for a horse worth £20, and £5 worth of harness; Exchanged a cart worth £30, and a quantity of fodder worth £25, for 7 sheep worth £5 each, and 2 bicycles worth £10 each; Bought from W. Brown, on credit, 6 sheep @ £5 10s. each, and a horse for £15 15s.; Sold to James Wright, on credit, 2 sheep @ £6 2s. 6d. each, and a horse for £16 10s.; Transferred from the Personal Ledger Account of A. Brown (to which account it had been incorrectly debited by the Ledger-keeper) a sum of £162 5s. 9d. paid by me to W. Brown & Co. on March 3 last; Made Williams Bros. a special allowance of £20 as compensation for delay in executing one of their orders, and credited them with this sum in their account. On March 3 last I drew two cheques as under: (1) for telephone subscription, £15 15s., (2) for Neave Bros., on account, £30 17s. 9d.; my Ledger keeper has posted cheque No. 1 to the debit of Neave Bros.' account, and has posted cheque No. 2 to the debit of "Telephone subscription" account. Prepare the Journal entries which are necessary in order to correct these errors.

EXERCISE 6F.

Prepare the Journal entries which are necessary in order to correct the following errors, ruling the necessary forms. Date the entries May 19, 1910.

£60 was received from A. Day on March 4, 1910, and was credited to his account. It now appears that he remitted the money, not on his own behalf, but on behalf of his father, Richard Day, with whom I have had dealings. My Ledger-keeper made, on January 10, 1910, the following entries on the debit side of his Cash Book: (a) To *Commission Account*, cheque from C. Way, £27 2s. 9d.; (b) To *Horses Account*, proceeds of one horse sold to C. Way, £25; (c) To *C. Way*, cheque for credit of his account, £17 2s. 9d.; he posted the entries accordingly. It now appears that the £17 2s. 9d. was the purchase-price of the horse sold by me for cash to C. Way, that the £27 2s. 9d. was a cheque remitted by C. Way for credit of his account as one of my trade customers, and that the £25 was for commission remitted by C. Way to me for letting one of his farms. On Mar. 1, I paid £25 by cheque to R. Lucien, being his fee for surveying an estate owned by me; it should therefore have been debited to "Surveyor's Fees" account. My Ledger-keeper has, however, debited the amount to R. Lucien's Personal account. I paid in cash £3 10s. to W. Hughes, an injured workman, as compensation. My Ledger-keeper has debited this sum to "Workmen's Compensation" account; this sum was, however, paid by me, not on my own behalf, but on behalf of the Insurance Company with whom I am insured against this kind of loss; the Company later on sent me a cheque for the £3 10s., and the sum should, originally, have been debited to them.

Exercise 6G.

Construct, from the following details, the Journal entry necessary to open the books of V. Gray on July 1, 1910, ruling the necessary form. Show V. Gray's initial "Capital."

Cash at bank. £362 1s. 9d. ; stock-in-trade, £1471 14s. 2d. ; creditors : Eager & Co., £32 1s., Finch Bros., £176 15s. 4d.; cash on deposit account at the bank, £350 ; plant and machinery, £549 13s. 2d. ; Freehold premises, £1000 ; amount owing to W. Brown for loans, £5500 ; debtors : W. Good, £362 13s. 9d., R. Hall, £40 ; cash at office, £5 2s. 9d.

Exercise 6H.

From the following particulars prepare the necessary Journal entry in order to open the books of Robert Hart as on June 10, 1910 :

Leasehold office, valued at £2000 ; office furniture, valued at £200 ; stock-in-trade, valued at £1100 10s. ; loan to R. Walters, £500 ; debtors : J. Robinson £250 10s., B. Lawes £310 15s. 6d., R. Johnson £205 12s. 10d. ; cash in hand, £50 2s. 6d. ; loan from the bank, £200 ; interest due to the bank, £10 ; creditors: F. Gribble £500 10s., J. Colville £58 4s. 2d., B. Peat £112 11s. 10d.

CHAPTER VII

THE LEDGER

I HAVE already made several brief references to a book called the "Ledger." I must now explain more fully the form and the uses of this important book.

The Ledger is the book in which the whole of a trader's transactions are stored, or "laid up," in classified form for future reference. It is divided into a number of sections called "Accounts." A Ledger Account is a statement which shows the dealings the trader has had, (*a*) in a particular thing, or (*b*) with a particular person, or (*c*) as regards particular kinds of "profit" and "loss." Taken as a whole, a trader's Ledger accounts provide him with a permanent record of his transactions, the details relating to which can always be readily found if the Ledger has been kept in a proper manner.

I explained to you in Chapter II. that the Cash Book is a Ledger account, bound separately for the sake of convenience. You must be careful to bear this fact in mind. The Cash Book is used as a "book of first entry," as are also the various Journals, the uses of which I have already explained to you. The Cash Book, however, is always a necessary companion to the Ledger, and the Ledger is incomplete without it. The Journals, on the other hand, after they have been posted to the Ledger, can be dispensed with, as the Ledger is complete without them.

Every entry in the Cash Book forms one-half of a double-entry; the other half of the double-entry appears on the opposite side of some account in the Ledger.

As I have already told you, a Ledger account is a statement that shows the trader's dealings in relation to some particular matter, or with some particular person; in other words, it is a statement in which transactions are classified according to their *general* nature. I must now enter more fully into an explanation of this statement :

1. A trader's transactions in any particular "*thing*" may be of two kinds, (*a*) purchases, or (*b*) sales.

2. A trader's transactions with any particular "*person*" may also be of two kinds. They may result in making the trader either (*a*) the debtor, or (*b*) the creditor, of the person with whom he has dealt.

3. A trader's transactions for which nominal accounts are employed may also be of two kinds, *i.e.* (*a*) "Profits" or (*b*) "Losses," *e.g.* discounts allowed or discounts received, commission paid or commission earned.

All these various kinds of transactions are recorded in the Ledger, which is thus expected to do several different kinds of work. In view of the task imposed upon it, it becomes necessary that the Ledger shall be designed so as to record transactions not only under their appropriate *general* heading, but also according to the *relation which they bear to the trader himself*. An account kept for "things" must be ruled so as to separate the *purchases* of that particular "thing" from the *sales* of the same "thing." A "Personal" account must be so ruled that all deliveries of money or goods *to* a person are separated from the receipts of money or goods *from* him.

In order to fufil these various duties the Ledger is ruled as under :

Dr.   Specimen Ledger Account.   *Cr.*

A	B	C	D	E	F	G	H	I	J	K	L	M	N

The accounts contained in any Ledger may be grouped under three headings, viz.—"Real," "Personal," and "Nominal" accounts.

The name of the subject of each account is placed at the head of the account itself ; this name is determined as follows

(*a*) In the case of accounts of "things," *i.e.* **Real Accounts**, the name of the "thing" dealt in forms the heading of the account.

(*b*) In the case of accounts with persons, *i.e.* **Personal Accounts**, the name of the person dealt with is placed at the head of the account.

(c) In the case of the third section of Ledger accounts, *i.e.* Nominal Accounts, the name of the "loss" sustained, or of the "profit" earned, or the name, "Capital Account," supplies the necessary heading according to the nature of the account.

Transactions are entered in columns A to G, or in columns H to N, according to the relation which they bear to the trader owning the Ledger.

Taking first the left-hand side of the Ledger account: columns A and B are designed to record the date (month and day) of each transaction; column C is to record the details showing the nature of the item; column D contains a page reference to the book wherein appears a preliminary and fully detailed record of the transaction, while columns E, F, and G contain the amount of the transaction in pounds, shillings and pence.

The right-hand side of the Ledger account is designed to provide for the entry of transactions of similar general nature to those which appear on the left-hand side of the account, though they are, of course, opposite in their relation as regards the trader himself; consequently, columns H to N are a repetition of those on the other side of the account, the uses of which have already been described.

Columns A to G together make what is called the "Debit" side of the Ledger account, and columns H to N collectively form the "Credit" side. Abbreviations of these words appear at the top of the account under the forms **Dr.** and **Cr.**

Personal Accounts are Ledger accounts kept by a trader to record his dealings with *persons* and are constructed as follows:

The value of everything that is paid to, or transferred to, the person dealt with, is entered on the *debit* side of that person's account, and the value of everything that is received from the person dealt with is entered on the *credit* side.

Since everything paid by the trader to the other party is entered on the debit side, and all receipts from him are entered on the credit side, it follows that the difference between the totals of the two sides represents the net sum owing by one of the parties. The sum is owing to, or by, the trader, according as the debit side of the account is greater than the credit side, or the credit side greater than the debit side.

It is customary in the case of all Ledger accounts, whatever their nature may be, to add up the two sides of the account at periodical intervals, and after having inserted on one side the difference, or "Balance," necessary to make the two sides of the account equal in amount, to rule them off and to insert the balance afresh below the ruled lines. This "Balance brought down," as it is termed, forms the starting-point for further transactions, and relieves the account of unwieldy totals.

An example of a "Personal Account"—*i.e.* an account between persons—has already been explained on p. 3.

Real Accounts are Ledger accounts kept by a trader for the *"things"* which are dealt in by him, and are constructed as under:

Accounts are opened in the Ledger, headed with the names of the various "things" dealt in by the trader. All "things" received are entered on the *debit* side of the particular account to which they relate. All "things" parted with are *credited* to the account to which they relate.

In the case of accounts of this kind, the amount by which the items on the debit side of the account exceed the items on the credit side, at any particular date, represents the stock of the particular "thing" remaining in the trader's possession.

An example of a "Real" account, *i.e.* an account kept to record the trader's dealings in "things," appears on p. 136.

Real accounts record the trader's dealings in property, including material objects, such as Land, Cash, Machinery, Buildings, &c., but excluding, of course, debts due to him which come under the previous heading.

Nominal Accounts.—The accounts in a Ledger which are neither "Personal" accounts nor "Real" accounts, are called "Nominal," or "Impersonal," accounts. They are are of three kinds, viz.:

1. Accounts kept to record "Profits" or "Gains."
2. Accounts kept to record "Losses" or "Expenses."
3. The trader's "Capital" account.

The existence of these "Nominal" accounts arises, in the first place, from the necessity of completing the double-entry for certain transactions. "Profits" made and "losses" sustained cannot be recorded in the form of a double-entry except by using Nominal accounts. A trader cannot commence to keep his books by double-entry without using a "Capital Account," except in the very unlikely event of his assets exactly equalling in value the amount of his liabilities.

Nominal accounts, kept to record "profits"—or "gains"— are *credited* with all the profits, or gains, made. These accounts may, for the purpose of illustration, be regarded as if they were Personal accounts, all profits made being regarded as if they were receipts from an imaginary person, to whose account they are credited in the ordinary way. To be strictly accurate the trader would head all such accounts "*My* Profits Account," &c.

Nominal accounts, kept to record "losses," or "expenses," are *debited* with all the losses or expenses sustained. They may, for the purpose of illustration, be regarded as if they were Personal accounts, the losses being also regarded as payments to an imaginary person, to whose account they are debited in the ordinary way. To be strictly accurate, the heading of these accounts would be ,, *My* Office Expenses Account," &c.

The "Capital" account contains the entry which is necessary to record the excess of the trader's assets over his liabilities, or of his liabilities over his assets, as the case may be. The Capital account thus represents the "net worth" of the trader, or the amount to the extent of which he is insolvent. In the former case this account would show an entry on the credit side, or a "credit balance," while in the latter case it would show an entry on the debit side, *i.e.* a "debit balance."

If the Capital account shows a credit balance it can be regarded as a Personal account, kept by the business for its proprietor, in order to show the amount which the latter has invested in the concern, and for which he is, so to speak, its creditor. If the account shows a debit balance it can be regarded as a Personal account for the proprietor, showing the amount that he must contribute in order to place the business in a state of solvency.

When a set of books are "opened" on the double-entry system the trader's "Capital" account shows his net worth, or the net amount to the extent of which he is insolvent at the date on which the books are "opened." By a process which will be explained to you later in Chapters X. and XI., the net profit, or the net loss, made by the trader during each succes· sive year, or other period of trading, is transferred to the trader's Capital account. All net profits made are credited to the Capital account, and thus increase the "net worth" of the trader, or lessen the amount to the extent of which he is insol- vent, as the case may be. All net losses sustained are debited to the Capital account, and thus lessen his "net worth," or increase his insolvency, as the case may be. The "net worth," or the net amount to the extent of which the trader is insolvent, is thus periodically brought up to date.

I must again remind you that a trader's transactions are first entered, as and when they occur, in the various books of " original entry."

You already know that the books of " original entry " consist of :

1. The Cash Book.
2. The Journals.

    (a) The various " Special " Journals, *e.g.* the " Sales " Journal, " Purchases " Journal, &c.
    (b) The " Journal Proper."

The necessary records in the Ledger are made from the above books of " original entry." The process of making these records is called " Posting the Ledger."

Postings in the Ledger are effected as follows :

1. **The Cash Book.**—All items appearing on the debit side of the Cash Book, whether in the " Cash," " Bank," or " Discount " columns, are posted to the *credit* of some account in the Ledger, and all items appearing on the credit side of the Cash Book are posted to the *debit* of some account in the Ledger. Transfers of money between the office cash-box and the bank account form an apparent exception to this rule. Such transfers do not need to be posted in the Ledger. The entry in the Bank column, on the one side of the Cash Book, offsets, or " *contras*," the entry in the Office Cash column on the other side.

You will remember that the Cash Book is really a Ledger account bound separately. It will be clear to you, therefore, that transfers which already "balance" one another in a Ledger account do not need further posting.

If Discount columns are included in the Cash Book, they must be added at the date on which the Cash Book is balanced and ruled off, and the totals arrived at must be posted in the Ledger as follows :

    (a) The total of the Discount column on the debit side of the Cash Book must be posted to the debit of the " Discounts Account " in the Ledger.
    (b) The total of the Discount column on the credit side of the Cash Book must be posted to the credit of the " Discounts Account " in the Ledger.

This forms, at first sight, an exception to the ordinary rule which governs the posting of entries from the Cash Book to the opposite side of some account in the Ledger ; but in reality it has nothing whatever to do with the ordinary rule.

The Discount columns are inserted in the Cash Book solely for convenience, and form no real part of it. They are merely " memoranda " columns for the purpose of saving time.

Discounts entered in the " Discounts Allowed" column, *i.e.* that on the debit side of the Cash Book, are, as has already been explained, posted to the credit of the person to whom they are allowed, in company with the cash received from him. Having been thus *credited* to the various persons to whom they have been allowed, it is obvious that they must be *debited* to some other account in the Ledger. The two Discount columns, being merely memoranda columns, are not really part of the Cash Book proper, and for this reason they do not form part of a Ledger account. It will be clear, therefore, that entries made in these columns have not the same effect as entries made in a Ledger account. This being the case, it will be obvious that the total of the " discounts allowed " must be dealt with by means of a debit in a Ledger account, viz., the " Discount Account." The debit entry of the total of the discounts allowed in this account equalises and offsets all the various entries made on the credit side in the accounts of the persons to whom discount has been allowed.

In a similar manner, the total of the " Discounts Received " column, on the credit side of the Cash Book, needs to be posted to the *credit* of the " Discount Account " in the Ledger. This entry will then equalise and offset the various debit entries made in the accounts of the persons from whom discount has been received.

In cases where a Petty Cash Book is kept (see p. 40), the totals of the analysis columns (A to H) are posted to the debit of Nominal accounts headed with their respective names.

Each item appearing in the " Ledger Account " column (col. I) is posted *separately* to the debit of the particular Ledger account against which it is placed in the " Ledger Account " column.

Payments from the bank or office cash-box to the Petty Cashier are credited in the Bank, or Office Cash column of the trader's Cash Book, and are debited in the debit column (T1) of the Petty Cash Book. The Petty Cash Book is balanced—columns T1 and T2—in the ordinary way, and the balance brought down in column TI ranks as the balance of a Ledger account, just as is the case with the balance of the trader's Cash Book.

Cash Book items are usually posted as "To" or "By Cash," or, if discount is included, "To" or "By Cash and Discount." In some cases it may be necessary to give a little more detail than this.

2 (a) The Special Journals.

(1) Entries which appear in the "Sales Journal" are posted (a) in detail to the *debit* of the respective Personal accounts of the customers, and (b) in total to the *credit* of the "Sales Account" in the Ledger.

(2) Entries which appear in the "Purchases Journal" are posted (a) in detail to the *credit* of the respective Personal accounts of the sellers, and (b) in total to the *debit* of the "Purchases Account" in the Ledger.

(3) Entries which appear in the "Returns Outwards Journal" are posted (a) in detail to the *debit* of the accounts of the persons to whom the goods have been returned, and (b) in total to the *credit* of the "Returns Outwards Account" in the Ledger.

(4) Entries which appear in the "Returns Inwards Journal" are posted (a) in detail to the *credit* of the Personal accounts of the dissatisfied customers, and (b) in total to the *debit* of the "Returns Inwards Account" in the Ledger.

Items posted from the "Purchases" and "Sales Journals" are usually entered as "To" or "By Goods." In some business houses, however, it is usual, and even necessary, to give more detail, *e.g.* "To 5 bags of coffee at £2 10s., and 2 chests of tea at 48s."

Note.—Although kept in separate accounts, the "Sales," "Purchases," "Returns Inwards," and "Returns Outwards" accounts are in reality subdivisions of one "Real" account called the "Trading Account." I shall explain to you, at a later stage, how they are combined in one "Trading Account."

2 (b) The Journal Proper

Entries which appear in the *debit* column are posted to the *debit* of the various Ledger accounts indicated, and entries in the *credit* column are posted to the *credit* of the various Ledger accounts indicated.

You already know that the entries which appear in the

Journal Proper have been prepared in correct form for entry in the Ledger, and that they merely need to be copied into the Ledger as they stand.

The principles which I have just explained to you in this chapter, together with those explained in Chapters II. to **VI.**, are practically illustrated by the example I will now give you of a series of mercantile transactions. These transactions are shown as having been recorded in the proper books of "original entry," and afterwards, as having been posted to the proper accounts in the trader's Ledger. For the purpose of easy reference the following abbreviations have been used in the various "folio" columns in the Ledger:

Cash Book—C.B. ; Purchases Journal—P. ; Sales Journal—S. ; Returns Inwards Book—R.I. ; Returns Outwards Book—R O. ; the Journal Proper—J.

The numbers inserted in the "Folio" columns in the books of "original entry" refer to the Ledger folios on which the entry is posted.

EXAMPLE.

R. Jones started business on May 2, 1910, with the following assets :

	£	s.	d.
Cash at the London & Provincial Bank, Ltd. . .	655	10	9
Debtors :			
C. Powell	32	4	6
R. Lyon	324	11	7
Stock of tea on hand, 355 chests valued at .	902	11	4
Freehold warehouse and land . .	350	0	0
Jones owed the following liabilities :			
Creditors			
C. Samuel	499	3	5
W. Barber	125	0	0

Jones's transactions for the month of May, 1910, were as follows :

1910.		£	s.	d.
May 2	Drew from the Bank for office cash . .	30	0	0
„ 4	Bought from C. Samuel on credit 70 chests of tea at 50s. per chest net	175	0	0
„ 5	Sold to C. Powell on credit 28 chests of tea at 60s. per chest net	84	0	0
„ 7	Paid from office cash sundry petty expenses	2	1	2
„ 9	Paid C. Samuel by cheque	200	0	0
	Being allowed discount	2	5	0
„ 10	Received from R. Lyon cheque, and banked the same	165	4	9
	Allowed him discount		16	6

1910.		£	s.	d.
May 11	Returned to C. Samuel 4 chests of tea, invoiced at 50s. per chest, of inferior quality to that ordered	10	0	0
„ 14	Paid from office cash salaries and wages to date	24	8	10
, 16	Received from C. Powell cash (placed in office cash)	32		0
	Allowed him discount . . .		0¼	6
„ 17	Of the £24 8s. 10d. paid on the 14th May as "Salaries and Wages," it is now found that 16s. 9d. was not paid on account of "Salaries and Wages," but for travelling expenses. This sum must be transferred from "Salaries and Wages account" to a separate "Travelling Expenses account"		16	9
„ 18	Paid R. Brown, on account, from office cash, for sundry articles of furniture purchased	20	0	0
„ „	Sold to R. Lyon, on credit, 29 chests of tea at 59s. per chest, less 5 per cent. trade discount	81	5	5
„ 19	R. Lyon returned as "not equal to sample" 3 chests of tea sold to him yesterday at 59s. per chest, less 5 per cent. trade discount	8		2
„ „	Drew from the Bank for office cash . .	25	8	0
„ 20	Returned to C. Samuel 2 chests of tea invoiced at 50s. per chest, found, on opening, to have been damaged by water .	5	0	
„ „	Bought on credit from W. Barber 5 chests of tea at 52s. per chest net	13	0	
„ 21	Sold to C. Powell on credit 6 chests of tea at 61s. per chest, net	18	6	0
„ „	Paid from office cash for 2 office stools . .	1	0	0
„ 23	Made a special allowance to R. Lyon of 1s. per chest on the 29 chests of tea sold to him on the 18th inst., the tea having been despatched too late, and having reached him after he had already been obliged to buy other tea locally, in order to fulfil an order	1	9	0
„ „	Paid by cheque to R. Brown for additional furniture bought from him . . .	1	10	0
„ „	Paid by cheque to W. Barber . . .	120	0	0
	Being allowed discount . . .	5	0	0
„ 24	Sold to R. Lyon on credit 60 chests of tea at 60s. per chest, net	180	0	0
„ „	Received from R. Lyon cheque on account, and banked the same	50	0	0
„ 25	R. Lyon returned 6 chests of the tea sold to him on the 24th inst., on the ground that it was of inferior quality to that ordered. Allowed him full invoice price . .	18	0	0

1910.		£	s.	d.
May 28	Paid by cheque cost of trade advertisements for the month	2	10	0
„ 30	Paid from office cash, salaries and wages to date	23	5	0
„ 31	Paid from office cash for Stationery supplied	2	4	6
„ „	Paid from office cash, sundry General Expenses	1	19	3
„ „	Paid by cheque, carriage and freight on goods sold during the month	8	17	.
„ „	Sold R. Lyon, on credit, 7 chests of tea invoiced at 60s. per chest, less 5 per cent. Trade Discount	19	19	0

NOTE.—The stock of tea in hand as on May 31st, 1910, was valued at £805 11s. 9d.

PURCHASES BOOK.

Date.	Particulars.	Ledger folio. (Cr.)	Details. £ s. d.	Total. £ s. d.
1910. May 4	C. Samuel— 70 chests of tea at 50s. per chest net .	5		175 0 0
„ 20	W. Barber— 5 chests of tea at 52s. per chest net	6		13 0 0
	Debit Ledger folio . . .	16		£188 0 0

SALES BOOK.

Date.	Particulars.	Ledger folio. (Dr.)	Details. £ s. d.	Total. £ s. d.
1910. May 5	C. Powell— 28 chests of tea at 60s. per chest net	8		84 0 0
„ 18	R. Lyon— 29 chests of tea at 59s. per chest . Less 5 per cent. trade discount .	7	85 11 0 / 4 5 7	81 5 5
„ 21	C. Powell— 6 chests of tea at 61s. per chest net .	8		18 6 0
„ 24	R. Lyon— 60 chests of tea at 60s. per chest .	7		180 0 0
„ 31	R. Lyon— 7 chests of tea at 60s. per chest . Less 5 per cent. trade discount .	7	21 0 0 / 1 1 0	19 19 0
	Credit Ledger folio. . .	17		£383 10 5

I

Dr.   CASH

Date.	Particulars.	Folio.	Discount allowed.			Cash.			Bank.		
			£	s.	d.	£	s.	d.	£	s.	d
1910 May 2	To Balance . . .	J.							655	10	0
" "	" Bank . . .	Contra				30	0	0			
" 10	" R. Lyon, on account	7		16	6				165	,	9
" 16	" C. Powell . .	8		4	6	32	0	0			
" 19	" Bank . . .	Contra				25	0	0			
" 24	" R. Lyon, on account	7							0		0
	Ledger Dr. folio .	15	£1	1	0						
						£87	0	0	£870	15	6
1910. June 1	To Balances brought down	✓				12	1	3	482	18	2

RETURNS INWARDS BOOK.

Date.	Particulars.	Details.			Total.		
		£	s.	d.	£	s.	d.
1910. May 19	*R. Lyon—* 3 chests of tea at 59s. per chest Less 5 per cent. trade discount . "Not up to sample."						
" 25	*R. Lyon—* 6 chests of tea at 60s. per chest . "Not as ordered."						

BOOK.
Cr.

Date	Particulars.	Folio.	Discount received.			Cash.			Bank.		
			£	s	d.	£		d.	£	s.	d.
1910.											
May 2	By Cash . . .	Contra							30	0	0
„ 7	„ General Expenses— Sundry petty expenses paid .	11				2		2			
„ 9	„ C. Samuel . .	5	2		0				200		0
„ 14	„ Salaries and wages (to date) . .	10				24		10			
„ 18	„ Furniture and fittings, on account .	4				20		0			
„ 19	„ Cash . . .	Contra							25		0
„ 21	„ Furniture and fittings— Cost of 2 office stools . .	4				1		0			
„ 23	„ Furniture and fittings . . .	4							1	10	0
„	„ W. Barber . .	6	5	0	0				120	0	0
28	„ Advertising Account— Cost of 1 month's advertisements	13							2	1	0
„ 30	„ Salaries and wages to date . . .	10				23	5	0			
„ 31	„ Stationery Account .	12				2	4	6			
„ „	„ General Expenses— Sundry expenses paid . . .	11				1	19	3			
„	„ Carriage and freight on goods sold during the month .	14							8	17	4
	Ledger Cr. folio .	15	£7	5	0						
„	„ Balances carried down	✓				12	1	3	482	18	2
						£87	0	0	£870	15	6

RETURNS OUTWARDS BOOK.

Date.	Particulars.	Ledger folio (Dr.)	Details. £ s. d.	Total. £ s. d.
1910.				
May 11	C. Samuel— 4 chests of tea at 50s. per chest net . "Quality inferior to that ordered."	5		10 0 0
„ 20	C. Samuel— 2 chests of tea at 50s. per chest . . "Damaged by water."	5		5 0 0
	Credit Ledger folio . . .	19		£15 0 0

JOURNAL.

1910.			£		d.	£	s.	d.
May 2	Sundries Dr.							
	To Sundries—							
	Cash at the bank . .	C.	655	10	9			
	C. Powell	8	32	4	6			
	R. Lyon	7	324	11	7			
	Stock of tea in hand .	2	902	11	4			
	Freehold warehouse and							
	land	3	350	^	0			
	C. Samuel . . .	5				499	3	5
	W. Barber . . .	6				125	0	0
	R. Jones, Capital Ac-							
	count . . .	1				1640	14	9
	For assets, liabilities, and capi-							
	tal at this date.							
			£2264	18	2	£2264	18	2
„ 17	Travelling Expenses Ac-							
	count Dr.	-		16	9			
	To Salaries and Wages Ac-							
	count . . .	10					16	9
	For transfer of amount placed							
	in error to the debit of the							
	latter account.							
„ 23	Discounts and Allowances Ac-							
	count Dr.	15	1	9	0			
	To R. Lyon . . .	7				1	9	0
	For a special allowance for late							
	delivery of 29 chests of tea.		£2	5	9	£2	5	9

LEDGER.

1   R. JONES, CAPITAL ACCOUNT.   **1**

Dr.   *Cr.*

			1910.			£	s.	d.
			May 2	By Balance at this date .	J.	1640	14	9

2   STOCK.   **2**

Dr.   *Cr.*

1910.			£	s.	d.			
May 2	To Balance .	J.	902	11	4			

3   FREEHOLD WAREHOUSE AND LAND.   **3**

Dr.   *Cr.*

1910.			£	s.	d.			
May 2	To Balance .	J.	350	0	0			

LEDGER—*continued.*

4   FURNITURE AND FITTINGS.   **4**

Dr.   *Cr.*

1910.			£	s.	d.	1910.			£	s.	d.
May 17	To Cash— For sundry furniture and fittings bought	C.	20	0	0	May 31	By Balance carried down	✓	22	10	0
„ 21	„ Cash— For 2 office stools	C.	1	0	0						
„ 23	„ Cash— For sundry furniture bought	C.	1	10	0						
		£	22	10	0			£	22	10	0
1910. June 1	To Balance brought down	✓	22	10	0						

5   C. SAMUEL.   **5**

Dr.   *Cr.*

1910.			£	s.	d.	1910.			£	s.	d.
May 9	To Cash and discount	C.	202	5	0	May 2	By Balance	J.	499	3	5
„ 11	„ Returns	R.O.	10	0	0	„ 4	„ Goods	P.	175	0	0
„ 20	„ „	R.O.	5	0	0						
„ 31	„ Balance carried down	✓	456	18	5						
		£	674	3	5	1910.		£	674	3	5
						June 1	By Balance brought down	✓	456	18	5

6   W. BARBER.   **6**

Dr.   *Cr.*

1910.			£	s.	d.	1910.			£	s	d.
May 23	To Cash and Discount	C.	125	0	0	May 2	By Balance	J.	125	0	0
„ 31	„ Balance carried down	✓	13	0	0	„ 20	„ Goods		13	0	0
		£	138	0	0			£	138	0	0
						1910. June 1	By Balance brought down	✓	13	0	0

LEDGER—*continued.*

7   R. LYON.   **7**

Dr.   Cr.

1910.			£	s.	d.	1910.			£	s.	d.
May 2	To Balance	J.	324	11	7	May 10	By Cash and Discount	C.	166	1	3
„ 18	„ Goods	S.	81	5	5	„ 19	„ Returns	R.J	8	8	2
„ 24	„ „	S.	180	0	0	„ 24	„ Cash	C.	50	0	0
„ 31	„ „	S.	19	19	0	„ „	„ Allowance for late delivery of 29 chests of tea	J	1	9	0
						„ 25	„ Returns	R.J.	18	0	0
						„ 31	„ Balance carried down	✓	361	17	7
		£	605	16	0			£	605	16	0
1910. June 1	To Balance brought down	✓	361	17	7						

C. POWELL.   **8**

Dr.   Cr.

1910.			£	s.	d.	1910.			£	s.	d.
May 2	To Balance	J.	32	4	6	May 16	By Cash and discount	C.	32	4	6
„ 5	„ Goods	S.	84	0	0	„ 31	„ Balance carried down	✓	102	6	0
„ 21	„ „	S.	18	6	0						
		£	134	10	6				134	10	6
1910. June 1	To Balance brought down	✓	102	6	0						

9   TRAVELLING EXPENSES.   **9**

Dr.   Cr.

1910.			£	s.	d.
May 17	To Transfer from Salaries and Wages account	J.		16	9

10   SALARIES AND WAGES.   **10**

Dr.   Cr.

1910.			£	s.	d	1910.			£	s.	d.
May 14	To Cash	C.	24	8	10	May 17	By Transfer to Travelling Expenses account	J.		16	9
„ 30	„ „	C.	23	5	0	„ 31	„ Balance carried down	✓	46	17	1
		£	47	13	10			£	47	13	10
1910. June 1	To Balance brought down	✓	46	17	1						

LEDGER—*continued.*

11   GENERAL EXPENSES.   **11**

Dr.   Cr.

1910.			£	s.	d.	1910.			£	s.	d.
May 7	To Cash, sundry petty expenses	C.	2	1	2	May 31	By Balance carried down	√	4	0	5
„ 31	„ „ „	C.	1	19	3						
			£4	0	5				£4	0	5
1910. June 1	To Balance brought down	√	4	0	5						

12   STATIONERY.   **12**

Dr.   Cr.

1910.			£	s.	d.
May 31	To Cash	C.	2	4	6

13   ADVERTISING.   **13**

Dr.   Cr.

1910.			£	s.	d.
May 28	To Cash— For one month's advertisements in Trade papers	C.	2	10	0

14   CARRIAGE AND FREIGHT.   **14**

Dr.   Cr.

1910.			£	s.	d.
May 31	To Cash— Carriage and freight on goods sold	C.	8	17	4

15   DISCOUNT AND ALLOWANCES.   **5**

Dr.   Cr.

1910.			£	s.	d.	1910.			£	s.	d.
May 24	To R. Lyon, allowance for late delivery	J.	1	9	0	May 31	By Sundries— Discounts received as per Cash Book	C.	7	5	
„ 31	„ Sundries— Discounts allowed as per Cash Book	C.	1	1	0						
„ 31	„ Balance carried down	√	4	15	0						
		£	7	5	0	1910.			£	7	5	0
						June 1	By Balance brought down	√	4	15	0

LEDGER—*continued.*

16 ·   PURCHASES ACCOUNT.   **16**

Dr.   *Cr.*

		£	s.	d.				
1910. May 31	To Purchases for May as per Purchases Book . . P.	188	0	0				

17   SALES ACCOUNT.   **17**

Dr.   *Cr.*

						£	s.	d
		1910. May 31	By Sales for May as per Sales Book . S.	383	10	5		

18   RETURNS INWARDS ACCOUNT.   **18**

Dr.   *Cr.*

		£	s.	d.				
1910. May 31	To Returns Inwards for May, as per Returns Inwards Book . R.I.	26	8	2				

19   RETURNS OUTWARDS ACCOUNT.   **19**

Dr.   *Cr.*

						£	s.	d.
		1910. May 31	By Returns Outwards for May, as per Returns Outwards Book . R.O.	15	0	0		

In the foregoing example the various "special" Journals, *i.e.* the Sales, Purchases, and the two Returns Journals, are shown as having been added at the end of the month. The respective totals of these books have then been posted in their proper Nominal accounts in the Ledger, *i.e.* to the Sales, Purchases, and the two Returns accounts.

The discount column in the Cash Book (p. 130), is also shown as having been added, and ruled off at the end of the month. The total of the left hand discount column has been posted to the *debit* of the Discount account, and represents the total of the discounts allowed to customers during the month. The total of the right-hand side discount column represents the total of the discounts received from creditors during the mouth, and has been posted to the credit of the Discount account. Both these entries are therefore in accordance with the rule laid down on p. 124.

The only transactions that require special mention are two of those which have been passed through the Journal Proper, viz. ·

1. The error which occurred on May 17.
2. The special allowance made to R. Lyon on May 23.

Both these transactions have been passed through the Journal because there is no other " book of first entry " in which they could have been suitably recorded.

The Cash Book and all the Ledger accounts have been balanced on May 31, 1910, and the balances have been brought down as on that date. The balances which appear in the Cash Book and Ledger on May 31, 1910, have been entered in a special manner in a list, or schedule, shown in the following chapter (see p. 145). In this list the debit balances have been kept separate from the credit balances, and the total of each of these two classes of balance has thus been obtained. When the Ledger balances have been arranged in this way it will be found that the total of the debit balances exactly equals the total of the credit balances. This agreement is the direct result of the main principle of double-entry book-keeping, viz., " that every debit requires its credit, and *vice versa*," and furnishes a very valuable safeguard against error. If the totals of the two classes of balance fail to agree, a mistake must have been made, and diligent search must at once be made to discover where the error has occurred.

When you have gained a little more experience, you will find that, in business houses, it is usual to keep more than one Ledger. The various Ledgers employed are, however, merely convenient subdivisions of the Ledger I have been telling you about, and do not involve any new book-keeping principles.

The sums of money periodically withdrawn from a business by the owner for his private expenditure are called **Drawings**.

Before concluding this chapter I must explain to you how these drawings are treated in the trader's books.

All sums withdrawn for private purposes must be *debited* to an account called **Drawings account**; the *credit* entry for the corresponding amount appears, of course, in the Cash Book in which the payment is entered as and when it occurs.

At the end of any given period, usually yearly, the Draw ings account is closed by a Journal entry which transfers the total of the drawings during the period to the debit of the trader's Capital account, e.g. :

			£	s.	d.	£	s.	d.
Capital Account　　　　　　　　Dr.	15		350	0	0			
To Drawings Account　.　.　.	21					350	0	0
For sums withdrawn by Mr. Barclay during the year.								

You will remember that the sum which stands to the credit of the trader's Capital account represents the amount which he has embarked in the business. In other words, the under-taking is his debtor for the amount of his capital. It will be quite clear to you, therefore, that all sums paid to the owner of the business should be treated as reducing the liability of the concern to its proprietor.

EXERCISE 7A.

1. What is a Ledger? Is a Journal a Ledger Account? Is a Cash Book a Ledger Account? Is the Returns Inwards Book a Ledger Account? 2. What are the rules for preparing a Personal Ledger Account? Prepare a specimen Personal Account for Henry Jones and show six imaginary entries on each side, and bring down the balance. 3. What are (a) Nominal Accounts, and (b) Real Accounts? 4. What is a Cash Book? how is it related to the Ledger? 5. What is the object of a Journal? what is its relation to the Ledger? 6. Why are "Books of Original Entry" employed in practical book-keeping? 7. What is meant by "Posting the Ledger"? 8. What is the main principle of Double-Entry book-keeping? 9. Explain the uses of the different columns contained in the ordinary form of Ledger account and give a specimen ruling.

EXERCISE 7B.

1. What is a trader's "Capital Account," and what does its balance represent—(a) If it is on the debit side, and (b) if it is on the credit side? 2. Classify the following Ledger accounts as among (a) Real, (b) Personal, and (c) Nominal Accounts, viz. Capital Account, Machinery Account, Telegrams and Postages Account, J. Wilson & Co.'s Account, Discounts Received Account, Profit and Loss Account, Wages Account, R. Brown (Loan)Account, Buildings Account, Office Expenses Account.

3. In which Ledger or other accounts, and on which side of such accounts, would you expect to find the following items?—(a) £1000 paid for a plot of land ; (b) £70 paid for wages ; (c) £100 paid to-day to R. Jones in full settlement of an account for £104 12s. 6d. due to him two months hence ; (d) £200 received from J. Brown in repayment of money lent to him. 4. Give a specimen ruling of a Ledger account (Real) and enter therein three entries on the debit and three on the credit side, and bring down the balance. 5. Open the necessary Ledger (or other) accounts from the following items, employing the Journal : On January 1, 1909, John Jones had cash at the Bank, £150 ; freehold shop, value £1000 ; a horse and cart, value £110 ; debts owing to him, £560—viz., R. Brown, £400 ; J. Robinson, £160—whilst he owed £670—viz., J. Fitter, £420 ; R. Roberts, £250 ; he also had stock of goods in hand valued at £312. 6. What are the rules which govern the preparation of "Nominal" accounts? Prepare an imaginery Ledger account showing six items representing "expenses." 7. What are the books of original entry? 8. State how, and where, entries made in the following books of original entry are posted in the Ledger— (a) The Sales Book ; (b) The Cash Book ; (c) The Returns Outwards Book ; (d) The Journal Proper. 9. Explain carefully how Cash Discounts are recorded in the Ledger through the medium of the Cash Book.

EXERCISE 7C.

William Heath commenced business on January 1, 1906, with Cash £50. His transactions were :

Jan. 1, Paid for goods bought this day, £15 ; Jan. 2, Bought and paid for Hand-cart, £2 10s. ; Jan. 3, Bought goods from R. Valley & Co., £13 10s. ; Jan. 4, Bought goods from J. Dale & Co., £26 10s. 3d. ; Jan. 5, Sold goods to J. W. Moore, £2 14s. 6d. ; Jan. 6, Sundry Cash Sales, £8 4s. 2d. ; Jan. 9, Bought goods from J. Dale & Co., £14 10s. 8d. ; Goods sold to T. Hill & Son, £3 10s. ; Jan. 10, Goods sold to J. W. Moore, £1 9s. 3d. ; Jan. 11, Bought goods from J. W. Moore, £4 ; Jan. 13, Sundry Cash Sales, £7 12s. 5d. ; Jan. 16, Sold goods to Chas. Fenn, 18s. 6d. ; Sold goods to J. W. Moore, £2 6s. 5d. ; Jan. 17, Bought goods from J. Dale & Co., £12 6s. 4d. ; Jan. 20, Sundry Cash Sales, £9 5s. 4d. ; Paid R. Valley & Co. amount of their account, less 2½ per cent. discount ; Paid J. Dale & Co. £40, discount allowed £1 0s. 11d. ; Jan. 23, Sold goods to J. Dale & Co., £1 5s. ; Jan. 24, Sold goods to J. W. Moore, £1 4s. 10d. ; Jan. 26, J. W. Moore paid balance of his account less discount 3s. 9d. ; Jan. 27, Sundry Cash Sales, £8 9s. 1d. ; Jan. 31, Paid Rent, £3 6s. 8d., and Wages, £6 10s. ; W. Heath withdrew Cash for private use, £3.*

Enter up the Purchases and Sales Books, Cash Book, and Ledger, and bring down the balance of all accounts on January 31, 1906.

(West Riding County Council, 1906.)

EXERCISE 7D.

Open the necessary ledger accounts with the following balances as on Jan. 1, 1910 : Stock of timber, £500 ; Cash at Bank, £600. Debtors :

* Debit this £3 to W. Heath's Capital Account.

O. Child, £100; B. Nugent, £32 10*s.*; R. Jones, capital account £1232 10*s.* Pass the following transactions through the proper books, post the ledger from them, and balance the accounts as on Jan. 7, 1910.

TRANSACTIONS.

Jan. 1, Bought a cargo of timber from V. Oscarsson for £385, less 10 per cent. trade discount. Paid V. Oscarsson, by cheque, £340, in settlement of his account. Jan. 3, Sold to Smith Bros., on credit, timber, £663. Jan. 4, Received cheque from Smith Bros. for the timber sold to them, less 2½ per cent. cash discount. Drew from the bank, for office cash, £20; paid from office cash for printing and stationery supplied, £3 15*s.*, and for an office desk bought, £5; paid by cheque for one quarter's standing advertisement in the "Timber Trades Journal," £3 15*s.* Jan. 5, Sold to Brown & Co., on credit, timber, £365, less 5 per cent. trade discount; paid by cheque, clerks' salaries, £5 10*s.* Jan. 6, Brown & Co. returned faulty timber included in yesterday's sale to them, invoiced at £22 10*s.*, less 5 per cent trade discount; Brown & Co. paid by cheque the amount due from them, less 2½ per cent. cash discount. Jan. 7, Bought, on credit, from the Soderhamn Timber Co., timber, £775, less 10 per cent. trade discount; paid them, by cheque, £100 on account; drew from the bank, for office cash, £10; paid from office cash for stamps, 10*s.*, envelopes, 5*s.*, and housekeeper's expenses, £2.

EXERCISE 7E.

1. Explain fully how the following transactions should be recorded in a set of books kept by double-entry, and mention the ledger accounts to which they should be posted.

1910. Jan. 1, Started business with £500 cash capital; Jan. 3, opened an account with Lloyd's Bank, Ltd., and paid in £480 to my credit; Jan. 4, Bought goods, on credit, from Corress Bros., £742 16*s.* 5*d.*; Sold goods, on credit, to Hill & Co., £40; Jan. 4, Sold goods on credit to Markwell and Bros , £36 4*s.* 9*d.*; paid by cheque, £200, on account, to Corress Bros.; received cheque (and banked the same) for £35 10*s.* from Markwell and Bros, and allowed them 14*s.* 9*d.* discount; Jan. 5, Bought office furniture for cash (paid out of office cash-box) £10 2*s.* 6*d.*; paid by cheque, telephone rent for one year in advance, £16 16*s.*; sold for cash, goods, £37 10*s.*, which amount was paid direct into the bank; paid by cheque for repairs and alterations at office, £10 6*s.*

2. On December 1, 1905, H. Lloyd commenced business with a capital of £500 in cash. On this date he paid the following sums : Shop fittings, £50; purchase of goods, £200; one quarter's rent in advance, £20. Open the necessary ledger accounts to record the above; post the following transactions direct to the ledger; balance the accounts as on Dec. 31, 1905, and bring down the balances :

1905, Dec. 2, Sold goods to W. Hunt, £140; Dec. 4, Purchased goods from R. Johnson, £20; Dec. 11, Purchased goods from H. Hall, £150; Dec. 16, Sold goods to E. Jones for cash, £20; Dec. 20, Sold goods to W. Silver, £50; Dec. 21, Received from W. Hunt cash on account, £10; Dec. 22, Paid R. Johnson's account, less 5 per cent. discount.

(Society of Arts, 1906.)

EXERCISE 7F.

1. Write up the following transactions of Andrew Merryman, Cloth Merchant, in Purchases and Sales Books, Cash Book, and Ledger. Balance the accounts as on January 30, 1904.

1904. Jan. 1, A. M. commenced with cash in hand, £115 12s. 8d. Jan. 2, Opened Account with Lloyds' Bank and paid in £100; Paid stamps, 5s.; Bought goods from Bailey & Co., £64 13s. 9d.; Jan. 4, Bought warehouse fixtures for Cheque, £15; Jan. 8, Sold goods to H. Arundel, £13 10s.; Sold goods to Walker & Sons, £15 12s. 6d.; Sold goods for Cash, £24 17s. 5d., and paid Bank, £25; Paid travelling expenses, £1 14s. 3d., and wages, £4 10s.; Jan 10, Paid Fire Insurance, 10s.; Jan. 14, H. Arundel pays on Account, £8; Sold goods to Alfd. Hainsworth, £25 17s. 8d.; Jan. 15, Sold goods for Cash, £28 19s. 1d., and paid Bank, £30; Jan. 15, Paid Wages, £4 10s.; Jan. 17, Bought goods of West Riding Co., £80 10s. 8d.; Jan 19, Bought goods of B. Shaw & Co., £42, and paid them Cheque, £20, on Account. Discount, £1.

(*West Riding County Council*, 1904.)

EXERCISE 7G.

On June 1, 1910, Robert Buchanan commenced business with the following property and debts:

Cash at the Bank £500; Cash in hand, £5 15s. 10d.; Stock-in-trade, £685 10s. 2d.; Freehold warehouse, £1500. Debtors: R. Jenkins, £310 4s. 6d.; H. Henderson, £38 15s. 6d. Creditors: the Yorkshire Spinning Co. Ltd., £985 14s. 6d.; A. Tyke & Co., £421 3s. 6d.; Richard Aldridge, £62 8s. 9d.; R. Buchanan's transactions for the month of June were as follows:

June 3, Bought, on credit, from R. Aldridge, silk £120 10s., and velvet, £92 8s. 6d.; June 4, Sold to R. Jenkins, velvet, £48 10s., less 5 per cent. trade discount; June 6, Sold to Paul Verney, silk, £140 8s.; June 9, Received cheque from R. Jenkins for the amount of his account; June 13, Received cheque from P. Verney for the amount of his account, less 2½ per cent. cash discount; June 14, Paid trade expenses by cheque, £15 18s. 6d.; June 18, Paid salaries by cheque, £20; June 23, Sold to Harry Bates, tweed, £95 10s., less 5 per cent. trade discount; June 28, Bought, on credit, from Henry Moore, prints, £40 8s. 6d., and paid for the same by cheque, less 5 per cent. cash discount.

Open the necessary books to record the above entries, post them to the Ledger, and balance the accounts as on June 30, 1910.

EXERCISE 7H.

On March 1, 19—, Charles Henry Smithson commenced business as a grocer with £1000 capital, of which £950 was paid into his banking account, and £50 retained as cash in hand for business purposes. His transactions for the month were as follows:

19—, March 1, Purchased Goods at J. Robinson & Son's auction mart, and paid cheque, £731 5s.; Also bought Office Furniture and Fittings, for which he paid cash, £38; March 9, Sold to Mrs. B. Vero,

Goods, £7 5s. ; March 13, Purchased from Lipton's, Ltd., tea, £28 10s. ; March 15, Purchased from J. G. Cooper, sugar, £13 5s. ; March 16, Paid Lipton's, Ltd., a cheque in full settlement of account, £27 ; March 18, Goods bought at J. Robinson's auction mart and paid cash, £10 ; March 19, Sold to Mrs. A. Harker, Goods, £3 3s. ; March 25, Received from Mrs. B. Vero, cash, £7, and allowed her Discount, 5s.; March 29, Cash Sales for month, £152 ; Paid Shop Assistants' wages for month (cash), £5 6s. ; Paid Rent for month (cheque) £5. Open the necessary books to record the above entries, post them to the Ledger, and balance the accounts as on March 31.

(Lancashire and Cheshire Union of Institutes.)

CHAPTER VIII

THE TRIAL BALANCE

When dealing with the various books of account described in the preceding chapters, I have continually referred to the principal rule of double-entry book-keeping, viz.: "That every debit entry requires its credit entry, and every credit entry its debit entry," and I have endeavoured to point out how this rule is applied in practical business to each of the books which I have explained to you.

I now propose to explain how this important rule provides the trader with a means of detecting any errors which may have been made in writing up his books. No other system of book-keeping provides such means of disclosing errors, and this important advantage constitutes one of the many reasons which have led to the general adoption of double-entry methods in modern business houses.

Owing to the fact that every entry appears in the trader's Ledger twice, once on the debit side and once on the credit side, it necessarily follows that the total of the *debit* entries which have been made in the Ledger must be equal in amount to the total of the entries appearing on the *credit* side. The Ledger thus referred to includes, of course, the Cash account, which is a necessary part of it.

If you go through your Ledger, and extract on a separate sheet of paper the totals of the debit entries appearing in each account, and the totals of the credit entries appearing in each account, the grand total of the debit entries thus extracted should exactly equal the grand total of the credit entries treated in the same manner. If these two grand totals do not agree exactly you must assume either (1) that you have extracted the postings incorrectly, or (2) that a mistake has been made somewhere in posting your Ledger. It will be a simple matter to go through the totals which you have extracted in order to make sure that you have done the work correctly—

and if, after you have done this, the totals of the two sides still fail to agree, you will be obliged to conclude that a mistake has been made somewhere in the Ledger.

In olden times the process which I have just described to you was actually carried out. The totals of the debit and credit postings which appeared in each account in the Ledger were extracted on a separate sheet of paper, the debit postings being separated from the credit postings. The totals of both the debit and credit postings were added, and if the two grand totals agreed it was assumed that the Ledger entries had been correctly made. The statement, or schedule, in which the total postings appeared was called a **Trial Balance**.

Although the term "Trial Balance" has been retained, it is very unusual in modern practice, when extracting such a statement, to deal with the *totals* of the debit and credit postings that appear in each account. The modern method is to insert the *balance* only of each account in the Trial Balance. That is to say, the *difference* between the total of the debit and credit postings of every account is extracted, instead of the more unwieldy total postings.

It will be obvious that a Trial Balance composed of the balances of all the Ledger accounts must agree in just the same manner as one which has been prepared by extracting the total postings contained on both sides of each Ledger account. The balance of a Ledger account contains in itself the net result of the postings on each side of the account.

The debit balances are, of course, kept distinct from the credit balances, separate columns being provided for each class of balance. If the books have been correctly posted, and the balances properly extracted, the total of the debit balances should equal the total of the credit balances.

A Trial Balance prepared by extracting "balances" serves all the purposes of a Trial Balance extracted under the more cumbersome method, because it discloses the existence of mistakes with equal certainty ; in addition, it serves the useful purpose of furnishing a list of the debtors and creditors, and the other balances appearing in the Ledger.

The Trial Balance relating to the example given at the end of Chapter VII. is appended. You will notice that the form it takes is simply that of a list, or schedule, of the balances appearing as on May 31, 1910, in the ledger of R. Jones, the debit balances being placed in one column, and the credit balances in the other column. The total of the debit balances amounts to £2513 18s. 7d., and the total of the credit balances amounts to the same figure. The Trial Balance thus "agrees": it may be assumed, therefore, that the work has been correctly done.

TRIAL BALANCE, May 31, 1910.

			Dr.			Cr.		
		*	£	s.	d	£	s.	u.
1	A. Jones, Capital Account . .	E.				1640	14	9
2	Stock-in-trade, May 2, 1910. .	A.	902	11	4			
3	Freehold warehouse and land .	A.	350	0	0			
4	Furniture and fittings . .	A.	22	10	0			
5	Creditors : C. Samuel . .	C.				456	18	5
6	W. Barber .	C				13	0	0
7	Debtors : R. Lyon . . .	A.	361	17	7			
8	C. Powell . .	A.	102					
9	Travelling expenses . .	B		1				
10	Salaries and wages .	B.	46	1				
11	General expenses . . .	B.	4					
12	Stationery	B.	2					
13	Advertising . . .	B.	2	1				
14	Carriage and freight on sales .	B.	8	1				
15	Discount and allowances .	D.				4	15	0
16	Purchases . .	A.	188	0	0			
17	Sales	A.				383	10	5
18	Returns inwards . . .	A.	26	8	2			
19	Returns outwards . .	A.				15	0	0
C.B.	Cash at bank . . .	A.	482	18	2			
C.B.	Cash in hand . . .	A.	12	1	3			
			£2513	18	7	£2513	18	7

The Stock-in-trade on May 31, 1910, was valued at £805 11s. 9d.

If a Trial Balance fails to "agree" it must be assumed either (a) that the statement has been incorrectly extracted from the Ledger, or (b) that a mistake exists somewhere in the Ledger. The former kind of error can usually be readily discovered; and if, after the extraction of the Trial Balance has been proved to be correct, the totals still fail to agree, it is evident that a mistake exists in the Ledger, which the book-keeper must endeavour to discover.

A Trial Balance may, for instance, fail to agree because of the existence of one or more of the following errors:

1. If any addition, either in the Ledger or in any book of "original entry," is incorrect: for example, if the additions

* The letters in this column refer to the classification of Ledger accounts given on p. 147.

of any page of the Sales Book are £10 in excess of the correct amount, the totals of the Trial Balance will disagree by £10.

2. If an entry has been posted incorrectly in the Ledger, or has been posted on the wrong side of the Ledger.

For example, if a cash payment of £111 11s. 10d. made to S. Hubert has been posted to the debit of his Ledger account as £111 1s. 10d. the totals of the Trial Balance will disagree by 10s.

3. If an entry has been made on one side of the Ledger only, the entry on the opposite side of the Ledger having been accidentally omitted. For example, if goods of the value of £35 1s. 10d. purchased from C. Brown have been entered in the Purchases Book, but, owing to an oversight, have not been posted to the credit of C. Brown's account, the total of the Trial Balance will disagree by £35 1s. 10d.

The "agreement" of a Trial Balance is, in practice, generally taken to furnish a proof of the accuracy of the book-keeping. It is not, however, always wise to assume that the agreement of a Trial Balance proves *conclusively* that the books are correct. For example, the following two kinds of error may exist in a Ledger without causing the relative Trial Balance to disagree, viz. :

1. If an item has been posted correctly as to amount and on its correct side, in the *wrong* Ledger account, the agreement of the Trial Balance will not be disturbed. For example, if £10 paid to John *Bird* has been posted to the debit in John *Brown's* Ledger account, the accounts of both these creditors will be incorrect. The totals of the Trial Balance will, however, "agree."

2. If "compensating errors" exist, a Trial Balance may still agree. The term "compensating errors" implies that one or more errors in the Ledger exist in one direction, but are exactly offset by one or more errors in the other direction. For example, if the debit side of the Cash Book has been added £100 in excess of the correct amount, and the Purchases Book has been added £100 less than its true amount, the Trial Balance will not disagree. The Cash Book balance will be £100 in excess of the correct amount, and the Purchases Account will be £100 less than the true figure. These two errors off-set, or "compensate," each other.

A Trial Balance should always be made to agree before proceeding further with the book-keeping. The discovery of errors is sometimes a laborious matter; but every Trial Balance *could* and *should* be made to agree,

The balances of which a Trial Balance is composed—indeed, the balances appearing in any Ledger, may bo classified as follows :

On the Debit side :

(*a*) Accounts representing " Property " or " Assets," *e.g.* machinery, stock-in-trade, book debts, land, buildings, &c.

(*b*) Accounts representing " losses " or " expenses," *e.g.* salaries, advertising, general expenses, &c.

On the Credit side :

(*c*) Accounts representing " liabilities," *e.g.* the personal accounts of creditors.

(*d*) Accounts representing " profits" or " gains," *e.g.* commission and discounts received.

(*e*) The Trader's Capital Account.

Each balance in the Trial Balance given on p. 145 has an initial letter appended to it (A, B, C, D, or E) in order to indicate to which of the above five classes it belongs.

The Sales, Purchases, Returns Inwards, and Returns Outwards accounts are classified as belonging to class A, because, in fact, they are subdivisions of the Trading account.

EXERCISES.

8A.

1. What is a " Trial Balance " ? 2. Write, for the guidance of the book-keeper in charge of a set of books kept by double-entry, an explanation of the way in which he is to prepare his Trial Balance. 3. The book-keeper mentioned above has extracted his Trial Balance, but finds that the debit and credit totals do not agree. Write an explanation for him (*a*) showing how this disagreement has probably arisen, and (*b*) describing the steps he should take in order to make the sides agree.

8B.

1. State how and where, in a Trial Balance, the totals or balances shown by the following books appear: (1) Cash Book. (2) Petty Cash Book. (3) Sales Book. (4) Returns Inwards Book. 2. With what object is a Trial Balance prepared ? What does it show ? 3. If the two sides of a Trial Balance agree, does this fact prove without doubt that the books have been correctly written up ? 4. Will the following errors, which have occurred in a set of books, have any effect upon the Trial Balance extracted from the books ? If so, state the effect of each error—(1) The Cash Book has been added £10 too much. (2) An entry for £1 in the journal has been posted twice to the credit in different accounts, instead of once to the debit and once to the credit. (3) A payment of £131 11s. 11*d*., made by cheque, has been posted as £131 1s. 11*d*. in the ledger. (4) £5 received from J. Brown & Co. has

been posted to the credit of Brown Bros. (5) The Purchases Book has been added £1 17s. 2d. short, but one purchase appearing therein for 18s. 7d. has been posted to the debit of the person from whom the goods were bought. (6) The ledger-keeper has forgotten to post an item of 6d. appearing on the credit side of the Cash Book. (7) A credit balance of £22 11s. 9d. appearing in the ledger has been copied into the Trial Balance as £22 19s. 1d.

5. From the following particulars write up James Wilson's books, and prepare a Trial Balance on June 9, 1910:

Example.—James Wilson started business on June 1, 1910, as a cycle dealer. On June 3 he borrowed £100 from Robert Wilson in cash. On June 4 he bought on credit 10 bicycles from the Speed Manufacturing Company at £8 each. On June 6 he sold 5 bicycles to H. Brown on credit at £10 each. On June 6 he paid the Speed Manufacturing Company £40 on account. On June 7 he sold 5 bicycles for cash at £9 10s. each, receiving the money. On June 9 he paid £4 cash for expenses to date.

8c.

The following is a Trial Balance extracted from the books of Charles Weeks by his book-keeper. The latter has evidently made several mistakes in preparing it. You are requested to re-draw it in proper form so that the Trial Balance shall show totals which agree.

TRIAL BALANCE, June 30, 1910.

	Dr. £	s.	d.	Cr. £	s.	d.
C. Weeks, Capital Account (Credit Balance)				432	11	10
Freehold land and buildings				500	0	0
Salaries	142	19	6			
Rates and taxes	42	10	9			
Discounts allowed				4	10	2
Discounts received	6	1	9			
Stock, Jan. 1, 1910				361	14	9
Purchases	1110	16	3			
Returns inwards				14	2	6
Sales				2010	4	9
Furniture and fixtures	32	9	8			
Printing and stationery	36	9	4			
Cash in hand	12	4	9			
Cash at the bank	241	12	2			
Commission paid				10	10	0
Purchases returns	12	2	2			
General expenses	75	9	8			
Advertising expenses				5	6	6
Creditors: J. Brown				109	10	0
W. Jones				120	5	6
Debtor: W. Harris	100	0	0			
	£1812	16	0	£3568	16	0

8D.

A. Post the following entries in the Ledger, creating Ledger accounts " Dr." and " Cr." for each entry, and prepare a Trial Balance : Goods bought : (1) From John Jones, steel rails, £1000 ; (2) From William Smith, bolts and nuts, £1500 ; (3) From John Richardson, steel rails, £1400. Goods sold : (4) To Great Northern Railway, steel rails, £2000 ; (5) To ditto, bolts and nuts, £600 ; (6) To Midland Railway, bolts and nuts, £600.

(*Institute of Bankers Preliminary Exam.*, 1907.)

B. What is meant by the term "compensating errors" in a Trial Balance?

C. Explain the following statement : "Every Trial Balance *could* be made to agree, and *should* be made to agree."

8E.

The following are the balances appearing in my Ledger on May 31, 1910. From them prepare my Trial Balance, inserting the amount of my capital as on June 1, 1909.

Cash, £1740 2s. 1d. ; purchases, £32,046 19s. 3d. ; Debtors : C. Rowan, £1093 2s. 0d. ; W. Pitman, £2062 14s. 9d. ; J. Morgan, £149 6s. 2d. ; O. Grenfell, £32 1s. 4d. ; Creditors : Q. Huth, £1762 8s. 6d. ; M. Hambro, £21 0s. 4d. ; V. Gibbs, £1 2s. 6d. ; M. Cutler, £308 4s. 9d. ; Sales : £44,369 17s. 11d. ; Investment, £1000 Consols, at cost, £832 16s. 6d. ; returns inwards, £17 2s. 4d. ; purchases returns, £1221 17s. 9d. ; plant and machinery, £2046 3s. 9d. ; discount received, £34 9s. 11d. ; salaries, £1028 16s. ; donations and subscriptions, £83 4s. 6d. ; carriage, £236 9s. 3d. ; freehold land, £1025 11s. 8d. ; stock of packages in hand, £13 7s. 6d. ; petty cash, £5 ; commission paid, £122 14s. 1d. ; general expenses, £864 2s. 9d. ; rates and taxes, £103 0s. 8d. ; commission received, £10 10s. ; interest paid, £4 2s. 9d. ; dividends received on Consols, £23 11s. 10d. ; stock, June 1, 1909, £9024 16s. 7d.

Note.—The capital account on June 1, 1909, is represented by the difference between the debit and credit balances stated above.

8F.

George Smith, having purchased from William Watson, wine merchant, the assets, including the goodwill of his business, for which he gave £3000 for stocks of wines and spirits, £500 for utensils, bottles, and appliances, and £1000 for goodwill, commenced business on December 1, 1904. He opened an account at the Secure Bank, Limited, and paid in £2000, representing his working capital. Open the necessary Ledger accounts to record the above, and post the following transactions direct to the Ledger. Balance the account as on December 9, 1904, and bring down the balances. Also prepare a Trial Balance as at that date.

1904. Dec. 2, Bought from R. French three pipes of port, at £85 per pipe ; Dec. 3, Bought from C. Clare 50 dozen of sherry, at 90s. per dozen ; Dec. 5, Bought from R. Frost a bottle-washing machine for £18 10s. ; Dec. 6, Sold to Grand Hotel Company, Limited, 10 dozens of sherry, at 108s. per dozen ; Dec. 7, Bought from G. Keen 10 dozens of champagne, at 100s. per dozen ; Dec. 8, Sold to R. White one pipe of port for £95.; Dec. 9, Sold to R. Frost two dozens of champagne, at 110s. per dozen.

(*Society of Arts*, 1905. *Stage I.*)

8G.

On December 1, 1905, H. Lloyd commenced business with a capital of £500 in cash. On this date he paid the following sums: Shop fittings, £50; purchase of goods, £200; one quarter's rent in advance, £20. Open the necessary Ledger accounts to record the above; post the following transactions direct to the Ledger; balance the accounts as on December 31, 1905, and bring down the balances. Also prepare a Trial Balance as at that date.

1905. Dec. 2, Sold goods to W. Hunt, £140; Dec. 4, Purchased goods from R. Johnson, £20; Dec. 11, Purchased goods from H. Hall, £150; Dec. 16, Sold goods to E. Jones for cash, £20; Dec. 20, Sold goods to W. Silver, £50; Dec. 21, Received from W. Hunt cash on account, £10; Dec. 22, Paid R. Johnson's account, less 5 per cent. discount.

(*Society of Arts*, 1906. *Stage I.*)

8II.

Write up the following transactions of Joseph Granby in his Cash Book and Sold and Bought Day Books; post to his Ledger, and make out a Trial Balance as on June 30, 1900.

1900. Jan. 1, Cash in hand, £17 15s. 3d.; Cash at bank, £186 17s. 9d.; Goods in stock, £349 13s. 11d.; Jan, 8, Sold to Wells & Son, goods, £19 16s. 3d.; Jan. 12, Bought of Brown Bros., goods, £24 19s. 1d.; Feb. 12, Wells & Son pay £19s. 10s.—allowed them discount, 6s. 3d.; Feb. 3, Paid to Bank, £10; March 6, Drew cheque for Brown Bros., £12; March 13, Sold to Chas. Carr, goods, £34 15s. 1d.; March 31, Received cash for goods, £2 10s.; April 4, Bought goods of D. Dixon, £86 2s. 9d.; April 18, Joseph Granby withdraws cash, £20;* April 28, Received from Carr, and paid to bank, £33, discount £1 15s. 1d.; May 9, Wells & Son buy goods, £96 14s 3d.; May 25, Wells & Son pay cash, £40; June 6, Paid Brown cash, £12 10s., discount 9s. 1d.; June 14, Paid Dixon cash, £10, and cheque on bank, £30; June 23, drew cheque for rent, £25; Cash paid for sundry expenses, £14 17s. 3d.

(*West Riding County Council*, 1900.)

---

* Debit J. Granby's Capital account.

CHAPTER IX

THE TRADING ACCOUNT

I HAVE already explained to you how to post and balance the accounts in the Ledger, and how to test the accuracy of the work by means of a Trial Balance.

After a trader has extracted a Trial Balance from his books the next thing he naturally desires to know is the result of his trading operations. In other words, he desires to know what profit or what loss he has made. In order to obtain this interesting information it is usual to prepare two separate statements. These statements are called the **Trading Account** and the **Profit and Loss Account**. I have already explained to you (p. 6), that there are two kinds of Profit, known as **Gross** and **Net** profit. The object of the Trading account is to ascertain the amount of the "gross" profit made in any given period, and that of the Profit and Loss account is to arrive at the "net" profit.

Now let us consider, first, how to prepare a Trading account. You will remember that the term "gross profit" means the difference between the cost price and the selling price of the goods dealt in. That is to say, suppose that I buy a bale of cotton goods for £10 and sell it for £14, my gross profit on the transaction is £4. But, as you will see as we proceed, when we are ascertaining the gross profit on a number of transactions taken together it is necessary to take into account some other matters, in addition to the actual goods which have been bought and sold.

The simplest way of constructing a Trading account is to regard the statement as though it were the account of an *actual person* who is responsible for the goods which have been bought and sold by the trader.

We must therefore ascertain, first of all, what this imaginary person is responsible for.

151

Turning to the Trial Balance given on p. 145, we find that the items which concern him are as follows·

		£	s.	d.
1.	Stock-in-trade, May 2, 1910	902	11	4
2.	Purchases	188	0	0
3.	Purchases Returns (Returns Outwards) .	15	0	0
4.	Sales	383	10	5
5.	Sales Returns (Returns Inwards) . . .	26	8	2
6.	Stock-in-trade, May 31, 1910 .	805	11	9

Let us now consider these items in detail.

Item No 1. Stock-in-trade, May 2, 1910, £902 11s. 4d.

When the trader commenced his trading operations for the period May 2–May 31, 1910, he had goods in hand that were valued at £902 11s. 4d. As our imaginary person is to be regarded as being responsible for all the transactions in goods, it will be clear that we must "open" his account by debiting him with the value of the goods in hand when the trading period commenced. On referring to the specimen Trading account on p. 155, you will see that this item forms the first entry on the debit side of the account. We may assume that, at the commencement of the period, these goods were handed over to our imaginary person—he must therefore be debited with them.

Item No. 2. Purchases, £188.

This item represents the total of the goods bought by the trader during the period May 2–May 31, 1910. These goods must therefore be assumed to have been duly handed over to our imaginary person, and must be added to the stock of goods for which he is already responsible. They must, for this reason, be entered on the debit side of his account, as an addition to the stock with which he started.

Note.—For a reason to be explained in the next paragraph, the amount of the purchases (£188) should not be entered at once in the principal debit column of the account. It is customary to enter it, in the first place, in the left-hand or "detail" debit column.

Item No. 3. Purchases Returns, £15.

This item represents goods purchased by the trader but afterwards returned by him to the person from whom they were bought, owing to some defect in them.

The goods thus "returned" are included in the total goods bought, £188. When they were received by the trader they were placed in his warehouse in company with all his other purchases. It must therefore be assumed that our imaginary person has received these goods, together with all other purchases, with the cost price of which, £188, he has been debited.

As soon as the £15 worth of goods which we are now considering were found by the trader to be unsatisfactory, they were sent b: ck to the person ,from whom they were purchased. Our imaginary person must consequently be assumed to have parted with them. He must, in the ordinary course of events, be credited with their value (£15), on the principle that if he is *debited* with all the goods received by him, he must be *credited* with all the goods with which he has parted.

In practice, however, the entry for "purchases returns" is made, not on the credit side, but on the *deb:t* side, of the account, as a *deduction* from the purchases already entered there. The latter entry amounts in effect to exactly the same thing as the former.

We have assumed that our imaginary person has received goods of the value of £188 purchased by the trader, and that he has parted with, or "returned," goods to the value of £15; so you will see that he has actually only retained goods of the value of £173, as additional stock to hold on the trader's behalf.

By entering the £15 "Purchases Returns" on the debit side of our imaginary person's account in the "detail" column, and by deducting this £15 from the £188 worth of Purchases already standing there (see item 2) we get the true figure of purchases, £173, which we can now extend into the principal debit column as an additional charge to our imaginary person.

Item No. 4. Sales, £383 10s. 5d.

This item means that during the period May 2–May 31, 1910, goods have been parted with to various customers of the value of £383 10s. 5d.

Our imaginary person may be assumed to have parted with these goods at the trader's request, and, seeing that we *debited* him with all the goods bought, it is only fair that we should *credit* him with all the goods sold. It is necessary, therefore, to enter the amount of £383 10s. 5*. on the credit side of our imaginary person's account, as representing the value of the

goods with which he has parted, and for which he has ceased
to be responsible.

For a reason similar to that which applied in the case of the
Purchases, you must not enter the total of the Sales at once
in the principal credit column of our imaginary person's
account. There are, you will remember, some Sales Returns
to he thought of which must be dealt with in a similar manner
to the Purchases Returns. You must consequently enter
the £383 10s. 5d., in the first instance, in the "detail," or
left-hand, credit column.

Item No. 5.   Sales Returns, £26 8s. 2d.

This item indicates that during the period May 2–May
31, 1910, some of the trader's customers, being dissatisfied,
returned goods which they had bought from him, for which
they had been charged £26 8s. 2d.

When these goods were returned they were put back into
the trader's warehouse, and were added to the goods already
there. We must assume, therefore, that our imaginary friend
has again become responsible for them. He must consequently
be *debited* with their value.

Instead of actually placing this item on the debit side of the
Trading account, however, it is the custom in practical business
to *deduct* the amount from the total of the Sales for the period,
as shown in the accompanying account. The reason for this
procedure is the same as that already explained in the case of
Purchases Returns. It is, of course, true that sales to the
amount of £383 10s. 5d. were actually effected during the
period; but goods to the value of £26 8s. 2d., which formed
part of the total sales, were returned; and if we desire to
show the actual net amount of the sales for the period, we
must deduct the returns from the sales, and carry out the *net*
amount only, viz. £357 2s. 3d.

Item No. 6.   Stock-in-trade, May 31, 1910, £805 11s. 9d.

I find that some students, when they are preparing Trading
accounts, are apt to forget to deal with the value of the stock
of goods in hand at the close of the period. Perhaps the chief
reason for this forgetfulness is the fact that the "closing
stock" does not appear in the Trial Balance.

A little consideration will show you that the omission of
this item would be very unfair to our imaginary person. He

is responsible for all the goods which come into and go out of the warehouse. When we are preparing an account for the purpose of ascertaining what he has done with the goods for which he is responsible, it is just as necessary to give him credit for the value of the goods which he has left in hand as it is to credit him with the sales which he has effected. In order to ascertain what amount must be given credit for under this heading a process called **stock-taking** is carried out. That is to say, brief particulars of the nature, number, and value of all the unsold goods are written on sheets of paper, or in a memorandum book. The value placed against each item appearing in these lists should be the *actual cost price* of the goods. In cases where the goods have fallen in value below their original cost price, and are not likely to recover their value, the current *market price* of similar goods should be taken.

When the stock-taking has been completed, all the amounts on the sheets are added together, and the total, £805 11s. 9d. in this case, is credited in the Trading account.

We have now dealt with all the items in our Trial Balance relating to the goods, for which our imaginary person is responsible. The next and final step is to balance the account by finding the difference between the totals of the two sides, and inserting it as shown in the accompanying account. This difference, £87 2s. 8d. in this case, represents the **gross profit** for the period with which we are dealing.

20   TRADING ACCOUNT for the month of May 1910.   20

Dr. *Cr.*

1910.			£	s.	d.	1910.				£	s.	d.
May 2	To Stock in hand	J.	902	11	4	May 31	By Sales :					
„ 31	„ Purchases :						£383 10 5	J.				
	£188 0 0	J.					*Less*					
	Less						Returns 26 8 2	J.				
	Returns 15 0 0	J.							357	2	3	
			173	0	0	„ „	By Stock in hand	J.	805	11	9
„ „	To Balance, being Gross Profit carried to the Profit and Loss Account	J.	87	2	8							
		£	1162	14	0			£	1162	14	0

The Trading account constructed from the entries described in this chapter is given above. It is one of the accounts in R. Jones's Ledger, and bears the folio number 20.

I have explained to you the principles upon which this account has been constructed; it remains to describe the Journal entries by means of which the items composing it are "closed," or brought into the account.

The following items in the above account appear in R. Jones's Ledger, and form respectively the balances of various accounts appearing in that Ledger, viz.:

1910.

May   2. The commencing stock, £902 11s. 4d., is the balance of the "Stock account," folio 2.

 „ 31. Purchases, £188, is the balance of the "Purchases account," folio 16.

 „ 31. Sales Returns, £26 8s. 2d., is the balance of the "Returns Inwards account," folio 18.

 „ 31. Sales, £383 10s. 5d., is the balance of the "Sales account," folio 17.

 „ 31. Purchases Returns, £15 is the balance of the "Returns Outwards account," folio 19.

The balances of these five Ledger accounts are transferred to the Trading account by means of Journal entries. These Journal entries are, in practice, made directly *after* the Trial Balance has been taken out. They have, of course, the effect of leaving no balance at all in the five Ledger accounts in question. The Journal entries themselves are merely "transfer" entries, and they are set out in the form of Journal given on p. 158. You will notice that the Purchases Returns (£15) are stated in the Journal as being *credited* to the Trading account, whereas, as I have already explained, their actual appearance in the Trading account takes the form of a *deduction* from the "Purchases" item on the debit side. The net result is, of course, exactly the same. Similarly, the Sales Returns are stated in the Journal as being debited to the Trading account, whereas, as a matter of fact, they take the form of a *deduction* from the "Sales" item on the credit side. You will remember that I have already explained the reason for this procedure.

The entry for the stock-in-trade at the end of the trading period (£805 11s. 9d.) is made as follows: *Credit* the "Trading account" and *debit* the "Stock account" with the value of the stock. This rule never changes.

For example, turning again to our imaginary person's transactions, we may assume that, at the end of his stewardship, he discharged his responsibility by handing over to the owner of the business the stock of unsold goods remaining in his hands at the *close* of the trading period. In order to record this fact, the value of these goods must therefore be *debited* to an asset account (the "Stock" account), and must be *credited* to the account of the imaginary person from whom they have been received (the "Trading" account).

The entry for the "closing stock" forms the sixth of the entries given in the Journal on p. 158.

The last Journal entry, as far as the Trading account is concerned, is one which transfers the gross Profit from the Trading account to a new account called the "Profit and Loss account." The Profit and Loss account forms the second account of the two statements which are prepared in order to ascertain a trader's profits. It commences with an entry on the credit side of the amount of the gross profit shown by the Trading account. The next chapter will be devoted to an explanation of the construction of the Profit and Loss account.

If the Trading account should show a **gross loss**, the amount of the loss must be (1) *Credited* to the Trading account, and (2) *Debited* to the Profit and Loss account. A gross loss on Trading is not, however, a common experience in a properly managed business.

The Journal entries relating to the preparation of the Trading account are set out on p. 158. Their effect is to "close" the Purchases, Sales, Returns Inwards, and Returns Outwards accounts absolutely, leaving no balances standing in them. The Stock account is first closed as regards the May 2 stock, and then re-opened with the May 31 stock. The Stock account, and the other four Ledger accounts, are also illustrated on p. 158.

At a later stage of your studies you will learn that, in some businesses, Trading accounts are prepared of a more complicated nature than the example which is given in this chapter.

For instance, in cases where the trader manufactures the goods which he sells, it is usual to include in the Trading account, in addition to the cost of the raw material, the wages and other expenses which are necessary in order to produce the finished article sold by him.

At present, however, it will be quite sufficient for you to grasp thoroughly the meaning and effects of the *principle*

upon which all Trading accounts are prepared—the principle
which is fully explained in the simple example I have given you
in this chapter.

JOURNAL—*continued.*

1910.				£	s.	d.	£	s	d.
May 31	Trading Account Dr. To Stock Account . . . . For Stock as on May 2, 1910, transferred.	20 2A		902	11	4	902	1	4
„ „	Trading Account Dr. To Purchases Account . . . . For balance transferred.	20 16A		188	0	0	188		0
„ „	Trading Account Dr. To Returns Inwards Account . . For balance transferred.	20 18A		26	8	2	26		2
„ „	Sales Account Dr. To Trading Account . . . . For balance transferred.	17A 20		383	10	5	383	1	5
„ „	Returns Outwards Account Dr. To Trading Account . . . . For balance transferred.	19A 20		15	0	0	15	0	0
„ „	Stock Account Dr. To Trading Account . . . . For stock as on May 31, 1910.	2A 20		805	11	9	805	11	9
„ „	Trading Account Dr. To Profit and Loss Account . . . For gross profit for the month of May, transferred.	20 21		87	2	8	87	2	8
			£	2408	4	4	£2408	4	4

2a   STOCK ACCOUNT.   **2a**

Dr.   Cr.

1910.			£	s.	d.	1910.			£	s.	d.
May 2	To Balance .	J.	902	11	4	May 31	By transfer to Trading Account.	J.	902	11	4
1910. May 31	To Trading Account .	J.	805	11	9						

16a   PURCHASES ACCOUNT.   **16a**

Dr.   Cr.

1910.			£	s.	d.	1910.			£	s.	d.
May 31	To Purchases for May, as per Purchases Journal	P.	188	0	0	May 31	By transfer to Trading Account .	P.	188	0	0

17a   SALES ACCOUNT.   **17a**
Dr.   *Cr.*

1910.			£	s.	d.	1910.			£	s.	d.
May 31	To transfer to Trading Account . .	J.	383	10	5	May 31	By sales for May, as per Sales Journal	S.	383	10	5

18a   RETURNS INWARDS ACCOUNT.   **18a**
Dr.   *Cr.*

1910.			£	s.	d.	1910.			£	s.	d.
May 31	To Returns Inwards for May, as per Returns Inwards Book.	R.I.	26	8	2	May 31	By transfer to Trading Account . .	J.	26	8	2

19a   RETURNS OUTWARDS ACCOUNT.   **19a**
Dr.   *Cr.*

1910.			£	s.	d.	1910.			£	s.	d.
May 31	To transfer to Trading Account . .	J.	15	0	0	May 31	By Returns Outwards for May, as per Returns Outwards Book	R.O.	15	0	0

EXERCISES.

9A.

1. What is a Trading account and how is it prepared ? 2. State how the following items must be dealt with in a Trading account : (a) Stock in hand at the close of the period ; (b) Purchases ; (c) Returns Inwards. 3. What is meant by the term " Gross Profit " ? 4. Prepare an example of a Trading account without inserting any figures in it. 5. How is the Balance of the Trading account dealt with ? Explain how the Journal Entries which are necessary in order to construct a Trading account are prepared.

9B.

From the following particulars, prepare my Trading Account for the year ended December 31, 1909 :

Sales, £13,222 11s. 1d.; Purchases, £11,141 10s. 6d. ; Returns Inwards, £108 4s. 9d. ; Stock, January 1, 1909, £1326 0s. 9d. ; Stock, December 31, 1909, £1426 10s. 7d.

9C.

From the following particulars prepare my Trading account for the year ended December 31, 1909 :

Stock, Jan. 1, 1909, £252 16s. 8d. ; Purchases in 1909 on credit, £1072 1s. 9d. ; Purchases in 1909 for cash, £222 11s. 6d. ; Sales in 1909 on credit, £1412 2s. 8d. ; Sales in 1909 for cash, £21 4s. 6d. ; Stock,

December 31, 1909, £210 1s. 11d. ; Returns Inwards in 1909, £10 3s. 1d. ; Returns Outwards in 1909, £14 6s. 6d.

9D.

From the following particulars prepare my Trading account for the year ended December 31, 1909 :

Stock, January 1, 1909, £1428 9s. 6d. ; Sales, £5401 2s. 8d. ; Purchases, £6622 11s. 8d. ; Returns Inwards, £1101 2s. 9d. ; Stock, December 31, 1909, £3682 1s. 9d. ; Returns Outwards, £10 4s. 8d.

9E.

From the following particulars, extracted from the books of O. Law-rence, prepare his Trading account for the year ended December 31, 1909 :

Stock of goods in hand, Jan. 1, 1909, £11,246 9s. 8d. ; Sales for the year, £68,109 11s. 3d. ; Purchases for the year, £66,242 12s. 9d. ; Returns Outwards for the year, £1842 19s. 8d. ; Stock of goods in hand Dec. 31, 1909, £12,899 1s. 3d.

Show also the Journal Entries which are necessary in order to deal with the Stock, Sales, Purchases, and Returns Outwards accounts in O. Lawrence's ledger.

9F.

From the following particulars, extracted from the books of James Higgins, prepare a Trading account for the year ended December 31, 1909 :

Stock, Jan. 1, 1909, £1386 2s. 2d. ; Purchases for year, £7221 13s. 9d. ; Returns Inwards for year, £142 0s. 10d. ; Sales for year, £10,219 15s. 7d. ; Stock, Dec. 31, 1909, £122 8s. 9d. ; Returns Outwards for year £14 2s. 1d.

Show the Journal Entries which are necessary in order to prepare and close the Trading account in the Ledger of James Higgins.

9G.

From the following particulars, extracted from the books of C. Cooper, prepare a Trading account for the year ended December 31, 1909 :

Purchases on credit for year, £7219 8s. 4d. ; Purchases for cash for year, £108 14s. 6d. ; Stock, Jan. 1, 1909, £8642 11s. 1d. ; Stock, Dec. 31, 1909, £3055 0s. 10d. ; Sales Returns for year, £133 4s. 6d. ; Sales on credit for year, £13,866 4s. 9d. ; Cash Sales for year, £1029 8s. 3d. ; Returns Outwards for year, £521 4s. 2d.

9H.

The following is the Trading account of Arthur Rance, a merchant, as prepared by his book-keeper. The latter's knowledge of book-keeping is slight, and the amount of the gross profit arrived at is evidently incorrect. You are requested to correct the mistakes appearing in the statement, and to redraw it in proper form.

ARTHUR RANCE.

TRADING ACCOUNT for the year ended December 31, 1909.

Dr.   Cr.

1909.		£	s.	d.	£	s.	d.	1909.		£	s.	d.	£	s.	d.
Dec.31	To Purchases	724	2	9				Jan. 1	By Stock in hand at Jan. 1 1909						
	Add Returns Inwards	6	2	5									200	14	9
	Add Stock in hand at Dec. 31, 1909	198	4	11				Dec.31	„ Sales	1059	2	6			
					928	10	1		Less Returns Outwards	4	2	9			
	To Difference between the two sides, being the Balance of Gross profit.												1054	19	9
					327	4	5								
					£1255	14	6						£1255	14	6

CHAPTER X

THE PROFIT AND LOSS ACCOUNT

In the previous chapter I explained to you how to prepare a Trading account, for the purpose of ascertaining the amount of the **Gross Profit** made by a trader during a given period of trading. I told you that the Gross Profit shown by the Trading account was transferred to the *credit* side of an account called the "The Profit and Loss account."

The object of a Profit and Loss Account is to ascertain the **Net profit** made by a trader, *i.e.* the profit which remains after all expenses and "losses" of every kind have been duly deducted. The gross profit shown by the Trading account represents, as you know, the difference between the total cost of the goods purchased by the trader and the total amount produced by their sale. This difference, or "balance," is arrived at before any charge whatever has been made for the various expenses which are necessarily incurred in carrying on the trader's business. It is only after the expenses of the business, and all the other "losses" and "profits," together with the gross profit, have been arranged in proper order in a Profit and Loss account, that the trader can find out how much he has really gained or lost during any particular period of trading.

The form of a Profit and Loss account is very simple. The rule to remember when preparing a Profit and Loss account is to *debit all losses and credit all profits.*

The gross profit brought from the Trading account appears as the first entry on the *credit* side of the account.

Any occasional profits made by the trader, *e.g.* interest, discounts, &c., are also entered on the *credit* side.

All the "losses" and expenses incurred in carrying on the business are entered in the Profit and Loss account on the *debit* side.

The credit side thus consists of all the "profits" made, and the debit side of all the "losses" incurred.

If the total of the entries on the credit side, *i.e.* the "profits," is greater than the total of those on the debit side, *i.e.* the "losses," the difference between the two totals represents the trader's **net** profit for the period.

If the total of the entries on the debit side, *i.e.* the "losses," is greater than the total of the entries on the credit side, *i.e.* the "profits," the difference between the two totals represents the net amount that the trader has lost during the period, *i.e.* his **net** loss.

We can now prepare the Profit and Loss account of R. Jones on the basis of the above rules.

You will readily understand that, if each individual item of "loss" and "gain" was posted direct to the Profit and Loss account, the result would be a mass of confused detail which would not afford the trader a clear idea as to how his expenses compared with his profits.

You also know that one of the principal aims of the modern book-keeper is to group all items of the same kind together as much as possible. If you will refer to the Trial Balance, which we are considering, you will notice that all the "profits" and "losses" of the same kind have been grouped in accounts under suitable headings.

The Profit and Loss account commences with an entry on its credit side of £87 2s. 8d., representing the gross profit on trading brought from the Trading account.

For the remainder of the items we must refer to the Trial Balance given on p. 145. Let us deal first with the credit side. You will notice that there is only one account on the credit side which is classified by the letter D, *i.e.* as a "profit" account, viz., the "Discount and allowances account, £4 15s."

This balance represents the fact that R. Jones has, during the month of May 1910, received a net sum of £4 15s. for *discount;* this, therefore, is a "profit," and must be entered underneath the entry of the Gross Profit on trading which already appears in the Profit and Loss account.

You must enter £4 15s. on the credit side of the account as "Discounts and allowances," the date, May 31, 1910, being entered also.

If you will refer again to the Trial Balance you will notice there the following balances classed with the letter B, *i.e.* as "loss" or "expense" accounts, viz. :

	£	s.	d.
Travelling expenses . .		16	9
Salaries and wages	46	17	1
General expenses .	4	0	5
Stationery	2	4	6
Advertising	2	10	0
Carriage and freight on Sales . .	8	17	4

These are all balances representing "losses" or "expenses" incurred in carrying on the business, and must be entered on the *debit*, or "loss," side of the Profit and Loss account; they must be entered on the debit side underneath one another exactly as they are set out above, the date, May 31, 1910, being attached in each case.

The Profit and Loss account is now complete, with the exception of the necessary balance.

The items on the credit side, *i.e.* the "profits," amount in total to £91 17s. 8d.; those on the debit side, *i e.* the "losses," amount in total to £65 6s. 1d.; that is to say, the profits exceed the losses, therefore R. Jones has made a **net profit**, the amount of which is £91 17s. 8d., *less* £65 6s. 1d., *i e.* £26 11s. 7d.

The net profit made during the period is, of course, the property of the owner of the business, and increases his "net worth." Having accomplished the work for which it was designed, the Profit and Loss account is closed by *debiting* the balance as follows:

" *To balance, being net profit for the month transferred to Capital account, £26 11s. 7d.*"

The Profit and Loss account is thus closed, and the trader's Capital account is *credited* with the amount of the profit made during the month. The addition of this profit to the trader's original " net worth " at the beginning of the month produces a fresh figure of " net worth " with which the ensuing trading period is commenced.

If the total of the "losses" and expenses which have been *debited* in a Profit and Loss account should exceed the total of the profits credited there, the difference between the two totals represents the trader's **net loss** for the period. This net loss must be (1) *credited* to the Profit and Loss account in order to make the two sides agree, and (2) *debited* to the trader's Capital account. The net loss for the period, when dealt with in this way, reduces the trader's " net worth," as shown at the beginning of the period, and causes the final balance of the Capital account to show correctly the trader's " net worth " at the end of the trading period.

The original balance standing to the credit of R. Jones's Capital account on May 2, 1910, was £1640 14s. 9d., which represented his then " net worth." R. Jones has, according to his Profit and Loss account, made a net profit of £26 11s. 7d. by trading during the month of May 1910. This sum is credited to his Capital account, and increases the balance of that account to £1667 6s. 4d., which latter sum represents R. Jones's " net worth " on May 31, 1910.

The Profit and Loss account prepared on these lines is given below.

21   21

PROFIT AND LOSS ACCOUNT for the month of May 1910.

Dr.   Cr.

1910.			£	s.	d	1910.			£	s	d
May 31	To Travelling Expenses .	J.		16	9	May 31	By Gross Profit brought from the Trading Account .	J.	87	2	8
,, ,,	,, Salaries and Wages .	J.	46	17	1	,, ,,	,, Discount and Allowances .	J.	4	15	0
,, ,,	,, General Expenses .	J.	4	0	5						
,, ,,	,, Stationery .	J.	2	4	6						
,, ,,	,, Advertising .	J.	2	10	0						
,, ,,	,, Carriage and Freight on Sales .	J.	8	17	4						
,, ,,	,, Balance, being net profit for the month, transferred to Capital Account .	J.	26	11	7						
		£	91	17	8			£	91	17	8

The Profit and Loss account is prepared by means of Journal entries in much the same manner as the Trading account.

The last Journal entry on p. 158 records the transfer from the Trading account to the Profit and Loss account of the Gross Profit made during the month, viz., £87 2s. 8d.

As I have already pointed out, the Discount and Allowances account is the only account included in the Trial Balance that shows a balance of profit, viz., £4 15s. By means of a Journal entry this amount is transferred from the Discount and Allowances account to the credit of the Profit and Loss account. This entry has the effect of closing the Discount and Allowances account, and is the first entry illustrated in the form of Journal given below.

The six "expense" accounts mentioned on p. 164 (viz., Travelling Expenses, Salaries and Wages, General Expenses, Stationery, Advertising, and Carriage), show *debit* balances. All these balances must be transferred to the debit of the Profit and Loss account by means of a Journal entry, and the respective "expense" Ledger accounts will then show no balance.

You will notice that the effect of these Journal entries is that all the individual "loss" or "gain" accounts are closed, their balances being collected and offset against each other in the Profit and Loss account.

The only Journal entry remaining to be effected is that which transfers the net profit made, £26 11s. 7d., from the Profit and Loss account to the Capital account. This entry has the effect of closing the Profit and Loss account, and of increasing the balance of R. Jones's Capital account to £1667 6s. 4d.

The foregoing Journal entries are set forth in the form below. The various "loss" and "expense" accounts are also shown after they have been closed by posting the respective Journal entries which relate to them. The Discount and Allowances account is also shown, treated in a similar manner. Finally, the Capital account of R. Jones is given, wherein the original balance is shown as having been increased by the addition of the net profit for the month.

JOURNAL.

1910.				£	s.	d.	£	s.	d.
May 31	Discount and Allowances Account	Dr.	15A	4	15	0			
	To Profit and Loss Account . . .		21				4	15	0
	For balance transferred.								
"	Profit and Loss Account	Dr.	21	65	6	1			
	To Sundries, viz.:								
	Travelling Expenses Account . .		9A					16	9
	Salaries and Wages Account . .		10A				46	17	1
	General Expenses Account . . .		11A				4	0	5
	Stationery Account		12A				2	4	6
	Advertising Account		13A				2	10	0
	Carriage and Freight Account .		14A				8	17	4
	For balances transferred								
"	Profit and Loss Account	Dr.	21	26	11	7			
	To R. Jones's Capital Account . . .		1A				26	11	7
	For net profit for May 1910 transferred.								
			£	96	12	8	£96	12	8

9a
Dr.
TRAVELLING EXPENSES.
9a
Cr.

1910.			£	s.	d.	1910.			£	s.	d.
May 17	To transfer from Salaries and Wages Account	J.		16	9	May 31	By transfer to Profit and Loss Account . .	J.		16	9

10a
Dr.
SALARIES AND WAGES.
10a
Cr.

1910.			£	s.	d.	1910.			£	s.	d.
May 14	To Cash . .	C.	24	8	10	May 17	By Transfer to Travelling Expenses Account . .	J.		16	9
„ 30	„ „ . .	C.	23	5	0	„ 31	„ Transfer to Profit and Loss Account	J.	46	17	1
		£	47	13	10			£	47	13	10

11a
Dr.
GENERAL EXPENSES.
11a
Cr.

1910.			£	s.	d.	1910.			£	s.	d.
May 7	To Cash, sundry petty expenses	C.	2	1	2	May 31	By Transfer to Profit and Loss Account. .	J.	4	0	5
„ 31	„ Ditto . .	C.	1	19	3						
		£	4	0	5			£	4	0	5

12a
Dr.
STATIONERY.
12a
Cr.

1910.			£	s.	d.	1910.			£	s.	d.
May 31	To Cash . .	C.	2	4	6	May 31	By Transfer to Profit and Loss Account . .	J.	2	4	6

13a
Dr.
ADVERTISING.
13a
Cr.

1910.			£	s.	d.	1910.			£	s.	d.
May 28	To Cash, for one month's advertising in trade papers .	C.	2	10	0	May 31	By Transfer to Profit and Loss Account .	J	2	10	0

14a
Dr.
CARRIAGE AND FREIGHT.
14a
Cr.

1910.			£	s.	d.	1910.			£	s.	d.
May 31	To Cash, carriage and freight on goods sold .	C.	8	17	4	May 31	By Transfer to Profit and Loss Account . .	J.	8	17	4

15a   DISCOUNT AND ALLOWANCES.   **15a**

Dr.   Cr.

1910.			£		d.	1910.			£	s.	d.
May 24	To R. Lyon, allowance for late delivery . .	J.	1		0	May 31	By Sundries—Discounts received as per Cash Book .	C.	7	5	0
„ 31	„ Sundries—Discounts allowed as per Cash Book	C.	1	1	0						
„ „	„ Transfer to Profit and Loss Account .	J.	4	15	0						
			£ 7		5 0				£ 7	5	0

1a   R. JONES' CAPITAL ACCOUNT.   **1a**

Dr.   Cr.

1910.			£	s.		1910.			£	s.	d.
May 31	To Balance carried down .	√	1667	6	4	May 2	By Balance .	J.	1640	14	9
						„ 31	„ Net Profit for the month transferred from Profit and Loss Account . .	J	26	11	7
			£ 1667	6	4				£ 1667	6	4
						1910. June 1	By Balance brought down . .	√	1667	6	4

EXERCISES.

10A.

1. What is a Profit and Loss account ? Explain how it is prepared.
2. What is the difference between a Profit and Loss account and a Trading account?   3. Explain the terms : Net Profit, Net Loss, Gross Profit, Gross Loss, and distinguish between them.   4. Explain briefly the Journal entries which are necessary for the preparation of a Profit and Loss account.   5. How is the balance of the Profit and Loss account dealt with (a) if it is a profit, or (b) if it is a loss ?

10B.

From the following particulars prepare my Profit and Loss account for the year ended December 31, 1909 :

Gross profit brought from Trading account, £622 8s. 10d. ; Commissions paid, £10 4s. 8d ; Salaries and wages, £204 2s. 2d. ; Discounts allowed, £17 7s. 8d. ; Rent, rates and taxes, £104 2s. 3d. ; Interest received on deposit account at bank, £5 6s. 6d. ; General expenses, £60 8s. 8d. ; Travelling expenses, £15 5s. 5d. ; Gas and electric light,

£16 2s. 9d. Show also the Journal entries which are necessary in order to prepare the Profit and Loss account.

10c.

From the following particulars prepare my Profit and Loss account for the year ended December 31, 1908 :

Gross profit brought from Trading account, £1420 8s. 2d. ; Clerks' salaries, £605 2s. 9d.; Warehouse wages, £211 4s. 8d. ; Electric light, £20 4s. 2d. ; Telephone subscription, £25 10s. ; Rent, rates and taxes, £288 14s. 9d. ; General expenses, £224 8s. 9d. ; Interest paid on money borrowed, £314 3s. 8d. ; Commissions received, £5 5s.

10D.

From the following particulars prepare the Profit and Loss account of Abel Thomas for the year ended June 30, 1910 :

Gross profit brought from Trading account, £2429 1s. 3d. ; Salaries, £682 10s. ; Travelling expenses, £222 14s. 6d. ; Commissions received, £68 15s. 9d. ; Rent, rates and taxes, £182 11s. 5d. ; Gas and electric light, £38 14s. 2d. ; Advertising, £449 2s. 6d. ; Commissions paid, £239 8s. 10d. ; Discounts received, £22 4s. 8d. ; Bankers' discount paid, £12 14s. 9d. ; Discounts allowed, £39 1s. 2d. ; Printing and stationery, £148 1s. 6d. ; Interest paid on loans, £100 9s. 8d. ; Uniforms for porters and carmen, £15 2s. 8d. ; Dividends received on investments, £4 9s. 8d. ; Packing expenses, £17 4s. 6d. ; Telephone rent, £21 10s. ; Insurance, £3 2s. 6d. ; Telegrams and postages, £48 9s. 6d.

10E.

From the following particulars prepare the Profit and Loss account of Herbert Riches for the year ended December 31, 1909

Salary received, £560 ; Rent, rates and taxes, £85 2s. 10d. ; Gas, coal and electric light, £21 4s. 9d. ; Dividends received on investments, £70 15s. 6d. ; Housekeeping expenses, £235 16s. 8d. ; Doctor and dentist's fees, £15 2s. 8d. ; Clothing, hatter and bootmaker, £45 9s. 2d. ; Travelling expenses, £15 8s. 9d. ; Holiday expenses, £25 10s. ; Earnings by writing newspaper articles, £24 ; Subscriptions to clubs and charities, £10 10s. ; Personal expenses £126 9s. 1d. ; Sundry expenses, £22 14s. 6d. ; Income tax paid, £15 1s. 3d. ; Servants' wages, £36.

10F.

From the following particulars prepare the Trading and Profit and Loss accounts of R. Warren for the 6 months ended June 30, 1910 :

Stock, January 1, 1910, £1191 4s. 8d. ; Discounts allowed, £17 8s. 9d. ; Salaries and packers' wages, £521 8s. 6d. ; Fire insurance premiums paid, £2 1s. 4d. ; Purchases, £4421 2s. 2d. ; Returns outwards, £12 1s. 4d. ; Printing and stationery, £224 16s. 8d. ; Rent, rates and taxes, £442 1s. 9d. ; Returns inwards, £16 8s. 5d. ; Sales, £5584 2s. 10d. ; General expenses, £336 9s. 10d. ; Telephone subscription, £25 10s.; Postage and telegrams, £44 2s. 8d. ; Discounts received, £2 0s. 4d.; Interest paid on loans, £30 9s. 8d. ; Stock, June 30, 1910, £2112 1s. 8d.; Gas and electric light, £51 4s. 8d.

10G.

From the following Trial Balance which has been extracted from the books of Mr. Wiggins make out—

1. A Trading account for the year ended December 31, 1909.
2. A Profit and Loss account for the same period.
3. The Journal entries which are necessary for the construction of these two accounts.

	Dr.			Cr.		
	£	s.	d.	£	s.	d.
Cash in hand	150	2	6			
Stock, January 1, 1909 . . .	1042	12	9			
Purchases	3331	11	2			
Freehold land and buildings . .	1028	16	10			
Returns inwards	14	2	8			
Salaries	284	2	10			
Rent, rates, and taxes . . .	188	17	3			
Telegrams, postages, and telephone subscription	14	3	6			
Sales				4086	2	10
Debtors : C. Brown	114	11	0			
W. Hayes	39	0	10			
R. Norris	221	4	8			
Creditor : C. Finnemore . . .				100	5	6
General Expenses	111	4	2			
Discount	36	8	5			
Commissions received . . .				5	5	6
H. Wiggins's Capital Account . .				2385	4	9
	£6576	18	7	£6576	18	7

Note.—Value of stock of goods in hand December 31, 1909 = £1212 8s. 6d.

10H.

From the following particulars prepare the Trading account, and the Profit and Loss account of C. Willis for the year ended December 31, 1909 :

Stock of goods in hand, January 1, 1909, £3096 10s. ; Sales, £35,932 15s. 1d. ; Purchases, £34,364 3s. 9d. ; Returns inward, £3921 0s. 3d. ; Returns outward, £2091 17s. 10d. ; Wages, £425 16s. 4d. ; Salaries, £394 12s. 1d. ; Postages, £38 17s. 9d. ; Discounts received, £365 2s. 8d. ; Discounts allowed, £39 4s. 2d. ; Rent, rates, and taxes, £274 9s. 8d. ; General expenses, £214 0s. 11d. ; Telephone subscription, £36 10s. ; Stock of goods on hand, December 31, 1909, £4114 2s 6d.

CHAPTER XI

THE BALANCE SHEET

THE Trial Balance illustrated on p. 145 was extracted from the Ledger of R. Jones *after* the "books of first entry" had been posted, but *before* the Trading and Profit and Loss accounts had been prepared.

In the two previous chapters I instructed you how to prepare a trader's Trading and Profit and Loss accounts; and the books of R. Jones were used in these chapters by way of illustration.

When we were preparing the Trading and Profit and Loss accounts, sundry "transfers" and various entries in several ledger accounts became necessary. The accounts affected by these entries were shown in Chapters IX. and X. in the form of continuations of the relative accounts which appeared in Chapter VII. In order, therefore, to obtain a complete view of the Ledger balances of R. Jones, it is necessary for you to study the accounts given in Chapter VII. in conjunction with the continuations of the various accounts as shown in Chapters IX. and X.

I will assume that you have made an intelligent study of these Ledger accounts, so we can now extract a second Trial Balance from the books of R. Jones. This further Trial Balance is prepared *after* all the entries relating to the month of May 1910 have been passed through the books, and *after* all the Ledger accounts have been ruled off and balanced.

This second Trial Balance takes the form set out on p. 172. By means of the "pages" column on the left hand side you can readily refer to the Ledger account from which each balance has been taken.

The Trial Balance differs somewhat from the one given on p. 145. In the first place, it is considerably shorter, and, in the second place, it contains no accounts relating to "losses" or "gains." All accounts of this nature

have, as you know, been collected and offset against one
another by means of the Trading and Profit and Loss accounts
into which they were transferred, or closed, and the final
result of this process has been transferred to R. Jones's
Capital account, as representing the net profit for the month.

R. JONES.

SECOND TRIAL BALANCE, May 31, 1910
(prepared after "closing" the books).

Page of this book.	Ledger folio.	Account.	Dr.			Cr.		
			£	s.	d.	£	s.	d.
168	1 A	R. Jones's Capital Account .				1667	6	4
158	2 A	Stock-in-trade	805	11	9			
132	3	Freehold Warehouse and Land .	350	0	0			
133	4	Furniture and Fittings . .	22	10	0			
		Creditors—						
133	5	C. Samuel . . .				456	18	
133	6	W. Barber .				13	0	0
		Debtors—						
134	7	R. Lyon	361	17	7			
134	8	C. Powell .	102	6	0			
	C.B.	Cash at the Bank . .	48	18	2			
	C.B.	Cash in hand	12	1	3			
			£2137	4	9	£2137	4	9

The Trial Balance which we are now considering consists
solely of " Asset " and " Liability " accounts, together with
R. Jones's Capital Account. It consists entirely, therefore,
of those balances which, if properly arranged, will show the
financial position of R. Jones as on May 31, 1910.

In order to show the trader's financial position more clearly
and concisely than is apparent from the Trial Balance, a further
statement, called a **Balance Sheet**, is prepared. A Balance
Sheet is a statement in which the outstanding balances contained in any set of books are shown grouped and classified in
such a manner that the financial position which they disclose
may be readily understood.

In practice, a Balance Sheet is simply a second Trial Balance
prepared in a condensed and classified form, with the sides
reversed.

You must be careful to remember that a Balance Sheet is
not a Ledger account. It consists merely of a copy, or list, on
a sheet of paper, of those balances which are outstanding
in the Ledger on a certain date. The items of which it is

composed are not transferred to it, as was the case with the Trading and Profit and Loss accounts.

The construction of the Balance Sheet may be briefly stated as follows :

BALANCE SHEET.

Liabilities.	£	s.	d.	Assets.	£	s.	d.
Creditors— All the outstanding balances due to persons to whom the trader owes money. Capital.*— The balance due to tne owner of the business.				Property— The balance of every account which represents Property owned or employed in the business, i.e. "asset" accounts, such as Machinery, Stock, Cash, &c. Debtors— The outstanding balances of the accounts of all persons who owe money to the trader.			
£				£			

On the left-hand side of the Balance Sheet the balances of all accounts representing liabilities are shown together with the Trader's Capital account. All balances of a similar kind— e.g. amounts owing to creditors—are grouped together in one total under a distinctive heading, e.g. Sundry Trade Creditors.

On the right-hand side of the Balance Sheet appear the balances of all "asset" accounts, and of those accounts in which outstanding debit balances are shown. These balances are grouped and classified in the same manner as the balances which appear on the opposite side of the statement, e.g. Sundry Debtors, Cash in hand and at Bankers, &c. Care and thought must be given to the appropriate arrangement of the items of which a Balance Sheet is composed. The ideal result to be aimed at is the preparation of a statement which shall be clear to all, and incapable of being misconstrued. To secure this end, the grouping together of balances which are dissimilar in nature must be carefully avoided.

A Balance Sheet, a Trading account, and a Profit and Loss account are the three statements commonly submitted by

* If the owner of the business is insolvent, the debit balance of his Capital account appears on the right-hand side of the Balance Sheet.

those responsible for the conduct of a business to the owners of the undertaking. The Balance Sheet and the Profit and Loss Account are frequently all that the shareholders in a Limited Company receive in the way of financial information about their business. It is therefore of the highest importance that these statements shall be carefully prepared.

When constructing the right-hand, or "asset," side of a Balance Sheet it is customary to range the various assets in the order of the ease with which they can be converted into money, commencing with those which are the most difficult to sell, and ending with the cash in hand. This course has been followed in the annexed Balance Sheet, which has been prepared from the books of R. Jones.

R. JONES.

BALANCE SHEET, May 31, 1910.

Liabilities.	£	s.	d.	Assets.	£	s.	d.
To Sundry Creditors .	469	18	5	By Freehold warehouse and land .	350	0	0
„ R. Jones, Capital Account . .	1667	6	4	„ Furniture and fittings . . .	22	10	0
				„ Stock of tea in hand . . .	805	11	9
				„ Sundry debtors .	464	3	7
				„ Cash at the Bank and in hand . .	494	19	5
	£2137	4	9		£2137	4	9

EXERCISES.

11A.

1. What is a Balance Sheet? 2. How is a Balance Sheet prepared? 3. What is the difference (if any) between a Trial Balance and a Balance Sheet? 4. Name the headings which are used for the two sides of a Balance Sheet. 5. On which side of a Balance Sheet should the following balances appear—(a) Stock of goods in hand; (b) Cash in hand; (c) Debts owing to trade creditors; (d) Freehold land and buildings; (e) The proprietor's capital; (f) Debts owing to the proprietor of the business? 6. In a given Balance Sheet the balance of the proprietor's capital account appears on the right-hand side. What does this fact signify? 7. From the following particulars prepare my Balance Sheet dated June 30, 1910—Cash in hand, £60; Goods in hand, £100. Owing to C. Browning, £120. R. Way owes me £25. Balance of my capital account, £65.

11B.

1. How should the balances from which a Balance Sheet is constructed be arranged or grouped? 2 Is a Balance Sheet a Ledger

account? What Journal Entries (if any) are necessary in preparing it? 3. Give a skeleton form of a Balance Sheet, without inserting any figures, explaining briefly the nature of the various accounts of which it is composed. 4. In what order is it customary to arrange the assets which appear in a Balance Sheet? 5. From the following particulars prepare a Balance Sheet, dating it June 30, 1910 : Cash in hand, £10 ; Cash at the bank, £50 ; Stock of goods in hand, £200 ; Sundry creditors, £1300 ; Sundry debtors, £1600 ; Freehold land and buildings, £300 ; Amount owing to solicitors for law costs, £60 ; Investments—Consols (2½ per cent.) valued at £830, and India 3 per cent. stock valued at £840 ; Capital, £2470.

11c.

From the following particulars prepare the Balance Sheet of John Hall as on June 30, 1910, showing therein the amount of his capital at that date : Stock-in-trade, £1222 8s. 10d. Debtors—(1) C. Brown, £122 2s. 8d. ; (2) H. Brougham, £112 8s. 2d. ; (3) M. Wild & Co., £12 18s. 8d. Creditors—(1) C. Wray, £121 2s. 8d. ; (2) Daphne, Ltd., £188 12s. 2d. ; (3) The Pericles Process Co., £188 8s. 2d. ; Freehold land and buildings, £880 ; Plant and machinery, £280 2s. 10d. ; Fixtures and furniture (at cost), £600 ; Stock of loose tools and patterns, £80 10s. ; Patent rights (at cost), £300 10s. 6d. ; Loan from the bank, £1000 ; Cash at the bank, £322 4s. 4d. ; Cash in hands of cashier, £12 2s. 2d.

11d.

From the following balances, which were extracted from the books of Charles Martin, on June 30, 1910, prepare (1) a Trial Balance as at that date ; (2) a Trading and Profit and Loss account for the half-year, and (3) a Balance Sheet as on June 30, 1910. Cash at the bank, £100 14s. 8d. Debtors—W. Brown & Sons, £113 8s. 8d. Creditors—A. Child, £10 ; C. Rowe, £60 12s. 9d. Purchases, £1488 11s. 9d. ; Stock-in-trade, January 1, 1910, £200 ; Salaries and wages, £214 12s. 6d. ; General expenses, £86 ; Freehold land and buildings, £650 ; Rates and taxes, £22 4s. 2d. ; Sales, £2004 2s. 6d. ; Capital (credit balance), £800 16s. 6d.

Note.—The Stock-in-trade, as on June 30, 1910, was valued at £100 2s. 8d.

11e.

1. Enter the following Statements and Transactions in Invoice Book (Purchases Book), Sales Book, Cash Book (having Bank and Office columns) ; or Journalise. (N.B.—All cheques to be treated as Bank Transactions.) 2. Post these entries into the Ledger. 3. Balance the accounts. Ascertain how much cash I have both at the office and in the bank ; also how much is owing to me and by me. Find the Gain or Loss in trading by means of a Goods account (Trading account), the Net Gain or Loss by a Profit and Loss account ; the Net Capital by means of a Balance Sheet. (N.B.—A Trial Balance is not desired, as the time is limited.) On July 1, 1905, my books showed the following :—Liabilities—I owe Finch & Son £72 10s. Assets—I have cash at bank, £765 ; I have cash at office, £56 10s. ; Goods valued at £567 15s. ; L. Martin owes me £48 5s.

Transactions.—July 3, 1905, Sold goods to Wren & Rooke, £96 15s. ; Bought goods and paid by cheque, £124 12s. ; July 5, Paid Finch & Son by cheque, £72 10s.; Sold goods to R. Swan, £85; July 8, L. Martin paid me in cash, £28 5s.; Sold Goods to Wren & Rooke, £73 15s.; Bought goods of Drake & Co., £136 12s. 6d.; July 12, Received from Wren & Rooke, cash, £26 5s., by cheque, £120 (discount allowed, £3 15s.), £150; July 15, Sold goods to L. Martin, £67 7s. 6d.; Sold goods for cash up to this date, £149 8s.; Sent cash to bank, £175; July 18, Sold goods to R. Swan, £54; Received from R. Swan, cash £39, and his acceptance at 3 months for £100,* £139; July 20, Paid Drake & Co. by cheque, £114, and was allowed as discount £6, £120; July 24, Bought goods of Finch & Son, £217; Sold goods to Wren & Rooke, £105; July 28, Paid Finch & Son by cheque, £152, and was allowed discount £8, £160; Wren & Rooke paid to my bank account, £97 10s., (discount allowed, £2 10s.), £100; July 31, Sold goods for cash up to this date, £132 16s.; Sent cash to bank, £150; Paid wages, &c., in cash during the month, £48 15s.; Estimated value of goods on hand, £356.

(College of Preceptors [Junior], Christmas, 1905.)

* Debit this £100 to an asset account entitled "Bills Receivable,' and credit a like amount to R. Swan.

11f.

(N.B.—The Dates and the Initials of Names should be given.) •

1. Enter the following Statements and Transactions in Invoice Book (Purchases Book), Sales Book, Cash Book (having Bank and Office columns); or Journalise. (N.B.—All Cheques to be treated as Bank Transactions.) 2. Post these entries into the Ledger. 3. Balance the accounts. Ascertain how much cash I have both at the office and in the bank; also how much is owing *to* me and *by* me. Find the Gain or Loss in trading by means of a Goods account (Trading account); the Net Gain or Loss by a Profit and Loss account; the Net Capital by means of a Balance Sheet. (N.B.—A Trial Balance is not desired, as the time is limited.) On July 1, 1906, my books showed the following results: Liabilities—I owe Field & Co. £95 15s. Assets—I have cash at bank, £345; I have cash at office, £27 10s.; Goods valued at £864; C. Dale owes me £36 5s.

TRANSACTIONS.—July 2, 1906, Sold goods to G. Heath, £48 10s.; Sold goods for cheque (sent to bank), £56 15s.; July 4, Paid Field & Co., by cheque, £91 (discount allowed, £4 15s.), £95 15s.; Sold goods to C. Dale, £67 10s.; July 7, Bought goods and paid by cheque, £125; Sold goods to K. Lea, £72 8s.; July 10, Received from C. Dale, cash, £53 15s.; Paid rates and taxes in cash, £22 10s.; July 14, Sold goods for cash up to this date, £132 5s.; Sent cash to bank, £150; July 16, Sold goods to G. Heath, £84 12s.; Received from G. Heath, cash, £97 10s. (discount allowed, £2 10s.), £100; July 20, Sold goods and was paid by cheque, £45 6s. Bought goods of Field & Co., £146 10s.; Sold goods to K. Lea, £37 16s.; July 24, Bought goods for cash, £52 10s.; July 28, K. Lea paid me by cheque, £65; Paid Field & Co. by cheque, £75; July 31, Sold goods for cash up to this date, £115; Sent cash to bank, £136; Paid wages, &c., in cash during the month, £33 15s.; Estimated value of goods on hand, £612.

(College of Preceptors [Junior], Christmas, 1906.)

11 G.

1. What is meant by Capital ? If you were furnished with a Trial Balance how would you ascertain the amount of the Proprietor's Capital? 2. From the following transactions make out F. Pearson's account: Oct. 1, 1906, I owe F. Pearson £257 ; Oct. 4, I pay £200 ; Oct. 5, He sells me goods, £43 ; Oct. 7, I sell him goods, £38 ; Oct. 10, I buy goods of him, £71 ; Oct. 14, He buys goods of me, £62 ; Oct. 19, He sells me goods, £29 ; Oct. 17, He returns goods, £6 ; Oct. 25, I buy goods of him, £96 ; Oct. 27, I sell goods to him, £400 ; Oct. 28, He pays me cash, £150 ; Oct. 28, I receive bill from him (*credit F. Pearson*), £250 ; Oct. 31, He buys goods of me, £18.   3. Make out a Cash Account : Jan. 1, 1906, Capital in cash £500 ; Jan. 7, Cash sales, £50 ; Jan. 12, Sold goods for cash, £19 1s. ; Bought goods for cash, £47 2s. ; Jan. 18, H. Long pays me £63 5s. ; Jan. 20, I pay F. Smedley, £329 ; Jan. 23, I pay W. Thomas, £137 0s. 10d. ; Jan. 25, I draw for private expenses, £10 ; Jan. 27, I receive from R. Judson, £37 5s. ; Jan. 29, Sold goods for cash, £47 2s. ; Jan. 31, F. Smith pays me, £8 5s.; Jan. 31, Paid wages, £10 ; Jan. 31, Paid trade charges, £4 7s. 6d. ; Jan. 31, Paid rent, £15. 4. From the following Balance Sheet open a new Ledger :

BALANCE SHEET.
December 31, 1906.

LIABILITIES.			£	ASSETS.				£
J. Frost	⎱ Sundry	.	151	Cash .	.	.	.	45
T. Wilson	⎰ Creditors	.	49	Bank .	.	.	.	150
R. Ford		.	75	T. Wells ⎱ Sundry			.	215
Capital	. . .	.	670	S. Reeves ⎰ Debtors			.	96
				Stock .	.		.	439
			£945					£945

5. Draw out a Profit and Loss account : Jan. 1, 1906, Capital, £2675 ; Jan. 31, Gross profit, £425 ; Sundry expenses, £35 ; Rent, £70 ; Wages, £80 ; Bad debts, £20 ; Discounts received, £25 ; Discounts allowed, £30.

(*Auctioneers Institute of the U.K. Preliminary*, 1907

11 H.

1. Explain clearly the difference between Cash and Capital, and show by an intelligent statement that I may have £1000 cash in my business and yet be worth only £100.   2. Into what principal classes are accounts divided? Give the names of those classes and two examples of Ledger headings (names of accounts) under each. 3. From the following Transactions compile a Cash Account: Jan. 1, 1908, Commenced business with cash, £1000 ; Jan. 4, Borrowed from the Security Bank, £500 ; Jan. 6, Bought goods for cash, £460 ; Jan. 8, Bought goods of West & Co., £245 ; Jan. 10, Sold goods for cash, £525 ; Jan. 15, Paid West & Co, on account, £200 ; Jan. 21, Paid into Security Bank for my credit, £1200 ; Jan. 22, H. Green sells me

M

goods, £150; Jan. 24, I sell J. Ford goods, £170; Jan. 26, J. Ford pays his account (less discount, £8 10s.), £161 10s.; Jan. 28, Paid H. Green, £150; Jan. 31, Paid for rent, £50; Paid for wages, £35; Paid for trade expenses, £15. 4. Make out F. Walker's account as it would appear in your Ledger, and show the first entry for the month of July, supposing that monthly balances were taken: Jan. 1, 1908, Mr. Walker owes me £500 10s. 6d.; Jan. 3, I sell him goods, £55 0s. 4d.; Jan. 4, He buys goods of me, £73 5s. 2d.; Jan. 6, I sell him goods, £394 3s.; Jan. 9, He pays me, £22 19s.; Jan. 10, I buy goods of him, £420; Jan. 11, I return goods to him, £3; Jan. 16, He sells me goods, £90; Jan. 21, He pays me £400; Jan. 28, I sell him goods, £77 1s.; Jan. 31, I receive cash from him, £67 1s. 5. T. Wood commences business as a Coal Merchant on January 1, 1908, with a Capital in cash of £1200. His Gross Profits are: Mar. 31, £142; June 30, £105; Sept. 30, £75; Dec. 31, £160. His Trade Expenses are: Mar. 31, £35; June 30, £43; Sept. 30, £28; Dec. 31, £65. On Dec. 31, 1908, J. Ford owes him £75, and he has cash in hand, £1236, and stock of coal, £200. Make out a Profit and Loss Account and a Balance Sheet. 6. Show how the items in the following Balance Sheet would appear in the Ledger.

H. Frazer.
Balance Sheet at December 31, 1908.

LIABILITIES.	£	ASSETS.		£
Loan from Bank	1500	Cash		
Sundry Creditors	750	At Bank	£1200	
Capital	2500	In hand	70	
				1270
		House Property		430
		Stock		1500
		Sundry Debtors		1550
	£4750			£4750

(*Auctioneers Institute of the U.K. Preliminary*, 1909.)

CHAPTER XII

CHEQUES AND BILLS

I REFERRED briefly in Chapter I. to the nature of Cheques and Bills. I now propose to give you a few more details concerning these two important business documents.

In the course of your progress through the various chapters of this book you have already become familiar with the trader's almost universal custom of keeping his cash with his banker upon "Current Account," instead of in his cash-box, and of making his payments by means of cheques drawn on his banker.

A cheque is a written order addressed by a person to his banker directing him to pay a certain sum of money on demand to some person named in the cheque, or to the bearer of it. The cheque must be signed by the person who gives these instructions to his banker.

The person who signs the cheque and gives the instructions for the payment of the money from his banking account is called the **Drawer** ; the banker to whom the cheque is addressed is called the **Drawee** ; and the person who is named in the cheque as authorised to receive the money is called the **Payee.**

Every cheque must bear a penny impressed stamp, or a penny "postage and inland revenue" stamp. If the latter stamp is used the drawer must cancel it.

A form of cheque is given on p. 180.

In this cheque Messrs. Peter Jones & Co., who keep their banking account with the Union of London and Smith's Bank, Ltd., have directed their bankers to pay £15 10s. 6d. from their Banking Account to Messrs. James Clarke & Co., "or Order."

The words "or Order" mean that the cheque must be endorsed by the party, or parties, to whom it is made payable ; that is to say, the parties to whom it is made payable, Messrs.

179

James Clarke & Co., must write the name of their firm on the back of the cheque when they present it for payment. Cheques of this kind are called "order" cheques.

In some cheques the words "or Bearer" are used instead of the words "or Order." Cheques of this description are called "Bearer" cheques, and need no endorsement whatever.

The left-hand portion of the form given on this page is called the Counterfoil. This counterfoil is separated from the cheque by a perforated line.

When the cheque itself has been filled in it is torn off along the perforated line, and is handed, or posted, to the person in whose favour it has been made payable. The details of the cheque—viz., the date of it, the name of the payee, what the payment is for, the amount of it, &c.—are entered in brief on the counterfoil, and these details are subsequently used in writing up and checking the Cash Book, and for comparison, in due course, with the Bank Pass Book.

The **Bank Pass Book**, or briefly the **Pass Book**, is the book which is supplied by a banker to his customer; it contains a copy of the customer's ledger account with the banker, and is periodically returned by him to his banker to be written up to date.

An "Order" cheque is commonly used by business men for making payments. The special usefulness of this form of cheque lies in the fact that if it is lost or stolen the party into whose hands it may come cannot obtain payment of the cheque by any means other than by forging an endorsement. "Bearer" cheques, owing to the fact that they need no endorsement, are not so safe as "Order" cheques, and consequently they are not so generally used. The Payee of an "Order" cheque may, should he so desire, direct the cheque to be paid to some other person named by him. In order to do this he must write his instructions on the back of the cheque above his own signature.

For example, if Messrs. James Clarke & Co. had wished to direct that the cheque illustrated on p. 180 should be paid to Mr. Horace Johnston instead of to themselves, they could have "endorsed" it as follows:

Pay Mr. Horace Johnston, or Order,
James Clarke & Co.

In this case Mr. Horace Johnston would have to endorse his name on the back of the cheque before presenting it to the banker for payment.

The many advantages of the cheque system have become so generally recognised that by far the greater number of a trader's receipts come to him in the form of cheques. The trader does not, as a rule, present these cheques himself for payment at the bank upon which they are drawn—the labour of so doing would be excessive; he therefore deposits them with his own bank, and the bank collects the cash for them on his behalf.

As a consequence of the almost universal employment in business of cheques instead of a metallic currency, a custom has arisen of marking cheques in a special way so that they can only be collected by a banker. The marking most commonly adopted consists of two parallel lines drawn transversely across the face of the cheque, with or without the words "and Company" (or any abbreviation of them) between them.

This form of marking is known as a **Crossing**, and a cheque so marked is called a **Crossed Cheque**.

This form of crossing is illustrated below.

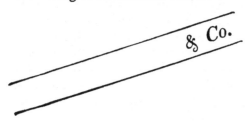

At the time when the custom of crossing cheques first came into practice, the words "and Company" formed the most usual ending of the names of banking firms. The employment of these words is not, however, compulsory when crossing a cheque.

If a crossed cheque be lost or stolen, it can only be cashed by being paid into some person's banking account.

A crossed cheque can be made still more difficult to cash should it fall into wrong hands, by using the following precautions :

1. By inserting in the crossing the name of the bank where the payee of the cheque keeps his account. It can then be cashed through that particular bank only, and through no other. This form of crossing is known as a **special crossing.**

2. By inserting the words **"not negotiable"** in the crossing.

Should a cheque which is crossed in the latter manner be stolen, the taint of theft, or any other legal defect which may be attached to it, remains associated with the cheque at the risk of any person who may become possessed of it.

The addition of the words "not negotiable" does not prevent the *bona-fide* transfer of the cheque from one person to another in the ordinary course of business.

As you proceed with your studies you will learn that other forms of crossed cheques are employed, but those which I have described for you are the most common, and form the bases of the various forms of crossings in common use.

Cheques can be drawn for any sums of money, however large or small, provided, of course, that they do not exceed the trader's credit balance with his banker.

A banker always expects, when opening a current account with a trader, that a sufficient balance will be kept by the trader to cover the banker's expenses, and to allow a small profit for the trouble of keeping the account. As a general rule a permanent balance, not less than £100 in London, and £50 in the provinces, will be regarded by the banker as sufficient in the case of an account where no very large number of cheques are drawn. If the balance frequently falls below these limits the banker will usually make an annual charge, called a "commission," for conducting the trader's banking account.

According to the custom of London bankers no interest is allowed to the trader on money placed by him to the credit of his Current account; but interest is allowed upon sums placed with the banker upon a special "**Deposit account.**' Deposit accounts cannot be drawn upon by cheque, nor is the money usually repayable on demand as in the case of Current accounts. A stated period of notice, usually seven days, is required before the withdrawal of any part of a Deposit account balance. Interest, varying with the value of money for the time being, is paid by the banker on the money deposited with him upon these terms. The rate allowed in London is usually $1\frac{1}{2}$ per cent. below the **Bank Rate,** i.e. the current official discount rate of the Bank of England. A trader who finds that his Current account contains a larger balance than he is likely to need for some time can transfer a round sum of money from his Current account to his Deposit account and thus earn interest upon a portion of his cash which would otherwise lie idle. When he foresees that a portion of his Deposit account balance will be needed for use in his business he can re-transfer whatever amount he may need to his Current account upon giving the necessary notice to his bankers.

In the north of England, and abroad, interest is commonly allowed by bankers on Current accounts, but, on the other hand, a charge is made for keeping the account.

BILLS OF EXCHANGE.

I have already told you that in practical business the majority of a trader's transactions are on the credit system. This system made the creation of Bills of Exchange a necessity.

An enterprising trader usually prefers to receive prompt payment for the goods sold by him, even though he may be obliged to forego some portion of his profit in order to obtain it—he has his own creditors to pay. His debtors, on the other hand, usually prefer to take the full length of time which was allowed for payment under the terms upon which they purchased his goods.

In order to meet the debtor's inclination to defer payment until the extreme limit of his credit, with the creditor's preference for prompt settlement, the "Bill of Exchange" has been brought into use.

A **Bill of Exchange** is, in effect, a short letter, addressed by a creditor to his debtor, requesting him to pay a certain sum of money at a stated future date to a person named in the letter itself. The debtor signifies his promise to comply with the request by writing his signature across the face of the letter itself. The creditor is said to **draw** the bill of exchange on the debtor, and the latter is said to **accept,** *i.e.* promise to pay it, by writing his name across the Bill.

Bills of Exchange are usually expressed as being payable after the expiration of fixed periods of time, *e.g.* "sixty days after date" (*i.e.* sixty days after the date of the bill), "three months after date," &c. The period of time is termed the **Tenor** of the bill. The law of this country allows the debtor three extra days, called **Days of grace,** beyond the time stated in which to pay the bill. These three extra days must always be added to the stated time in order to find the date on which a bill will fall due. For example, a bill drawn on June 2, 1910, payable "three months after date," will fall due, not on September 2, 1910, but on September 5, 1910.

The chief advantages of a Bill of Exchange may be briefly stated as follows :

1. **From the Creditor's standpoint.**

(*a*) It furnishes written evidence of the existence of the debt which is due to him, coupled with a promise for its payment on a definite date.

(*b*) If the commercial reputation of the debtor who "accepts" the bill is good, the creditor can readily sell it, even though it is not yet due for payment. Banks and Discount houses are always willing to buy, for something less than their face value, acceptances which bear the names of solvent traders. The deduction which is made by those who purchase bills before they are due is called "**discount.**" The operation of selling a bill subject to a "discount" is called "**discounting**" it.

2. **From** the Debtor's standpoint, the advantages are that:

The acceptor of a Bill of Exchange retains the benefit of the full term of credit for which he has bargained. It gives him time to convert into money the goods for which he has accepted the bill, and thus enables him to provide the cash to meet and discharge the bill when it becomes due.

The signature of the creditor, *i.e.* the "drawer," must appear on the bill as well as that of the debtor, *i.e.* the "acceptor." As a result of this rule the creditor is liable to pay the amount of the bill himself to any holder of it if the acceptor fails to do so at its maturity.

The person in whose favour a bill is made payable must "endorse" it, *i.e.* sign his name on the back of it, before he can sell it to any one else, or present it for payment when it becomes due. By thus endorsing it, he, as well as the drawer, becomes liable to pay the amount of the bill if the acceptor fails to pay it when it falls due. When endorsing a bill, the endorser may direct payment of the amount of it to any person he may choose to name. The person so named must endorse it in his turn,

BILL OF EXCHANGE.

London June 6th 1910

Nº 201   £24.10.6

Three months after date pay to our order the sum of Twenty-four pounds ten shillings and sixpence for value received

Whitebois & Goodman.

To Mr John Attree.
346 Canongate Street,
York.

and he thereby incurs liabilities similar to those incurred by the previous endorser.   In short, whoever endorses the bill becomes responsible for the payment of it in common with the drawer and acceptor.

You will now understand why bankers like to purchase good bills as temporary investments, as such bills are, by reason of the different signatures they bear, twofold, threefold, or fourfold promises to pay the amount of the bill at its maturity.

The actual form of a Bill of Exchange is given on p. 185.

In this bill Messrs. Child, Sons & Goodman request Mr. John Attree to pay £24 10s. 6d. to their "Order," i.e. to themselves, or to any person who may obtain the bill from them, on the expiration of the period named in the bill.   Mr. John Attree will signify his assent to the conditions stated in the bill by writing his signature across the face of it, as previously explained ; he may also add the word " accepted," and state a place, commonly his own bank, where the bill must be presented for payment.

Upon accepting this bill, therefore, John Attree would write as follows across the face of it :

Accepted, payable at the
London Joint Stock Bank, Ltd., York.
John Attree.

This bill must be endorsed by Messrs. Child, Sons & Goodman before they can part with it to another person, or before they can present it for payment.   The bill is due, not on September 6, 1910, but on September 9, 1910, by reason of the fact that the three additional days of grace must be added to the term of the bill.

The bills which a trader receives from his debtors are called his **Bills Receivable** ; those which he accepts himself in favour of his Creditors are called his **Bills Payable**.

We will deal first with the entries necessary in order to record the former class of bills.

BILLS RECEIVABLE.

When one of your debtors hands you a bill receivable in discharge of a debt that he owes to you, you must enter the transaction in your books in the following manner :

1. As though your debtor had discharged his original debt by giving you a bill for it ; and

2. As though you had acquired a new kind of asset, called a "Bill Receivable," in place of the debt.

You must therefore open a "Bills Receivable" account in your Ledger, and *debit* the amount of the bill receivable therein. You must, at the same time, *credit* a like amount to the Personal account of your debtor.

When the bill receivable is paid to you at maturity, you must *credit* your Bills Receivable account with the amount of the bill, because you have parted with the bill receivable in exchange for the money, and you must *debit* the money which you receive to your Cash or Bank account, because one or other of these accounts has received the cash.

If, having received a bill receivable, you decide not to hold it until it is due, but to sell it to a Bank, or Discount house, you must treat the matter in your books—(a) As though the Bank, or Discount house, had paid you the full amount of the bill before it was due, and (b) as though you had immediately paid them the amount charged by them as discount.

You must therefore:

1. *Credit* your Bills Receivable account with the face value of the bill;
2. *Debit* the face value of the bill in your Cash or Bank account;
3. *Credit* your Cash or Bank account with the amount of the discount; and
4. *Debit* the same amount to Bankers' Discount account —which thus forms one of your "loss" or "expense" accounts.

The following example illustrates the rules which I have just given you:

On January 1, 1910, I owed to Abel Brown £60, and to Robert Giles £102 10s. On January 3 I accepted Abel Brown's draft, at three months' sight, for £60, and on January 10 I accepted Robert Giles's draft, dated January 8, for £100, payable one month after date, paying him by cheque £2 10s. These bills were duly paid at maturity by my banker on my behalf. Prepare the Ledger entries for these transactions.

1   ABEL BROWN.   **1**

Dr.   Cr.

1910.			£	s.	d.	1910.			£	s.
Jan. 3	To Bill payable	3	60	0	0	Jan. 1	By Balance brought forward .	✓	60	0

2   ROBERT GILES.   **2**

Dr.   *Cr.*

1910.			£	s.	d.	1910.			£	s.	d.
Jan. 10	To Bill payable	3	100	0	0	Jan. 1	By Balance brought for-ward . .	√	102	10	0
„ „	„ Cash . .	4	2	10	0						
		£	102	10	0			£	102	10	0

3   BILLS PAYABLE.   **3**

Dr.   *Cr.*

1910.			£	s.	d.	1910.			£	s	d.
Feb. 11	To Cash .	4	100	0	0	Jan. 3	By Abel Brown	1	60	0	0
April 6	„ „ .	4	60	0	0	„ 10	„ Robert Giles	2	100	0	0

4   BANK.   **4**

Dr.   *Cr.*

						1910.			£	s	d.
						Jan. 10	By Robert Giles	2	2	10	0
						Feb. 11	„ Bills payable (R. Giles's draft due) .	3	100	0	0
						April 6	„ Bills payable (A. Brown's draft due) .	3	60	0	0

If the nature of your business is such that you frequently receive Bills Receivable from your debtors, it will become necessary for you to employ a "special" Journal, known as a **Bills Receivable Book**, or Journal, to contain the details recording their receipt and subsequent history.

I have already explained, on p. 47, that if you are constantly buying and receiving goods from a person, the most xpeditious way of dealing with the necessary records is by means of a Purchases Journal. Every purchase is entered in the Purchases Journal, as and when it takes place, and is then posted to the *credit* of the Personal account of the person from whom the goods have been received. The *total* of the purchases, as shown by the Purchases Book, is periodically posted to the *debit* of the Purchases account in the Ledger. A number of credit entries in the Ledger are thus offset by one debit entry equal in amount to their total.

The method of using a Bills Receivable Book is based upon precisely the same principles as those which are employed in the construction of a Purchases Book, the only difference being

1	2	3	4	5	6	7	8	9	10	11	12
Date.	Number of Bill.	Acceptor.	Drawer.	From whom received.	Where payable.	Date of Bill.	Tenor.	Due date.	Folio of Ledger account credited.	£ s. d.	Remarks.
1910. Jan. 1	81	Horsman & Co.	Myself	Horsman & Co.	Parr's Bank, Lombard Street.	Dec. 30, 1909	3 m/d	April 2, 1910	32	614 0 0	Paid at maturity
"	82	Wilson Bros.	Myself	Wilson Bros.	Yorkshire Bank, York.	Dec. 31, 1909	2 m/d	Mar. 3, 1910	64	50 0 0	Do.
"	83	Brown & Co.	J. Atkins & Co.	J. Atkins & Co.	Bank of England, Hull.	Dec. 27, 1909	3 m/s	Mar. 31 1910	14	500 0 0	Do. { Paid with bank Feb. 5, 1910
										£1164 0 0	

NOTE.—If there were no further Bills double transactions during the trading period (e.g. the 3 or 6 months), the double entry would be completed by debiting £1164 to Bills Receivable account in the (...

BILLS PAYABLE BOOK.

1	2	3	4	5	6	7	8	9	10	11	12
Date.	Number of Bill.	Drawer.	In whose favour drawn.	To whom given	Where payable.	Date of Bill.	Tenor.	Due date.	Folio of Ledger account debited.	£ s. d.	Remarks.
1910. Jan. 1	101	Brown & Co	Brown & Co.	Brown & Co.	London.	Jan. 1, 1910	1 mth from the	Feb. 4, 1910	36	200 0 0	
"	102	Jones Bros.	R. Hill	Jones Bros.	do.	Jan. 1, 1910	3 months from date	April 4, 1910	42	1000 0 0	
"	103	J. H. Beck	Smith & Co.	J. H. Beck	do.	Dec. 30, 1909	3 months after sight	April 4, 1910	64	785 16 2	
										£1985 16 2	

NOTE.—If there were no ... the Bills able transactions during the trading period (e.g. the 3 or 6 months), the double entry would be completed by crediting £1985 16s. 2d. to Bills Payable Account in the (...

that the Bills Receivable Book is ruled with a number of additional columns designed to contain useful information concerning the bills that are received. Consequently, a Bills Receivable Book presents a slightly more complicated appearance to the young student than a Purchases Book.

The additional columns provided in the Bills Receivable Book are not, however, necessary in order to effect a complete double entry; the majority of them are only employed in order to contain, in a classified form, such useful details as the date of the bill, the date when it must be presented for payment, the names of the parties whose names appear on it, and other needful details.

A form of Bills Receivable Book is illustrated on p. 189.

Each bill is entered on a separate line in the Bills Receivable Book, as and when it comes in; the information indicated by the headings of the columns is entered in the case of each bill, and in this manner the full history of every bill is available by reading the details which appear across the page.

The columns to which you must devote special attention are the following:

(a) Column 1. Which gives the date on which the bill was received.

(b) Column 5. Which gives the name of the person from whom the bill has been received—i.e. the name of the person to whose account the bill must be credited.

(c) Column 10. Which gives the folio of the Personal account of the person who has been credited with the bill.

(d) Column 11. Which gives the amount of the bill.

From the information contained in these four columns, each bill is posted to the *credit* of the Personal account of the debtor from whom it has been received. The Bills Receivable book is added (in column 11), and the total is carried forward from page to page until the end of any given period. The total then shown is posted to the *debit* of the Bills Receivable account; it there equalises and offsets the numerous credit entries previously made in the Personal accounts of the persons from whom the bills have been received.

When a Bill Receivable is paid at maturity, or is sold under discount, the Bills Receivable account is *credited* with the face value of the bill, and the Cash account is *debited*. In the case of bills which have been sold under discount, there will, of course, be a further entry in the Cash Book, on the credit side, for the amount of the discount, which, in due course, the ledger-keeper will post to the debit of the Bankers' Discount, or Bank Charges, account.

In the "Remarks" column of the Bills Receivable book it is usual to note the ultimate fate of the bill—*e.g.* Discounted, Paid at Maturity, &c.

In practical business the majority of traders pay their Bills Receivable into their banking accounts for collection when they fall due. Such bills are usually paid in two or three days before the date of their maturity. When bills are paid in, the Bank account of the trader is *debited* with the full nominal amount represented by the bills, and the Bills Receivable account is *credited*. The trader does not wait until he is informed that the bill has actually been met before he debits his banker with the amount, as the delay would, in the majority of cases, cause confusion in his books. He debits the banker with the bill *immediately* he pays it in for collection, and assumes, for the moment, that it has been paid.

If, as sometimes happens, the bill is **dishonoured**, *i.e.* not paid, by the acceptor to whom the banker presents it for payment, the trader must make suitable entries to record this fact, and to reverse the double-entry already made in his books as described above. He must, in the first place, credit his Bank account with the face value of the bill, in order to reverse the debit entry previously made in that account. He must offset this credit entry by debiting the amount of the dishonoured bill to the person who has failed to pay it. He can then deal with the defaulting party as one of his ordinary debtors. Any charges—*e.g.* for *noting,** or *protest*, of the dishonoured bill incurred by his banker—must be credited in the Bank account and debited to the account of the defaulting acceptor.

BILLS PAYABLE.

I have explained in the preceding pages how to treat your Bills Receivable. I must now explain how to deal with the bills which you accept and hand to your creditors, viz., your **Bills Payable**.

* *Note.*—When a bill is dishonoured, it is handed by the collecting Banker to a Notary Public, who re-presents it for payment, and formally records the fact that it has been dishonoured. A slip is attached to the bill *noting* the charges of the Public Notary. A formal document called a **Protest** is also sometimes drawn up.

If one of your creditors draws a bill on you which you accept and return to him, you must record the transaction in your books in a special way. You must *debit* your creditor with the amount of the acceptance, and you must open an account called **Bills Payable** Account to contain the necessary *credit* entry for the like amount.

You will probably wonder why, in view of the fact that you have not actually paid your creditor anything, you should debit him with the face value of a document which is merely a promise to pay at a future date. The reason is this : You know that the creditor, to whom you have given your acceptance, may very likely sell that acceptance before it becomes due, in order to raise money for the needs of his business. Your acceptance may probably change hands more than once before it is presented to you for payment, and you will be in the position of owing money, first to one person and then to another, without knowing the name of the actual person to whom the money is payable. One thing, however, is certain, viz., that it would not be wise to assume that the creditor to whom you originally gave the bill will necessarily be the person who will present it for payment when it becomes due.

In order to prevent confusion, it is customary to credit the amount of outstanding Bills Payable to an account called Bills Payable account. This heading is a convenient way of expressing, "the holders of my acceptances, whosoever they may be." The debts owing by you to the creditors who originally drew the bills on you are treated as having been discharged by the acceptance of the bills.

When you pay, or "meet," your Bills Payable at maturity, the money paid is *credited* to the Bank or Cash account, and is *debited* to the Bills Payable account, thus cancelling the Bill Payable in question.

This rule will be made clearer to you by the following example :

On January 1, 1910, H. Stanley owed me £40 15*s*., and C. Smith owed me £150. On January 3 I drew a bill on H. Stanley for £40 15*s*., payable one month after date, which he accepted ; I paid this bill into my bank at its maturity, and it was duly met. On January 5 I drew a bill for £150 on C. Smith, payable two months after date, which he accepted I discounted this bill with my bank on January 8 at 6 per cent. per annum. Show the Ledger entries for these transactions.

1   H. STANLEY.   **1**

Dr.   *Cr.*

1910.			£	s.	d.	1910.			£	s.	d.
Jan. 1	To Balance brought forward .	√	40	15	0	Jan. 3	By Bill receivable .	3	40	15	0

2   C. SMITH.   **2**

Dr.   *Cr.*

1910.			£	s.	d.	1910.			£	s.	d.
Jan. 1	To Balance brought forward .	√	150	0	0	Jan. 5	By Bill receivable .	3	150	0	0

3   BILLS RECEIVABLE.   **3**

Dr.   *Cr.*

1910.			£	s.	d.	1910.			£	s.	d.
Jan. 3	To H. Stanley .	1	40	15	0	Jan. 8	By Bank (C. Smith's bill discounted).	4	150	0	0
„ 5	„ C. Smith .	2	150	0	0	Feb. 6	„ Bank (H. Stanley's bill paid) . .	4	40	15	0

4   BANK.   **4**

Dr.   *Cr.*

1910.			£	s.	d.	1910.			£	s.	d.
Jan. 8	To Bills receivable (C. Smith's bill discounted).	3	150	0	0	Jan. 8	By Banker's discount (discount on C. Smith's bill)	5	1	10	0
Feb. 6	„ Bills receivable (H. Stanley's bill paid) . .	3	40	15	0						

5   BANKER'S DISCOUNT.   **5**

Dr.   *Cr.*

1910.			£	s.	d.						
Jan. 8	To Bank . .	4	1	10	0						

If your Bills Payable transactions are numerous, you will find it convenient to use a special Journal for recording the acceptance of them. A **Bills Payable Book** or **Journal** is employed in the same way as the Bills Receivable Journal which I have already described, except that the entries in the

Ledger are made in different accounts, and on the opposite sides of those accounts.

Each bill is recorded, as and when accepted, in the Bills Payable Book on a separate line; and from this record it is posted to the *debit* of the Personal account of the creditor to whom it has been given. The Bills Payable Book is added at the bottom of the page, and the total is carried forward from page to page until the end of a given period. At the end of this period the total of the Bills Payable book is posted to the *credit* of the Bills Payable account in the Ledger, and this entry equalises and offsets the various debit entries previously made in the creditors' personal accounts.

A form of Bills Payable Book is given on p. 189. The four columns which are of importance for double-entry purposes are the following

(*a*) Column 1. For the date on which the bill was accepted.

(*b*) Column 5. For the name of the creditor to whom it was given, and who must therefore be debited with it.

(*c*) Column 10. The "folio" column, in which the folio of the creditor's Ledger account when posting the bill is entered.

(*d*) Column 11. For the amount of the bill.

All the other columns in the Bills Payable Book contain useful information, but they are not actually required for the purpose of framing the necessary double entries.

EXERCISES.

12A.

1. What do you understand by the phrase "Keeping a current account with a bank"? 2. What is a cheque? 3. Who are (*a*) the Drawer, (*b*) the Drawee, and (*c*) the Payee of a cheque? 4. Is it necessary for a cheque to be stamped? If so, what stamp must it bear? 5. If a postage and inland revenue stamp is affixed to a cheque in payment of the stamp duty, what rule exists as to its cancellation? 6. Explain the word "endorse" in relation to cheques. 7. What are "Bearer" cheques? Do they need endorsement? 8. What are "Order" cheques? Do they need endorsement? 9. Make out an "Order" cheque for £5, dated July 1, 1910, payable to R. Heath, drawn by O. Wray on the Union of London and Smith's Bank, Ltd., Princes Street, London.

12B.

· 1. What is the use of the counterfoil in a cheque book? 2. What is a Bank Pass Book? Explain briefly how it is employed. 3. Are *Order* cheques more commonly used than *Bearer* cheques by business men for making payments? State the reason why most business men prefer one form of cheque rather than the other. 4. If the payee of a cheque desires to direct payment of it to some other person, what must he do? 5. What is a "crossed" cheque? 6. What is the object of "crossing" a cheque? 7. If a cheque is crossed can it be presented for payment by the payee of it? 8. Give a simple form of crossing, and explain where it should be placed on the cheque.

12c.

1. How can a crossed cheque be made more difficult to cash should it go astray? 2. What do the words "not negotiable" mean? Explain briefly the advantage of employing these words in the crossing of a cheque. 3. I draw a *bearer* cheque for £65 on the Bank of Australasia, London, dated July 15, 1910, in favour of Robert Tryll, who banks with the London Joint Stock Bank, Ltd. I cross this cheque "specially" to his bank. Prepare the form of cheque. 4. C. Verity drew, on June 20, 1910, an *Order* cheque for £100, in favour of R. Small, on the London and Provincial Bank, Ltd., Lothbury, London, E.C.; this cheque being crossed "not negotiable," Parr's Bank, Ltd. Prepare this cheque. 5. Draw an Order cheque, dated to-day, for £10, in favour of the Universal Stores, Ltd., on a bank chosen by yourself. 6. Why has the custom of keeping a Current account with a banker, and of making payments by cheque, become so generally adopted?

12d.

1. Name one or two ways in which a banker derives a profit by employing the moneys entrusted to his keeping. 2. If a customer fails to keep a sufficient balance with his banker on his Current account, what does the banker do? 3. Is interest allowed on money kept with a banker on Current account? 4. What is a Deposit account? 5. What is the difference between a Deposit account and a Current account? 6. At what rate is interest usually allowed in London on the balance of Deposit accounts? 7. A trader has a larger balance in his Current account than he will need for business purposes for some time to come— what would you advise him to do?

12e.

1. What is a bill of exchange? 2. What is the use of a bill of exchange (*a*) to the person who receives it in discharge of a debt; (*b*) to the person who "accepts" it to satisfy a debt? 3. What is meant by the term "days of grace"? 4. What is meant by the phrase "to endorse a bill of exchange"? 5. How does a bill of exchange (*a*) resemble, and (*b*) differ from a cheque? 6. What are (*a*) bills payable, (*b*) bills receivable? 7. What is meant by "discounting" a bill with a banker? 8. Explain the following terms when used in connection with bills of exchange: (*a*) the "drawer," (*b*) the "acceptor," (*c*) the "payee," (*d*) the "endorsers," (*e*) the "tenor" of a bill.

12f.

1. A Bill of Exchange is drawn by A.B. upon C.D. in favour of E.F. It is duly accepted by C.D. E.F. endorses it in favour of G.H. to whom he sends it. Explain the liabilities of A.B., C.D., E.F., and G.H. in

connection with the bill. 2. What is meant by "dishonouring" a bill of exchange? 3. I receive a bill of exchange from one of my debtors in discharge of a debt owing by him to me. Explain the entries which I must make in my books (a) when I receive the bill, (b) when it falls due and is paid. 4. I accept a bill of exchange for £100, drawn on me by one of my creditors. Explain the entries which I must make in my books (a) when I accept the bill, and (b) when it falls due and is paid by me in cash. 5. I hold a bill of exchange for £300, accepted by a well-known firm of merchants. Being in need of ready money, I discount this bill with my bankers some time before it falls due. My bankers charge me £3 6s. 8d. for discounting the bill. Explain the entries which I must make in my books in order to record this transaction?

12G.

Pass the following transactions through the proper books (including a Bills Receivable Book to be ruled by you), and make all the entries which are necessary to comply with the double-entry system :
1910. Jan. 6, Received from Hubert & Co. their acceptance (No. 1), drawn by me in my own favour, payable 3 months from to-day, at 394 Lime Street, E.C., for £200 ; Jan. 18, Received from Miles Bros. a bill of exchange (No. 2), drawn by me on them in my favour, payable 2 months after date at the Bank of England, London, dated January 18, 1910, for £250 ; Jan. 21, Received from Wrilding & Co., a bill of exchange (No. 3), drawn by myself on them in my favour, payable 10 days after date at 222 Little Mill Street, Leeds, dated January 21, 1910, for £600 ; Jan. 31, Bill Receivable (No. 3), due to-day, was presented by my bankers, and was duly paid to them for my account ; March 9, I discounted Bill (No. 1) with my bankers, being charged discount 15s. ; March 21, Bill Receivable (No. 2), due to-day, was paid by me into my bank account for collection, but was returned dishonoured, the bank having charged me 1s. 6d. for "noting expenses" in connection with the bill ; March 22, Received from O. Jones his acceptance, drawn by me in my favour, payable 1 month after date, dated March 22, 1910 (No. 4), for £200.

12H.

Pass the following transactions through my books in double-entry form, including a properly ruled Bills Payable Book. All bills are made payable at my bankers. The total of the Bills Payable account is to be posted in its proper place.
1910. June 2, Accepted J. Jones's draft 3 months from date, in his own favour, dated June 2, 1910 (bill payable No. 36), for £300 ; June 3, W. Brown drew on me, in his own favour, at 10 days after date, dated June 3, 1910—accepted this draft (No. 37), £250 ; June 9, Handed to C. Miles my acceptance, in his favour, due June 25-28, 1910 (No. 38), for £100 ; June 16, Accepted Warren & Sons' draft, in their own favour, dated June 16, payable 1 month after date (No. 39), for £200 June 16, Bill payable (No. 37) was paid by the bank, £250 ; June 28, Bill payable (No. 38) was paid by the bank, £100 ; July 19, Bill payable (No. 39) was paid by the bank, £300 ; Sept. 5, Bill payable (No. 36) was paid by the bank, £300 ; Sept. 7, Gave C. Drew my acceptance, in his favour, dated to-day, payable 3 months after date, drawn by him (No. 40), for £100.

CHAPTER XIII

A MERCHANT'S ACCOUNTS

IN the preceding chapters I have explained to you in detail the uses of the various books which are necessary in order to fulfil the requirements of the double-entry system of book-keeping.

In this chapter I propose to give you a practical illustration of the manner in which these books are employed in actual business.

The transactions which follow are recorded in correct double-entry form in the various books just as they would be in an actual business. In addition to this, I propose to describe in detail each necessary step as we proceed to work out the exercise. I wish you to carefully read these detailed explanations, and at the same time to follow each item in its progress through the subsidiary books to the Ledger.

If you do this intelligently, you will not only learn how a trader records his transactions in actual business, but at the same time you will be acquiring the knowledge which is necessary to enable you to answer examination exercises in a proper manner.

You will readily understand that in the illustration given many kinds of transactions occur less frequently than they would in actual business—*e.g.* the sales and purchases are far less numerous than they would be in actual business. This course has been followed in order to economise space, and to avoid the unnecessary repetition of similar transactions.

The books illustrated are enumerated hereunder. The initial letters placed against the name of each book of first entry are used in the Ledger in place of the usual posting "folios."

Cash Books.
{
Cash Book, with columns for " Bank,"
" Office Cash," and " Discount" . C. B.
Petty Cash Book . . . . P. C.
}

Journals.
{
Purchases Book . P.
Sales Book . . . S.
Returns Inwards Book . . . R. I
Returns Outwards Book . . . R. O.
}

Ledger.

A Trial Balance is given on p. 231, and a Balance Sheet on p. 232.

TRANSACTIONS.

C. Leslie, a cigar merchant, commenced on June 1, 1910, to keep his books by double-entry.

His position at that date was as follows :

	£	s.	d.
Cash at the London County & Westminster Bank, Ltd	240	10	8
Debtors : W. Miles	265	9	6
Lightwood Bros., Ltd. . . .	104	2	10
Creditors : Garcia Brothers	35	16	6
Sasso & Escobal . .	227	11	0
Arrietta and Co. .	514	0	10
Stock of cigars in hand .	686	3	5
Freehold premises (valued at cost)	655	10	0
Furniture, fittings, and fixtures .	32	8	2

C. Leslie's transactions for the month of June 1910 were as follows ·

		£	s	d.
June 1.	Drew from the bank for office cash . . .	50	0	0
	Drew from the bank for petty cash . .	20	0	0
,, 2.	Bought from Sasso and Escobal, on credit—			
	3000 Especiales, at 22s. per 100 net . . .	33	0	0
,, 4.	Sold to Lightwood Bros., Ltd., on credit—			
	2000 Especiales, at 25s. per 100 . .	25	0	0
	3000 Esquisitos, at 27s. per 100 .	40	10	0
	10,000 Prima Donnas, at 25s. per 100 .	125	0	0
,, 6.	Paid from petty cash—			
	For envelopes and letter paper . . .	1	4	9
	For brass door-plates (debit Furniture and Fixtures account)	3	8	6
	For stamps		15	0
,, 8.	Paid by cheque to Garcia Bros. . . .	35	10	0
	Being allowed discount by them . .		6	0
,, 10.	Lightwood Bros., Ltd., returned as " out of condition " 500 of the Esquisitos cigars, sold to them on June 4, at 27s. per 100	6	15	0
	Also 500 Especiales, sold them at 25s. per 100	6	5	0
	Allowed them therefor full invoice price.			
,, 15.	Paid from office cash salaries and wages to date	6	15	0
,, 15.	Paid from office cash for electric-light fittings purchased . : . .	5	7	9

A MERCHANT'S ACCOUNTS

		£	s.	d.
June 15. Sold to W. Miles, on credit—				
10,000 Flor de Cuba cigars, at 22s. per 100 net		110	0	0
10,000 Reina Victoria, at 21s. per 100 net		105	0	0
„ 15. Returned to Sasso & Escobal, as "damaged by damp," 500 Especiales, bought frcm them on the 2nd inst., at 22s. per 100		5	5	0
„ 16. Received from W. Miles, cheque on account (paid to bank).		262	10	0
Allowed him discount		2	19	6
„ 18. Bought from Arrietta and Co., on credit				
10,000 Princesas cigars, at 20s. per 100, less 5 per cent. trade discount		95	0	0
10,000 Madeiras, at 26s. per 100 net		130	0	0
„ 18. Paid from petty cash				
Housekeeper and cleaning to date		2	5	0
Fires to date			8	6
Postages and telegrams to date			9	6
„ 18. Paid by cheque on account to Arrietta and Co.		150	0	0
„ 20. Sold to W. Miles—				
5000 Princesas, at 24s. 6d. per 100, less 5 per cent. trade discount		58	3	9
„ 20. Received from Lightwood Bros., Ltd.—				
Cheque (paid to bank) for		104	0	0
Allowed them discount			2	10
„ 21. W. Miles returned, as being of inferior quality, 500 of the Princesas sold him on June 20, at 24s. 6d. per 100, less 5 per cent. discount. Allowed him therefor		5	16	5
„ 21. Returned to Arrietta & Co., 500 Princesas, bought from them on June 18, at 20s. per 100, less 5 per cent. trade discount, as being of inferior quality		4	15	0
„ 23. Sold for cash (placed in office cash)				
3000 Superbas, at 22s. 9d. per 100		34	2	6
„ 24. Paid by cheque on account to Sasso & Escobal		100	0	0
Being allowed discount thereon		1	0	0
„ 24. Received from W. Miles in cash (placed in office cash)		12	17	0
Received from W. Miles by cheque (paid to bank).		200	0	0
Allowed him discount thereon		2	3	0
„ 24. Paid from office cash to the bank.		80	0	0
„ 25. Bought from Garcia Brothers, on credit—				
1000 Conquistadores, at 20s. per 100, less 2½ per cent. Trade Discount		9	15	0
1000 Infantes, at 18s. 6d. per 100 net		9	5	0
4000 Reina Isabella, at 23s. per 100 net		46	0	0
„ 27. Paid Garcia Bros., by cheque, on account		50	0	0
„ 27. Sold to W. Miles, on credit—				
500 Infantes, at 20s. 6d. per 100, less 5 per cent. trade discount		4	17	5
2000 Reina Isabella, at 26s. per 100 net		23	0	0

		£	s.	d
June 28.	Returned to Garcia Bros., 1000 Conquistadores, as not being of the quality ordered, bought from them on June 25, at 20s. per 100, less 2½ per cent. trade discount .	9	15	(
„ 28.	Paid, by cheque, to Wright & Co., carriers' charges for carriage on sundry parcels of cigars forwarded to purchasers by them	3	2	6
„ 29.	Drew from the bank for office cash , . .	20	0	0
„ 30.	Paid from petty cash—			
	'Housekeeper and cleaning to date . .	2	8	10
	Fires to date		9	10
	Postages and telegrams to date .	4	4	3
	Travelling expenses to date . . .	4	3	7
„ 30.	Paid from office cash salaries and wages to date	12	15	0
„ 30.	Drew from the bank to restore the Petty Cashier's balance to £30	19	17	9
„ 30.	Granted to W. Miles a special allowance of 6d. per 100 on the 2000 Reina Isabellas sold to him on the 27th inst., owing to the fact that some of these cigars were of inferior colour		10	0

Note.—The stock of cigars on hand on June 30, 1910, was
valued at 612 13 4

Unless otherwise stated, all moneys are to be assumed as having been paid into the bank as and when received, and all payments to have been made by cheque.

Write up C. Leslie's books. from the foregoing particulars, and prepare Trading and Profit and Loss Accounts for the month ending June 30, 1910, and a Balance Sheet as on that date.

Taking the above transactions in the order in which they occur, the manner in which they are dealt with is as follows ·

The first matter requiring attention is the opening of the books as on June 1, 1910, by means of a Journal Entry marshalling the Assets and Liabilities at that date, and disclosing the amount of Capital with which C. Leslie commenced business.

I mentioned in Chapter VI. that the Assets are set out on the debit side of the Journal Entry, while the Liabilities are arranged on the credit side. The amount which is necessary to make the two sides of the Journal Entry agree is entered on the credit side, and represents the net worth of C. Leslie on June 1, 1910.

The opening Journal Entry is given on p. 222. The amount of C. Leslie's starting capital appearing in it is the amount which is necessary to make the two sides of the Journal Entry agree, viz. £1206 16s. 3d.

Having thus opened C. Leslie's books by means of this Journal Entry, the transactions for the month must be dealt with as under

June 1. Drew from Bank for Office Cash, £50.

The £50 is entered in the Cash Book, on the credit side, in the Bank column, to record the withdrawal of that amount from the Bank, and on the debit side in the "Office Cash" column, to record the receipt by the Office Cashier of the same sum, the Bank having parted with £50, and the Cashier having received it. Office Cash is thus *debited* with the £50 received by it, and the Bank is *credited* with the £50 with which it has parted.

June 1. Drew from Bank for Petty Cash, £20.

The £20 is entered in the Bank column of the Cash Book, on the credit side, and a debit entry is made in the Petty Cash Book recording the receipt of £20 by the Petty Cashier. The former entry is made by the Chief Cashier, or other official entrusted with the Cash Book, and the latter entry is made by the Petty Cashier, who, wherever possible, should be a different person. The Petty Cashier is thus *debited* with the £20 because he has received it, and the Bank is *credited* with the £20 with which it has parted.

June 2. Bought from Sasso & Escobal, on credit, 3000 Especiales Cigars at 22s. per 100 net = £33.

Immediately the invoice relating to the above purchase is received from Sasso & Escobal, the book-keeper copies the details given above in the Purchases Book.

From the Purchases Book the goods supplied must be posted to the credit of the Personal account kept for Messrs. Sasso and Escobal, the folio of their Ledger account being entered in the folio column of the Purchases Book as an indication that this purchase has been duly posted to the credit of the proper account in the Ledger.

The total of the Purchases Book, in which the £33 in question has, of course, been included, must afterwards be posted to the debit of the Purchases account in the Ledger.

The Purchases account is thus *debited* with goods to the value of £33 received by C. Leslie, and Sasso & Escobal are *credited* with the £33 worth of goods which they have sold and delivered.

June 4. Sold to Lightwood Bros., Ltd., on credit :	£	*s.*	*d.*
2000 *Especiales, at* 25*s. per* 100 . .	25	0	0
3000 *Esquisitos, at* 27*s. per* 100 . .	40	10	0
10,000 *Prima Donnas, at* 25*s. per* 100 .	125	0	0
	£190	10	0

When C. Leslie sells goods he sends to the purchaser a statement known as an Invoice (see p. 2). This invoice is press-copied in an " Invoice Press Copy Book."

From this press copy book the book-keeper makes an entry in the Sales Book. In this entry, as I have already explained to you, each parcel of goods sold is entered separately in the " details " column, and the total—in this case, £190 10*s.* 0*d.*—is entered in the " total " column.

From the Sales Book the total of the sale made is posted to the debit of Lightwood Bros., Ltd., in the Ledger. The Sales Book is added at a later stage, and its total, which, of course, includes the £190 10*s.* 0*d.* above referred to, is posted to the credit of Sales account.

Lightwood Bros., Ltd., are thus *debited* with the £190 10*s.* 0*d.* worth of goods received by them, and " Sales " account is *credited* with the £190 10*s.* 0*d.* worth of goods which have been parted with.

June 6. Paid from Petty Cash :	£	*s.*	*d.*
For envelopes and letter-paper . .	1	4	9
For brass door-plates (debit " Furniture and Fixtures" account) . . .	3	8	6
For stamps		15	0

When the above payments are made by the Petty Cashier, he enters them in his Petty Cash Book, on the credit side, in the total column. Such of them as are for expenses coming under any of the headings set out in the analysis columns of the Petty Cash Book are at once extended (*i.e.* entered more to the right-hand side of the book) in their proper analysis columns. In this class are the payment for envelopes and letter-paper (£1 4*s.* 9*d.*), and for stamps (15*s.*), which are therefore extended in the " Stationery " and " Postages and Telegrams " columns respectively.

The remaining payment, that for brass door-plates (£3 8*s.* 6*d.*), must be debited to the real Ledger account headed " Furniture and Fixtures." This sum is therefore extended into the "Ledger" column on the extreme right-hand side of the Petty Cash Book, with the name of the Ledger account (Furniture and Fixtures) appended. From this item, a debit entry is made by the Ledger-keeper in Furniture and Fixtures account in his Ledger, and the double-entry is thus completed. The Ledger folio is inserted in the folio column in the Petty Cash Book in the ordinary way, to show that the item has been duly posted.

The various expense accounts, Stationery, Postages, &c., are thus *debited* with the sums spent for such necessities, and the Furniture and Fixtures account is *debited* with the brass door-plates acquired; the Petty Cash being *credited* with the money parted with.

		£	s.	d.
June 8.	*Paid by cheque to Garcia Bros* . .	35	10	0
	Being allowed discount by them .		6	0
		£35	16	0

The payment of £35 10s. is entered on the credit side of the Cash book in the Bank column because a cheque has been drawn on the bank for this amount; the discount is placed in the Discount column on the same side of the Cash Book. The total of these two items, viz. £35 16s., is posted to the debit of Garcia Brothers in the Ledger.

Garcia Bros., are thus *debited* with £35 16s. for "cheque and discount" because they have received the one and allowed the other. The Bank is *credited* with £35 10s. because it has parted with that sum, and Discount account is *credited*—via the Cash Book—with the 6s. discount received.

		£	s.	d.
June 10.	*Lightwood Bros., Ltd., returned as out of condition 500 Esquisitos sold them on June 4, at 27s. per 100* . . .	6	15	0
	500 Especiales sold them on June 4, at 25s. per 100	6	5	0
	Allowed them full invoice price therefor .	13	0	0

Returns Inwards are, for book-keeping purposes, as has already been explained, treated in the original seller's books as re-purchases of goods previously sold. They must be recorded in the Returns Inwards Book as if they were goods bought in the ordinary way of business from Lightwood Bros., Ltd.

Each of the two parcels of cigars returned is entered in the Returns Inwards Book, the amounts allowed for them, viz. £6 15s. and £6 5s., being entered in the details column. The total of the goods thus taken back, viz. £13, is then "extended" into the total column.

From the Returns Inwards Book the total of the goods taken back is posted to the credit of Lightwood Bros., Ltd. The Returns Inwards Book is added at a later stage, and its total, which, of course, includes the items now being dealt with, is posted to the debit of " Returns Inwards account."

Returns Inwards account is thus *debited* with £13 for the value of the goods received back, and the persons from whom they were received, Lightwood Bros., Ltd., are *credited* with £13 for the value of the goods which have been received back from them.

	£	s.	d.
June 15. Paid from Office Cash Salaries and Wages to date	6	15	0

The Office Cash column on the credit side of the Cash Book is credited with the £6 15s. paid away, and the double-entry completed by posting £6 15s. to the debit of Wages and Salaries account in the Ledger.

"Salaries and Wages" account is thus *debited* with £6 15s. because this expense has been incurred, and Office Cash is *credited* with £6 15s. because it has parted with the money.

	£	s.	d.
June 15. Paid from Office Cash for Electric Light Fittings.	5	7	9

The Office Cash column on the credit side of the Cash Book is credited with £5 7s. 9d., representing the payment of that sum from Office Cash, and the " Furniture and Fixtures " Ledger account is debited with the same amount. Furniture and Fittings are thus *debited* with £5 7s. 9d., representing property received, and Office Cash is *credited* with £5 7s. 9d., representing money parted with.

June 15.	*Sold to W. Miles, on credit—*	£	s	d.
	10,000 *Flor de Cuba, at* 22s. *per* 100 *net.*	110	0	0
	10,000 *Reina Victoria, at* 21s. *per* 100			
	net.	105	0	0
		£215	0	0

These sales are entered in the Sales Book in the same manner as the sales already explained above (June 4th).

W. Miles is *debited*—from the Sales Book—with the £215 worth of goods received by him, and Sales account is eventually *credited* with the same sum (in company with other sales) representing the value of goods parted with.

		£	s.	d.
June 15.	*Returned to Sasso & Escobal, as* "*dam-aged by damp,*" 500 *Especiales bought from them on the 2nd instant* . .	5	5	0

This " Return Outwards " is entered, when it takes place, in the Returns Outwards Book, and from this book a posting for £5 5s. is made to the debit of the Ledger account of Sasso & Escobal. The transaction is treated as if it were a resale to Sasso & Escobal of cigars previously bought from them. The Returns Outwards Book is afterwards added, and its total is posted to the credit of Returns Outwards account.

Sasso & Escobal are thus *debited* with £5 5s. for the value of goods returned to them, and " Returns Outwards " account is *credited* with the same sum because goods of that value have been parted with.

		£	s.	d.
June 16.	*Received from W. Miles, cheque on account* (*paid to Bank*) . . .	262	10	0
	Allowed him discount	2	19	6
		£265	9	6

The £262 10s. received is entered in the debit Bank column in the Cash Book, while the amount of the discount allowed is placed on the same line in the Discount column on the same side of the Cash Book. The total, £265 9s. 6d., is then posted to the credit of W. Miles's Ledger account. At a later date the total of the debit discount column in the Cash Book is posted to the debit of "Discount" account in the Ledger.

The Bank is thus *debited* with £262 10s. because it has received that sum, Discount account is *debited*—*via* the Cash Book—with £2 19s. 6d., because that amount has been lost, or parted with, in that direction, and W. Miles is *credited* with the total of the two items, £265 9s. 6d., because he has parted with a cheque for £262 10s., and has been allowed, in addition, £2 19s. 6d. in the shape of discount.

	£	s.	d.
June 18. *Bought from Arrietta & Co., on credit :*			
10,000 *Princesas,* at 20s. *per* 100, *less*			
5 *per cent. trade discount* .	95	0	0
10,000 *Madeiras, at* 26s. *per* 100 *net*	130	0	0
	£225	0	0

This sale is recorded in the Purchases Book, and is afterwards posted in the Ledger on similar lines to those already explained in the case of the transaction dated June 2.

The 10,000 Princesas bought are entered in the Purchases Book as on June 18, and under the name of Arrietta and Co. the gross amount of the purchase, £100, is entered in the detail column against the description of the goods, and is followed by a deduction of the trade discount, £5, as follows :

	£	s.	d.
Arietta & Co. :			
10,000 *Princesas, at* 20s. *per* 100 . .	100	0	0
Less 5 *per cent. trade discount* . .	5	0	0
	95	0	0
10,000 *Madeiras, at* 26s. *per* 100 *net* . .	130	0	0
	£225	0	0

The 10,000 Madeiras, bought at 26s. net per 100, are entered underneath the net cost of the Princesas, and the total of the purchase, £225, is extended in the right-hand set of money columns.

The £225 is posted to the credit of Arrietta & Co. in the ordinary way, and the total of the Purchases Bill, including these items, is afterwards posted to the debit of Purchases account.

The Purchases account is thus *debited* with the £225 worth of goods received by the business, and Arrietta & Co. are *credited* with the £225 worth of goods they have sold and delivered.

June 18. Paid from Petty Cash:	£	s.	d.
Housekeeper and cleaning to date . .	2	5	0
Fires to date		8	6
Postage and Telegrams to date .		9	6
	£3	3	0

These payments are entered on the credit side of the Petty Cash Book in the Total column.

They are then extended in their proper expense-analysis columns on the same horizontal line. Thence the £2 5s. and the 8s. 6d. are inserted in the "Housekeeper, Fires and Cleansing" analysis column, and the 9s. 6d. is entered in the "Postages and Telegrams" column.

At a later date these expense-analysis columns are added, and their totals are debited to their appropriate nominal accounts in the Ledger. The various expense accounts are thus *debited* with the sums spent in the respective directions, and Petty Cash is *credited* with £3 3s., in all, because it has parted with the money.

	£	s.	d.
June 18. Paid by cheque on account to Arrietta & Co.	150	0	0

The payment of £150 is entered on the credit side of the Cash Book in the Bank column because a cheque for that amount has been drawn. In due course the item is posted to the debit of Arrietta & Co.'s account in the Ledger.

Arrietta & Co. are thus *debited* with £150 because they have received a cheque for that amount, and the Bank is *credited* with the same sum because it has parted with the money.

	£	s.	d.
June 20. Sold to W. Miles 5000 Princesas, at 24s. 6d. per 100, less 5 per cent. Trade Discount	58	3	9

This sale is entered in the Sales Book in the same way as that made to W. Miles on June 15th. The gross selling price of the cigars, £61 5s., is entered in the details column, followed by a deduction of the Trade Discount, £3 1s. 3d. The net selling price, £58 3s. 9d., is extended in the right-hand set of money columns, and is posted to the debit of the Ledger account of W. Miles. The total of the Sales Book, including this item, is afterwards posted to the credit of Sales account.

W. Miles is thus *debited* with £58 3s. 9d., the value of goods received by him, and Sales account is *credited* with the same sum representing the value of the goods parted with.

	£	s.	d.
June 20. *Received from Lightwood Bros. Ltd., a cheque paid to Bank for* . . .	104	0	0
Allowed them discount		2	10
	£104	2	10

The £104 is entered in the debit Bank column in the Cash Book, and 2s. 10d. is entered in the debit discount column. The total of the two items, £104 2s. 10d., is posted to the credit of Lightwood Bros., Ltd.

The Bank is thus *debited* with £104, the money received by it; Discount account is *debited* with 2s. 10d. for a loss made in this direction; and Lightwood Bros., Ltd., are *credited* with £104 2s. 10d., the cash received from them and the discount allowed to them.

	£	s.	d.
June 21. *W. Miles returned, as being of inferior quality, 500 of the Princesas sold him on the 20th June. Allowed him for them, at 24s. 6d. per 100, less 5 per cent. trade discount*		5	16	5

This Return Inwards is treated in similar manner to that already explained under date June 10—the only difference being that there is a trade discount to be deducted.

The gross value of the goods returned, £6 2s. 6d., is entered in the details column in the Returns Inwards Book, and the trade discount, 6s. 1d., is deducted from it. The net invoice value of the goods returned, £5 16s. 5d., is then extended in the total column, and is afterwards posted to the credit of W. Miles.

Returns Inwards account is *debited*, via the Return Inwards

Book, with the value of the goods returned, £5 16s. 5d., because they have been received by the business. W. Miles is *credited* with the same sum because he has parted with the cigars in question.

£ s. d.

June 21. *Returned to Arrietta & Co., 500 Princesas bought from them on the 18th June, as being of inferior quality, being allowed therefor at 20s. per 100, less 5 per cent. trade discount* 4 15 0

In this transaction the goods returned to C. Leslie by W. Miles are returned by the former in his turn to Arrietta and Co., the dealers from whom he originally bought them.

This Return Outwards is treated on similar lines to those explained under date June 15, except for the fact that there is a trade discount to be dealt with.

The gross invoice price of the goods sent back, £5, is entered in the details column in the Returns Outwards Book, and is then followed by the deduction of the 5 per cent. trade discount, 5s.; the net value, £4 15s., is then extended in the total column for posting in due course to the debit of Messrs. Arrietta & Co.'s account, and for inclusion in the total of the Returns Outwards book.

Arrietta & Co. are *debited* with the £4 15s. representing the value of the goods returned to them, and Returns Outwards account is *credited* with the like sum because goods to that value have gone out of the business.

£ s. d.

June 23. *Sold for cash (placed in Office cash), 3000 Superbas, at 22s. 9d. per 100* . . 34 2 6

Office Cash is *debited* with £34 2s. 6d. because it has received the money, and Sales account is *credited* with £34 2s. 6d. because goods to that value have been parted with.

£ s. d

June 24. *Paid by cheque to Sasso & Escobal* 100 0 0
Being allowed discount thereon . . 1 0 0

£101 0 0

The Bank is *credited* with £100 because a cheque for that amount has been drawn, and £1 is entered in the " discount

o

received " column in the Cash Book, to be posted later to the *credit* of Discount account, representing the profit made in that direction. Sasso & Escobal are *debited* with £101 because they have received a cheque for £100, and have made C. Leslie an allowance of £1 as discount.

	£	s.	d.
June 24. Received from W. Miles in cash (placed in Office cash)	12	17	0
Received from W. Miles by cheque (paid to Bank)	200	0	0
Allowed him discount thereon . .	2	3	0
	£215	0	0

£12 17s 0d. is entered in the *debit* cash column in the Cash Book because that sum has been placed in the Office cash-box ; £200 is entered in the *debit* Bank column in the Cash Book because the Bank has received that sum ; and £2 3s. 0d. is placed in the *debit* discount column in the Cash Book because discount to that amount has been allowed. The last item is, at a later date, debited, as part of a total, to Discount account.

W. Miles is *credited* with the total of these three items, £215, because cash has been received from him, and because discount has been allowed to him.

June 24. Paid from Office cash to the Bank, £80 0s. 0d.

The Bank column, on the left hand side of the Cash Book, is *debited* with £80 because the Bank has received this sum, and Cash, on the credit side of the Cash Book, is *credited* with £80 because that sum has been parted with by the Office Cashier,

June 25. Bought from Garcia Brothers on credit :	£	s.	d.
1000 *Conquistadores*, at 20s. per 100, less 2½ per cent. trade discount . .	9	15	0
1000 *Infantes*, at 18s. 6d. per 100 net .	9	5	0
4000 *Reina Isabellas*, at 23s. per 100 net .	46	0	0
	£65	0	0

These purchases are entered in the Purchases Book, and are dealt with in a precisely similar manner to those which occurred on June 18.

Purchases account is *debited* with the total of the invoice, £65, because cigars of that value have been received, and Garcia Bros. are *credited* with the same sum because they have parted with the goods.

June 27. Paid to Garcia Bros., by cheque, on account, £50 0s. 0d.

Garcia Bros. are debited with £50 because they have received that sum, and the Bank, in the credit Bank column of the Cash Book, is *credited* with a like amount, because it has parted with the money.

June 27. Sold to W. Miles on credit :	£	s.	d.
500 *Infantes*, at 20s. 6d. per 100, less 2½ per cent. trade discount .	4	17	5
9000 *Reina Isabellas*, at 26s. per 100 net	23	0	0
	£27	17	5

This sale resembles those already explained on June 4 and June 20. The 500 Infantes sold are entered " short " in the detail column of the Sales Book at their gross invoice price, £5 2s. 6d., the 5 per cent. trade discount, 5s. 1d., being deducted. To the net cost of the Infantes, £4 17s. 5d., the cost of the Reina Isabellas, £23, is then added, and the total of the sale, £27 17s. 5d. is extended in the Total column.

From the Sales Book W. Miles is *debited* with the value of the cigars because he has received them, and " Sales " account is *credited* with a like amount in the total of the Sales Book, because the cigars have gone out of the business.

June 28. Returned to Garcia Bros. 1000 Conquistadores as not being of quality ordered, bought from them on June 25, at 20s. per 100, less 2½ per cent. trade discount, £9 15s. 0d. ·

This Return Outwards is entered in the Return Outwards Book, the gross value of the cigars, £10, being placed in the detail column followed by a deduction of the trade discount, 5s. The net amount £9 15s. 0d., is then extended in the Total column.

Garcia Brothers are *debited* with £9 15s. because the cigars have been returned to them. Returns Outwards account is *credited* with the same sum in the total of the Returns Outwards Book, because goods of that value have gone out of the business.

June 28. Paid to Wright & Co., Carriers, charges for carriage on sundry parcels of goods forwarded to purchasers by them, £3 2s. 6d.

It is not necessary to go to the trouble of opening a Ledger account for Wright & Co. for an isolated item like this. By means of a Journal entry, " Carriage and Cartage " account could have been debited, while Wright & Co.'s account was credited, the cheque drawn being posted to the debit of the latter account. The simple and more usual way, however, of recording a transaction of this nature is to debit the amount of the cheque direct from the Cash Book to " Carriage and Cartage " account in the Ledger. The entry is consequently :

Credit the Bank column in the Cash Book with £3 2s. 6d., because the Bank has parted with the money, and *debit* Carriage and Cartage account with £3 2s. 6d., because that sum has been expended on Carriage and Cartage.

June 29. Drew from Bank for Office Cash, £20.

The Bank account is *credited* with £20 because it has parted with the money, and " Cash " is *debited* with the same sum because the cashier has received it.

June 30. Paid from Petty Cash :	£	*s.*	*d.*
Housekeeper and cleaning to date . .	2	8	10
Fires to date		9	10
Postages and telegrams to date . .	4	4	3
Travelling expenses to date . .	4	3	7

The foregoing payments are first entered in the Total column on the credit side of the Petty Cash Book, and are then extended in their proper analysis columns in that book as in the case of previous similar items already explained.

The £2 8s. 10d. and 9s. 10d. are extended in the column for Housekeeper, Fires, and Cleaning, the £4 4s. 3d. as Postages and Telegrams, and the £4 3s. 7d. as Travelling Expenses. There are no items requiring separate posting to the debit of Ledger accounts, and consequently there is nothing to extend in the Ledger column.

Petty Cash is *credited* with these payments because it has parted with the money, and —*via* the Petty Cash Book—the respective expense accounts are *debited* because the money has been parted with on their account.

June 30. Paid from Office cash Salaries and Wages to date, £12 15s.

The Cash Book is *credited* with £12 15s. in the cash column on the credit side because that sum has been parted with. Salaries and Wages account is *debited* with the same amount because it is for this purpose that the £12 15s. has been paid.

June 30. Drew from the Bank to restore the Petty Cashier's Balance to £20, £19 17s. 9d.

The Petty Cash must be *debited* with £19 17s. 9d. because the Petty Cashier has received the money. The Bank account must be *credited* with £19 17s. 9d. because that sum has been withdrawn from the Bank.

June 30. Granted to W. Miles a special allowance of 6d. per 100 on the 2000 Reina Isabellas sold to him on the 27th inst, owing to their being of inferior colour, 10s.

There is no book of first entry, except the Journal, in which this transaction can be stated in proper double-entry form. An entry in the Journal (p. 222) must therefore be made *crediting* W. Miles with the allowance of 10s. granted to him, and *debiting* Discount and Allowances account with the same sum. The latter account must be debited because a loss in the shape of a special allowance has been made.

Having entered all the foregoing transactions as I have explained, we must now proceed to deal with the various postings which are necessary in order to complete the double-entry in certain instances.

To begin with, the discount columns in the Cash Book must be added; the total of the *debit* discount column must be posted to the *debit* of the Discount account in the Ledger, and the total of the *credit* discount column must be posted to the *credit* of the same account.

You will remember that all discounts allowed on the receipt of money from debtors have been entered in the debit discount column in the Cash Book, and that it has been posted to the *credit* of the Personal accounts of the debtors to whom it has been allowed. The posting of the total of this column to the *debit* of the Discount account equals and offsets all these separate credits, and completes the double entry for them.

Similarly, the posting of the total of the credit discount column in the Cash Book to the *credit* of the Discount account in the Ledger offsets and completes the double entry for the various items of discount which were received from creditors, and were posted to their *debit* on the payment of their accounts.

Next in order the following work should be completed :

(1) The total of the Purchases Book (p. 223), £323 0s. 0d., must be posted to the *debit* of the Purchases account in the Ledger.

(2) The total of the Sales Book (p. 223), £491 11s. 2d., must be posted to the *credit* of the Sales account in the Ledger.

(3) The total of the Returns Inwards Book (p. 224), £18 16s. 5d., must be posted to the *debit* of the Returns Inwards account in the Ledger.

(4) The total of the Returns Outward Book (p. 224), £19 15s. 0d., must be posted to the *credit* of the Returns Outwards account in the Ledger.

These postings are necessary in order to complete the double-entry for the respective transactions which they represent, and they all proceed on the principle of offsetting a *number* of detail postings to the debit or credit of customers' or creditors' accounts, by *one* entry, for their total to the credit or debit in a single Ledger account.

All the purchases made have been posted from the Purchases Book to the credit of the persons from whom the goods have been purchased. The posting of the total of the Purchases Book to the *debit* of the Purchases account offsets all these various *credit* postings and completes the double entry.

Precisely the same principle underlies the posting of the total of the Sales and Returns, Inwards and Outwards, in their respective Ledger accounts.

(5) It is also necessary to complete the double entry for the transactions entered in the Petty Cash Book.

These are of two kinds : (1) those entered in the Analysis columns, and (2) those entered in the Ledger column.

The Analysis columns (*e.g.* Postages and Telegrams, &c.), must all be added, and the totals of the various columns must be posted to the *debit* of their proper loss or expense accounts in the Ledger. The making of this debit entry equalises and offsets the *credit* entry made in the credit " total " column in the Petty Cash Book.

The single item which appears in the " Ledger " column,

" brass door-plates bought, £3 8s. 6d.," must be *debited*, not to a loss or expense account in the Ledger, but to an asset account, viz., Furniture Fittings and Fixtures. This item is consequently debited to that account on p. 225.

This course is followed because certain property, namely, door-plates, has been acquired by the expenditure in question.

The total columns of the Petty Cash Book are balanced in the ordinary way, and the balance in hand, £20, is brought down as on July 1st. The Petty Cash Book is then ruled off.

The Bank and Cash Columns of the Cash Book are similarly balanced and ruled off.

We have now completed the double-entry for every transaction, and may therefore proceed to extract a Trial Balance. The latter is prepared, as you will remember, with a view to discover whether any errors have been made in posting the Ledger.

In order to prepare the Trial Balance, the balance of every account, *i.e.* the difference between the total debit postings and the total credit postings appearing in that account, is ascertained, and is entered in a list of balances prepared in the form illustrated on p. 145. The balances of Cash (£12 1s. 9d.) and of the Bank account (£438 10s. 5d.) shown in the Cash Book are included in the Trial Balance on the side on which they appear in the Cash Book, viz., the *debit* side. The balance of Petty Cash in hand is similarly entered on the debit side.

The Trial Balance thus prepared appears on p. 231. It shows that the total of the debit balances appearing in the Ledger equals the total of the credit Balances, £2496 2s. 3d in each case, and we may therefore assume that the Ledger has been correctly posted.

This is not, as you know, an assumption which is always justifiable, for, as I have explained to you, errors may exist in a Ledger although the trial balance extracted from it " agrees." In practice, however, the book-keeper usually assumes that his work has been done correctly if his Trial Balance does "agree."

Having completed the Trial Balance it now becomes possible—

    (1) To prepare C. Leslie's Trading account and Profit and Loss account for the month of June ; then

    (2) To prepare C. Leslie's Balance Sheet as on June 30, 1910.

I have already fully explained, in Chapters IX. and X., how

you must prepare a Trading account, and a Profit and Loss account. I shall not, therefore, repeat in detail the instructions I there gave you because I want you to re-read these chapters in conjunction with the description of the preparation of C. Leslie's Trading and Profit and Loss accounts which follows.

All the transactions in cigars have, as I have already explained to you, been placed in their proper Ledger accounts according to their nature, viz., Stock, Sales, Purchases, Returns Inwards and Returns Outwards.

In order to prepare C. Leslie's Trading account all these classified accounts must be closed, and their balances must be transferred to the Trading account.

The first item to be placed in the Trading account is the stock of goods which was in hand on June 1. This stock amounted to £686 3s. 5d. For this sum a Journal entry must be made *debiting* the Trading account and *crediting* the stock account.

The next class of transaction to be dealt with is the Purchases—and here we must bear in mind the Returns Outwards. You will remember that goods purchased and afterwards returned to the sellers were allowed to remain in the Purchases Book, although they had been sent back, and that later on they were dealt with separately, when returned, by being entered in the Returns Outwards Book.

The true figure of Purchases for the month is not the amount, £323 0s. 0d., shown in the Purchases account, but that figure *minus* the total of the goods sent back as Returns Outwards, £19 15s. 0d., as shown in the Returns Outwards account.

In order to close the Purchases account a Journal entry is passed crediting Purchases account with the total appearing in it, and debiting this sum to the Trading account. This entry is posted "short" in the Trading account, *i.e.* not in the main set of money columns in the account but to the left-hand side of them.

In order to close the Returns Outwards account, a Journal entry is passed *debiting* this account with the total of the postings appearing in it, and *crediting* the Trading account.

This entry is posted to the Trading account, not on the credit side, but on the *debit* side, immediately under the purchases, and as a deduction from them. The net amount of purchases thus obtained is the true figure for the period, and is extended in the main set of money columns on the debit side of the Trading account.

This entry appears in the Trading account as follows:

		£	s.	d.	£	s.	d.
June 30. To *Purchases*	. . .	323	0	0			
Less Returns .	. .	19	15	0			
					303	5	0

The Sales and the Returns Inwards are treated in the same manner on the other side of the Trading account, and similar Journal entries are passed to record the closing of these accounts.

The next item to be brought into the Trading account is the value of the stock of cigars on hand at the end of June, viz., £612 13s. 4d. For this sum a Journal entry is made *debiting* Stock account (an asset account) and *crediting* the Trading account.

After this entry has been posted in the Trading account, it is possible to find out what gross profit C. Leslie has made by his trading for the month of June, as shown below:

					£	s.	d.
Total of the credit money column	.	.	.	1119	10	7
Total of the debit money column	.	.	.	989	8	5
Difference .	.	.	.	.	.	£130	2	2

This difference is the **gross profit**. It must be debited to the Trading account, and has the effect of causing the two sides of that account to add up to the same total, £1119 10s. 7d. It must be credited to a new account, called the Profit and Loss account, in which it forms the first entry.

A Journal entry is passed for this transaction, *debiting* the Trading account, and *crediting* the Profit and Loss account.

The gross profit brought from the Trading account to the Profit and Loss account represents the difference between the prices at which C. Leslie has sold his cigars and the prices at which he purchased them. It includes no allowance or deduction for the expenses incurred by C. Leslie in carrying on his business. All the expenses incurred in making the gross profit must be deducted from it before the trader can ascertain what profit he has really made, and the Profit and

Loss account is the account in which this process is carried out.

There are seven accounts contained in the Ledger which represent losses made or expenses incurred, viz., Salaries and Wages (folio 9), Stationery (10), Postage and telegrams (11), Discount and allowances (12), General Expenses (13), Carriage (14), and Travelling Expenses (20).

The balances of all these accounts must be transferred, by means of a Journal entry, to the debit of the Profit and Loss account. This Journal entry is given on p. 222.

After these losses and expenses have been debited in the Profit and Loss account it is possible to find out the amount of the net profit made by Mr. C. Leslie during the month of June. The net profit is, as you know, the difference between the Gross Profit, £130 2s. 2d., entered on the credit side of the Profit and Loss account, and the total of the losses and expenses, £43 11s. 1d., entered on the debit side. The net profit is, therefore, £130 2s. 2d. − £43 11s. 1d. = £86 11s. 1d.

By means of a final Journal entry this net profit is *debited* to the Profit and Loss account, and is *credited* to C. Leslie's Capital account. This entry, when posted, closes the Profit and Loss account, and increases the balance of C. Leslie's Capital account to £1293 7s. 4d.

The next step is the balancing and ruling off of all the accounts in the Ledger which still remain open. Since all the accounts which relate to goods, returns, loss, and expense accounts have been closed by means of transfers to the Trading or Profit and Loss accounts, the accounts still remaining open in the Ledger are either (1) asset accounts, (2) liability accounts, or (3) the Capital account. When all these accounts have been balanced and ruled off, a Balance Sheet is prepared from them in accordance with the rules given you in Chapter XI. This Balance Sheet is set forth on p. 232, and shows totals on each side which agree.

In the preparation of this Balance Sheet, the balances due to the various creditors, and from the various debtors, have been grouped together under the heading of Sundry Creditors and Sundry Debtors respectively.

The assets appearing in the Balance Sheet have been ranged in the order of the ease with which they could be converted into money, beginning with the most difficult to realise—that is, with Freehold Premises—and ending with the cash in hand.

PETTY CASH BOOK.

Dr.

Date.	Details.	Folio.	Total. £ s. d.
1910. June 1	To Bank	C.	20 0 0
" 30	" "	C.	19 17 9
			£39 17 9
1910. July 1	To Balance brought down	/	20 0 0

Cr.

Date.	Details.	Total. £ s. d.	Postages and telegrams.	House-keeper and cleaning.	Stationery.	Fires.	Travelling expenses.	Ledger Folio.	Ledger Account.	Ledger £ s. d.
1910. June 6	By Envelopes and letter paper	1 4 9			1 4 9					
1 "	" Brass door-plates	3 8 6						3	Furniture and fittings	3 8 6
"	" Stamps	15 0	15 0							
" 18	" Housekeeper and cleaning	2 5 0		2 5 0						
"	" Fires to date	8 6				8 6				
"	" Postage and telegrams to date	9 6	9 6							
" 30	" Housekeeper and cleaning	2 8 10		2 8 10						
"	" Fires to date	9 10				9 10				
"	" Postage and telegram to date	4 3	4 3							
"	" Travelling expenses	4 3 7					4 3 7			
"	" Balance carried down	20 0 0								
		£39 17 9	£5 8 9	£4 13 10	£1 4 9	£18 4	£4 3 7			£3 8 6
			Debit Ledger Folio 11.	Debit Ledger Folio 93.	Debit Ledger Folio 10.	Debit Ledger Folio 13.	Debit Ledger Folio 20.			

CASH

Dr.

Date.	Details.	Folio.	Discount.		Cash.			Bank.		
			£	c	£	s.	d.	£		d.
1910. June 1	To Balance . . .	J.						240	0	8
„ 1	„ Bank— Cheque per contra .	Contra			50	0	0			
„ 16	„ W. Miles— Cheque and discount .	5	2	19 6				262	0	0
„ 20	„ Lightwood Bros., Ltd. Cheque and discount .	4	^	1'				104	0	0
„ 23	„ Sales— 3000 Superbas sold for cash at 22/9 per 100	17			34		6			
„ 24	„ W. Miles— Cheque, cash and discount . . .	5	2	3 0	12	1	0	200	0	0
„ 24	„ Office cash— Cash paid to bank .	Contra						80	0	0
„ 29	„ Bank— Cheque, per contra .	Contra			20		0			
	Debit ledger folio . .	12	£5	5 4						
					£116	19	6	£887	0	8
1910 July 1	To balances brought down	7			12	1	9	438	10	5

BOOK.

Cr.

Date.	Details.	Folio.	Discount.			Cash.			Bank.		
			£	s.	d.	£	s.	d.	£		d.
1910. June 1	By office cash— Cheque per contra .	Contra							ʀ0		0
„ 1	„ Petty cash— Cheque to petty cashier	P.C.							،0	◡	0
„ 8	„ Garcia Bros— Cheque and discount .	6		6	0				۱5	10	0
„ 15	,; Salaries and wages— Amount due to date .	9				6	15	0			
„ 15	„ Furniture and fittings Cost of electric light, fittings purchased	3				5	7	9			
„ 18	„ Arrietta & Co.— Cheque on account .	8							150	0	0
„ 24	„ Sasso & Escobal— Cheque and discount .	7	1	0	0				100	0	0
„ 24	, Bank— Cash paid to bank .	Contra				80	0	0			
„ 27	Garcia Bros.— Cheque on account .	6							50	0	0
„ 28	,: Carriage— Cheque to Wright & Co. for carriage on goods sold	14							3	2	6
„ 29	, Office cash— Cheque per contra .	Contra							20	0	0
„ 30	„ Salaries and wages— Amount due to date .	9				12	15	0			
„ 30	„ Petty cash— Cheque to restore Petty cashier's balance to £20	P.C.							19	17	9
	Credit Ledger Folio .	12	£1	6	0						
„ „	, Balances carried down	✓				12	1	9	438	10	5
					£	116	19	6	£887	0	8

J   Sundries   *Dr.*

To Sundries, viz. :—
- Bank . . .
- W. Miles .
- Lightwood Bros., Ltd.
- Stock in hand .
- Freehold Premises . .
- Furniture, Fittings and Fixtures
  - Garcia Bros. . . .   0
  - Sasso & Escobal .   6
  - Arrietta & Co. . .   10
  - C. Leslie, Capital Account . .   3

For Assets, Liabilities, and Capital at this date.

7

	Particulars		Fol.	Dr. £	Dr. s	Dr. d	Cr. £	Cr. s	Cr. d
„ 30	Discount and Allowances	*Dr.*	12		1	0			
	To W. Miles		5					10	0
	For special allowance of 6*d.* per 100 on 2000 Reina Isabellas of inferior colour.								
„ „	Trading Account	*Dr.*	21	6 6		5			
	To Stock Account		15				686	3	5
	For Stock as on June 1 transferred.								
„	Trading Account	*Dr.*	21	3 1 1		5			
	To Sundries, viz.:								
	Purchases Account . . .		16				323	0	0
	Returns Inwards Account . . .		18				18	16	5
	For balances transferred.								
„ „	Sundries	*Dr.*							
	To Trading Account		21				545	8	8
	viz.:								
	Sales		17	525	13	8			
	Returns Outwards		19	19	15	0			
	For balances transferred.								
„ „	Stock Account	*Dr.*	15	6 2 1					
	To Trading Account . . .		21				612	13	4
	For stock at this date.								
„ „	Trading Account	*Dr.*	21	1 0					
	To Profit and Loss Account . . .		22				130	2	2
	For gross profit transferred.								
„ „	Profit and Loss Account	*Dr.*	22	3 1					
	To Sundries, viz.:								
	Salaries and Wages . . .		9				19	10	0
	Stationery		10				1	4	9
	Postages and Telegrams . .		11				5	8	9
	Discount and Allowances . .		12				4	9	4
	General Expenses . . .		13				5	12	2
	Carriage		14				3	2	6
	Travelling Expenses . . .		20				4	3	7
	For balances transferred.								
„	Profit and Loss Account	*Dr.*	22	86	11	1			
	To Capital Account . . .		1				86	11	1
	For Net Profit for the month of June transferred.								
			£	2446	16	2	£2446	16	2

Purchases Book.

Date.	Particulars.	Ledger folio.	£	s.	d.	£	s.	d.
1910.								
June 2	Sasso & Escobal.							
	3000 Especiales at 22s. per 100 net	7				33	0	0
„ 18	Arrietta & Co.							
	10,000 Princesas at 20s. per 100		100	0	0			
	Less 5 per cent. trade discount		5	0	0			
			95	0	0			
	1000 Madeiras at 26s. per 100		130	0	0			
		8				22	0	0
„ 25	Garcia Brothers.							
	1000 Conquistadores at 20s. per 100		10	0	0			
	Less 2½ per cent. trade discount			5	0			
			9	15	0			
	1000 Infantes at 18s. 6d. per 100 net		9	5	0			
	4000 Reina Isabellas at 23s. per 100 net		46	0	0			
		6				65	0	
	Debit Ledger folio	16				£323	0	0

Sales Book.

Date.	Particulars.	Ledger folio.	£	s.	d.	£	s.	d.
1910·								
June 4	Lightwood Bros., Ltd.							
	2000 Especiales, at 25s. per 100		25	0	0			
	3000 Exquisitos, at 27s. „ „		40	10	0			
	10,000 Prima Donnas, at 25s. „		125	0	0			
		4				1 0	10	0
„ 15	W. Miles,							
	10,000 Flor de Cuba, at 22s. per 100		110	0	0			
	10,000 Reina Victoria, at 21s. „ „		105	0	0			
		5				2 5	0	0
„ 20	W. Miles,							
	5000 Princesas, at 24s. 6d. per 100		61	5	0			
	Less 5 per cent. trade discount		3	1	3			
		5				8	3	9
„ 27	W. Miles,							
	500 Infantes, at 20s. 6d. per 100		5	2	6			
	Less 5 per cent. trade discount			5	1			
			4	17	5			
	2000 Reina Isabellas, at 26s. per 100		23	0	0			
		5				27	17	5
	Credit Ledger folio	17				£491	11	2

RETURNS INWARDS BOOK.

Date.	Particulars.	Ledger folio.	£	s.	d.	£	s.	d.
1910. June 10	Lightwood Bros., Ltd. 500 Esquisitos, at 27s. per 100　.　.		6	15	0			
	500 Especiales, at 25s. „　„ out of condition　.　.　.　.　.　.		6	5	0			
		4			--	13	0	0
„ 21	W. Miles. 500 Princesas, at 24s. 6d. per 100 .　.		0	2	6			
	Less 5 per cent. trade discount, quality inferior .　.　.　.			6	1			
		5				5	16	5
	Debit Ledger folio　.　.　.	18				£18	16	5

RETURNS OUTWARDS BOOK.

Date.	Particulars.	Ledger folio.	£	s.	d.	£	s.	d.
1910. June 15	Sasso & Escobal. 500 Especiales at 22s. per 100, damaged by damp .　.　.　.　.　.　.	7						0
„ 21	Arrietta & Co. 500 Princesas at 20s. per 100 .　.　.		5	0				
	Less 5 per cent. trade discount, inferior quality　.　.　.　.			5	0			
		8				4	15	0
„ 28	Garcia Bros. 1000 Conquistadores at 20s. per 100		10	0				
	Less 2½ per cent. trade discount, not of quality ordered .　.　.　.　.			5	0			
		6				9	15	0
	Credit Ledger folio　.　.	19				£19	15	0

LEDGER.

1   C. LESLIE, CAPITAL ACCOUNT.   **1**

Dr.   Cr.

1910.			£	s.	d.	1910.			£	s.	d.
June 1	To Balance carried down .	√	1293	7	4	June 1	By Balance .	J	1206	16	3
						„ 30	„ Net Profit for the month of June 1910, transferred from the Profit and Loss Account .	J.	86	11	1
		£	1293	7	4			£	1293	7	4
						1910. July 1	By Balance brought down .	√	1293	7	4

2   FREEHOLD PREMISES.   **2**

Dr.   Cr.

1910.			£	s.	d.				
June 1	To Balance .	J.	655	10	0				

3   FURNITURE, FITTINGS AND FIXTURES.   **3**

Dr.   Cr.

1910.			£	s.	d.	1910.			£	s.	d.
June 1	To Balance .	J.	32	8	2	June 30	By Balance carried down	√	11	4	5
„ 1	„ Cash, for electric light fittings purchased .	C.	5	7	9						
„ 6	„ Petty Cash, brass doorplates purchased .	PC.	3	8	6						
		£	11	4	5			£	11	4	5
1910. July 1	To Balance brought down	√	11	4	5						

LEDGER—*continued.*

4   LIGHTWOOD BROS., LTD.   **4**

Dr.   *Cr.*

1910.			£	s.	d.	1910.			£	s	d.
June 1	To Balance .	J.	104	2	10	June 10	By Returns .	R.I.	13	0	0
„ 4	„ Goods . .	S.	190	10	0	„ 20	„ Cash and dis-count . .	C.	104	2	10
						„ 30	„ Balance car-ried down .	✓	177	10	0
			£	294	12	10			£	294	12	10
1910.											
July 1	To Balance brought down . .	✓	177	10	0						

5   W. MILES.   **5**

Dr.   *Cr.*

1910.			£	s.	d.	1910.			£	s.	d.
June 1	To Balance .	J.	265	9	6	June 16	By Cash and dis-count . .	C.	265	9	6
„ 15	„ Goods .	S.	215	0	0	„ 21	„ Returns in-wards .	R.I.	5	16	5
„ 20	„ „ .	S.	58	3	9	„ 24	„ Cash and dis-count . .	C.	215	0	0
„ 27	„ „ .	S.	27	17	5	„ 30	„ Allowance .	J.		10	0
						„ 30	„ Balance car-ried down .	✓	79	14	9
			£	566	10	8			£	566	10	8
1910.											
July 1	To Balance brought down . .	✓	79	14	9						

6   GARCIA BROS.   **6**

Dr.   *Cr.*

1910.			£	s.	d.	1910.			£	s.	d.
June 8	To Cash and dis-count . .	C.	35	16	0	June 1	By Balance .	J.	35	16	0
„ 27	„ Cash . .	C.	50	0	0	„ 25	„ Goods . .	P.	65	0	0
„ 28	„ Returns out-wards .	R.O.	9	15	0						
„ 30	„ Balance car-ried down .	✓	5	5	0						
			£	100	16	0			£	100	16	0
						1910.					
						July 1	By Balance brought down . .	✓	5	5	0

LEDGER—*continued.*

7   SASSO & ESCOBAL.   **7**

Dr.   Cr.

1910.			£	s	d.	1910.			£	s.	d.
June 15	To Returns outwards	R.O.	5	5	0	June 1	By Balance	J.	227	11	6
„ 24	„ Cash and discount	C.	101	0	0	„ 2	„ Goods	P.	33	0	0
„ 30	„ Balance carried down	✓	154	6	6						
		£	260	11	6			£	260	11	6
						1910. July 1	By Balance brought down		154	6	6

8   ARRIETTA & CO.   **8**

Dr.   Cr.

1910.			£	s.	d.	1910.			£	s.	d.
June 18	To Cash	C.	150	0	0	June 1	By Balance	J.	514	0	10
„ 21	„ Returns outwards	R.O.	4	15	0	„ 18	„ Goods	P.	225	0	0
„ 30	„ Balance carried down	✓	584	5	10						
		£	739	0	10			£	739	0	10
						1910. July 1	By Balance brought down	✓	584	5	10

9   SALARIES AND WAGES.   **9**

Dr.   Cr.

1910.			£	s.	d.	1910.			£	s.	d.
June 15	To Cash, salaries and wages to date	C.	6	15	0	June 30	By Transfer to Profit and Loss Account	J.	19	10	0
„ 30	„ Cash „	C.	12	15	0						
			19	10	0				£19	10	0

10   STATIONERY.   **10**

Dr.   Cr.

1910.			£	s.	d.	1910.			£	s.	d.
June 30	To Sundries, as per Petty Cash Book	P.C.	1	4	9	June 30	By Transfer to Profit and Loss Account	J	1	4	9

LEDGER—*continued.*

11   POSTAGE AND TELEGRAMS.   **11**
Dr.   *Cr.*

1910.		P.C.	£	s.	d.	1910.			£	s.	d.
June 30	To Sundries, as per Petty Cash Book.	P.C.	5	8	9	June 30	By Transfer to Profit and Loss Account.	J.	5	8	9

12   DISCOUNT AND ALLOWANCES.   **12**
Dr.   *Cr.*

1910.			£	s.	d.	1910.			£	s.	d.
June 30	To W. Miles, allowance on cigars of inferior colour .	J.	0	10	0	June 30	By Sundries, as per Cash Book .	C	1	6	0
„ 30	„ Sundries, as per Cash Book .	C.	5	5	4	„ 30	„ Transfer to Profit and Loss Account.	J.	4	9	4
		£	5	15	4			£	5	15	4

13   GENERAL EXPENSES.   **13**
Dr.   *Cr.*

1910.			£	s.	d.	1910.			£	s.	d.
June 30	To Sundries, as per Petty Cash Book— Housekeeper and Cleaning	P.C.	4	13	10	June 30	By Transfer to Profit and Loss Account	J	5	12	2
	Fires . .	P.C.		18	4						
		£	5	12	2			£	5	12	2

14   CARRIAGE.   **14**
Dr.   *Cr.*

1910.			£	s.	d.	1910			£	s.	d.
June 28	To Cash, Wright & Co., carriage on sundry goods delivered by them to the purchasers .	C.	3	2	6	June 30	By Transfer to Profit and Loss Account	J.	3	2	6

LEDGER—*continued*.

15 **STOCK.** **15**
Dr. *Cr.*

1910.		£	s.	d.	1910.			£	s.	d.
June 1	To Balance . . J.	686	3	5	June 30	By Transfer to Trading Account . . J.		686	3	5
1910.										
June 30	To Trading Account . . J.	612	13	4						

16 **PURCHASES.** **16**
Dr. *Cr.*

1910		£	s.	d.	1910.			£	s.	d.
June 30	To Sundries, as per Purchases Book . . P.	323	0	0	June 30	By Transfer to Trading Account . . J.		323	0	0

17 **SALES.** **17**
Dr. *Cr.*

1910.		£	s.	d.	1910.			£	s.	d.
June 30	To Transfer to Trading Account . . J.	525	13	8	June 23	By Cash Sales . C.		84	2	6
					„ 30	„ Sundries, as per Sales Book . . S		491	11	2
		£ 525	13	8				£ 525	13	8

18 **RETURNS INWARDS.** **18**
Dr. *Cr.*

1910.		£	s.	d.	1910			£	s.	d.
June 30	To Sundries, as per Returns Inwards Book . . R.I.	18	16	5	June 30	By Transfer to Trading Account . . J		18	16	5

19 **RETURNS OUTWARDS.** **19**
Dr. *Cr.*

1910.		£	s.	d.	1910.			£	s.	d.
June 30	To Transfer to Trading Account . . J.	19	15	0	June 30	By Sundries, as per Returns Outwards Book . . R.O.		19	15	0

LEDGER—*continued.*

20   TRAVELLING EXPENSES.   **20**

Dr.   *Cr.*

1910.			£	s.	d.	1910.			£	s.	d.
June 20	To Sundries, as per Petty Cash Book . .	P.C.	4	3	7	June 20	By Transfer to Profit and Loss Account	J.	4	3	7

21   C. LESLIE.   .   **21**

Dr.   TRADING ACCOUNT for the month of June 1910.   *Cr.*

1910.			£	s.	d	1910.			£	s.	d.
June 1	To Stock . .	J.	680	3	5	June 30	By Sales— £ s. d. 525 13 8 *Less* Returns 18 16 5	J.	506	17	3
„ 30	„ Purchases— £ s. d. 323 0 0 *Less* Returns 19 15 0	J.	303	5	0	„ „	By Stock . .	J.	612	13	4
„ „	To Balance, being gross profit, transferred to Profit and Loss Account. .	J.	130	2	2						
		£	1119	10	7			£	1119	10	.

22   C. LESLIE.   **22**

PROFIT AND LOSS ACCOUNT for the month of June 1910.

Dr.   *Cr.*

1910.			£	s.	d.	1910.			£	s.	d.
June 30	To Salaries and Wages .	J.	19	10	0	June 30	By gross profit, brought from Trading Account . .	J	130	2	
„	„ Stationery .	J.	1	4	9						
„	„ Postage and telegrams .	J.	5		8						
„	„ Discount and Allowances.	J.	4		9						
„	„ General Expenses .	J.	5	12	2						
„	„ Carriage .	J.	3	2	6						
„ „	„ Travelling Expenses .	J.	4		3						
„	„ Balance, being net profit, transferred to Capital Account. .	J	86	11	1						
		£	130	2	2			£	130	2	2

C. LESLIE.

TRIAL BALANCE, June 30, 1910.

		Dr. £	s.	d.	Cr. £	s.	d.
1	Capital Account				1206	16	3
2	Freehold premises	655	10	0			
3	Furniture, fittings and fixtures .	41	4	5			
4	Lightwood Bros., Ltd . . .	177	10	0			
5	W. Miles	79	14	9			
6	Garcia Bros.				5	5	0
7	Sasso & Escobal				154	6	6
8	Arrietta & Co.				584	5	10
9	Salaries and wages	19	10	0			
10	Stationery	1	4	9			
11	Postage and telegrams . . .	5	8	9			
12	Discount and allowances . . .	4	9	4			
13	General expenses	5	12	2			
14	Carriage	3	2	6			
15	Stock in hand (June 1, 1910) . .	686	3	5			
16	Purchases	323	0	0			
17	Sales				525	13	8
18	Returns Inwards	18	16	5			
19	Returns Outwards				19	15	0
20	Travelling expenses . . .	4	3	7			
C.B.	Cash at bank	438	10	5			
C.B.	Cash in hand	12	1	9			
P.C.	Petty Cash	20	0	0			
		£2496	2	3	£2496	2	3

C. LESLIE.

BALANCE SHEET, JUNE 30, 1910.

Liabilities.	£	s.	d.	£	s.	d.	Assets.	£	s.	d.	£	s.	d.
*Sundry Creditors—							Freehold premises				655	10	0
?ia Bros.	5	5	0				Furniture, fittings and fixtures				41	4	5
Sasso & Escobal	154	6	6				Stock of cigars in hand				612	13	4
A?h & G.	584	5	10				*Sundry Debtors						
				743	1	4	I. Glitwood Bs., L d.	177	10	0			
C. Leslie, Capital account				1293			W. Miles	79	14	9			
											257	4	9
							Cash—						
							At the bank	438	10	5			
							In hand	32	1	9			
											470	12	2
				£2037	4	8					£2037	4	8

* NOTE.—I have set out the details com- for the items Sundry Creditors and Sundry Deb ts, in order that you may f le ach account to the balance sheet. In actual business, and in r to an examination question, the items would simply appear in one tota as—

	£	s.	d.
Sundry Creditors	743	17	4
Sundry Debtors	257	4	9

CHAPTER XIV

EXAMINATION PAPERS

THE following pages contain a selection of examination papers set during recent years at various public examinations in elementary book-keeping. The papers reproduced have been issued by nine different examining bodies, and the standard of each of these nine examinations differs, in certain respects, from the others.

The papers set by any given examining body often resemble each other very closely from year to year, but as between d.fferent examining bodies, the papers issued vary greatly as regards form and style.

The author desires to record his indebtedness to each of the public bodies whose examination papers are reproduced here, for their courteous permission to reprint the questions.

UNIVERSITY OF OXFORD LOCAL EXAMINATIONS.

March 1909.

SENIOR AND JUNIOR CANDIDATES.

Reproduced by special permission of the Delegates.

(1½ hours allowed.)

(You will receive, with this paper of questions, six pages of ruled paper representing the "Cash Book." The work is to be done on these.)

The following is a Trial Balance of my accounts as on December 31, 1907. The Stock on hand at that date was £1200.

Prepare

    (a) Trading Account showing Gross Profit.*

    (b) Profit and Loss Account showing Net Profit.*

    (c) Balance Sheet.†

	Dr.			Cr.		
	£	s.	d.	£	s.	d.
Purchases	8500	0	0			
Bills Payable				620	0	0
Machinery and Plant	1200	0	0			
Capital Account				10,000	0	0
Carried forward .	£9700	0	0	£10,620	0	0

* Questions marked thus were to be worked by all Candidates.

† The question marked thus was only to be worked by "Senior" Candidates.

	Dr.			Cr.		
	£	s.	d.	£	s.	d.
Brought forward .	9700	0	0	10,620	0	0
Drawings Account	2000	0	0			
Buildings . . .	6000	0	0			
Mortgage on Buildings				3,000	0	0
Manufacturing Wages	2700	0	0			
Salaries	1300	0	0			
Rates and Taxes	210	0	0			
Sales				21,980	0	0
Purchase Returns				815	0	0
Rates and Taxes (Manufacturing Charge) .	300	0	0			
Lighting and Power (Manufacturing Charge)	290	0	0			
Cash Sales				1,200	0	0
Sales Returns	1000	0	0			
Cash in hand and at Bank . .	1600	0	0			
Depreciation of Machinery . .	110	0	0			
Repairs to Plant and Premises .	85	0	0			
Bills Receivable	3400	0	0			
Sundry Debtors	6500	0	0			
Depreciation of Buildings . .	90	0	0			
Interest on Mortgage . . .	150	0	0			
Stock on hand (Jan. 1, 1907)	1900	0	0			
Discounts allowed . .	92	10	0			
Travelling and General Expenses . .	187	10	0			
	£37,615	0	0	£37,615	0	0

Interest on Capital must be written up at the rate of 10 per cent. per annum,* and provision of £1000 made for Bad and Doubtful Debts.†

UNIVERSITY OF OXFORD LOCAL EXAMINATIONS.
July 1909.
SENIOR AND JUNIOR CANDIDATES.

Reproduced by special permission of the Delegates.

(1½ hours allowed.)

(You will receive, with this paper of questions, sheets of ruled paper representing the "Cash Book," "Journal," and "Ledger," together with a sheet for the Trial Balance. The work is to be done on these.)

1. On July 1, 1907, I had a balance at my Bankers of £1200, being my Capital. I purchased from Messrs. Snell & Co. their business of Leather Dressers, taking over the whole of their Assets and Liabilities for the sum of £1000, which I paid by cheque the same day.

* Debit Profit and Loss account with £1000 and credit Capital account.
† Debit Profit and Loss account with £1000 and credit Reserve for Bad and Doubtful Debts account; the latter account is a liability, and appears in the Balance Sheet as a deduction from the £6500 Sundry Debtors.

The Assets and Liabilities comprised—

	£	s.	d.		£	s.	d.
Goodwill	200	0	0	Trade Creditors	250	0	0
Plant	500	0	0	Bill Payable	150	0	0
Debtors.	300	0	0				
Stock-in-trade	300	0	0				
Bill Receivable	100	0	0				

2. The following were the transactions for July, August and September: July 3, Received at bank on account sundry debtors, £285 ; And allowed as discount, £15 ; July 12, Sold to Jones, goods value £120 ; July 15, Bought from Taylor, goods value £200 ; July 19, Jones advised damage of goods in transit, allowed for same, £10 ; July 23, cash sales, £45 ; July 28, I advised Taylor shortage in quantity of goods bought from him, he allowed me £25 ; Aug. 6, Accepted Taylor's bill at one month for £175 ; Aug. 10, Drew bill on Jones for one month, he accepted same, £110 ; Aug. 14, Paid repairs to plant by cash, £22 ; Aug. 19, Sold to Smith small portion of plant, received cash, £30 ; Sept. 4, Sold goods to Evans, £160 ; Sept. 5, Received cheque from Evans, £160 ; Sept. 9, Bill payable, duly paid by bank, £150 ; Sept. 10, Taylor's bill duly paid by cash, £175 ; Sept. 12, Cash for Jones's bill duly received by bank, £110 ; Sept. 15, Paid to trade creditors by cheque, accounts amounting to £220, they allowed me discount of £12 ; Sept. 16, Sold goods to Robinson value £200. He paid cash and I allowed him discount of £10 ; Sept. 18, Sold goods for cash, value £85 ; Sept. 19, Purchased goods for cash, value £60 ; Dec. 30, Petty expenses paid by cash, £10 9s. ; Paid wages by cheque, £25 6s. 8d. ; Paid rent by cheque, £50 13s. 4d. ; Paid rent by cash, £5 ; Paid cash to bank, £50.

Senior and Junior Candidates.—Write up the Cash Book with Columns for Discount, Cash, and Bank. Make the necessary Journal Entries for the above, and post all items to their respective accounts in the Ledger. Show in Cash Book the Cash and Bank Balances as on September 30. Also prepare Trial Balance.

Senior Candidates only.—The Stock on hand on September 30 was £223 4s. After making provision for depreciation of Plant at the rate of 10 per cent. per annum,* you are required to prepare—

(1) Profit and Loss Account.
(2) Balance Sheet.

(*Note.*—Cash and cheques are not to be journalised, nor is it necessary to open a Cash and Bank Account in the Ledger. All cheques are paid direct into Bank.)

UNIVERSITY OF CAMBRIDGE LOCAL EXAMINATIONS.

July 24, 1909.

JUNIOR STUDENTS.

(2 hours allowed).

(*Handwriting and neatness of work will be considered in awarding marks.*)

1. On May 1, 1909, my books showed the following balances: Creditors in account, C. Deeler, £321 10s. 6d. ; H. Deeler, £95 ; Debtor

---

* Debit Profit and Loss account and credit Plant account.

in account, O. Johnston, £37 15s. 6d.; Stock of sheep, £487 10s. 6d.; Balance at bank, £291 3s. 4d.; Stock of cattle, £537 10s.; Bills receivable, £250. All payments are made by cheque, and all amounts received are paid into the bank upon receipt. The accounts for sheep and cattle are to be kept separate.

The following are the transactions during the month of May :

1909. May 1, Settled C. Deeler's account as follows : accepted his draft (at one month) for £150, gave him bill receivable (No. 3) for £100, and my cheque for the remainder £71 10s. 6d., £321 10s. 6d. ; May 8, Bought cattle from H. Deeler, £87 5s. 6d. ; Bought sheep from C. Deeler. £51 ; Also bought at auction, paying by cheque, cattle, £13 7s. 6d., and sheep, £94 17s. 3d., £138 4s. 9d.; May 22, Sold to O. Johnson, sheep, £110 17s. 7d., and cattle, £66 10s., £177 7s. 7d. ; May 31, Cash sales during the month :, Sheep, £135 10s., £263 ; My acceptance to C. Deeler paid by the Bank, £150 ; Paid wages and expenses for the month, £31 17s. 3d. Open the Books on May 1, 1909, by means of the proper Journal entries, and (a) Journalise all the transactions in order of date. The Cash entries are not to be summarised. Bills are to be inserted in the Journal ; supplementary books, such as Bill books or Bought and Sold books, are not to be opened. (b) Post the Ledger from the Journal. No marks will be given for the Ledger posted otherwise than as directed. (c) Take out the Trial Balance. (d) Having struck the Trial Balance, close the books, and draw up a Balance Sheet, taking the stock of cattle as worth £570, and the stock of sheep as worth £310, and making the necessary Journal entries for Profit and Loss. 2. On February 15 I despatched goods valued at £21 10s. to A. Train & Sons, Calcutta, to be sold by them on commission. Freight cost me £4 13s. 10d.; Dock dues, £1 19s. 3d. ; Insurance, £2 15s. ; and Cartage 15s. 6d. On June 23 I received from Messrs. Train & Sons Account Sales with cheque for £240 13s. 4d., the balance due to me after deducting their expenses and commission. Make the Journal entries necessary to record these transactions and to show the resulting profit or loss.

UNIVERSITY OF CAMBRIDGE LOCAL EXAMINATIONS.

December 17, 1909.

JUNIOR STUDENTS.

(2 hours allowed.)

(Handwriting and neatness of work will be considered in awarding marks.)

1. At the end of October 1909 my books showed the following balances : Creditor in account, T. Brian, £219 11s. 6d. ; Debtors, J. Clark, £88 12s. 9d., and H. Penn, £57 19s. 5d. ; Bills payable, £293 ; Bills receivable, £750 ; Bank, £273 7s. 3d. ; Goods, £1280. All payments are made by cheque, and all amounts received are paid into the bank upon receipt.

The following are the transactions for November 1909 :

1909. Nov. 3, Bought goods from C. Hicks, £117 12s. ; Nov. 5, Settled Brian's account by cheque. He allowed me £4 11s. 6d. discount, £215 ; Nov. 9, Sold goods to H. Penn, £34 17s. 6d. ; Nov. 13, Bill receivable (No. 2) for £150 matured and was paid into my bank,

£150 ; Nov. 16. Sold goods to H. Penn, £53 8s. 6d.; Nov. 17, Accepted from H. Penn in full settlement for goods purchased before the beginning of November, £54 13s. 5d. ; Nov. 25, J. Clark, having failed, paid a composition of 13s. 4d.* in the £, £59 1s. 10d. ; Nov. 31, Cash purchases during the month, £50 ; Cash sales during the month, £233 15s. ; Paid all trade expenses for the month, £53 12s. 4d. Open the Books on November 1, 1909, by means of the proper Journal entries, and (a) Journalise all the transactions in order of date. The cash entries are not to be summarised ; bills are to be inserted in the Journal ; supplementary books, such as Bill books or Bought and Sold books are not to be opened. (b) Post the Ledger from the Journal. No marks will be given for the Ledger posted otherwise than as directed. (c) Take out the Trial Balance. (d) Having struck the Trial Balance, close the books, and draw up a Balance Sheet, taking goods on hand as worth £1160, and making the necessary Journal entries for Profit and Loss. 2. On April 17 H. Kennedy received from R. Tamplin goods (ordered by Kennedy) to the value of £35. At the same time Tamplin sent Kennedy an order for goods amounting to £53 17s. 9d. Kennedy despatched these on April 19 and sent with them certain other goods on approval valued at £27 13s. 5d. On April 27 Tamplin wrote accepting a portion of these invoiced at £12 19s. and returned the rest together with some of his own goods on approval invoiced at £23. Kennedy accepted these and on May 11 received a cheque from Tamplin balancing the account. Write out (i) Tamplin's account in Kennedy's Ledger, and (ii) Kennedy's account in Tamplin's Ledger.

UNIVERSITY OF CAMBRIDGE LOCAL EXAMINATIONS.
December 18, 1909.
JUNIOR STUDENTS.
(2 hours allowed.)

(*Handwriting and neatness of work will be considered in awarding marks.*)

1. At the end of October 1909 my books showed the following balances : Creditor, C. Fisher, £217 10s. ; Goods, £817 ; Bills payable, £219 ; Debtors, T. Carpenter, £73 2s. 9d. ; S. Fry, £69 8s. 4d. ; R. Joiner, £53 17s. 5d.; Bank, £119 4s. 11d. All payments are made by cheque, and all amounts received are paid into the bank upon receipt.

The following are the transactions for November 1909.

1909. Nov. 4, Bill payable (No. 2) matured and was paid by bank, £18 10s. ; Nov. 6, Bought goods from C. Fisher, £35 ; Nov. 11, R. Joiner settled his account by cheque ; I allowed him £1 17s. 5d. discount, £52 ; Nov. 16, Sold goods to T. Carpenter, £29 13s. 3d. ; Nov. 19, Accepted C. Fisher's draft for £200, and gave him my cheque for £52 10s. ; Nov. 23, Sold goods to S. Fry, £41 3s. 4d.; Nov. 25, T. Carpenter paid on account, £40 ; Sold goods to B. Merry, £27 16s. 5d. ; Nov. 31, Cash purchases during the month, £43 5s. ; Cash sales during the month, £123 17s. 2d. ; Paid trade expenses for the month, £41 11s. 9d. Open the Books on November 1, 1909, by means of the proper Journal

* Credit the irrecoverable 6s. 8d. in the £ to J. Clark's account and debit it to Profit and Loss account.

entries, and (*a*) Journalise *all* the transactions in order of date. The Cash entries are not to be summarised. Bills are to be inserted in the Journal; supplementary books, such as Bill books or Bought and Sold books, are not to be opened. (*b*) Post the Ledger from the Journal. No marks will be given for the Ledger posted otherwise than as directed. (*c*) Take out the Trial Balance. (*d*) Having struck the Trial Balance, close the books and draw up a Balance Sheet, taking goods on hand as worth £750, and making the necessary Journal entries for Profit and Loss. 2. The Trial Balance below contains three errors which you should be able to detect, and no others. Make any alterations which you think necessary, state why you make them, and show by adding the columns that the Dr. and Cr. totals then agree.

£	s.	d.		£	s.	d.
49	3	4	R. Leslie	85	14	1
847	3	11	Goods	219	4	4
			F. Fairfax	53	14	6
275	3	6	Bank	159	7	10
420	0	0	Bills Receivable	629	10	0
79	10	0	K. Longhurst			
29	3	6	Discount	35	11	9
103	14	4	Salaries and Wages			
			Trade Expenses	39	19	6
200	0	0	Bills Payable	375	0	0
845	15	7	Capital			
£2849	14	2		£1598	2	0

COLLEGE OF PRECEPTORS.

2ND CLASS (OR JUNIOR) EXAMINATION.

Midsummer, 1909.

(1½ hours allowed.)

1. Enter into a Cash Book, with Discount columns, the following transactions of a business firm. Then balance cash and discount. No Journal required.

1909. Jan 1, The firm has in hand, £179 15*s*. 4*d*.; Jan. 2, Cash sales for the day, £13 11*s*. 9*d*.; Jan. 5, Pay for office expenses, £3 7*s*. 11*d*.; Jan. 12, T. Wyld settles his account, £82 4*s*., less discount allowed, £1 2*s*. 9*d*.; Jan. 15, Discounted with Fry & Co., bills amounting to £250, less discount allowed, £3 10*s*.; Sundry cash purchases, £5 6*s*. 7*d*.; Jan. 16, My acceptance due this day duly met, £36 2*s*. 9*d*.; Jan. 18, Forward to S. Williams the amount of his account, £300; Less discount allowed, £7 10*s*.; Jan. 20, A composition is made by Phillips of 12*s*. 6*d*. in £; I receive my dividend on £64, £40; Jan. 25, Various amounts paid in by debtors, £27 15*s*. 9*d*; Less discount allowed, £1 7*s*. 9*d*.; Withdrew for private expenses, £10; Jan. 26, I discharge debts to creditors, £17 10*s*.; and am allowed a rebate of 5 per cent.; Jan. 27, Wilson & Co. in settlement of debt of £150 pay this to me, less discount, £2 10*s*.; Jan. 30, Amounts forwarded by collector, R. Brown's account, £15 19*s*. 9*d*.; T. Smith's account, £16 17*s*. 4*d*.; Pinnock & Co., £14 13*s*. 3*d*.; less his expenses, £4 7*s*. 9*d*.; Monthly expenses paid, £13 18*s*. 9*d*.; Salaries, £18 14*s*. 3*d*.; Received rent for part of premises let, £4 15*s*.; Monthly rent and taxes paid, amounting to £14 17*s*. 4*d*

2. Journalise the following transactions in an unclassified form. Then post into a ledger. Then balance the ledger, ascertain the net capital and the net profit or loss. No Trial Balance to be made. Separate accounts for port and sherry.

1909. Feb. 1, On hand, 3 butts sherry (duty paid) at £70, £210; debts due to firm—A. Savage, £42 7s. 6d.; F. Romer, £119 2s. 8d.; Debts owing by firm—J. Porter, £68 3s. 5d.; Feb. 5, Bought of E. Wedgwood, 6 pipes of port, at £60, £360; Sold to W. J. Ross, 1 butt sherry, at £80, £80; Feb. 6, Sold James Hagger, 2 butts sherry, at £71, £142; Feb. 8, Received of W. J. Ross his acceptance at 2 months, £80; Feb. 10, Received of James Hagger, £138 9s. (for amount of his account, £142, less discount, £3 11s.); Feb. 11, Sold A. W. Hemming, 5 pipes of port, at £65, £325; Feb. 12, Received of F. Romer, cash, £119 2s. 8d.; Feb. 13, Paid into a bank account, £170; Accepted draft of E. H. Wedgwood at 1 month, £360; Feb. 15, Paid duty, by cheque, for A. W. Hemming, on 1 pipe port, £31 1s. 9d.; Feb. 16, Drew cheque for clerk on account of petty cash, £10, for salary in advance, £12; A. W. Hemming paid into my bank account, £31 1s. 9d. 3. Change 425 dollars 45 cents into English coinage, reckoning that £1 = 4 dollars 85 cents. 4. What is meant by (a) *Dishonoured Bill*, (b) *Discounted Bill*, (c) *Bill of Exchange*, (d) *a Promissory Note*?

COLLEGE OF PRECEPTORS.

2ND CLASS (OR JUNIOR) EXAMINATION.

Christmas, 1909.

(1½ hours allowed.)

A.

1. After reading the Statements below, open the Books by the usual Journal entries. 2. Write up the Cash, Bank, and Discount entries in the Cash Book. 3. Enter the remaining Transactions in the Journal. 4. Write up from these Books separate Ledger accounts for tea, coffee, and the consignment, and show gain or loss on each. 5. Ascertain, by means of a Profit and Loss account, the net gain or loss for the period.

(*Note.*—All receipts are at once paid into the Bank and all payments are made by cheque, unless otherwise stated.)

BALANCE SHEET OF MR. R. REDHED AT DECEMBER 31, 1908

Liabilities.	£	s.	d.	*Assets.*	£	s.	d.
Sundry Creditors—				Bank	234	10	0
Black & Co., Ltd.	200	0	0	Cash	20	0	0
W. White & Co.	186	15	0	Bill Receivable (P.			
Bill Payable	105	5	0	Pink, due Jan.			
Capital Account	2600	0	0	24/27, 1909) .	100	0	0
				B. Brown & Co.	152	0	0
				Tea .	850	0	0
				Coffee	735	10	0
				Goodwill .	1000	0	0
	£3092	0	0		£3092	0	0

The following are his transactions during January, 1909 :

1909. Jan. 2, Sold B. Brown & Co.—300 lb. tea, £23 15s.; 240 lb. coffee, £13; Jan. 4, Discounted P. Pink's bill, due January 24/27 at bank, being charged 5s. discount, £99 15s.; Jan. 8, Bought of W. White & Co., 2700 lb. tea at 1s. 2½d. per lb. and gave them our acceptance at 3 months for same, paid carriage thereon, £7 ; Jan. 11, Received from B. Brown & Co. their acceptance at 1 month, £100, together with their cheque to settle their account outstanding on December 31, 1908, £49 10s.; Jan. 14, Sold to Gold & Co.—220 lb. tea, £19 5s. ; 100 lb. coffee, £5 16s. 8d. ; Jan. 16, Consigned to M. Vert & Cie., Paris, 4000 lb. tea, value £233 6s. 8d. ; Expenses thereon due to S.E. Railway Co., £11 10s. ; Jan. 20, My acceptance due this day met at bank, £105 5s. ; Jan. 25, Bought of W. White & Co, 2000 lb. tea at 1s. 2d. per lb. ; Jan. 26, Bought of Black & Co., Ltd, 3000 lb. coffee at 1s. 3d. per lb. ; Jan. 27, Bill receivable (P. Pink) dishonoured, noting charges, &c., paid from bank, 10s. 6d. ; Jan. 28, Paid W. White & Co., to settle their account due 1st inst., £174 ; Jan. 29, Received from M. Vert & Cie., Paris, sight draft (being proceeds of sale of one-half of the tea consigned to them, less their commission £17), £150 ; Jan. 30, Paid salaries, £20 ; Paid wages, by cash, £5 ; Paid sundry charges, by cash, £3 10s. ; Rent of shop, due to Mr. Yellow (landlord), for month, £8 6s. 8d.; Drew for self, £5 ; Values of stock on hand—Tea, £920 ; Coffee, £880.

(*Note.*—Salaries, Wages, Sundry Charges, and Carriage may be posted to one Ledger account—"Trade Expenses.")

B.

1. Explain briefly and concisely these terms in connection with cheques—*endorsed, dishonoured, not negotiable, forged, refer to drawer*, and *& Co.* 2. B. Black owed Robert Red £40. Black became bankrupt and his estate realised a first and final dividend of 6s. 8d. in the £. What is meant by "a first and final dividend"? What did Red receive ? What entries would you expect to find in his books ?

ROYAL SOCIETY OF ARTS EXAMINATIONS, 1908.
Stage I.—Elementary.
(3 hours allowed.)

1. What is a voucher ? Briefly describe the system upon which you would arrange vouchers in a business.

2. What entries are necessary in my books to record the fact that A. has become my creditor for goods supplied by him to me?

3. In the following account—

JOHN JONES in account with WILLIAM SMITH.

1908.

Feb. 22. To Welsh coal supplied, by J. Jones's order to S. McNeil, at Glasgow £256 5 10

Who owes the £256 5s. 10d., and to whom is it owing ?

4. Write up a Cash Book recording the following transactions—

Jan. 1, 1908. Balance in hand this day, £217 10s. 1d. ; Jan. 3, Paid into bank, £100 ; Jan. 4 Received from Tom Smith, £69 10s. ; Jan. 4,

Allowed discount to him, 10s. 9d. ; Jan. 7, Received from E. Owen and paid into bank, £116 1s. 9d. ; Jan. 10, Paid one quarter's rent, £30 ; Jan. 10, Paid G. Nash by cheque on bankers, £151 12s. 10d. ; Discount allowed thereon, £4 7s. 2d.

Balance the account and bring down the balance.

5. On which side of the following accounts should the balance, if any, always be, and why ?—

Bills Payable, Bills Receivable, Cash.

EXERCISE.

6. On December 1, 1907, Charles Dickson commenced business with following assets : Cash at bank, £500 ; Cash in hand, £100 ; and Fixtures, £150. The following transactions took place during December—

Dec. 2, Purchased goods of T. Bell, value £100 ; Dec. 3, Purchased goods of Black & Co., value £80, for cash, and paid him for same ; Dec. 9, Sold to W. Brown goods value £50 ; Dec. 16, Paid T. Bell's account by cheque, less 5 per cent. discount ; Dec. 18, Sold goods to R. Walters value £10 ; Dec. 31, Received of W. Brown cash in settlement of his account, less 2½ per cent. discount. Open the necessary Ledger accounts and post direct the above facts and transactions. Balance these accounts as on December 31, 1907, and bring down the balances.

ROYAL SOCIETY OF ARTS EXAMINATIONS, 1909.
STAGE I.—ELEMENTARY.
(3 hours allowed.)

1. What do you understand by the terms "balance down," "trial balance," and "balance sheet" ? What is the chief difference between the last two ? Does the term "balance down," closing the debit side of an account, mean that the account is in credit, or in debit, and why ?

2. Give a form of Cash Book you would recommend as suitable for recording both cash and bank transactions. Start the book with a balance at the bank, and draw a cheque in favour of "self," the proceeds of which are to be used in making cash payments. Make six further entries on the debit side, paying all receipts into the bank, and six further entries on the credit side, three being cash payments and three payments by cheque ; balance the Cash Book and carry down the balances.

3. On February 27, 1909, John Jones sold William Smith 3 lb. of tea at 1s. 9d., 2 lb. of sugar at 6½d., 2 ozs. of Jordan almonds at 2s. 6d. per lb., and 3 tins of potted salmon at 5s. 4d. the dozen. Make an Invoice of the goods supplied.

4. On April 3, 1908, Thos. Fisher sold George Kent goods to the amount of £30 15s. ; on May 4, Kent paid Fisher £20 5s. on account ; on April 30, Fisher sold Kent £45 10s. of goods ; on May 31, Kent paid Fisher £31 10s. on account ; on June 4, Kent returned to Fisher £5 10s. goods (not being up to sample) ; on June 12, Fisher sold Kent £42 8s. of goods ; on June 30, Kent paid Fisher the balance owing upon the transactions of April 3 and 30, after deducting 2½ per cent. discount.

Q

together with a further amount of £20 on account. As on June 30; Fisher sent a three months' statement to Kent. Draw the statement so sent.

5. On May 31, 1908, George Kent paid Thos. Fisher £32 10s. He paid this by cheque on the Credit Banking Company, Ltd. Sketch the form of cheque he would use, and "draw" it, making it as secure as you can against loss by theft or mischance.

EXERCISE.

6. On January 1, 1908, J. Ferguson started business as a grocer, and paid £200 into the Union Bank by way of capital. On that day goods were delivered by McDonald & Co. to him which he had previously ordered to the value of £50, and for which he paid by cheque, deducting 5 per cent. discount for cash. The same day he made "cash sales" amounting to £4 6s. 2d., which he paid into the bank.

On January 2, he drew and cashed a cheque for £5 for petty cash purposes and purchased for cash 5s. worth of stamps and 15s. worth of stationery. The cash sales on this day amounted to £1 7s. 7d., which he paid into the bank ; and he also sold goods on credit to Mrs. Murphy amounting to £2 4s. 6d., and to Mr. Graham amounting to £1 4s. 4d.

On January 3, he bought further goods from McDonald & Co. amounting to £25 16s. 10d., but this time the purchase was on "credit terms." On January 4, Mrs. Murphy paid £1 on account of the goods supplied to her, and this amount (together with the cash sales for two days, £4 3s. 7d.) was paid into the bank. On the same day he supplied goods amounting to £1 16s. 10d. on credit to Mr. Graham, who, at the time of ordering, paid for the goods supplied on January 2, less 4s. 4d. discount, and this amount was paid to the bank. On January 5, he bought goods on credit from W. McNab & Sons amounting to £14 12s. 8d., and paid McDonald & Co.'s account, less 5 per cent. discount, by cheque.

Open Ledger Accounts and post direct the above transactions. Then balance the accounts, and bring down the balances.

ROYAL SOCIETY OF ARTS EXAMINATIONS.
STAGE I.—ELEMENTARY, 1910.
(3 hours allowed.)

Candidates are expected to rule the necessary Cash columns and other lines for themselves, with the exception of the Ledger accounts, which will be found provided in the working pages.

1. Give three "business terms" and three "business abbreviations," and explain the meaning of each. 2. When goods are sent to a customer, what is said to be sent with them (or by an early post) recording the transaction? Give an example. How does this document differ from a "statement"? 3. On January 4, 1909, John Brown purchased goods of Thomas Smith to the amount of £252 4s. 3d. On January 8, Brown returned £51 2s. 5d. of these goods as being faulty, and sent Smith £50 on account. On January 15, Brown purchased of Smith £72 5s. 8d. of goods and paid him £60 on account. On January 31, Smith sent Brown a statement showing the balance owing to Smith, and this Brown paid to him on February 1. How much was-

this balance? Give a copy of Brown's account in Smith's Ledger recording the above transactions. 4. Explain the meaning of the word "discount." In what books of a trader do the records of discounts usually appear? 5. Write up a Bank account recording the following transactions:

Dec. 1, 1909, balance at my bank, £3215 14s. 1d.; Dec. 2, Drew cheque for self, £25; Dec. 4, Paid in £9634 received from W. Porter; Dec. 6, Drew cheque for T. Kerr, £161 10s.; E. Milner paid into my Bank account, £864; Dec. 10, Drew cheque for J. Coleman, £10,000; Dec. 15, Drew cheque for Black & White, £241 6s. 3d.; Dec. 24, Drew cheque £50 for rent, and paid into bank £91 6s. 8d. received from H. Jackson; Dec. 31, Drew cheque £25 for self; Paid into bank £51 received from Duff Bros. Interest allowed on the account by the bank, £18 9s. 3d., and commission charged £1 2s. 3d. Balance the account and bring down the balance.

EXERCISE.

James Cripps started business as a coal merchant on July 1, 1909, paying (as his capital) to his bankers, £250; purchasing, for £50, a horse and van from Timothy Toogood, and 60 tons of coal at 11s. 6d. from the Stiff Colliery Co., Ltd., which were duly delivered. On July 2, he sold 15 cwt. of coal at 1s. per cwt. for cash. On July 3, he sold 12 cwt. of coal at 11d. per cwt. for cash, and 5 tons at 19s. a ton to Miss Graham on credit. He paid the Stiff Colliery Co. Ltd. (by cheque) £25 on account and drew a cheque for £1 for petty cash. On July 4, he sold 14 cwt. of coal at 1s. 1d. per cwt. for cash, and 2 tons at 19s. 6d. a ton to Mrs. Smith on credit. He received and paid into his bank a cheque from Miss Graham, in payment of her account, less 10s. allowed for short weight. On July 5, he sold 20 tons of coal at 18s. 6d. a ton to A. Evans and received from him £10 on account, which he paid into his bank. He sent the Stiff Colliery Co. Ltd., a cheque in settlement of their account, less 2½ per cent. discount. On July 6, he paid Timothy Toogood £50 by cheque. Open Ledger accounts and post the above transactions *direct* thereto. Balance the accounts, and bring down the balances.

THE LONDON CHAMBER OF COMMERCE.

JUNIOR EXAMINATION, 1909.

(2 hours allowed.)

1. State the objects of the following books and the methods of using the same, upon the basis of the double entry system: Cash Book, Purchase Book, Returns Inwards Book, Bills Receivable Book. 2. Some of the balances in John Jones's Ledger on October 1, 1907, were: A. Fell, Cr., £300; R. Lion, £165; B. Smith, Dr., £171; A. Seal, £300; Bills payable, £200; Stock on hand, £855; Rent due, £75; Petty cash in hand, £18; Cash at bank, £550 5s. Open the Ledger.

Enter the following transactions in the proper subsidiary books, and post the same to the Ledger:

Oct. 1, Bought of A. Fell, cloth, £180; Bought of R. Lion, cloth, £335; Oct. 4, Sold to A. Seal, cloth, £220; Oct. 6, Sold to B. Smith, cloth, £112 10s.; Oct. 8, Paid A. Fell, by cheque, £300; Oct. 10,

Accepted R. Lion's draft, £500, at three months from this date; Oct. 13, Received from A. Seal, cheque, £292 10s.; Allowed A. Seal, discount, £7 10s.; Paid cheque for rent £75; Oct. 15, Sold A. Seal, cloth, £118 5s.; Oct. 18, Sold B. Smith, cloth, £216 10s.; Oct. 20, At B. Smith's request drew on him for £500 at three months; Oct. 23, Discounted B. Smith's acceptance at my bankers, who charged for discount, £4; Oct. 24, Paid bills payable, £200; Oct. 26, Bought of R. Lion, cloth, £250; Oct. 28, Sold B. Smith, cloth, £225 10s.; Oct. 31, Drew the following cheques: Salaries, £30; Petty cash expenditure for month, £16; Private drawings, £40; B. Smith returned cloth damaged, £25. Balance the Ledger accounts and bring down the balances.

3. On June 30, 1908, after the first twelve months' trading, W. Boyce obtained from his books, &c., the following information:

He had stock in hand on June 30, 1908, £2000. His purchases and wages had amounted to £15,000, and his sales to £16,500. He had paid or brought into account rent, rates and taxes £753, salaries £400, travelling expenses £300, travellers' commission £360, trade expenses £482, carriage outwards £150. Discounts allowed by him were £250, discounts received by him £225. After allowing £15 for depreciation, the furniture, &c., was valued at £285. Private drawings amounted to £700, book debts due to him £4000, creditors (including bills payable) £2500, cash at bank and in hand £715. Prepare the trial balance (bringing into account W. Boyce's capital at commencement, which is the sum required to complete the trial balance). Also prepare Trading and Profit and Loss Account and a Balance Sheet as on June 30, 1908.

4. What is a contingent liability? Give an example.

THE LONDON CHAMBER OF COMMERCE.

JUNIOR EXAMINATION, 1910.

(2 hours allowed.)

1. On July 1, 1909, George Field, who then commenced business as a merchant, borrowed, free of interest, from B. Tree, the sum of £750 in cash, with which sum he on the same day opened an account with the London Banking Co., from whom he received a cheque book, containing sixty cheques.

During the month of July, George Field's transactions appeared from his books to be as follows:

July 2, Drew from bank for petty cash, £10; Purchased from A. Smith, goods, £750; July 4, Sold to B. Tree, goods, £375; July 8, Purchased from A. Smith, goods, £1500; A. Smith drew on George Field at three months for the sum of £1125; July 10, Sold to B. Tree, goods, £900; July 11, Drew from bank for petty cash, £22 10s.; July 13, B. Tree paid by cheque, £525; July 14, Consigned to G. Tom, of Paris, on own account and risk, goods valued at £750; July 18, Purchased from A. Smith, goods, £1050; Drew from bank for petty cash, £22 10s.; July 21, Sold goods for cash, which sum was paid into bank on the same day, £20; July 23, Sold goods to B. Tree, £450, and drew on him at three months from this date for a like amount, £450; July 24, Repaid by cheque, £81 15s. standing at debit of an account in George Field's name with the City Banking Co., £81 15s.; Returned to A. Smith soiled goods invoiced at £75; July 25, Drew from bank for petty cash, £22 10s.; Paid A. Smith, by cheque, £750; July 27, Discounted with the London Banking Co. bill receivable, £450, and was charged for discount, £5 10s.; July 31, Received from G. Tom account sales of consignment, together with draft on Abel & Co. for net proceeds, £825; Paid draft into bank, £825; Paid A. Smith, by cheque, £750; Received from B. Tree invoice for agreed price of office furniture and fixtures, £75, which sum was placed to the credit of B. Tree's account, £75; Sold B. Tree, goods, £525.

The summary of petty cash payments for the month was: Salaries, £20; Trade expenses, £21 10s.; Fire insurance paid on July 8, £6 Personal drawings, £25. Stock on hand, July 31, was valued at £400 Outstanding liabilities not yet brought into account were: Printing and stationery, £22 10s.; Office repairs, £7 10s. Accrued liabilties were: Gas, £2; Rent, one month at £300 per annum. Pass the entries through the usual books of account, take out Trial Balance and prepare Trading Account, Profit and Loss Account, and Balance Sheet as on July 31, 1909.

2. State the errors, if any, which appear in the following Trial Balance made out by a merchant's clerk for the year ended December 31, 1909.

	£	£
Capital Account		2000
Sundry Debtors	1000	
Sundry Creditors		800
Goods Account		1250
Trading Expenses, Rent, &c.	500	
Salaries and Wages	300	
Goodwill		600
Bank overdraft	500	
Furniture and Fixtures	200	
Drawings Account	450	
Leasehold Premises, value at January 1, 1909	1600	
	£4550	£4550

3. What are the principal books of account in a merchant's office? State very briefly their uses.

4. What do you understand by "reconciliation of bank balance"? What is the procedure to effect it?

MIDLAND COUNTIES UNION OF EDUCATIONAL INSTITUTIONS.

ELEMENTARY, 1908.

Part I. Compulsory.

On September 1 Messrs. Carter and Co.'s position was as follows:

Cash in hand, £750; Cash at bank, £1100; Bills receivable: Adams and Co., £215; Cope & Co., £360; Coal on hand, 1500 tons at 15s., £1125; Coke on hand, 900 chaldrons at 10s., £450; they owed the Gas Company £375 10s.; Rainsford & Co., £284 5s.; and Smith & Co. £340 5s.

The following were their transactions for the month:

September 3, Purchased from Smith & Co., gravel, 185 loads at 7s., £64 15s.; Sept. 4, Forwarded to Smith & Co. (acceptance payable in 10 days), £64 15s.; Sept. 5, Adams's bill paid at bank, £215; Sept. 6, Forwarded to Adams & Co., coals, 360 tons at 18s., £324; Sept. 8, Forwarded to Gas Co., cheque, £150; Sold to Burchell, G., coals 240 tons, at 17s. 6d., £210; Sold to Burchell, G., coke, 144 chaldrons, at 12s. 6d., £90; Sold to Burchell, G., gravel, 36 loads, at 10s.; £18; Sept. 12, Received from Burchell, G., cheque, and paid same into bank, £180; Sept. 15, Sold to Adams & Co., coal, 160 tons, at 18s., £144; Sold to Cope & Co., coal, 72 tons, at 18s., £64 16s.; Sold to Burchell, G., coal, 36 tons, at 18s., £32 8s.; Sept. 17, Bank honour acceptance, £64 15s.; Adams & Co., paid cash for goods—discount, £3 12s. 6d., £140 7s. 6d.; Sept. 20, Paid to Bank, £137 7s. 6d.; Purchased coal from Rainsford & Co., 820 tons, at 10s., £656; Purchased coal from Smith & Co., 120 tons, at 17s. 6d., £105; Purchased coke from Gas Co., 64 chaldrons, at 12s., £38 8s.; Purchased gravel from Smith & Co., 24 loads, at 6s., £7 4s.; Paid Ransford by cheque for goods—discount £16, £640; Sept. 22, Gave Smith & Co. acceptance for 1 month, £340, and cash £7 4s.; Sept. 23, Sold Cope & Co., coal, 180 tons, at 19s., £171; Sold Cope & Co., coke, 140 chaldrons, at 15s. 6d., £87 10s.; Sold Cope & Co., Gravel, 42 loads at 7s. 6d., £15 15s.; Sept. 30, Cash paid for salaries and expenses, £136 15s. 10d.; Cope & Co. settle their account by paying cash, £330.

Coal on hand on Sept. 30, £1401 12s.; Coke on hand, £358; Gravel on hand, £45 17s.

Post the above transactions into the proper books of account, take out a Trial Balance, and prepare a Profit and Loss Account and Balance Sheet on Sept. 30.

Part II.

(Four questions only are to be attempted. Answers are to be given briefly.)

1. Define Capital, and show clearly how I could have £1000 Capital, and at the same time only £1 cash. 2. What do you do with each of the following balances—Balance of Profit and Loss Account; Capital Account; Trade Expenses; Goods Account; Discount Account? 3. Explain clearly the terms—Acceptance, Promissory Note, Draft, Assets and Liabilities. 4. Rule a form of Sales Day Book, suitable for a manufacturer who makes three distinct classes of articles, and give three specimen entries. 5. What do you understand by B/R, B/P, Days of Grace? What is meant by Discounting a Bill? 6. Write out a Silk Mercer's Invoice for Goods Sold, amounting to more than £100, and give the form of a Bill at 3 months' date, drawn by the mercer on his customer for the amount.

THE MIDLAND COUNTIES UNION OF EDUCATIONAL INSTITUTIONS.

ELEMENTARY EXAMINATION, 1910.

(3 hours allowed.)

Part I. Compulsory.

Mr. F. Connor's books disclosed the following assets and liabilities on June 30, 1909:

	£	s.	d.	£	s.	d.
Cash in hand	74	9	6			
Cash at London and City Bank . .	477	19	2			
C. Porter, Dr.	35	9	4			
H. Willis, Dr. . .	24	17	2			
C. W. Harrison, Dr. .	10	17	3			
Stock on hand . . .	500	6	0			
J. Berry				54	17	2
P. White .				21	18	0
R. Spencer				14	15	7
Hy. Smithson				64	9	6
Capital				967	18	2
	£1123	18	5	£1123	18	5

Open the books by a Journal entry, enter up and post the following, after which make out a Trial Balance, a Profit and Loss Account, and a Balance Sheet, as at July 31, 1909.

Note.—Candidates may (a) write up and balance the Cash Book, and journalise the remaining transactions, or (b) journalise all the transactions. Additional marks will be given for writing up and balancing the Cash Book.

1909. July 1, Paid cheque to J. Berry in settlement of his account, £53 10s.; July 3, Sold goods to D. Kemp, £67 14s.; Received cash from H. Willis, £23 18s. 6d.; Allowed discount, 18s. 8d.; July 5, Paid H. Smithson, cheque, £62 17s. 3d.; Discount, £1 12s. 3d.; July 7, Sent C. Porter credit note for goods soiled, £1 18s. 6d.; July 10, Purchased from R. Spencer, goods, £43 19s. 7d.; July 11, Paid cheque to R. Spencer, £14 8s.; Was allowed discount, 7s. 7d.; July 13, Lent to C. Scotson, cheque, £25; July 14, C. Porter, paid on account, £20; July 17, C. W. Harrison, paid in settlement, £10 10s.; July 18, Sold to H. Willis, goods, £38 19s. 5d.; July 20, Paid rent, £25; July 21, C. Porter, bought goods, £43 17s.; July 22, Cash received from D. Kemp, £50; Paid into London and City Bank, £120; July 23, Received cash from C. Porter, £13 10s. 10d.; July 27, Sent cheque to R. Spencer, £41 15s. 7d.; Discount, £2 4s.; July 30, Sales for cash for the month, £47 10s.; July 31, Sundry trade expenses (cash), £7 16s.; Wages paid for the month (cash), £25; Stock of goods on hand, £413 10s.

Part II.

(Four questions only are to be attempted. Answers are to be given briefly.)

1. Give the meanings of the following: º/ₒₒ, º/ₒ, I O U, folio, consign. 2. What stamp is required on an I O U? 8. Write out a receipt for £3 14s. 7d. as if F. Connor received it from C. Sharpe on December 30, 1909. 4. It is proposed to charge C. Scotson £1 5s. for interest on the loan made July 13, in Part I. Show the entry you would make to charge him. 5. What is a Balance Sheet? 6. What do you understand by a 'crossed cheque'?

THE MIDLAND COUNTIES UNION OF EDUCATIONAL INSTITUTIONS.

PRELIMINARY CERTIFICATE EXAMINATION, 1910.

(1 hour allowed.)

Part I. Compulsory.

On January 1, 1910, Mr. George Watson commenced business with £600 in cash, and he made the following purchases, sales, &c ·

1910. Jan. 2, Purchased goods of J. Wild, £35 ; Jan. 6, Sold goods to G. Morgan, £25 10s. ; Jan. 9, Paid for office ooals, 18s. 9d. ; Purchased of T. Parkes, goods, £56 14s. ; Jan. 11, Sold to H. Walker, goods, £37 19s. 6d. ; Jan. 12, Bought sundry goods from auction for cash, £125 15s. 5d. ; Jan. 14, Received cash from G. Morgan in settlement of his account, allowing him discount for the balance, £24 17s. 3d ; Jan. 15, Paid premium for insurance, 16s. ; Jan. 18, Paid J. Wild his account, less $2\frac{1}{2}$ per cent. ; Jan. 20, Received from H. Walker on account, £15 10s. ; Jan. 25, Sold goods to G. Harvey and received cash same time, allowing him a discount for prompt payment, £33 15s. ; Jan. 30, Paid petty cash expenses, £4 4s. 7d. ; Paid wages of man and boy, £7 12s. You are required to enter the above transactions in the Journal and Cash Book, post to the Ledger, and take out a Trial Balance.

Part II.

(*Two questions only are to be attempted.*)

1. What is a Credit Note? 2. What do you understand by Trade as compared with Cash Discount? 3. From information received a merchant decides to "write off" as a bad debt, owing by S. Pearce, for £7 10s. Show the entry you would make to give effect to this. 4. What is a Debit Balance?

COUNTY COUNCIL OF THE WEST RIDING OF YORKSHIRE.

FIRST STAGE, 1909.

(3 hours allowed.)

1. Define fully the use of a Sales Day Book. 2. Two traders A. and B. carry on the same kind of business. A. has a set of books which are properly kept, whilst B. keeps no books, but only has incomplete memoranda of a portion of his transactions. What will A.'s advantages be as compared with B. at the end of a year's trading? 3. What are the points which you would consider it necessary to watch if you were entrusted with the keeping of a Cash Book? 4. On March 9, 1909, Chas. Read commences business and borrows from his father, John Read, £250. March 1, He pays £200 into Commercial Bank ; He becomes tenant of a shop at £4 a month rent ; Paid cash for shop fixtures, £20 : Paid to G. Ellis for stock in shop by cheque, £80 ; Mar. 2, Bought goods from A. Reynolds, £30 8s. 7d. ; Mar. 4, Paid plate glass insurance, 10s. 6d. ; Sold goods to Beale & Co., £10 0s. 5d. ; Sold goods to Ashton & Mills, £3 16s. 4d. ; Paid for cleaning shop, £3 10s. ; Mar. 6, Receipts per shop-

till for week, £18 5s. 6d. ; Mar. 7, Ashton & Mills return goods, 2s 6d. ; Mar. 8, Paid to bank, £30 ; Mar. 11, Sold goods to Beale & Co., £5 19s. 7d. ; Mar. 12, Ashton & Mills pay cash (discount allowed, 3s. 10d.), £3 10s. ; Mar. 13, Receipts per shop-till for week, £19 14s. 3d. ; Paid self for household expenses, £2 10s. ; Paid wages, 2 weeks, £8 16s. 8d.; Mar. 15, Received cheque from Beale & Co., and paid into bank (discount allowed, 8s.), £15 12s. ; Paid to bank, £15 ; Paid for advertising, £2 10s. ; Mar. 16, Sold goods to Beale & Co., £2 0s. 5d. ; Mar. 16, Bought goods from A. Reynolds, £5 4s. 9d. : Mar. 18, Paid rates by cheque, £4 13s. 3d. ; Paid A. Reynolds cheque (discount, 13s. 4d.), £35 ; Mar. 19, Sold goods to Ashton & Mills, £14 3s. 7d. ; Mar. 20, Receipts per shop-till for week, £27 6s. 4d. ; Bought goods from A. Reynolds, £4 3s. 7d. ; Mar. 24, Sold goods to Beale & Co., £4 6s. 11d. ; Mar. 27, Receipts per shop-till for week, £18 9s. 2d. ; Paid month's rent, £4 ; Paid self for household expenses, £3 10s. ; Sold goods to Beale & Co., £1 18s. 4d. ; Paid wages, 2 weeks, £11 ; Mar. 28, Goods returned by Beale & Co., 8s. 11d. ; Mar. 29, Paid for repairs to premises, £4 13s. 6d. Enter in the proper books and prepare Trial Balance. 5. J. Rhodes has the following transactions with B. Sharp—On Jan. 1, 1909, Sharp owes Rhodes £15 8s. 6d. Rhodes sells goods to Sharp : Jan. 28, £4 16s. 9d. ; Feb. 3, £8 17s. 5d. ; Feb. 9, £5 12s. 11d. ; Mar. 4, £13 12s. 9d. ; Mar. 18, £6 14s. 5d. ; Mar. 24, £3 11s. 9d. Sharp returns goods, Feb. 6, £2 16s. 4d. ; Mar. 1, 17s. 11d. Rhodes buys goods from Sharp : Jan. 16, £10 10s. ; Feb. 18, £14 15s. 9d. ; Mar. 25, £3 9s. 2d. ; and on Feb. 28, Rhodes returns goods, £3 5s. 9d. Rhodes allows Sharp discount 5 per cent., and Sharp allows Rhodes 2½ per cent. Make out an account showing how much Sharp owes net at March 31.

COUNTY COUNCIL OF THE WEST RIDING OF YORKSHIRE.

TECHNICAL SCHOOL EXAMINATIONS, 1910.

Third " Year."

(3 hours allowed.)

1. Write up in the Cash Book, Sales and Purchase Day Books, and Ledger the following transactions of John Wilson. Prepare Trial Balance, Profit and Loss account and Balance Sheet, March 31, 1910. Use Journal for closing entries only.

Jan. 1, Cash in hand, £16 15s. ; Jan. 3, Bought goods of M. Noble & Co., £35 ; Jan. 8, Sold goods to S. James, £7 16s. 8d. ; Jan. 19, Bought goods of M. Noble & Co., £4 13s. 4d. ; Jan. 28, Paid trade expenses, £1 11s. ; Paid wages, £7 ; Jan. 31, Sold goods to S. James, £19 2s. ; Feb. 5, Sold goods for cash, £2 7s. 6d. ; Feb. 12, Bought goods from M. D. Knox, £12 16s. 4d. ; Feb. 14, Paid rent, £5 10s. ; Feb. 24, Sold goods to B. Marshall & Sons, £9 19s. ; Feb. 29, Sold goods to S. James, £2 12s. 10d. ; March 5, Received cash from S. James, £29 11s. 6d. ; March 8, Bought goods from M. D. Knox, £9 15s. 4d. ; March 9, Paid cash to M. D. Knox, £22 11s. 8d. ; March 12, Bought goods for cash, £1 13s. 10d. ; March 14, Bought goods from M. Noble & Co., £52 12s. 4d. ; March 19, Paid wages, £7 ; March 24, Paid trade expenses, £1 16s. ; March 31, Stock on hand, £10. 2. Write up in Thomas Walker's Cash Book with columns for Discount, Cash, and Bank, the following items balance the Cash and Bank columns on April 30 :

April 1, Cash in hand, £13 17s. 10d.; April 2, Paid into Bank, £10; April 4, Sold goods for cash, £1 4s. 9d.; April 5, Paid advertisements, 2s. 4d.; April 6, Paid by cheque to Martin & Co., £7 12s. 2d., discount 2s. 10d.; March 8, Received from Barnett & Co. and paid to Bank, £9 5s., discount 25s.; April 9, Received from Hy. Hirst, £1 18s. 4d., discount 1s. 8d.; April 11, Bought goods for cash, £4 5s.; April 13, Received from Benjamin Wright, £1 19s., discount 1s.; April 15, Paid for coals, 15s. 3d.; April 18, Paid to self, £1 17s. 10d.; April 23, Received from Chas. Dearman, £2 18s. 6d., discount 1s. 6d.; Received for goods sold, 17s. 6d.: Paid into Bank the last two items; April 26, Paid to Andrews & Son, £1 10s.; April 28, Cash drawn from Bank, £2 10s.; April 29, Paid Nasmith Bros. by cheque, £9 7s. 6d., discount 12s. 6d.; April 30, Paid sundry expenses, £1 8s. 4d. 3. Give a full description of a Petty Cash Book and the method of using it. 4. State five different kinds of mistake which will cause the totals of the Trial Balance to disagree. Mention an error which will *not* affect the Trial Balance totals. 5. Explain what is meant by "Taking Stock" and describe the process as completely as you can.

LANCASHIRE AND CHESHIRE INSTITUTES.
JUNIOR GRADE, 1909.
(3 hours allowed.)

(*You must first attempt not more than four of the questions in Part I. and afterwards attempt the Statements of Account in Parts II. and III. of this grade.*)

Part I.

1. What is the use of the Journal? Give two examples illustrating the class of items which can be passed through the Journal. 2. What is meant by "Consignment Account"? Albert Jones sends to Jamaica, on consignment account, goods of the value of £600. He also pays for freight and insurance charges £22. What books would these entries be passed through, and how? 3. What do you understand by a "Returns Book"? Make the ruling of such a book for a company who have a number of returns, and whose business is divided into the three following departments: Woollens, cottons, silks. 4. William Robinson owes to you for goods sold to him on July 2, 1908, £275 16s. On July 6, 1908, he sends a Bill for £125 due on October 1, 1908, and also cash on account of the balance, £62 17s. 6d. On October 1, 1908, he fails to meet his Bill, and you pay for noting the dishonoured Bill, 1s. 6d. On December 31, 1908, you receive from his Trustee in Bankruptcy a first and final dividend of 6s. 8d. in the £. Show William Robinson's Ledger Account in your books.

   5. What is meant by—

     (a) Gross profit?
     (b) Net profit?

A man's turnover for the year ending October 31, 1908, is £12,500, his gross profit is £2500, his net profit is £750.

What is the rate per cent. on the turnover for gross profit and also for net profit.

   6. You supply Mr. Lloyd Asquith with goods of the value of £550, and he gives you in payment a Bill of Exchange due on January 1,

1909. On November 1, 1908, you discount the Bill at the rate of 5 per cent. per annum. How much cash will you receive? and give the entry that you will make in your Cash Book on this date.

Part II.

7. On February 1, 1909, Henry Wood commenced business with the following assets: Cash in hand, £50 1s. 6d.; Cash at bank, £864 7s. 6d.; Stock-in-trade, £560. William Jones owes him £162 1s. 3d.; James Slater owes him £124 2s. 6d. His liabilities are: John Jackson, £400 2s. 9d.; A. Wilson, £103 15s.; Webster & Co., £156 15s.

The transactions for the month of February were as follows:

Feb. 1, Sold goods to Wm. Jones, £80 10s.; Feb. 2, Gave bill to A. Wilson at 3 months in settlement of his account, £101; Feb. 3, Paid John Jackson on account (by cheque), £100; Feb. 4, Drew from bank for petty cash, £10; Feb. 5, Cash sales, £125; Feb. 6, Paid into bank, £150; Feb. 9, Bought of Webster & Co., goods, £250; Feb. 11, Received from William Jones, bill at 4 months, in full settlement of his account, £236; Feb. 12, Bought office furniture and fittings (by cheque) £50; Feb. 13, Henry Wood withdraws from bank, for private purposes, £180; Paid out of petty cash, stamps and sundry expenses, £3; Feb. 15, Sold goods to Jas. Slater, £200; Feb. 17, Jas. Slater returns goods as being inferior to sample, £20; Feb. 19, Paid Webster & Co. by cheque, £300, and received discount, £7 10s., £307 10s.; Feb. 23, Paid John Jackson on account, by cheque, £100, and received discount, £5, £105; Feb. 28, Received rent from sub-tenant, £6; Feb. 28, Drew cheque for wages, £60, and paid £57; Feb. 28, Rent *due* to landlord, £36; Credit capital with interest, £6 10s.; Depreciate office furniture, £4.

Enter the above items in the proper books, post to Ledger, and take out Trial Balance.

Part III.

8. From the foregoing, close the accounts, bring down the balances, make out Profit and Loss Account and Balance Sheet. On February 28 the Stock amounted to £484 10s.

LANCASHIRE AND CHESHIRE UNION OF INSTITUTES.

(3 hours allowed).

JUNIOR GRADE, 1910.

You must first attempt not more than FOUR *of the questions in Part I., and afterwards attempt the statements of account in Parts II. and III. of this grade.*

Part I.

1. What do you understand by an "Inward invoice"? Into what book would it be entered and to which side of a personal account in the Ledger would the amount be posted? How would it be dealt with for easy reference? 2. What is the difference between "bankers' discount" and "true discount"? You discount with your banker a bill of exchange at three months for £200, the bank rate being 4 per cent. What amount would your banker charge for discounting such bill? 3. Who are the parties to a bill of exchange? Make out a

bill of exchange, showing the amount of stamp duty, drawn by K. Hindley on J. Thompson for £312 9s. 6d., dated March 5, 1909, at three months' date. Show also the acceptance and endorsement of such bill. 4. On January 1, 1910, John Mason supplies you with goods amounting to £200. His terms are 5 per cent. discount if you pay cash on January 31, or net if you pay by a six months' bill dated from January 1. Which method would you adopt in paying Mason's account, assuming that on January 1, 1910, you had £400 in the bank on which interest was being earned at 3 per cent. per annum? Give reasons for your answer. 5. Define the following terms: (a) Capital expenditure, (b) Revenue account, (c) Depreciation, (d) Mortgage. 6. In taking out the balances of your books you find that your book-keeper has made the following errors: £25 paid for office furniture has been debited to "Trade Expenses Account." Invoice for £23 for goods purchased has not been passed through books, although the goods are included in stocktaking. How would you rectify these errors?

Part II.

7. On December 1, 1909, the balances in Joseph Penn's books stood as follows: Cash in hand, £20 18s. 3d.; Cash at Bank, £123 4s. 2d.; Stock-in-trade, £517 8s.; Fixtures and fittings, £82 3s. There is owing to him by L. Max, £35; by Williams & Son, £26 10s. 7d.; and by Kay & Co., £5 9s. He owes to H. Simpson £408 10s., and to H. Taylor £302 3s. His transactions for the month were as follows:

Dec. 1, Borrowed from W. Sykes on loan, £100; Dec. 2, Bought goods (from H. Simpson for cash £23 12s. 8d., and for credit £55 6s. 2d.) £78 18s. 10d.; Dec. 4, Paid into Bank, £90; Dec. 5, Received bill of exchange at six months in payment of L. Max's account, £35; Dec. 6, Sold to Williams & Son, goods, £87 10s.; Sold goods for cash, £12; Dec. 8, Paid H. Simpson on account (by cheque £200, and received discount £10), £210; Dec. 9, Received from Williams & Son (cheque on account, which was paid into Bank same day £50, and allowed them discount £2 10s.), £52 10s.; Dec. 10, Received credit note from H. Taylor for goods returned, £38 2s. 8d.; Dec. 11, Sold goods to H. Taylor, £100 1s. 6d.; Dec. 12, Drew cheque for petty cash, £10; Dec. 13, Bought stamps out of petty cash, £3 10s.; Dec. 15, Bought of William Smith, goods, £93 1s. 6d.; Dec. 18, Repaid W. Sykes by cheque, being £50 part repayment of loan, and £1 interest to December 31, £51; Dec. 20, Received from Kay & Co. in settlement of their account, £5 2s.; Dec. 22, Received notice from Official Receiver that L. Max has been made bankrupt and has no assets; Dec. 23, Paid salaries out of cash, £8; Dec. 28, Paid carriage out of petty cash, 18s. 6d.; Dec. 31, Railway accounts due but not paid, £5 8s.; John Mason withdraws for private purposes, £15; Credit capital with interest: £2; Depreciate fixtures and fittings, £2 3s. Enter the above items in the proper books, post to Ledger, and take out Trial Balance.

Part III.

8. From the foregoing, close the accounts, bring down the balances, make out Profit and Loss Account and Balance Sheet. On December 31, 1909, the stock amounted to £480 2s. 10d.

NATIONAL UNION OF TEACHERS EXAMINATIONS.
ELEMENTARY, 1909.
(3 hours allowed.)
(*You may answer* ALL *the questions.*)

1. Give the meanings of the following: Account, Commission, Posting, Solvent, Sterling, Voucher. 2. Rule a model Sales Book, and enter two of the following items to each of two names (and dates) of your own choice: 6 gross buttons, at 5*d.* per doz.; 29 yds. silk, at 10*s.* 6*d.* per yd.; 5 doz. hats, at 2*s.* 6*d.* each; 90 ties, at 21*s.* per doz. 3. Each day, from Monday to Saturday (six days), a costermonger bought 17*s.* 6*d.* worth of fruit. His takings were 23*s.* daily. On Saturday night he reckoned he had 2*s.* 6*d.* worth of fruit left. Make out an account, showing his profit for the week.

EXERCISE.

On January 1, 1909, the state of Francis Fair's business was as follows: Cash in hand, £365; Goods on hand, £420. Debtors: B. Best, £115; D. Dean, £80; K. Kew, £315; Creditors: L. Lord, £205; Y. Young, £90. You are requested to find and credit his Capital. Then enter the transactions given below in suitable books, post them to the Ledger, draw out a Trial Balance, balance the Accounts, and make out a Profit and Loss Account and Balance Sheet.

Jan. 1, 1909, Paid rent, £25; Jan. 2, Received of K. Kew, £197 10*s.* (discount in addition, £2 10*s.*), £200; Jan. 4, Paid water rate, £5 5*s.*; Jan. 6, Sales to K. Kew, £120 15*s.* 6*d.*; Jan. 7, Received cash for a bad debt written off last year, £24 12*s.* 8*d.*; Jan. 8, Bought goods of L. Lord, £65 10*s.* 6*d.*; Jan. 9, Received cash of B. Best, £102 12*s.* 6*d.*; Wrote off the balance of his debt as bad, £12 7*s.* 6*d.*; Jan. 11, Cash sales, £90 3*s.* 4*d.*; Jan. 12, Cash purchases, £70 13*s.* 4*d.*; Jan. 13, Received cash of K. Kew, £113 12*s.* 6*d.* (discount in addition, £1 7*s.* 6*d.*), £115; Jan. 14, Paid L. Lord cash, £146 5*s.* (discount in addition, £3 15*s.*), £150; Jan. 15, K. Kew bought goods, £32 8*s.* 4*d.*; Jan. 16, Paid wages, £8 15*s.*; Jan. 18, Y. Young purchased goods, £35 7*s.* 6*d.*; Jan. 19, D. Dean paid me, £78 8*s.* (discount in addition), £1 12*s.*), £80; Jan. 20, Purchases from N. Nash, £136 10*s.*; Jan. 21, Paid Y. Young, cash, £53 (discount in addition, £1 12*s.* 6*d.*), £54 12*s.* 6*d.*; Jan. 22, Sales to D. Dean, £120 13*s.* 4*d.*; Jan. 23, Paid wages, £8 15*s.*; Jan. 25, Paid L. Lord, cash, £53 12*s.* 6*d.* (discount in addition, £1 7*s.* 6*d.*), £55; Jan. 26, D. Dean bought goods, £24 16*s.* 8*d.*; Jan. 27, Paid to N. Nash cash, £35 (discount in addition, £1 10*s.*), £36 10*s.*; Jan. 28, Y. Young sold me goods, £85 10*s.* 9*d.*; Jan. 29, Drew cash for self, £25; Jan. 30, Paid salaries, £35; Jan. 30, Interest on capital, £4 3*s.* 4*d.*; Jan. 30, Stock on hand, £495.

NATIONAL UNION OF TEACHERS EXAMINATIONS.
BOOK-KEEPING.
ELEMENTARY EXAMINATION, 1910.
(3 hours allowed.)
You may answer ALL *the questions.*

1. If you were a clerk in an office, and somebody brought you the Purchases Book and told you to post it, describe fully what you would

do. 2. John Baker, merchant, had cash in hand £100 and goods on hand £200. His creditors were : B. Black, £130 ; G. Green, £250 ; W. White, £120. His debtors were : B. Bray, £50, and M. May, £80. Make out a balance sheet and say what it tells you about the state of his business. 3. Open a Ledger Account for Geo. Scott. Debit him with balance £20. Charge him £1 interest. Credit him with cash £15 and goods £20. Debit him with goods £40, and charge him £2 carriage. Balance his account, bring down the balance, and say whether he or you must pay it.

EXERCISE.

On January 1, 1910, the state of George German's business was as follows : Cash in hand, £420 ; Goods on hand, £510. Debtors : A Ayres, £120 ; B. Baird, £75 ; C. Cass, £250. Creditors : D. Dan, £145 and E. Euston, £55.

You are requested to find and credit his capital. Then enter the transactions given below in suitable books, post them to the Ledger, draw out a Trial Balance, balance the accounts, and make out a Profit and Loss Account and Balance Sheet.

1910. Jan. 1, Received cash of A. Ayres, £104 12s. 6d. ; Wrote off his balance as bad debt, £15 7s. 6d. ; Jan. 2, Received cash (of C. Cass, £147 17s. 6d., allowed him discount £2 2s. 6d.), £150 ; Jan. 3, Paid for stationery, £2 13s. 4d. ; Jan. 4, Cash sales, £95 4s. 6d. ; Jan. 5, Cash purchases, £85 3s. 4d. ; Jan. 6, Sold goods to C. Cass, £145 10s. 4d. ; Jan. 8, Paid wages, £7 15s. 6d. ; Jan. 10, Purchased goods of D. Dan, £75 10s. 8d. ; Jan. 11, Received cash for a bad debt previously written off, £25 5s. ; Jan. 12, Paid for painting premises, £10 3s. 6d. ; Jan. 13, Drew cash for self, £15 ; Jan. 14, Charge B. Baird interest on his overdue account, £1 1s. 6d. ; Jan. 15, C. Cass paid me cash £98 13s. 4d. (and was allowed discount £1 6s. 8d.), £100 ; Jan. 17, Cash paid to D. Dan, £107 12s. 9d. (discount in addition £2 7s. 3d.), £110 ; Jan. 18, Sales to C. Cass, £47 15s. 2d. ; Jan. 19, E. Euston bought goods, £32 10s. 9d. ; Jan. 20, Received cash of B. Baird, £76 1s. 6d. ; Jan. 21, F. France sold me goods, £160 7s. 6d. ; Jan. 22, Paid E. Euston (cash £20 10s., discount in addition £1 19s. 3d.), £22 9s. 3d. ; Jan. 22, Paid wages, £7 15s. 6d. ; Jan. 24, Sales to B. Baird, £110 10s. 8d. : Jan. 25, Paid D. Dan (cash £33 18s. 6d., discount in addition £1 1s. 6d.), £35 ; Jan. 26, Bought goods of E. Euston, £130 15s. 6d. ; Jan. 27, B. Baird purchased goods, £34 9s. 4d. ; Jan. 28, Paid F. France (cash £58 10s. ; he allowed discount £1 10s.), £60 ; Jan. 29, Paid salaries, £32 17s. 6d. ; Jan. 31, Interest on capital, £5 ; Goods on hand, £482 13s. 9d.

COMMERCIAL DEFINITIONS

The simplest points only have been dealt with in these definitions, and in a way which, it is hoped, will enable the young student readily to grasp them. More advanced students will require fuller details, and are referred to the Author's text-book "Book-keeping and Accounts," *Crown 8vo., 760 pp., 3s. 6d. net.*

ACCEPTANCE is the term frequently applied to a Bill of Exchange which has been duly accepted and issued. The amount of money named in the bill is known as its contents.

ACCOUNTS, a term which comes to us from the old French word *compte.* In modern business the word has acquired many meanings, and is capable of wide extension. For present purposes, however, accounts may be simply described as statements recording the nature and history of commercial transactions. **Ledger Accounts** disclose in concise form a trader's dealings (*a*) with persons, (*b*) with things, or (*c*) with regard to profits and losses. The Ledger accounts with persons are periodically (usually monthly or quarterly) copied from the Ledger on ruled and printed forms, and sent to the persons to whom they relate. A Ledger account thus copied it called a **Statement of Account,** or simply a **Statement,** and when it is forwarded to the customer it is referred to as an **Account Rendered.** A Statement gives the dates and amounts of all goods delivered, or services rendered, to a particular customer within a particular period, and also the dates and amounts of any cash paid by him and of any credits to which he has become entitled during that period. The balance of the statement shows the net amount due to date. When an account has been rendered, and it is either (1) unpaid, or (2) only partially paid, so that a balance is outstanding when the time for rendering the statement again comes round, the old statement is not re-copied in its entirety, but the new statement is begun with the balance outstanding on the old statement. The entry in (1) will take the following form, "To Account Rendered, £35"; in (2) "To Balance Brought Forward, £6 7s. 6d."

ACCOUNT CURRENT.—This is a somewhat specialised form of statement sent by one merchant to another, where the relationship between them is not purely that of seller on one side and buyer on the other, but where both merchants sometimes buy from and sometimes sell to each other, and frequently pay money to third parties on each other's account. In this relationship it is customary for merchants to charge and allow interest on the various items. When moneys placed with **a** banker may be added to at any time and withdrawn on demand, the account kept by the banker with his customer is called a **Current Account** (literally a "running account").

ACT OF BANKRUPTCY.—An act which renders a person liable to be made a bankrupt. The following are Acts of Bankruptcy : If an insolvent debtor has (*a*) made an assignment of his property in trust for his creditors generally ; (*b*) made a fraudulent assignment of his property ; (*c*) given any creditor a fraudulent preference over the other creditors ; (*d*) departed out of the reach of his creditors ; (*e*) suffered execution on his goods ; (*f*) filed a declaration that he is unable to pay his debts, or committed certain other specified acts to the injury of his creditors. See "**Bankruptcy.**"

ADMINISTRATOR.—A person appointed by the High Court of Justice to administer, *i.e.* to realise and distribute, an intestate's estate among the persons entitled to it. An **intestate** is a deceased person who has left property but made no will. An administrator must give security to the Court for the faithful performance of his duties. In this respect he differs from an **executor,** who is appointed by a testator, *i.e.* by a person who has made a will, to perform similar duties, but who is not required to provide security.

AD VALOREM (AD. VAL.).—Latin, according to value, a term chiefly applied to the duties levied by the Customs and Inland Revenue departments of the Government. Such duties take the form of a *percentage* of the value involved.

AFFIDAVIT.—A written statement which the maker of it declares on oath to be true before a Commissioner for Oaths, or some other person legally appointed to administer oaths.

AGENT.—(Latin—*agens* = one who acts.) A person authorised to do certain acts on behalf of another, called the **Principal.** The acts of an agent, acting within the scope of his authority, are as binding upon his principal as though the latter had done them himself. The relation of Agent and Principal is very wide in its application. Within certain limits every employee of a trading concern is an agent.

AGREEMENT.—A binding promise or contract between two or more persons. An agreement may be made (1) orally, (2) in writing, (3) partly in writing and partly by word of mouth, or (4) be inferred from the conduct of the parties. See "**Deed.**"

ANNUITY (Latin, *annus* = a year).—A yearly payment of money made either for a stated number of years or during the lifetime of one or more persons. Persons entitled to the benefit of an Annuity are called **Annuitants.**

ARBITRATION.—When disputed questions arising between two or more persons are settled, not by process of law, but by an independent person, or persons, whose decision the contending parties agree to accept, the questions at issue are said to be submitted to arbitration. The person, or persons, selected to **arbitrate** are called **Arbitrators,** and their decision is termed the **award.** Arbitration avoids the expense and delay of a lawsuit. In cases where the arbitrators fail to agree, **a** third party called an **Umpire** is sometimes appointed

ASSETS.—(French, *assez* = enough.) Property of any description. Some assets are called **Liquid** or **Circulating Assets.** These consist of property that can be easily converted into money. Other assets, because they are held by a trader for permanent use in his business, and not for sale, are termed **Fixed Assets.**

AUDIT.—An examination of the accounts and books of a trader, or company, by an independent person, usually a professional accountant. An auditor states the result of his examination in his **Certificate,** or his **Report.**

BAD DEBTS.—Debts which are believed to be irrecoverable.

BANKRUPT.—Legally an insolvent person who, after certain proceedings, has been **adjudicated** a bankrupt by the Court.

BILL OF LADING (B/L).—A receipt, bearing a sixpenny stamp, given by the captain acting for the owners of a vessel for goods received on board for transportation. It sets forth full particulars of the goods and their destination. It is also an agreement, or contract, setting forth the terms on which the goods are accepted for transportation. The effect of a Bill of Lading is that any one who has become lawfully possessed of it is the legal owner of the goods it represents. The B/L represents the goods, which may be bought and sold simply by transferring the B/L. Hence, a merchant who has shipped goods to another merchant abroad often draws a Bill of Exchange on the consignee (*i.e.* the person to whom he has shipped the goods), attaches the B/L to the Bill of Exchange, and sells the documents to a banker. The B/L operates as security for the payment of the B/E, and if the person on whom the B/E is drawn does not pay or "honour" it when it is presented to him, the agents of the bank whose duty it is to secure payment of the B/E may sell the goods and recover the amount due to them.

BILL OF SALE (B/S).—A document by which one person conveys his title to personal property to another. It is usually given as security for a loan which must not be less than £30. If the conditions of the B/S are not complied with, the holder may seize the property mentioned in the B/S and sell it. A B/S must be registered in the proper public office.

BOOK DEBTS.—Debts shown by the Ledger to be owing to a trader by his customers.

CODICIL.—See "Will."

COMMISSION.—When a trader employs an agent to buy or sell goods for him, he usually agrees to pay the agent a percentage on the amount of the goods bought or sold. This percentage is termed **commission.** Similarly, a stockbroker buying or selling stocks and shares for a principal is paid by a commission on the amount of the business transacted.

COMMITTEE.—A limited number of persons selected from a larger body of persons for some particular purpose, *e.g.* persons selected by the members of a club, or company, from amongst their own number to manage the affairs of the club, or company, or to transact such other business as the general body requires to be done.

CONSOLS.—An abbreviation of the word "consolidated," commonly used as part of the names of stocks. When used in this connection it signifies that stocks of various kinds have been merged, or consolidated,

R

into one class of stock. "Consols" or "Consolidated Stock" is the name given to the bulk of the National Debt of this country.

COUPONS.—Small detachable warrants which entitle the holder to obtain payment of the interest due upon bonds, bearer certificates, and bearer debentures. They are commonly in sheets somewhat resembling a sheet of postage stamps, and each bears a date when the interest will become due for payment. See "**Dividend.**"

CREDIT NOTE (C/N).—A statement giving particulars of an amount placed to the credit of the person to whom it is sent. Credit notes are usually printed in red and relate to allowances, returns inwards, &c.

CURRENCY.—(Latin, *currere* = to run.) That which is used in any particular country as the medium of exchange. It is either (*a*) metallic currency or (*b*) paper currency. In the United Kingdom, the metallic currency consists of gold, silver, and bronze coins. The paper currency consists of the notes issued by the Bank of England, the Bank of Ireland, the Scotch Banks, and a few others. These banks are termed **Banks of Issue**, in contradistinction to the other banks which are not allowed to issue notes.

DEBENTURES.—When a Trading Company, Railway, or other institution borrows money the borrower frequently issues to the lenders documents called **debentures.** A debenture is a document promising to repay a certain sum of money at a stated time, and usually undertaking that interest at a stated rate per cent. shall be paid at certain intervals, commonly half-yearly. A debenture frequently also adds that certain assets of the borrower are pledged as security for the due payment of the interest and the repayment of the loan. See "**Coupon.**"

DEBIT NOTE (D/N).—The reverse of a Credit Note. A memorandum giving particulars of an amount which has been placed to the debit of the person to whom it is sent. Debit Notes usually relate to overcharges, returns outwards, &c.

DEED.—It was explained under the heading "**Agreement**" that a binding promise or contract could be made, amongst other ways, "in writing." The most important class of written contracts are **deeds,** *i.e.* contracts made under seal. All other contracts are called **simple** contracts. A deed is a writing sealed and delivered by the persons making it and usually signed by them. The seal or seals are the visible sign that the writing is a deed, but in order to be valid a sealed writing must also be delivered. Delivery is effected by each party to the deed placing a finger upon his seal, after he has signed the deed, and saying, "I deliver this as my act and deed." There is one other point that should be mentioned, viz., that in all **simple** contracts no promise is binding unless it is made for valuable consideration. In a **deed** a promise, then termed a **covenant,** is binding without valuable consideration.

DEPRECIATION.—Machinery, fixtures, leases, and other assets wear out by use, or become lessened in value by effluxion of time. In order to provide for this shrinkage in value a percentage is periodically (usually yearly) deducted from the original cost, or the present value, of wasting assets as disclosed by the trader's books. The amount thus deducted is debited in the Profit and Loss account, and is called **Depreciation.**

DIVIDEND.—That part of the profits made by a company which is distributed amongst the shareholders. Dividends are usually stated as a percentage of the nominal, *i.e.* the face value, of the shares. An **Interim Dividend** is a dividend declared and paid in advance of the final distribution of profits on completion of the yearly audit of the company's books. **Ex-Dividend** (x/d) is a Stock Exchange term meaning that the price at which a particular security is offered for sale does not include the dividend declared, or about to be declared ; **Cum-Dividend** (cum. div.), on the contrary, means that the price does include the dividend declared, or about to be declared.

DOCK WARRANT.—A receipt issued by the dock authorities certifying that certain specified goods have been warehoused for the party in whose favour the warrant has been issued.

ENTRY.—The first record made in the proper book of account is called the **Original Entry** ; other entries, in other books, arising out of this original entry are termed **Posted Entries.** The act of entering the latter is called **Posting** the entries.

ESTATE.—The aggregate property owned by a person. The term is applied specially to the assets of an insolvent debtor, and also to the property left by a deceased person.

EXECUTOR.—A person appointed by a testator in his will to carry out his instructions. See also **Will** and **Administrator.**

FIRM.—Two or more persons who carry on business together with a view to making profit. The name under which the business is carried on is called the **Firm-name.** The members of a firm are called **Partners,** and the association of partners a **Partnership.** Each member of a partnership usually shares in the management of the business, and also shares in the profits or losses in agreed proportions.

FIXED ASSETS.—Property owned and held by a trader for use in his business, and not for sale. See **Plant,** also **Depreciation.**

FIXED CHARGES.—Regularly recurring obligations chargeable against the profits of an undertaking—*e.g.* rent, rates, taxes, interest on mortgages, &c.

FLOATING ASSETS.—Assets whose character is continually changing. Cash, for example, is exchanged for goods ; goods sold are exchanged for either cash or book-debts ; book-debts, in turn, may become cash, and so on.

F. O. B. (Free on Board).—Merchants quote prices for goods in a variety of ways. An F. O. B. price is a price which, in addition to the actual cost of the goods, includes also the cost of packing, removal to the docks, and placing on board the transporting vessel.

F. O. R. (Free on Rail).—This is another form in which the price of goods is frequently quoted by merchants. In addition to the price of the goods, it includes the cost of placing them in railway trucks.

FREIGHT.—The name given (1) to the charge made for transporting goods by sea ; (2) to the actual goods transported.

GUARANTEE.—An undertaking by one person, called the Guarantor, to be responsible for the payment of some debt, or the performance of some act, in case of the failure of another person, who is, or is about to become, liable for such payment or performance. A guarantee must be in writing.

GUARD-BOOK.—A book of blank leaves of cartridge paper to which invoices, vouchers, or other documents are attached and preserved for reference.

HIRE PURCHASE.—A system by which a person called the Hirer, in exchange for instalments of the purchase price of certain goods, paid in agreed sums at fixed dates, enjoys the use of the goods until such time as the instalments paid amount to the full price of the goods, when they become the hirer's own property. In the event of the hirer failing to pay any instalment at the agreed time, the owner may forfeit the instalments already paid, and resume possession of the goods.

INCOME.—Money derived from property, or received as remuneration for services, usually stated at so much per annum.

INCOME TAX.—A tax granted by an Act passed each year by the British Government, and levied on the income of every person whose income is liable to taxation under the regulations of the law. The subject of Income Tax is extremely complicated. No satisfactory instruction can be given in the brief space available here, and the student is therefore referred to the author's treatise, "**Book-keeping and Accounts,**" where the subject is fully treated.

INFANT.—In law, a person under twenty-one years of age. An infant has many legal privileges, and suffers some restraints. The restraints are designed for his benefit. They prevent him from being imposed upon, or injuring himself through improvident acts. He can only be sued in company with his guardian.

INSURANCE OR ASSURANCE.—A contract whereby in exchange for the **premium**, which is sometimes a lump sum, and sometimes consists of equal periodical payments, a company, or person, undertakes (1) to pay a stated sum, called the **sum assured**, on the happening of a particular event, or (2) to make good any loss covered by the contract. The company, or person, is termed the **Insurer**, and the payer of the premium the **Insured**. The contract itself is called the insurance **Policy**. In (1) the event is either the reaching of a certain age by, or the death of, the assured. In (2) the loss made good may be : (a) Loss by fire—**Fire Insurance**; (b) Loss through shipwreck, or other peril of the sea—**Marine Insurance**; (c) Loss through accident—**Accident Insurance**; (d) Loss through death or injury of live stock—**Live Stock Insurance**; (e) Loss through claims awarded under the Employers' Liability and Workmen's Compensation Acts—**Workmen's Compensation Insurance**, &c. &c. The principle of insurance has extended in all directions, and practically every description of loss may now be insured against.

INTEREST.—A charge made by one person for a loan of money to another. It may be likened to rent paid for the use of money lent. The rate of interest, stated at so much per cent., is usually determined by the adequacy of the security offered, and the abundance or scarcity of loanable capital. The latter depends upon (1) the state of trade, (2) political and social conditions.

INVESTMENTS.—Money expended in the purchase of houses, land, stocks and shares, or lent on mortgage, or in other ways, in order to secure the interest or profit to be derived from their possession.

INVOICE.— A written statement of the quantity, description, and price of goods sold by a trader to his customer. It is usually forwarded with the goods. A *Pro Forma* **Invoice** or **Consignment Note** is used instead of an invoice when the goods have been forwarded on consignment, *i.e.* when the customer is not acting as a principal but as selling agent for the trader. At other times a *Pro Forma* invoice is used in order that a prospective buyer may know what the goods will actually cost him before he orders them. But in this case the *Pro Forma* invoice is an actual copy of the invoice, as it would appear if the goods were really bought. A *Pro Forma* invoice is also sometimes used by way of intimation that the goods will only be supplied for cash in advance.

INVOICE BOOK.— A book in which outward invoices are press-copied for office reference. The name is also somewhat loosely applied to a guard-book used for preserving inward invoices, and to a Sales or a Purchases Journal.

I O U.— These letters are the recognised contraction of the words, **I owe you.** An I O U is a written acknowledgment of indebtedness, and does not require a stamp. The following is the common form:

To Mr. A. Harris.
I O U
Ten Pounds.
Joshua Jones.

LEASE.— A document which conveys the use of lands or tenements for life, or for a period of years, in exchange for rent usually payable quarterly, half-yearly, or yearly, or for a fixed sum of money (a **premium**) paid at the outset. The person who conveys or grants the lease is called the **Lessor**; the person to whom he conveys it, the **Lessee.**

LEGACY.— A gift of personal property by will. Government Duty is payable on all legacies, the rate varying with the nearness of the relationship between the testator and the **Legatee,** *i.e.* the person benefiting by the legacy.

LIABILITIES.— The debts owing by traders and companies. For **Limited Liability** *see* **Limited Company. Employers' Liability** is the liability of employers to pay compensation should any of their servants be injured, or killed, in pursuance of their employment. Successive Acts of Parliament have made this liability so serious that prudent business men protect themselves, either by taking out a policy of Insurance, or by creating an "Accident Fund." See " Insurance."

LIFE INSURANCE.— See " Insurance."

LIMITED COMPANY.— A company consisting of a number of persons called **Shareholders,** whose risk of losing money by the operations of the company is *limited* by law to the amount which each has agreed to contribute to the capital, *i.e.* the funds of the company. Thus if one has agreed to contribute £1000, and another £100, the utmost loss they can respectively suffer, in the event of the insolvency of the company, is £1000 and £100.

LIQUIDATION.— Winding up and settling the affairs of a public company. Insolvency is the most frequent cause of liquidation. The person appointed to carry out the work is known as a **Liquidator.** He collects all moneys due to the estate, converts all assets into cash, and divides amongst the creditors and shareholders whatever surplus may remain after all expenses and preferential liabilities have been met. The company whose affairs are being wound up is said to be **In Liquidation.**

MANIFEST.—A document made in accordance with the requirements of the Custom House, and signed by the captain of a vessel, stating, amongst other particulars, the nature and quantity of the goods carried in the ship, and the names of the consignors and consignees. See "**Bill of Lading.**"

MONEY.—Pieces of stamped metal of a definite degree of weight and fineness used as the medium of exchange, and the measure of value. These pieces are called coins, and, as the student knows, the coinage of different countries is not only differently named, but also varies in both weight and fineness. These variations, and also the fact that some countries have adopted gold and some silver as the medium of exchange, give rise to the business of **Foreign Exchange.** Great Britain has adopted gold, and the sovereign is the standard coin. It will be useful to explain "medium of exchange." and "standard of value." In early times **Barter** prevailed, i.e. one thing was directly exchanged for another thing. Thus six sheep might have been exchanged for one horse. Nowadays, the owner of a horse who wishes to exchange it for sheep, first of all exchanges his horse for so much money, and then exchanges the money for so many sheep, Thus money is the medium of exchange. Again, in early times, the value of a thing was measured in other things. Thus, in the illustration given, the value of the horse was six sheep, and *vice versa.* Now we measure the value of a horse, and of all other things, by the amount of money for which it can be exchanged. Thus, we say, e.g. the value of a certain horse is £40. The amount of money anything will exchange for is termed the price of that thing. Just as barter gave way to the use of a medium of exchange, and in course of time the medium adopted was money, so, in turn, the use of metallic money is very largely dispensed with by the employment of representatives of money, e.g. Bank Notes, Cheques, Bills of Exchange, Promissory Notes, &c. The bulk of modern commerce is transacted, not with actual coin, but by means of these representatives of money, and in this way the danger (from robbery), the labour (in counting and transporting heavy metals), and the loss (through coinage and the wear and tear of the coins) attending the use of vast sums in actual coin is avoided, and the operations of commerce greatly facilitated. It was explained earlier in this section that currency consisted of (1) Metals, (2) Paper. The two things must not be confounded, for while both are currency, paper currency is not money, because it is no real standard of value.

MORTGAGE.—A pledge of real estate (lands, buildings, &c.) by the owner as security for a loan. The borrower on mortgage is called the **Mortgagor,** and the lender, the **Mortgagee.** Should the mortgagor fail to pay the interest on the loan, or to repay the sum lent, when called upon to do so under the terms of the mortgage, the mortgagee may sell the property, and deduct from the proceeds the amount of the loan, and also all expenses incurred and all interest accrued. There are many points in connection with mortgages about which the student will have to learn, but these must be left till he is further advanced in his studies.

NEM. CON.—(Latin, *Nemine contradicente* = No one contradicting.) If a proposal, or motion, is made at a shareholders' or other meeting, and when put to the vote is agreed to by all, the proposal is said to be "carried" **nem. con.** The proposal or motion then becomes a **Resolution.**

NET.—The term applied to the price of an article, or to the balance of an account after all allowable deductions have been made. The opposite to **Net** is **Gross.** Thus, if an invoice amounts to, say, £100 gross, and the discount allowed is 5 per cent.—*i.e.* £5—the net amount is £95. When, in a merchant's trade list, you see that a price is marked net, you will know that no discount will be allowed to a purchaser of the article so marked. (See "Net Profit and Gross Profit," Chapter IX.)

NOT NEGOTIABLE.—A cheque is a negotiable instrument. That is to say, if a person becomes possessed of a cheque in good faith, and by giving value for it, he is the lawful owner of the cheque, and is entitled to payment of it. In order to prevent cheques being wrongfully converted, it has become the practice to add to the crossing of the cheque the words "not negotiable." The addition of these words does not affect the *bona fide* transfer of a cheque, but it restricts its negotiability, and no one who takes a cheque so marked can acquire any better title to it than is possessed by the person from whom he takes it. Except when inserted in the crossing of a cheque, the words "not negotiable" have no legal signification when attached to commercial documents. (See Chapter XII.)

PAR.—(Latin, *equal.*) The nominal, or face, value of a security. If a hundred-pound share in a Company were sold for £100 it would be said to have been sold **at par;** if the share in question were sold for £110 it would be said to have been sold at 10 per cent. **above par,** or at 10 per cent. **premium;** if sold for £90 it would be said to have been sold at 10 per. cent. **below par,** or 10 per cent. **discount.**

PATENT.—An official grant giving to the inventor of a new article or process, or the improver of an old one, the exclusive right, *i.e.* the **monopoly** of his invention for a period of fourteen years. In special cases the period of monopoly may be extended for a further limited time. The rights of a **Patentee,** *i.e.* a person who has patented an article or process, cease if certain prescribed annual fees are not duly paid. Where a patent right forms part of a manufacturer's or trader's assets, care must be taken that the cost of it shall be gradually "written off" in the owner's books. "Writing off" in this case means that an annual sum shall be deducted from the Ledger balance representing the cost of the patent, so that, at the end of its estimated "life," *i.e.* at the end of the period during which the patent may be assumed to exist or remain profitable, the Ledger balance shall become extinguished, or reduced to the residual value of the patent.

PERCENTAGE.—The ratio which other figures bear to 100. Thus 5 in relation to 100 is 5 per cent. (five per hundred). So also 50 in relation to 1000 is 5 per cent., 45 in relation to 1000 is 4½ per cent.

PLANT.—The tools, machinery, and other things held by a manufacturer for use in his business. (See "**Depreciation**," also "**Fixed Assets**.")

POST-DATED CHEQUE.—A cheque dated forward. A cheque will not be paid by a banker in advance of the date it bears. Hence a person owing, say £10, due for payment on, say, January 15, and being unable to pay the amount on that date, might, with the consent of his creditor, hand him on January 15 a cheque for the amount, dated January 30. The creditor must then wait till January 30 before he can cash the cheque. Such cheques are possibly a breach of the stamp laws. The opposite of post-date is ante-date.

PROSPECTUS.—A published statement giving full particulars (1) of Government or municipal loans offered for subscription, or (2) of a newly formed company with the object of obtaining shareholders and purchasers of debentures. Severe penalties attach to the publishers of a company prospectus containing untrue statements or omitting essential information.

REBATE.—A deduction or allowance made from specific charges. Thus shippers who undertake to ship their goods by certain companies are given a rebate of so much per cent. on the annual amount paid for freight. Rebate is also used to express the allowance of interest made by a Bank to an acceptor taking up a Bill of Exchange before its due date.

RECONCILIATION STATEMENT. See Chapter II

REMITTANCE.—A sum of money sent by one person to another, whether in the shape of coin, cheque, postal order, money order, or other form.

ROYALTY.—A payment made for the right to use a patent or copyright, or for the right of "winning" minerals from a mine.

SALVAGE.—The money paid for the services of persons, *not of the salved ship's company*, who have saved a ship or cargo from shipwreck, fire, or other disaster. The amount is commonly agreed upon between the owners and the salvors, but in cases of disagreement it is fixed by the Admiralty Court. The goods saved are also described as salvage.

SAMPLES.—Small portions of goods used to represent the quality of the whole. Goods are very frequently bought and sold on sample. The seller guarantees that the characteristics of the sample are the essential characteristics of the bulk; and the buyer on sample has the right, should the bulk not correspond with the sample, to reject the goods.

SET-OFF. If A. claims £100 from B. for goods delivered, or other good reason, and B. has a claim against A. for £50 for money lent, or in respect of any other matter, B. has the right to set-off his claim of £50 against A.'s claim of £100, and A. could only recover from B. the difference of £50. Negotiable instruments are an exception to this general rule.

STATEMENT.—See "Account."

TRUSTEE.—Whenever, by a legal instrument, property of any description is conveyed from one person to another on condition that the property shall be applied to certain specified purposes, a trust is created. The person appointed to administer a trust is called a **Trustee**. An **Executor** (see p. 259) is a trustee, so also in bankruptcy is the person appointed to settle the affairs of an insolvent debtor.

TURNOVER.—A trader's total sales during a given period. The word is usually applied to the total annual sales.

VOUCHER.—A receipt for money paid. A **debenture** is a voucher that the company issuing it has received the amount mentioned therein. Share or stock certificates are vouchers that the amounts due upon them have been paid.

WILL.—The document whereby the **testator,** *i.e.* the maker of the will, gives directions as to the disposal of his property after his decease. A will must be signed by the testator in the presence of two witnesses, who must also sign it, as witnesses, *in his presence and in the presence of each other.* If, at a later time, the testator desires to revoke or otherwise alter any part of his will, he does so by means of a codicil. He may make as many **codicils** as he likes, but each must be signed and attested with the same formality as the will itself. See "**Executor.**"

LIST OF ABBREVIATIONS

@	at	Col.	Column
a/c, acct.	account	Com.;	
a/ce.	acceptance	Comm.	Commission
Admor.	Administrator	Cr.	Credit; Creditor
ad val.	According to value (Latin—*ad valorem*)	Ctge.	Cartage
		Cum. div.	with the dividend
Agt.	Agent	cur.	current
A1	The description of a First-Class Ship in Lloyd's Register of Shipping	C.W.O.	Cash with Order
		cwt.	hundredweight
		D/A	Documents against acceptance
amt.	amount	Dbk.	Drawback
a/o	account of	d/d	days after date
a/or	and or	Deld.	Delivered
A/S	Account Sales	Dely.; D/y	Delivery
Av.	Average	Dept.	Department
Bal. b/d	Balance brought down	Dft.	draft
Bal. b/f	„ brought forward	Dis.	Discount
Bal. c/d	„ carried down	Div.	Dividend
Bal. c/f	„ carried forward	D.L.O.	Dead Letter Office
Bal. trd.	„ transferred	D/N	Debit Note
B/E	Bill of Exchange	do.	ditto
Bkg.	Banking	D/O	Delivery Order
Bkpt.	Bankrupt	dol. ($)	dollar
B/L	Bill of Lading	D/P	Documents against payment
B/P	Bill Payable		
B/R	Bill Receivable	Dr.	Debit
B/S	Balance Sheet; Bill of Sale	d/s	days after sight
		dwt.	pennyweight
bt.	bought	e.g.	for example
C.A.	Chartered Accountant	Enclo(s).	Enclosure(s)
C/B	Cash Book	E. & O.E.	Errors and omissions excepted
c. ct.	American coin, 100 c. = 1$		
c/d	carried down	eq.	equal
cent.	hundred	et seq.	and that which follows
C/F	Carried forward	et sqq.	and the things following
c.f.	cost and freight		
cf. cp.	compare	etc.	and the rest (Latin—*et cetera*)
Chq. Chqe.	Cheque		
c.i.f.	cost, insurance, and freight	ex.	out of, without
		ex cont.	from contract
C/N	Credit Note	ex div.	without dividend
Co.	Company	Exd.	Examined
c/o	care of	Exes.	Expenses
C.O.D.	Cash on Delivery	Exor.	Executor

Exp.	Export	%	per cent.
f.a.a.	free of all average	Ord.	Ordinary (shares)
f.a.s.	free alongside ship	O/S	On Sale ; out of stock
fcs.	francs	p. (pp.)	page (pages)
F.G.A.	Foreign General Average (Insce.)	p.c.	postcard ; per cent.
fl.	florin	P'd.	Paid
fo.	folio	P & L a/c	Profit and Loss Account
f.o.b.	free on board	per ann. } p.a. }	By the year (Latin—*per annum*)
f.o.r.	free on rail		
f.o.s.	free on steamer	per pro. } p. pro. } p.p. }	On behalf of (Latin *per procurationem*)
f.o.t.	free on truck		
F.P.A.	Free of particular average (Insce.)		
		P.M.G.	Postmaster-General
		P.N.	Promissory Note
Frt.	Freight	P.O.	Postal Order ; Post Office
G.A.	General Average	P.O.O.	Post Office Order
G.M.Q.	Good Merchantable Quality	P.O.D.	Pay on delivery
		pro. tem.	for the time being (Latin —*pro tempore*)
G.P.O.	General Post Office		
Id.	the same (Latin—*idem*)	prox.	next month (Latin— *proximo*)
i.e.	that is (Latin—*id est*)		
Ier.	first (French—*premier*)	qr.	quarter
Inc./tax	Income Tax	q.v.	which see (Latin—*quod vide*)
Insce.	Insurance		
inst.	instant (*i.e.* the current month)	qy.	query
		r/d	refer to drawer (Banking)
Int.	Interest	Re	with reference to
Inv.	Invoice	Recd.	Received
I O U	I owe you	Recpt.	Receipt
I.R.O.	Inland Revenue Office	Ref.	Reference
L/C.	Letter of Credit	Regd.	Registered
£ s. d.	Pounds, Shillings, and Pence (Latin—*Libra, solidi, denarii*)	Retd.	Returned
		Rly., Ry.	Railway
		R.P.	Reply Paid
Ltd.; Ld.	Limited (Companies)	R.S.O.	Railway Sub Office
M.	Marks (German)	Rs.	Rupees
Mem.,		Sec., Secy.	Secretary
Memo.	Memorandum	ss.	Steamship
Mfrs.	Manufacturers	Ster., stg.	Sterling
M.O.	Money Order	Stk.	Stock
M.O.O.	Money Order Office	T/B	Trial Balance
Mo(s)	Month(s)	T/C	Till countermanded (Advertising)
m/s	months after sight		
MS(S)	Manuscript(s)	Testor	Testator
Mtge.	Mortgage	T.M.O.	Telegraph Money Order
n/a	no account (Banking)	T.T.	Telegraph Transfer
N.B.	Take note (Latin—*nota bene*)	ult. } ulto. }	last month (Latin— *ultimo*)
N/P	Net Proceeds	v.	see, *e.g.*: *v.p.* 100 = see page 100
n/s	not sufficient (Banking)		
o/a	on account	val.	value
o/d	on demand	via	by way of
O.H.M.S.	On His Majesty's Service	viz.	namely
On a/c	On Account	x.d.	without dividend

INDEX

SUPPLEMENTARY EXERCISES

CHAPTER I

Ex. 1. (*a*) What is an "Invoice"? Wherein does it differ from an Account? (*b*) A. Stumps & Co., wholesale toy dealers, sold the following goods to C. Brown on September 3, 1910, on credit :—10 gross marbles @ 2¾*d*. per gross; ½ gross large glass marbles @ 3¼*d*. per doz.; 2 doz. model aeroplanes @ 9½*d*. each; 10 doz. dolls @ 6*s*. 9*d*. per doz. Prepare a form of Invoice from the above particulars. (*c*) Supposing that in addition to the preceding, A. Stumps & Co. sold to C. Brown during September 1910 the following goods :—September 7, £11 16*s*. 9*d*., September 20, £4 4*s*. 2*d*., and received cash from him on September 29, £20, show all the transactions as they would appear in an account kept by A. Stumps & Co. (*d*) What are ": Profits"? How are they usually made?

Ex. 2. (*a*) Explain how money may be paid by means of a cheque. Does a cheque require a stamp? (*b*) What is the meaning of the word "Discount"? What does "net" mean? (*c*) A dealer in cricket bats buys two doz. cricket bats from The Games Supply Co. Ltd. on March 31, 1910. These are priced in the Company's catalogue at 15*s*. each, less a Trade Discount of 10%, and a Cash Discount of 5% if paid for within one month. How much would the dealer have to pay altogether if he paid on April 20? How much if he paid on May 1? (*d*) If you sold to Madame Cecile on September 30, 1910, 2 gross of lace pocket-handkerchiefs @ 11*s*. 6*d*. per doz. less 5% Trade Discount, and 1 doz. Fancy Belts @ 4*s*. 9*d*. each net, how much would the Invoice come to altogether?

Ex. 3. (*a*) You have received a Bill dated September 1, 1910, promising to pay you £200 in two months' time. You, however, require some money at once. How can you turn the Bill into ready money? (*b*) When do the following Bills of Exchange fall due for payment? (i) A Bill dated August 23, 1910, payable three months after date; (ii) A Bill dated August 23, 1910, payable 90 days after date. (*c*) If the Bill marked (i) in the previous question was for £500, how much would you receive for it if you discounted it on September 23, 1910, @ 4% per annum? And how much would the Bill marked (ii) realise under the same conditions? (*d*) Is there any difference between ": simple interest" and "banker's discount"?

Ex. 4. (*a*) Explain the terms—": Consignment," ": Consignor," ": Consignee." How is the Consignee usually paid for his services? (*b*)

Give two transactions which do not in themselves involve the payment of cash, but which would be recorded in a trader's books. (c) A boy buys a second-hand bicycle for £2. He thoroughly cleans, repairs, and generally overhauls it at a cost of 7s. 6d. He then sells it for £3 5s. What was his gross profit, and what was his net profit on the transaction ? (d) A girl wishing to do some work for a bazaar bought a doll for 9½d. and spent 3½d. on materials for its dress. If the doll was sold for 3s. 6d., what profit would be made ? How much per cent. would this profit represent ? If the girl spent 3 hours on making a dress for the doll, and valued her time at 2d. per hour, how much might she reckon the net profit at then ? (e) What different kinds of Accounts would you expect to find in a Ledger ? (f) What are the Accounts called which show your dealings in things ? Give the names of two such Accounts.

Ex. 5. (a) If George Nelson purchased goods from you of the value of £75 on September 1, 1910, and paid you £25 on September 8, and £20 on September 15, what would be the balance of his Account at the end of the month ? On which side of the Account would it appear ? (b) Draw up an imaginary Invoice containing six items. (c) If, in question (a), George Nelson returned part of the goods to you on September 29, and you gave him credit for £35 for them, would the balance then be a debit or a credit ? (d) What are ": Drawings " ? What do they represent ?

CHAPTER II

Ex. 1. (a) Where does a trader usually keep most of his money, and why ? (b) How would you ": balance " a Cash Book ? If the book was for the record of office cash only, with what could you compare the balance shown by it ? (c) Thomas Brown, having just obtained a post as a junior clerk in the City, determines to keep an account of his money in a businesslike way. The following are his transactions during a fortnight :—1910. September 3 (Saturday), Balance in hand 2s. 3d. ; received salary 10s. ; gave mother 5s. ; admission to football match 3d. September 4, church collection 3d. September 5, lunch 4d. September 6, lunch 4d., *Tit-Bits* 1d. September 7, lunch 5d ; Uncle Thomas came in the evening and gave him 5s. to celebrate his start in life. September 8, lunch 6d., new tie 9d.; took his sister to a living picture theatre, admission 3d. each. September 9, lunch 4d., lent Jenkins 9d. September 10, salary 10s. ; gave mother 5s.; went out for cycle ride and spent 5d. ; Jenkins repaid the loan of 9d. September 11, collection 3d. September 12, received from father for season ticket £1 11s. 8d. ; paid for ticket during the day ; lunch 4d. September 13, sold camera for 5s. 6d. ; lunch 4d. ; present for mother on her birthday 2s. 6d. September 14, lunch 4d.; *Answers* 1d.; bought a pocket knife 1s. 6d. September 15, lunch 5d. ; in the evening went for a 'bus ride, fare 2d. each way. September 16, lunch 4d. ; hair-cut 3d. Rule a form for the proper record of these transactions, making a " balance " as on each Friday night.

Ex. 2. From the following particulars prepare the Cash Book of R. Crusoe and balance it as at the end of August 1910. August 1, 1910. Balance of Cash brought forward from last month, £15 0s. 4d. August 3, received from A. Selkirk amount owing by him £3 8s. 9d.

August 6, received from M. Friday amount owing by him £2 17s. 2d.
August 10, paid A. Parrott for goods supplied £9 9s. 3d.   August 10,
received from W. Gunn £13 13s. 8d.   August 12, paid B. Sheepskin &
Co. 9s. 4d.   August 15, paid F. Stepp amount owing to him £10 0s. 10d.
August 19, lent G. Savage £5.   August 23, paid the plumber for repairing
taps 10s. 6d.   August 28, G. Savage repaid loan £5.

Ex. 3.   K. Arthur is a trader who keeps no cash at his office, but
pays all moneys received direct into his banking account, and makes
all payments by cheque.   From the following particulars prepare his
Cash Book and balance it at the end of the month.   1910.   Oct. 1,
Balance at Bank £491 0s. 7d. ; Oct. 4, received from Lancelot & Co.
£209 11s. 3d. ; Oct. 5, paid L. Gawaine £300 ; Oct. 9, received from
F. Tristram cash £11 0s. 9d. ; Oct. 12, lent H. Merlin £10 ; Oct. 15,
received from S. Galahad Postal Orders for 14s. 9d. ; Oct. 18, paid
F. Dagonet & Co. £301 9s. 8d. ; Oct. 21, received from Geraint & Enid
on account £150 ; Oct. 26, H. Merlin repaid his loan ; Oct. 29, received
from B. Balin three £10 and two £5 notes.

Ex. 4.   A trader named R. Barr keeps the whole of his cash with his
Bankers, The London County & Westminster Bank Ltd., paying all
his receipts into the Bank and making all payments by cheque.   The
following are his cash transactions for July 1910.   Prepare his Cash
Book and balance it as on July 31, 1910.   July 1, 1910.   Balance at
Bank £227 13s. 7d. ; July 4, received from M. Quaver £27 14s. 2d. ;
July 8, paid to F. Crotchett £102 13s. 11d. ; July 10, received from
T. Trebble & Co. two £5 notes, Postal Orders value £1 4s. 6d. and
£3 0s. 9d. in cash ; July 14, drew out of bank £2 and paid it to P. Bass ;
July 17, drew cheque for Gas Bill to June 30 in favour of the Peckham
Gas Co. £4 17s. 11d. ; July 24, received cheque from Messrs. Drumm &
Fife £42 ; same date, lent G. Sharp £10 ; July 25, paid landlord, A.
Trill, £22 10s. ; July 28, G. Sharp repaid the loan of £10 ; July 31,
drew cheque for salaries £10, drew cheque for self for house-keeping
£12 10s.

Ex. 5.   W. C. Smith is a trader who keeps the greater part of his cash
at his Bank, but also keeps a small sum in his office cash-box.   The
following are his transactions for Dec. 1910.   Prepare Smith's Cash
Book in double-column form, and balance it at the end of the month.
1910.   Dec. 1, Balances at this date, cash in hand £2 1s. 9d., cash at the
bank £307 19s. 2d. ; Dec. 2, drew from bank for office cash £20 ; Dec. 3,
received from J. T. Hearne in cash (placed in cash-box) £2 19s. 9d. ;
Dec. 4, received from W. Rhodes by cheque £47 and banked the same ;
Dec. 6, paid to L. B. & S. C. Ry. by cheque for season ticket £2 5s. ;
Dec. 8, paid from office cash for repairing window 2s. 6d. ; Dec. 11,
paid by cheque to J. T. Tyldesley £147 19s. 2d. ; Dec. 14, received
cheque from J. Gunn £91 7s. 2d. and banked the same ; Dec. 17, paid
from office cash for goods bought at auction £15 2s. 3d. ; Dec. 18, sold
a second-hand typewriter for £1 10s. and received cash for same ;
Dec. 23, drew from bank for personal expenses £25 ; Dec. 27, paid
Christmas boxes in cash, postman 5s., telegraph boy 1s., dustman
2s. 6d., office cleaner 5s., lamplighter 1s. ; Dec. 28, received from Relf
Bros. cash £13 1s. 9d. ; Dec. 31, drew cheque for salaries £9 10s., paid
£15 to the Bank from office cash.

Ex. 6.   B. Rackett is a trader who keeps part of his cash at his
Bankers and part in his office cash-box.   Many of his transactions

involve discount, to record which he employs discount columns in his Cash Book. From the following particulars prepare his Cash Book in "three-column" form, and balance it at the end of the month, and total the discount columns. 1910. Oct. 1, Balances in hand, Cash £7 0s. 4d., at Bank £872 16s. 3d.; Oct. 2, paid to B. Nett by cheque £213 5s., discount £11 15s.; Oct. 4, received from C. Lett cheque for £39, allowing him £1 discount; Oct. 5, paid water rate in cash £3 11s. 3d., paid carpenter for odd jobs 11s. 6d., paid woman for cleaning office 5s. 6d.; Oct. 6, drew £10 from Bank and placed it in the office-cash box; Oct. 7, paid D. Sett from office cash, £2 5s. 4d., being allowed discount 2s. 2d.; Oct. 9, received from E. Lyne cash, and put it in the cash-box, £15 7s. 2d., discount 12s. 10d.; Oct. 14, paid to F. Ascourt cheque value £363 17s. 4d., discount £6 2s. 8d.; Oct. 17, received cheque from Doherty Bros. £22 16s., discount £1 4s.; Oct. 25, paid cheque to F. Handel, £10 19s. 2d. net; Oct. 26, bought goods for cash (paid for out of cash-box) £3 13s. 7d., paid fire insurance premium in cash 6s. 3d.; Oct. 31, drew cheque for office salaries, £10 12s. 6d., paid into Bank from office cash £15, drew cheque for self for housekeeping £25.

Ex. 7. From the following particulars prepare the Petty Cash Book of Dr. Robertson for the month, using analysis columns for the following classes of expenditure: (a) Postage, Telegrams, &c., (b) Stationery, (c) Advertisements, (d) Carriage, (e) Fares, (f) Sundries, and a "Ledger column." Balance the Cash Book as on May 14, 1910. May 1, 1910. Drew from Bank for Petty Cash £20; May 1, postage 1s. 7d., telegrams 2s. 6d.; May 3, fares to Turnham Green 9d., advertisements in the *Ryetown Gazette* 13s. 5d., postage 7d.; May 4, paid man for cleaning windows 1s. 6d., telegrams 1s. 3d., parcel to Potters Bar 9d., cab to Westminster 4s.; May 5, sent boy out for pens 6d., blotting paper 4d., parcel to Brighton 1s. 1d., stamps 10s.; May 7, surcharge on un-stamped letters 2d., advertisement in the *Pedlington Mirror* 5s., new lock to office cupboard 2s. 6d., tram to Hackney 3d.; May 10, paid R. Jones his account 5s. 6d., hire of barrow 4d.; May 11, postage 2s. 2d., parcels 5s. 6d., fares 9d.; May 11, telegram 9d., train to Hastings on business 10s.; May 12, bottle of ink 2s. 6d., paid W. Harris his account 7s. 3d.; May 13, stamps 7s. 6d., insertion of name in Directory 5s.; May 14, fare 4d., telegram 7d., new waste-paper basket 2s. 6d. (debit "Furniture" account in Ledger Column).

CHAPTER III

Ex. 1. Enter the following transactions in my Purchases Book: 1910. Oct. 1, Bought from J. H. Taylor, 6 Brassey bulger socket drivers @ 3s. 6d. each; Oct. 3, Bought from J. Braid 3 lofting irons @ 3s. 3d. each; Oct. 4, Bought of H. Vardon 4 Niblicks @ 3s. 3d. each; Oct. 5, Bought of A. Massey 2 doz. "Resilient" golf balls @ 10s. 6d. per doz.; Oct. 6, Bought from J. Ball 1 pigskin caddy, complete, 12s. 6d.

Ex. 2. From the following particulars prepare the Purchases Book of Toby Veck Ltd., Toy Dealer:—1910. Nov. 2, Bought of Martin Chuzzlewit 2 dolls' houses @ 5s. 3d. each, 2 ditto @ 9s. 9d. each, 1 ditto @ 17s. 6d.; Nov. 9, Bought of Dombey & Son 1 doz. fish-ponds

@ 1*s*. 7*d*. each, 2 doz. Spellicans @ 1*s*. 7*d*. each, 6 doz. Ludo @ 15*s*. per doz., 6 doz. Word-making and Work-taking @ 9*s*. per doz. ; Nov. 13, Bought of Samuel Pickwick 1 gross assorted soldiers @ 11*s*. the lot, 3 forts @ 2*s*. 9*d*., 4*s*. 9*d*., & 7*s*. 9*d*. respectively, 1 box of Army Medical Corps @ 1*s*. 8*d*., 1 box Zulus @ 2*s*. 3*d*. ; Nov. 18, Bought from Nicholas Nickleby & Co. 6 sets of chessmen @ 4*s*. each, 6 boards @ 1*s*. 3*d*. each, 1 doz. Halma @ 1*s*. 3*d*. each, 1 doz. draughts @ 9*s*. per doz. ; Nov. 25, Bought of Edwin Drood 1 table billiards, 6 ft. × 3ft., with cues, rest, marking board and balls, £4 15*s*.

Ex. 3. From the following particulars prepare the Purchases Book of R. Dolland, Optician :—1910. Sept. 1, Purchased from " The Longsight Co. Ltd." 3 Voightlander Service binocular field-glasses @ £3 2*s*. 6*d*. each ; Sept. 4, Bought of V. Quixy 1 doz. motor goggles @ 3*s*. 1*d*. each, 2 doz. ditto ventilated gauze mask @ 6*s*. 6*d*. each, 1 doz. blue tinted goggles @ 4*s*. 3*d*. a pair ; Sept. 7, Bought from R. Keen 3 school microscopes, ball and socket joint, high magnifying power, @ 11*s*. 9*d*. each, 6 doz. microscopic slides, assorted, @ 8*s*. 3*d*. per doz. ; Sept. 8, Purchased from " The Longsight Co. Ltd." 6 doz. pocket magnifying glasses @ 3*s*. 3*d*. each ; Sept. 12, Purchased from The Bellevue Co. ½ doz. pince-nez 9 carat gold @ 31*s*. 6*d*. each, ½ doz. ditto 12 carat @ 39*s*. 6*d*. each, ¼ doz. ditto 15 carat @ 48*s*. 6*d*. each, 1 gross ditto steel frames astigmatic @ 33*s*. 9*d*. per doz. ; Sept. 16, Bought of The Star Co. Ltd. 1 astronomical telescope, brass fittings, star finder with stand complete, £42 10*s*. ; Sept. 26, Bought of " The Weather Bureau Ltd." 3 aneroid barometers in heavy oak frames @ 41*s*. 9*d*. each ; 3 watch aneroid barometers, to register 20,000 feet elevation, @ 37*s*. 6*d*. each.

Ex. 4. From the following particulars prepare the Purchases Book of R. Harper & Co., Musical Instrument Dealers :—1910. Nov. 1, Bought of "The Melody Co." 3 Anglo-German concertinas, 26 keys, rosewood, @ 21*s*. 9*d*. each ; Nov. 4, Purchased from G. Sharp 3 zither banjos, inlaid, @ £7 2*s*. 6*d*. each ; Nov. 7, Purchased from T. Stave 6 bugles @ 4*s*. 9*d*. each, 6 cords and tassels for ditto @ 1*s*. 11½*d*. each, 1½ doz. fifes @ 2*s*. each, 6 side drums, 14 inch, @ 12*s*. 6*d*. each, 1 big drum £5, tiger skin for ditto £2 12*s*. 6*d*., being complete outfit for the St. Mark's Co. of the Boy Scouts ; Nov. 20, Bought of L. Crotchett 2 violins, superior quality, @ £9 each ; Nov. 27, Bought of T. Ledger 1 grand piano, £127 10*s*.

Ex. 5. From the following particulars prepare the Purchases Book of The Travelling Requisites Co. Ltd. :—1910. Aug. 1, Bought of S. Peary 3 regulation Orient cabin trunks, brown mail canvas, @ 56*s*. each ; 3 light overland trunks, dull black canvas, leather corners, @ 23*s*. 3*d*. each ; Aug. 8, Bought of D. Shackleton 6 railway portmanteaux, leather capped, steel bands, @ £4 15*s*. each, less 10% trade discount ; Aug. 12, Bought of L. de Rougemont 12 saratoga trunks @ 39*s*. each, less 2½% trade discount ; Aug. 16, Bought of R. Stanley 6 gentlemen's fitted dressing-bags, silver fittings, ebony brushes, &c., @ £4 5*s*. each net ; Aug. 20, Bought of Marco Polo 9 picnic baskets, nickel-plated fittings, @ 41*s*. each, less 7½% trade discount and 2½% for prompt cash ; Aug. 24, Bought of G. Munchausen 1 doz. Scout luminous night-marching compasses @ 14*s*. 9*d*. each, less 5% trade discount.

Ex. 6. From the following particulars prepare the Returns Outwards

Book of V. Summers, Gentlemen's Outfitter :—1910. Sept. 9, Returned to the Premier Outfit Co. Ltd. 1 chauffeur's jacket, wrong size sent, 24s. 6d. ; Sept. 11, Returned to R. Hall & Co. 1 doz. pairs boys' boots @ 54s. the doz., inferior quality, ¼ doz. slippers @ 24s. the doz., wrong colour sent ; Sept. 18, Returned to the West End Co. Ltd. 3 doz. gentlemen's collars @ 5s. 6d. per doz., sent in excess of order.

Ex. 7. From the following particulars prepare the Purchases Returns Book of H. Brown, Furniture Dealer :—1910.   March 17, Returned to Turner & Co. 3 arm-chairs, "not as ordered," invoiced at 37s. 6d. each, less 5% trade discount ; March 24, Returned to Carpenter Bros. 1 overmantel, warped, invoiced @ 42s. net ; March 26, Returned to S. Joiner 1 set of fireirons, invoiced @ 12s. 6d., less 10% trade discount ; March 31, Returned to L. Carver, 1 bracket, broken in transit, 17s. 6d. net.

CHAPTER IV

Ex. 1. (a) Give another name for the Sales Returns Book. (b) On Sept. 23 I sold B. Rose two rustic garden arches, Gothic pattern, @ 10s. 9d. each, less 10% trade discount.   Enter this sale in my Sales Book.   (c) On Sept. 25 B. Rose returned one of the above arches, stating that it was faulty, and I agreed to take it back.   How would you enter this return in my books ?   (d) Enter the following sales in my Sales Book.   1910.   June 2, Sold to A. Morgan 2 doz. travelling inkstands, spring caps, @ 9d. each ; June 8, Sold to J. Jenkins 2 letter balances, engraved with letter rates, @ 5s. 6d. each ; June 15, Sold to W. Williams 1½ doz. autograph albums @ 3s. 6d. each ; June 21, Sold to D. Rees 1 doz. gilt metal photograph frames @ 2s. 3d. each ; June 27, Sold to R. Evans 3 scrap books, half morocco, royal 4to, @ 6s. 6d. each.

Ex. 2. From the following particulars make out the Sales Book of G. Winter, wholesale grocer. 1910. Sept. 1, Sold to G. Thrush 1 gross bottles Bouillon Fleet @ 5s. per doz., 2 doz. 2-lb. jars mincemeat, Lazenby's, @ 15s. per doz., 1 doz. tomato and onion pickles, Lily Brand, @ 6s. 3d. per doz. ; Sept. 4, Sold to C. Finch 6 doz. each apricot, black-currant, greengage, red plum, and strawberry jam, 3-lb. pots, @ 11s. 6d. per doz., 1 gross Cairn's bramble jelly, 1-lb. pots, @ 4s. 9d. per doz., 3 doz. large boxes Guava jelly @ 12s. 3d. per doz. ; Sept. 11, Sold to M. Nightingale 1 doz. bottles evaporated horse-radish @ 7¾d. per bottle, 1 doz. 1-lb. packets Swinborne's patent refined isinglass @ 4¼d. per packet, 1 doz. tins Maggey's Consommé @ 1s. 4¼d. per tin, 2 doz. pots Patum Peperium @ 7s. 3d. per doz. ; Sept. 18, Sold to C. Gull 168 lb. hemp seed @ 9½d. for 7 lb., 1 cwt. German rape @ 1s. 2½d. for 7 lb., 84 lb. Spratt's parrot food @ 3¾d. for 7 lb. ; Sept. 26, Sold to K. Lark 2 doz. tins Blanchflower's kippered herrings @ 3s. 9d. per doz., 2 doz. glasses herrings' roes @ 4s. 3d. per doz., 1 doz. tins curried lobster @ 10½d. per tin.

Ex. 3. From the following particulars write up the Sales Book of Messrs. Grant & Co., glove merchants. 1910. Oct. 2, Sold to Samuel Pickwick 1 gross black cloth gents' gloves, 1 button, @ 15s. 3d. per doz. pairs, ½ gross tan cape, 1 button, @ 2s. 4½d. per pair, 3 dozen Havannah tan, lined Shetland, @ 4s. 1½d. per pair, 6 doz. imitation reindeer, assorted shades, 1 button, @ 1s. 10d. per pair ; Oct. 3, Sold to Nathaniel Winkle 3 doz. tabac-tan Bohemian chevrette driving gloves @ 2s. 11d. per pair, 6 doz. coloured kids, 2 buttons, @ 33s. per doz., 6 doz. white kids @ 21s. per doz. ; Oct. 4, Sold to Mrs. Bardell 1 gross black piqué suède, 3 buttons, 27s. per doz., ½ gross white mousquetaire kid, 16 buttons, @ 4s. 11d. per pair ; Oct. 5, Sold to Miss Nupkin 3 doz. ladies' black fur gauntlet gloves, lined lambs-wool, @ 6s. 9d. per pair. 3 doz. ladies' white doe cycling gloves, 3 buttons, @ 21s. per doz., 6 doz. fancy heather wool gloves @ 11s. 11d. per doz.

Ex. 4. From the following particulars make out the Sales Book of The Neptune Angling Supply Co. Ltd. 1910. Feb. 1, Sold to G. Cod 1 white cane roach rod, bronzed fittings, 2 tops, cork handle, 18 ft., 25s., 1 superior bronzed gunmetal winch, 3½ inches diameter, 21s., 1 drab fustian bag, No. 2 size. 10s. 6d.; Feb. 2, Sold to M. Herring ¼ doz. each of the following flies :—sand fly, grannom, yellow dun, black palmer, grouse hackle, jenny spinner, hare's ear, and red tag @ 2s. 3d. per doz. ; Feb. 3, Sold to R. Sturgeon artificial baits as follows : 1 wagtail, size 5, 1s. 9d., 2 silk phantoms, size 6, 1s. 6d., 1 sarcelle 8d., 1 serpentanic, 1s. 9d., 3 spoon baits @ 7d. ; Feb. 4, Sold to R. Minnow 3 japanned bait boxes @ 7d. each ; 1 doz. disgorgers @ 9d. per doz., 2 bottles rod and tackle varnish @ 6d. per bottle, ¼ lb. Hercules gimp @ 6d. per ¼ oz.

Ex. 5. Make out the Sales Book of the Isle of Dogs Furnishing Co. Ltd. from the following particulars. 1910. Dec. 1, Sold M. Turtle & Co. 1 Sheraton drawing-room suite for £27 19s. 6d., less 10% trade discount ; Dec. 2, Sold to W. Rabbit 1 52-piece dinner service @ £1 17s. 6d., 1 40-piece tea service @ 13s., 1 doz. tumblers @ 3s. 3d. net, case for packing same 3s. ; Dec. 3, Sold to T. Carpenter 1 fumed oak bedroom suite @ £22 10s., 1 bedstead @ £3 3s., 1 mattress @ 18s. 6d., 1 overlay @ £2, 1 bolster @ 9s., and 2 pillows @ 12s. each, all subject to 5% trade discount ; Dec. 4, Sold to M. Hatter 1 oak roll-top desk, 50 inches wide, for £7 15s. net ; Dec. 5, Sold to W. Knight 1 fourfold screen, descriptive panels, @ £1 12s. 6d., 1 music cabinet @ £1 16s. 6d., 1 Davenport, walnut inlaid, @ £6 6s., all less 15% trade discount.

Ex. 6. From the following particulars make out the Returns Inwards Book of Messrs. Cartridge & Co., stationers. 1910. June 1, James Cannon returned 10 quires notepaper, headed Cannon's Hostel, in mistake for Monk's Hostel, charged @ 4s. 6d. per 5 quires ; June 9, James Cannon returned 15 quires fancy notepaper, sent in mistake for sermon paper, charged at 4d. per quire ; June 17, Signor Caruso returned 5 quires ruled MS. music paper, sent in excess of order, charged 1s. per quire ; June 23, Miss Vine returned 2 doz. valentines, sent in mistake for birthday cards, charged @ 3d. each.

Ex. 7. From the following particulars write up the Sales Returns Book of Messrs. Sillicker & Co., glass merchants. 1910. Oct. 3, Messrs. T. Quart & Co. returned 1 doz. and 4 tumblers, broken in transit, charged @ 4d. each, less trade discount of 25% ; Oct. 4, Messrs. Flint & Co. returned one packing-case, charged @ 4s. 6d. ; Oct. 6, J. Taylor returned 1 quart decanter, badly engraved, charged @ 21s. the pair, less 10% trade discount ; Oct. 7, Messrs. Tantalus & Co. returned 3 cut-glass jugs, wrong colour sent, charged @ 2s. 6d. each net.

CHAPTER V

Ex. 1. From the following particulars prepare E. Taylor's Account, as shown in my books, and balance it as on Sept. 30, 1910. Sept. 1, E. Taylor owed me £47 16s. 2d.; Sept. 2, Sold to E. Taylor 6 canvases @ 2s. each; Sept. 4, Received from E. Taylor cash on account £30; Sept. 7, Sold to E. Taylor 3 Spanish mahogany palettes @ 2s. 1d. each; Sept. 11, Received from E. Taylor £15 8s. 4d., which, with 5% discount, will settle his August account; Sept. 14, Bought from E. Taylor 1 picture, "The Ruined Mill," £25; Sept. 19, Sold to E. Taylor 2 doz. assorted hog's-hair brushes @ 2s. 6d. a doz. ; Sept. 26, Paid to E. Taylor £15; Sept. 30, E. Taylor returned ½ doz. brushes, inferior quality, allowed him 1s. 3d.

Ex. 2. Show how the following transactions may be expressed in double-entry form. (a) The cash purchase of a bicycle for £7 10s. (b) The accidental loss of a sovereign from the cash-box. (c) The lending (by cheque) of £2 2s. to Mr. Hunt. (d) The payment of cash, amounting to £2 3s. 6d., for repairs to office desks and stools. (e) The gift of £1 1s. to the local hospital. (f) The sale, on credit, of two bicycles @ £10 10s. each to Mr. Trent. (g) The receipt of a cheque, value £25, from J. Martin, in settlement of an account which he owed. (h) The payment of £20 from the cash-box into the Bank. (i) The payment of 1s. 6d. for telegrams from the Petty Cash. (j) The payment of £17 10s. by cheque for advertisements. (k) Mr. Hunt repaid his loan by cash.

Ex. 3. Show how the following transactions may be expressed in double-entry form. 1910. Oct. 2, Bought a motor-car from F. Hopkins for £400, on credit; Oct. 3, Paid rent to Sept. 29, £22 10s. by cheque; Oct. 4, Bought a new roll-top desk at an auction, handing the auctioneer a cheque for £6 10s.; Oct. 5, Gave the men who brought the desk 1s. 6d. from the petty cash; Oct. 9, Sold 500 shares in the Eldorado Gold Mining Co. to G. Nokes for £50, the money to be paid on the 26th inst. ; Oct. 15, Exchanged a second-hand motor-car, worth £105, for three new motor-bicycles worth £35 each; Oct. 18, Received from A. Tyler cheque for £40, on account of money he owed me; Oct. 26, Received from G. Nokes £50 for the shares sold to him on the 9th inst. ; Oct. 30, Drew cheque for office salaries, £16 3s. 6d.

Ex. 4. From the following particulars prepare (a) My Cash Account, (b) My Dogs Account, (c) J. Learoyd's Account, and (d) My Expenses Account. Bring down the balances of these accounts as on Sept. 30, 1910. 1910. Sept. 1, Balance of cash in hand £33 2s. 9d., value of dogs in hand £69 10s. ; Sept. 2, Bought of J. Learoyd 2 Newfoundland dogs @ £15 each; Sept. 5, Paid carriage for dogs bought on the 2nd inst. 7s. 6d. ; Sept. 6, Sold to J. Learoyd 2 Irish terriers @ £1 1s. each ; Sept. 8, Paid to J. Learoyd cash on account £10 10s. ; Sept. 9, Sold 1 Schipperke for cash, £2 10s. ; Sept. 14, Bought of J. Learoyd 1 Pomeranian @ £3; Sold the Pomeranian the same day for £4 in cash; Sept. 18, Bought from J. Learoyd 6 foxhounds @ 15s. each, 3 greyhounds @ £3 each; Sept. 19, Paid to J. Learoyd £12 10s. ; Sept. 20, Travelling expenses 7s. 3d., stamps 5s. ; Sept. 23, Paid subscription to *The Dog Fancier* for 6 months, 15s. ; Sept. 30, Paid veterinary surgeon's fee for month £1 1s., kennelmen's wages £4 10s.

Ex. 5. From the following particulars prepare (a) My Cash Account with " Cash " and " Bank " columns, (b) The Personal Accounts of G. O. Smith and S. Bloomer in my Ledger, (c) My Trade Expenses Account, (d) My House Account, and (e) My Purchases Book. Balance the first four of these accounts as at Oct. 31, 1910. 1910. Oct. 2, Balance at Bank £1792 14s. 4d. ; Oct. 4, Drew from Bank for office cash £35 ; Oct. 5, Bought of G. O. Smith goods value £75 on credit ; Oct. 6, Paid telephone subscription for year by cheque £15 15s. ; Oct. 7, Paid clerks' salaries in cash £4 15s. ; Oct. 10, Bought of S. Bloomer on credit goods value £227 14s. 6d. ; Oct. 11, Paid G. O. Smith by cheque on account £50 ; Oct. 12, Bought at auction " Sunny Bank " for £1250 and paid cheque for the same, paid legal charges in connection with same in cash £7 19s. 2d. ; Oct. 13, Bought of S. Bloomer for cash goods value £15 ; Oct. 14, Drew out of bank for office cash £50 ; paid clerks' salaries in cash £4 15s. ; Oct. 20, Bought of S. Bloomer on credit goods value £227 ; Oct. 21, Paid clerks' salaries in cash £4 15s. ; Oct. 26, Gave orders for the construction of a motor-house at " Sunny Bank," and paid cheque £20 to builder on account ; Oct. 27, Paid cheque to S. Bloomer on account £150 ; Oct. 28, Paid clerks' salaries in cash £4 15s. ; Oct. 30, Paid from office cash into Bank £20.

Ex. 6. (a) S. Martin commenced to keep his books by double-entry on Jan. 1, 1910. His position at that date was as follows : Trade Creditors, J. Wren £429 6s. 3d., S. Sparrow £250 4s. 9d. ; stock of goods £77 9s. 4d. ; freehold premises value £575 ; owing to P. Starling £129 7s. 2d. ; cash at bank £49 7s. 5d. ; cash at office £7 6s. 3d. ; owing to J. Nightingale for charge in connection with purchase of shop £7 6s. 3d. State in what accounts the foregoing balances should be entered and upon which side, also state the amount of S. Martin's capital on Jan. 1, 1910. (b) Classify the following Ledger Accounts as among (1) real, (2) personal, and (3) nominal, viz., machinery, telegrams and postages, J. Wilson & Co., wages, discounts allowed, E. Brown (loan), premises, insurances, capital.

Ex. 7· (a) R. White commenced to keep his books by double-entry on July 1, 1910, when his position was as follows :—He possessed premises valued at £1500, machinery valued at £700, his stock-in-trade was worth £550 at cost price, and he had cash in hand amounting to £117 6s. 2d. He was owed £47 16s. 4d. by J. Hill and £32 17s. 9d. by J. Field, while he owed £99 4s. 2d. to S. Mountain. What was the amount of his capital as at July 1, 1910 ? (b) Open Nominal Accounts under suitable headings for the following :—1910. Aug. 7, Received £5 interest due from B. Rivers on my loan to him ; Aug. 10, Received £15 as discount from the Prairie Supply Company on paying them their account due for goods supplied ; Aug. 12, Allowed £4 6s. 9d. to K. Lake in settlement of his claim that the goods supplied to him were short weight ; Aug. 13, Received £4 from the G.W. Railway Co. in settlement of my claim re goods damaged in transit.

CHAPTER VI

Ex. 1. (a) What are " Opening Entries " ? How do you bring them into the Books ? (b) Pass the following transactions through the Journal, dating them Oct. 13, 1910 : Bought on credit from Alexander McTavish goods worth £47 6s. 2d. ; Sold on credit to Hector McAlpine goods worth £9 17s. 4d. ; Exchanged with Donald Fraser goods worth £10 and furniture worth £15 for a typewriter worth £20 and stationery worth £5 ; Returned part of the goods bought of A. McTavish to the value of £7 6s. 2d.

Ex. 2. Journalise the following transaction : Patrick O'Flinn commenced business as a pig and potato merchant on Nov. 1, 1910, with the following assets : Cash at Bank, £50 ; premises, £500 ; pigs on hand, £75 ; potatoes, £15. During Nov. the following transactions took place : Nov. 4, Sold pigs to Terence Macguire, £50 on credit ; Nov. 7, Sold potatoes to Bridget Malone, £5 for cash ; Nov. 10, Received cash from T. Macguire, £20 ; Nov. 17, Bought pigs on credit from Shiel O'Connel, £25 ; Nov. 24, Paid S. O'Connel by cheque £15.

Ex. 3. Journalise the following transactions : On Oct. 1, 1910, William Polperro commenced business with £400, to the credit of his account at Parr's Bank. His transactions were : Oct. 1, Bought goods from H. Treloar, £250 on credit ; Oct. 3, Paid for advertisement by cheque £10 10s., Drew cheque for Petty Cash, £15 ; Oct. 5, Sold goods on credit to R. Penjerrick, £75 ; Oct. 8, Received from M. Constantine a goods delivery cart worth £5 and gave him goods to the same value in exchange ; Oct. 15, Bought goods from S. Perranwell, £50 on credit ; Oct. 17, Gave H. Treloar a Bill for £250 ; Oct. 19, Paid S. Perranwell's account, £47 10s. by cheque and £2 10s. discount ; Oct. 30, Paid by cheque for travelling expenses £7 10s., Received from R. Penjerrick cheque £50 on account and paid same into Bank ; Oct. 30, Paid salaries by cheque, £5 10s.

Ex. 4. Journalise the following transactions, dating the entries Oct. 15, 1910 : Exchanged two horses worth £30 each for a van worth £60 ; Exchanged a motor-bicycle worth £30 for a horse worth £25 and harness worth £5 ; Exchanged a cart worth £25 and fodder worth £30 for 7 sheep worth £5 each and 2 bicycles worth £10 each ; Bought from W. Black on credit 6 sheep @ £6 each and a cow for £15 ; Sold to B. White, on credit, 3 sheep @ £6 10s. each and a horse for £30. On Oct. 4 I drew two cheques, as follows : (1) telephone subscription £15 15s., (2) G. Green £17 2s. 6d., but these amounts had been posted in the Ledger (1) to the debit of G. Green, and (2) to the debit of Trade Expenses. Make the necessary Journal entries to rectify these errors in posting.

Ex. 5. Prepare Journal entries to correct the following errors : Oct. 1, Received a cheque for £15 which was posted to the credit of M. Brown, although it really came from W. Brown & Co. ; Oct. 3, I paid a solicitor named L. Mauve a cheque for £10 10s. for some legal work he had done for me, which should have been posted to Legal Expenses ; my book-keeper, however, opened an account for L. Mauve and posted it to that account ; Oct. 6, I returned some unsatisfactory goods worth £10 to G. Chrome, part of a lot he had sent me, these returns were entered in the Sales Book ; Oct. 10, an item of £50 was posted to the " Furniture " account instead of to the " Premises " account.

Ex. 6. From the following details write up the Journal entry necessary to open the books of B. Scarlett as on Oct. 1, 1910, showing the commencing " Capital " : Cash at Bank £271 3s. 9d. ; Stock £475 0s. 8d.

Creditors, G. Gray £27 2s. ; S. Madder £47 3s. 1d. ; Premises £800 ; Plant & Machinery £247 6s. 3d. *Debtors*, G. Bice £73 6s. 9d. ; M. Steyne £32 4s. 2d.

Ex. 7. From the following details prepare the Journal entry necessary to open the books of R. Wagner as on Jan. 1, 1911. Leasehold premises £1500 ; furniture and fittings £75 ; stock £1122 7s. 3d. *Debtors*, L. Beethoven £47 6s. 2d. ; F. Mendelssohn £6 0s. 2d. ; F. Schubert £47 9s. 9d. ; bill receivable £225 ; cash at Bank £62 0s. 4d. *Creditors*, G. H. Handel £99 4s. 7d.; A. S. Sullivan £62 0s. 4d. ; F. Chopin £30. Cash in hand £22 4s. 2d. Owing to F. Liszt (money lent by him to start the business) £4000.

CHAPTER VII

Ex. 1. (a) In which Ledger Accounts would you expect to find the debit entries for the following transactions ? (1) Paid cheque £500 for a new gas engine, (2) Drew cheque for wages £50, (3) Received from R. Jones £47 10s. by cheque, which, with £2 10s. discount allowed, will settle his account. In which accounts would you look for the corresponding credits ? (b) Open the necessary Ledger Accounts from the following items, first entering them in the Journal : On Oct. 1, 1910, W. Hudson had cash at the Bank £100 ; a shop worth £800 ; a cart worth £60 ; two horses worth £35 each ; debts owing to him, B. Baffin £27 0s. 2d., S. Smith £13 0s. 9d. ; Stock in hand £27 3s. 9d. ; while he owed L. Behring £49 0s. 6d.

Ex. 2. On Jan. 1, 1904, John Jones had £500 as his Capital in his business, while James Green was his debtor for £350, and he owed William Paul £400. He had £450 at his Bankers, and £100 in his safe. Open the necessary Ledger Accounts and post direct to the Ledger the following transactions : Jan. 1, Sold goods to Wm. Paul £350 ; Jan. 4, Purchased goods from J. Robinson £150 ; Jan. 7, Purchased goods from Wm. White £220 ; Jan. 10, Purchased goods from P. Frean £140 ; Jan. 15. Sold goods to Charles Carter £340 ; Jan. 20, Sold goods to J. Farlow £140 ; Jan. 25, Purchased goods from Wm. Paul £480 ; Jan. 31, Returned goods to J. Robinson £50.

(Society of Arts, Grade I., 1904.)

Ex. 3. Open the necessary Ledger Accounts with the following Balances as on July 1, 1910 : Stock of eggs, £27 9s. 2d. ; Cash at Bank, £42 0s. 4d. Debtors : G. Cruttenden £2 17s. 9d. ; J. Tutt £3 0s. 10d. ; Capital Account, R. Weatherseed £75 8s. 1d. Pass the following transactions through the proper books, and rule off the accounts as on July 8, 1910, and bring down the balances. July 1, Bought eggs on credit from S. Cantler £7 0s. 9d. ; July 3, Sold eggs to J. Tutt £4 19s. 2d. ; July 4, Received from J. Tutt cheque £7 12s., which, with discount at 5 per cent., will balance his account ; July 5, Bought eggs from A. Farmer £15, less 10 per cent. trade discount ; July 6, Drew from Bank for office cash £5, paid by cheque for advertisement in the *Fowlkeeper*, £1 5s. ; July 8, Paid wages to man 15s. by cash ; paid carriage 2s. 9d.

Ex. 4. The following items appear in W. Robinson's Books, in the month of Jan. 1902. Post up the Ledger, opening new accounts where necessary, and bring down the balances of the Ledger and Cash Book, as on Jan. 31, 1902.

LEDGER BALANCES, JANUARY 1, 1902.

	Dr.	Cr.
W. Robinson .	—	.. £2000
Stock-in-Trade	£569	
Owen Williams	—	.. £323
Tom Turnbull .	£254	—
Safe Bank Co. Ltd. .	£1039	—
Furniture and Fittings	£650	—
Cash	£15	—
Morgan Lewis & Co. .	—	.. £204
	£2527	. £2527

CASH BOOK (as kept by Robinson).

Dr. 1902		Dis.	Bank	1902		Dis.	Bank
Jan. 1	To Balance		£1054	Jan. 15	By O. Williams	£3	£320
Jan. 20	T. Turn-			Jan. 30	Morgan,		
	bull	£4	£250		Lewis & Co.	£4	£200
Jan. 30	W. Smith			Jan. 31	Robinson's		
	(loan)		£300		drawings		£25
					Wages		£30
					Warehouse		
					expenses		£5

Purchases Book, 1902. Jan. 4, Owen Williams, £551 5s. ; Sales Book, Jan. 5, Tom Turnbull, £418 ; Jan. 9, R. Butcher, £243 15s.

(Society of Arts, Grade I., 1902.)

Ex. 5. Enter the following transactions of a firm into the following books : Day Book, Invoice Book, Cash Book, and add up the entries. Then transfer these entries into the Ledger. Then balance the Ledger. 1898. Jan. 1, The firm have on hand : Cash £200 ; Goods worth £2420 ; Premises worth £1500 ; Cash at Bank £1800. Jan. 1, Buy goods from T. Inde & Co. £225 ; Jan. 3, Sell goods to Dansie & Co. £360 ; Jan. 4, Kneller & Co. sell goods £234 5s. 6d. ; Jan. 5, Deans & Co. purchase goods £104 ; Jan. 7, Place in Bank £104 ; Jan. 9, Pay T. Inde & Co. by cheque £220, by discount allowed £5 ; Jan. 10, Dansie & Co. forward Bill at three months £200 ; Jan. 11, The firm forward to Kneller & Co. acceptance at one month £100 ; Jan. 12, Withdraw cash from Bank £180 ; Jan. 13, Goods received from King & Co. £248 12s. ; Jan. 14, Firm sell goods to Dansie & Co. £117 5s. 9d., Firm sell goods to Deans & Co. £213 4s. 7d., Firm sell goods to Dansie & Co. £72 ; Jan. 15, Cheques forwarded to Kneller & Co. £134 5s. 6d. ; Jan. 16, Sell goods to Deacon & Co. for cash, £77 9s. 5d., for credit £100 ; Jan. 17, Cheque received from Deacon & Co. £70 ; Jan. 20, Dansie & Co. pay by cash £110, and are allowed discount £7 5s. 9d. ; Jan. 21, Carpenter's account for new Desks paid by cheque £23 4s. 6d. ; Paid by cash to King & Co. £140 ; Jan. 31, Monthly Cash sales £82 17s. 9d. ; incidental expenses paid by cash £50 7s. 2d., goods on hand at end of month valued at £2500.

(College of Preceptors' Examination : Christmas, 1898.)

Ex. 6. On June 1, 1910, S. Dawes commenced business with the following property and debts : Cash at Bank £300 ; Cash in Hand £7 14s. 2d. ; Stock £593 15s. 7d. ; Premises £800 ; Debtors : R. Hills £272 15s. 7d. ; W. Johnson £33 6s. 3d. Creditors : The Lincolnshire Lace Co. £75 7s. 2d. ; A. Scard £330 19s. 7d. ; E. Egglesfield, £63 9s. 8d.

S. Dawes' transactions for the month of June were as follows : June 3, Bought on credit from A. Scard silk £69 19s. 2d., and lace £47 3s. 4d. ; June 4, Sold to W. Johnson lace £363, less 5 per cent. trade discount ; June 9, Received cheque from W. Johnson for the amount of his account, less 2½ per cent. cash discount ; June 14, Paid trade expenses by cheque £14 19s. 7d. ; June 23, Sold to L. Biggs silk £57 9s. 2d., less 5 per cent. trade discount ; June 29, Bought from M. Pinnett velvet £33 17s. 5d., and paid for same by cheque, less 5 per cent. cash discount ; June 30, Paid wages by cheque £15 15s. 6d. Open the necessary books to record the above entries, post them into the Ledger, and balance the accounts as on June 30, 1910.

Ex. 7. George Smith, having purchased from Wm. Watson, wine merchant, the Assets, including the goodwill, of his business, for which he gave £3000 for stocks of wines and spirits, £500 for utensils, bottles, and appliances, and £1000 for goodwill, commenced business on Dec. 1, 1904. He opened an account at the Secure Bank Ltd., and paid in £2000, representing his working Capital. Open the necessary Ledger Accounts to record the above, and post the following transactions direct to the Ledger. Balance the accounts as on December 9, 1904, and bring down the balances. Dec. 2, Bought from R. French 3 pipes of port @ £85 per pipe ; Dec. 3, Bought from C. Clare 50 doz. of sherry @ 90s. per doz. ; Dec. 5, Bought from R. Frost a bottle-washing machine for £18 10s. ; Dec. 6, Sold to Grand Hotel Co. Ltd. 10 doz. of sherry @ 108s. per doz. ; Dec. 7, Bought from G. Keen 10 doz. of champagne @ 100s. per doz. ; Dec. 8, Sold to R. White one pipe of port for £95 ; Dec. 9, Sold to R. Frost 2 doz. of champagne @ 110s. per doz.

(Society of Arts, Grade I., 1905.)

CHAPTER VIII

Ex. 1. (a) What effect, if any, will the following errors in a set of books have upon the Trial Balance ? (1) The debit side of the Cash Book has been over-added £5, (2) an entry of £2 in the Journal has been posted to the debit of two accounts instead of once to the debit and once to the credit, (3) a cheque received for £19 14s. 2d. has been posted as £19 4s. 2d., (4) £50 received from J. Simpson has been posted to the credit of Simpson & Co. in error, (5) an item of 2s. 6d. on the credit side of the Cash Book has not been posted at all. The Purchases Book has been added 10s. too much, and the discounts received column in the Cash Book has been added 10s. too little. (b) From the following particulars write up Hugh Thompson's books, and prepare a Trial Balance as at Nov. 10, 1910. Hugh Thompson started business on Nov. 1, 1910, as a cycle dealer. On Nov. 2 he borrowed £250 from D. Hardy in cash. On Nov. 3 he bought on credit 20 bicycles from the Speedwell Co. Ltd. @ £7 each. On Nov. 5 he sold 10 bicycles to H. Cowham @ £9 10s. each on credit. On Nov. 7 he paid £75 on account to the Speedwell Co. Ltd.

Ex. 2. The following is a Trial Balance extracted from the books of H. Wood. Several items, however, are entered on the wrong side. Correct the Trial Balance so that the totals agree.

TRIAL BALANCE—SEPTEMBER 30, 1910.

	£	s.	d.	£	s.	d.
H. Wood, Capital Account . . .				1972	10	3
Freehold Land & Buildings . . .				750	0	0
Salaries	73	19	3			
Rates & Taxes	42	0	2			
Discounts allowed				10	17	4
Discounts received	19	19	2			
Stock, July 1, 1910				1349	16	3
Purchases				864	6	3
Returns Inwards	11	13	7			
Sales	1590	16	3			
Furniture & Fittings	50	0	0			
Printing & Stationery	22	4	9			
Cash at Office				11	16	3
Cash at Bank	229	14	7			
General Expenses				22	0	4
Sundry Debtors	492	6	3			
Sundry Creditors				347	9	4
	£2532	14	0	£5328	16	0

Ex. 3. Wm. Richardson commences business on Jan. 1, 1900, and the following are his transactions for the first month : 1900. Jan. 1, Capital paid into the Bank, £2000, paid for furniture (cheque), £100, paid for fixtures (cheque), £50 ; Jan 3, Bought from Murray, goods, £250 ; Jan. 4, Bought from Badcock, goods, £150 ; Jan. 5, Sold to Couper, goods, £150, Cash Sales paid into Bank, £50 ; Jan. 7, Paid Murray on account (by cheque £95, discount allowed £5) £100 ; Jan. 8, Accepted Murray's bill for balance, £150 ; Jan. 10, Sold goods to Hoskins £50, Sold goods to Bird £40 ; Jan. 12, Received from Couper bill receivable, £145, allowed Couper discount £5 ; Jan. 20, Paid wages (by cheque), £30, paid salaries (by cheque), £20 ; Jan. 25, Cash Sales (paid to Bank), £30 ; Jan. 26, Bought goods from McGechie, £120, paid Badcock (cheque), £150 ; Jan. 29, Paid taxes, £30 ; Jan. 31, Private drawing of Wm. Richardson, £50. Enter the above transactions in the Day Book, Cash Book, and Ledger, and the Bills in the Journal, and post the same to the Ledger, after which draw up a Trial Balance.

(Institute of Bankers, Preliminary, May 1900.)

Ex. 4. The following are the balances appearing in my Ledger on Nov. 30, 1910. From them prepare a Trial Balance, inserting the amount of my Capital as on Nov. 1, 1910. Cash, £332 0s. 9d. ; Purchases, £1790 14s. 7d. Debtors : L. Wilson, £37 16s. 9d., F. Lime, £69 0s. 3d. Creditors : G. Watson, £114 17s. 3d., S. Simpkins, £6 17s.4d., B. Allison, £43 16s. 9d. ; Sales, £3463 16s. 3d. ; Premises, £700 ; Investment, £1000, India 3½ per cent. Stock, at cost, £933 17s. 3d. ; Returns Inwards, £11 14s. 2d. ; Returns Outwards, £9 19s. 2d. ; Plant and Machinery, £450 ; Discounts received, £29 0s. 4d. ; Discounts allowed, £25 0s. 10d. ; Salaries, £260 10s. 6d. ; Stock in hand, Nov. 1,

1910, £4672 13s. 3d. ; Petty Cash, £10 ; General Expenses, £430 16s. 9d.; Rates and Taxes, £129 19s. ; Bank Charges, £3 13s. 9d.

Ex. 5.   Austin Brown, whose Capital consisted of £2500 in the Assets Bank Ltd., commenced business on Feb. 1, 1904, by opening stores for the sale of tea and coffee, having adapted the front room of his house (his own freehold) for use as a shop by an outlay of £200 and expended £50 in furniture and fittings.   He paid for both items by cheque on Feb. 1, 1904.

The following were Brown's transactions for the period ended Feb. 18, 1904 : Feb. 2, Drew cheque for £10, Petty Cash ; Feb. 3, Bought from F. Thompson & Co. 8 chests of Indian tea for £43 4s. and paid the Government duty thereon of £2 12s. 6d. ; Feb. 4, Purchased a coffee-roasting machine from the Machine Supply Co. for £38 10s. ; Feb. 5, Sold one chest of tea to A. James & Co. for £6, allowing 2½ per cent. discount for one month ; Purchased from G. Mager 1 cwt. of coffee @ 87s. 6d. per cwt. and 1½ cwt. do. @ 92s. per cwt., Purchased from R. Phillips 2 cwt. of coffee @ 81s. 3d. per cwt. ; Feb. 6, Bought stationery, string, &c., for £6 4s. 2d. and paid cash for same ; Feb. 7, Drew cheque for £12 10s. for Rates ; Feb. 9, Bought from the Ceylon Tea Co. three chests of tea @ £4 16s. per chest, duty paid ; Feb. 10, Cash sales for the week amounted to £7 3s. 4d., Ordered advertisement in Geo. Smith's Time Tables to the amount of £7 10s., Drew cheque for wages £3 4s. 6d., Drew cheque for Petty Cash £6 4s. 2d. ; Feb. 12, Finding that his roasting machine was unsuitable, sold it for £33 cash down and purchased a larger one from the Machine Supply Co. for £64 ; Feb. 13, Paid the Machine Supply Co. for the first machine less 5 per cent. cash discount ; Feb. 14, Sold to the Royal Tea Co. 56 lb. of " A.B.'s special Blend " @ 2s. a lb., Received cheque from James & Co. in settlement of their account, less 2½ per cent. cash discount ; Feb. 15, Purchased two bales of Mocha coffee @ 192s. per bale from the Coffee Syndicate Ltd. and gave them an acceptance at one month for the amount of their invoice ; Feb. 16, Paid from Petty Cash a fine of 40s. and 5s costs for inaccurate scales, Sold G. Mager 1 cwt. of " A.B.'s pure coffee " @ 94s. per cwt., Paid Geo. Smith one-half of the advertisement, having settled the proof ; Feb. 17, Drew cheque for £3 4s. 6d. wages, Cash sales for the week amounted to £11 16s. 2d. ; Feb. 18, Drew cheque for £10 for private purposes.   All moneys received were paid into the Bank and (unless otherwise stated) all payments were made by cheque.   Pass the above transactions through the proper books to the Ledger.   Balance the accounts as on Feb. 18, 1904 ; bring down the balances and extract a Trial Balance.

(*Royal Society of Arts, Grade* II., 1905.)

Ex. 6.   William Smith began the year 1902 with the following balances in his Ledger ·

	£	s.	d.	£	s.	d.
Wm. Smith, Capital Account . . .				1000	0	0
Cash	100	0	0			
Town Bank, Limited	385	0	0			
Stock-in-Trade	520	0	0			
James Ball				125	0	0
John Green	120	0	0			
	£1125	0	0	£1125	0	0

He made the following purchases and sales during the first week in January 1902 : Purchased from James Ball (goods), £110 ; Purchased from William Paul (goods), £48 ; Purchased from Edward Parker (goods), £15 14s. 11d. ; Purchased from John Robinson (goods), £21 5s. 6d. ; Sold to John Green (goods), £58 5s. 6d. ; Returned to William Paul (goods), £8 7s. 6d. ; Sold to Edward Parker (goods), £21 8s. 9d. ; Sold to William Peek (goods), £121 ; Sold to John Robinson (goods), £2 7s. 5d. ; Returned by William Peek (goods), £6 10s. 6d. Post the above items, opening where necessary new accounts. Balance and rule off these Ledger Accounts and bring down the Balances. Prepare a Trial Balance. (*Royal Society of Arts, Grade* I., 1903.)

Ex. 7. John Smith commenced business as a general and colonial merchant on Jan. 1, 1900. The undermentioned transactions took place during January. Pass the necessary entries through the proper books to the Ledger and extract a Trial Balance as on Jan. 31 : Jan. 1, Opened an account with his bankers by paying in £2000 ; Purchased office furniture and stationery for £110 ; Jan. 2, Purchased from Paul & Co., commission agents, 2 gross boxes of pens @ 10s. per doz. boxes net, 3 cases of 100 each cycle lamps @ £12 per doz. lamps (trade discount 25 per cent.), and 12 gross electro-plated table spoons @ 60s. per doz. spoons (less trade discount 50 per cent.). Gave Paul & Co. a three months' bill for the amount of the invoice. Consigned the whole purchase to his agent in Canada, paying shipping charges, £8 2s. 6d., and marine insurance, £3 5s. 6d. ; Jan. 4, Drew cheque for Petty Cash, £10, cashed same and opened petty cash book ; Jan. 5, Made the following cash sales of goods received on consignment from Black & Co. of Ceylon, viz., 20 chests of tea @ £4 15s. 6d. a chest, 30 packages of coffee @ 60s. a package, and 10 bags of cocoa at 30s. a bag. Received and banked the cash ; Deducting 1 per cent. Commission, sent Black & Co. cheque for balance. Jan. 8, Drew cheque for £50 for private purposes ; Jan. 12, Paid sundry trade expenses, £4 8s. 8d., from Petty Cash ; Jan. 16, Paid other trade charges, £25 ; Jan. 20, Purchased at an auction a bankrupt stock of cycles for £200, and paid for same ; Jan. 22, Sold Paul & Co. 10 cycles @ £6 each, with one month's credit ; Jan. 23, Sold Paul & Co. 12 cycles @ £6 each, with 5 per cent. cash discount, Received net cash for same ; Jan. 29, Received cash (by cable) from his Canadian Agent, £490, being proceeds of the sales of the cycle lamps and spoons consigned on the 2nd inst. (the pens remaining unsold), less £10 his commission ; Jan. 31, Paid from Petty Cash, month's salaries (trade charges) £4.

N.B.—Unless otherwise stated, all moneys received were at once paid into the Bank and all payments made by cheque.

(*Royal Society of Arts, Grade* II., 1900.)

CHAPTER IX

Ex. 1. From the following particulars prepare my Trading Account for the year ended Sept. 30, 1910. Stock, Oct. 1, 1909, £641 7s. 2d. ; Sales £4472 6s. 3d. ; Purchases £2609 7s. 4d. ; Stock, Sept. 30, 1910, £422 14s. 7d. ; Returns Outwards £47 6s. 2d.

Ex. 2. From the following particulars prepare my Trading Account for the year ended Dec. 31, 1909 : Sales on Credit £3692 4s. 7d. ; Sales for cash £964 0s. 5d. ; Purchases on credit £2002 0s. 11d. ; Purchases for cash £1724 6s. 2d. ; Stock, Jan. 1, 1909, £597 16s. 3d. ; Stock, Dec. 31, 1909, £742 16s. 4d. ; Returns Inwards £16 0s. 4d. ; Returns Outwards £14 19s. 2d.

Ex. 3. From the following particulars prepare my Trading Account for the six months ended June 30, 1910. Stock, Jan. 1, 1910, £1472 6s. 3d. ; Sales £2964 18s. 7d. ; Purchases £2507 3s. 3d. ; Returns Inwards £47 6s. 2d. ; Returns Outwards £19 0s. 7d. ; Stock, June 30, 1910, £547 6s. 9d.

Ex. 4. From the following particulars prepare the Trading Account of J. Goldsmith for the three months ended Sept. 30, 1910, making the necessary Journal entries : Stock of goods in hand, July 1, 1910, £632 13s. 2d. ; Sales for the quarter £9692 0s. 7d. ; Purchases for the quarter £6005 7s. 2d. ; Returns Outwards for the quarter £15 7s. 1d. ; Stock of goods in hand, Sept. 30, 1910, £881 7s. 3d.

Ex. 5. From the following particulars draw up the necessary Journal entries to close the various accounts and construct the Trading Account, closing off the latter by means of a further Journal entry : Stock, July 1, 1909, £4769 0s. 4d. ; Purchases £10,487 9s. 4d. ; Sales £16,042 17s. 5d. ; Returns Outwards £29 19s. 4d. ; Stock, June 30, 1910, £5964 17s. 3d.

Ex. 6. From the following particulars, extracted from the books of Marcus Oldroyd, prepare a Trading Account for the month ended Sept. 30, 1910 : Sales for cash during month £764 9s. 2d. ; Sales on Credit during month £636 0s. 4d. ; Returns Inwards £97 6s. 4d. ; Purchases for cash during month £964 0s. 2d. ; Purchases on credit during month £550 9s. 7d. ; Returns Outwards £67 0s. 4d. ; Stock, Sept. 1, 1910, £1476 4s. 2d. ; Stock, Sept. 30, 1910, £1006 17s. 5d.

Ex. 7. The following is the Trading Account of Balham Brown, a trader, as prepared by his book-keeper. The latter has evidently no proper knowledge of book-keeping, and there are several errors in the account. You are required to draw up the account correctly.

BALHAM BROWN,
Trading Account for the Year Ended
Sept. 30, 1910.

1910.		£	s.	d.	1909.		£	s.	d.
Sept. 30	To Purchases	699	0	7	Oct. 1	By Stock	220	6	2
	Add Returns				1910.				
	Inwards	14	7	0	Sept. 30	Sales			
	Add Stock @					£820 7s. 2d.			
	30–9–10	517	6	3		Less			
						Returns			
						Outwards			
						£17 0s. 3d.			
						──── = 803	6	11	
						Difference—			
						being			
						Balance of			
						Gross Profit	207	0	9
		£1230	13	10			£1230	13	10

CHAPTER X

Ex. 1. From the following particulars prepare my Profit and Loss Account for the year ended Dec. 31, 1909. Gross Profit brought from Trading Account £371 1s. 9d. ; Salaries and Wages £125 6s. ; Commissions paid £5 0s. 4d. ; Discounts allowed £17 16s. 2d. ; Rent, Rates, and Taxes £84 6s. 1d. ; General Expenses £24 19s. 9d. Show also the necessary Journal entries.

Ex. 2. From the following particulars prepare my Profit and Loss Account for the half-year ended June 30, 1910 : Gross Profit brought from Trading Account £704 6s. 3d. ; Salaries £420 ; Gas and Electricity £25 0s. 9d. ; Rent, Rates, and Taxes £167 4s. 2d. ; General Expenses £133 0s. 4d. ; Interest paid on Money borrowed £50.

Ex. 3. From the following particulars prepare the Profit and Loss Account of Andrew Jackson for the year ended Sept. 30, 1910 : Gross Profit from Trading Account £2698 4s. 7d. ; Salaries £790 ; Wages £447 6s. 3d. ; Travelling Expenses £37 0s. 9d. ; Discount on Purchases £47 8s. 5d. ; Discount on Sales £99 0s. 4d. ; Rent, Rates, and Taxes £377 19s. 7d. ; Gas and Electricity £57 3s. 9d. ; Interest paid on overdraft at Bank £17 6s. 3d. ; Dividends on Investments £37 0s. 6d. ; Printing and Stationery £157 6s. 3d. ; Insurance £9 ; General Expenses £247 6s. 3d.

Ex. 4. From the following particulars prepare the Profit and Loss Account of Hiram Grant for the year ended June 30, 1910 : Salary received £500 ; Rent, Rates, and Taxes £76 0s. 4d. ; Heating and Lighting £23 0s. 7d. ; Housekeeping expenses £208 ; Earned by coaching in evenings £26 5s. ; Interest from Investment £15 0s. 7d. ; Doctor's fees £10 10s. ; Clothing. &c. £37 3s. 3d. ; Travelling Expenses £17 17s. 9d. ; Holiday £25 ; Charity £11 5s. ; Personal expenses £63 0s. 4d. ; Servants' wages £25.

Ex. 5. From the following particulars prepare the Trading and Profit and Loss Accounts of L. Hare for the year ended June 30, 1910 : Stock, July 1, 1909, £747 6s. 3d. ; Discounts allowed £14 0s. 3d. ; salaries and wages £630 4s. 2d. ; Purchases £6329 17s. 2d. ; Returns Outwards £17 6s. 11d. ; Stationery £127 6s. 4d. ; Rent, Rates, and Taxes £490 6s. 3d. ; Returns Inwards £16 4s. 3d. ; Sales £10,040 16s. 3d. ; Postages, &c. £65 0s. 3d. ; General Expenses £170 3s. 9d. ; Discounts received £10 11s. 3d. ; Gas, &c. £65 0s. 4d. ; Stock, June 30, 1910, £590 16s. 4d.

Ex. 6. From the following particulars prepare the Trading and Profit and Loss Accounts of H. Rainbow for the six months ended Dec. 30, 1909 : Stock, July 1, 1909, £1473 6s. 2d. ; Sales £4763 9s. 8d. ; Purchases £3631 17s. ; Returns Inwards £127 0s. 9d. ; Returns Outwards £47 9s. 9d. ; Wages £322 0s. 7d. ; Salaries £207 6s. 3d. ; Postages £69 0s. 3d. ; Rent, Rates, and Taxes £473 6s. 3d. ; General Expenses £221 4s. 1d. ; Stock, Dec. 31, 1909, £807 6s. 3d.

Ex. 7. From the following Trial Balance, which has been compiled from the books of J. Melton, prepare : (a) A Trading Account for the quarter ended Sept. 30, 1910. (b) A Profit and Loss Account for the same period. (c) The Journal entries necessary for the construction of these two accounts.

	Dr.			Cr.		
	£	s.	d.	£	s.	d.
Purchases	2796	14	3			
Premises	800	0	0			
Salaries	390	4	2			
Returns Inwards . . .	17	3	3			
Sales				4003	6	3
Rent, Rates, and Taxes	63	17	3			
Sundry Debtors . . .	421	6	3			
Sundry Creditors . . .				570	6	3
Returns Outwards . . .				14	0	9
Discount (balance) . . .	22	6	3			
General Expenses . . .	121	4	7			
Stock, July 1, 1910 . . .	880	6	2			
Cash in hand	87	9	6			
J. Melton's Capital Account				1012	18	5
	£5600	11	8	£5600	11	8

Stock, Sept. 30, 1910, was valued @ £950 4s. 7d.

CHAPTER XI

Ex. 1. From the following particulars prepare the Balance Sheet of W. Shakespeare as on June 30, 1910, showing the amount of his Capital : Stock £672 3s. 3d. ; Debtors : J. Milton £33 6s. 3d., P. B. Shelley £17 6s. 2d. ; Creditors : A. Tennyson £90 0s. 4d., W. Wordsworth £16 19s. 11d. ; Premises £627 10s. 4d. ; Plant and Machinery £220 6s. 3d. ; Furniture and Fittings £79 9s. 3d. ; Loan from Bank £500 ; Cash at Bank £54 6s. 3d. ; Cash in the office £17 0s. 4d.

Ex. 2. From the following balances, which were extracted from the books of Henry Tompkins on Sept. 30, 1910, prepare (a) a Trial Balance as on that date, (b) a Trading and Profit and Loss Account for the half-year, and (c) a Balance Sheet as on Sept. 30, 1910. Cash at Bank £75 6s. 4d. ; Debtors : H. Fawcett £63 0s. 4d., Bright and Son £17 2s. 6d.; Creditors : E. Granville £57 9s. 4d., S. Spencer £39 0s. 4d. ; Purchases £2467 3s. 4d. ; Stock, April 1, 1910, £237 6s. 2d. ; Salaries and Wages £290 7s. 3d. ; General Expenses £47 17s. 2d. ; Freehold Land and Buildings £1840 ; Rates and Taxes £33 0s. 4d. ; Sales £3502 17s. 3d. ; Capital Account £1471 16s. 6d. *Note.*—Stock at Sept. 30, 1910, £307 16s. 3d.

Ex. 3. (a) Enter the following statements and transactions for Jan. 1899 into Invoice Book, Sales Book, Cash Book, and Bank Book. (b) Post into Ledger ; balance the accounts ; ascertain how much is owing to M. Self and by M. Self. (c) In Double Entry, ascertain the Gross Gain, Net Gain, Net Capital. On Jan 2, 1899, M. Self has Cash in hand £125, at Bank £875, Goods (cost price £1250), R. Spring owed him £150, he owed Summer & Co. £320. His transactions during the month were as follows : 1899. Jan 5, Sold V. Winter goods £67 10s. ; Jan. 6, Bought of Summer & Co. goods £240 ; received from R Spring, Cash £144, having allowed him Discount £6, £150 ; Jan. 9, Sold L. May goods £75 ; paid into Bank, Cash £200 ; Jan. 11, Sold R. Spring goods

£84 ; paid Summer & Co. by cheque, £304, having been allowed Discount £16, £320 ; Jan. 14, R. Spring paid into Bank £64 ; Jan. 16, Sold L. May goods £97 10s. ; Received from V. Winter, Cash £50 ; Jan. 18, Sold goods for cheque and sent it to Bank £108 ; Received from L. May, Cash £115, having allowed him as Discount £5, £120 ; Bought goods and paid by cheque £100 ; Jan. 24, Bought goods and paid in Cash £65 ; Jan. 31, Sold goods for Cash during the month £187 10s. ; Sent to Bank, Cash £300 ; Paid rent of Warehouse by cheque £45 ; Paid Trade Expenses for the Month in Cash £15 15s. ; He has goods unsold valued @ £1125.

(College of Preceptors ; Midsummer, 1899.)

Ex. 4. The firm of Brown & Collins on Jan. 2, 1900, have the following Balances from old Ledger : Cash on hand £800 ; Balance at Bank £2800 ; Port on hand £750 ; Sherry on hand £550 ; Dobson & Co. owe the firm £365 ; The firm owes W. Crediton £145.

Jan. 3, Sell to J. Derby, Port, £220 ; Sell to J. Derby, Sherry, £180 ; Jan. 6, Place in Bank, Cash, £425 ; Jan. 7, Pay weekly current expenses by Cash, £19 14s. ; Jan. 11, Sold Port to S. Cardius, £120 10s. ; Jan. 12, J. Derby forwards cash in payment of Port, £220, less Discount, £5 ; Jan. 13, Purchase Sherry for Cash, £140 ; Jan. 14, Pay weekly current expenses, £7 5s. 7d. ; Jan. 17, Forward cheque to W. Crediton, £140 ; Jan. 18, Sell Sherry to J. Doughty on Credit, £130 ; Sell Sherry to J. Doughty for Cash, £25 ; Jan. 21, Pay weekly current expenses, £12 7s. 6d. ; Jan. 23, Dobson & Co. forward to the firm £45, and their acceptance at two months for £250 ; Purchase Port from W. Crediton, £100 ; Jan. 24, Forward to J. Derby, Cash, £220 ; Jan. 25, S. Cardius pays into the Bank £80 10s. ; Jan. 28, Pay weekly current expenses, £10 12s. ; Jan. 31, Sundry small sales for Cash during month : Port, £19 7s. 9d. ; Sherry, £14 11s. 6d. ; On hand estimated : Port, £600 ; Sherry, £400.

(a) Enter the above transactions by any system of Book-keeping you have been taught, opening separate Accounts for Port and Sherry. (b) Post these entries into the Ledger. (c) Balance the Ledger. (d) Ascertain the Net Profit or Loss ; ascertain the Capital.

N.B.—No Trial Balance required.

(College of Preceptors ; Midsummer, 1900.)

Ex. 5. Enter the following set of transactions by any system of Book-keeping that you have been taught, and then post into the Ledger ; afterwards balance the Ledger. List of transactions. 1894. Sept. 1, In hand £195, At Bank £450, goods on hand £358 1s. 6d., J. Fowler's acceptance due Oct. 9, £135, Debts owing by me to J. Torrington £102, T. Dolman £78 16s. ; Sept. 2, Paid into Bank, £150 ; Sept. 3, Bought of J. Thompson, goods valued @ £67 10s. ; Sept. 4, Sold to J. Burton, goods, £47 16s. ; Sept. 5, Paid T. Dolman by cheque, £78 16s. ; Paid wages by Cash, £9 3s. ; Sept. 11, Sold goods to W. Herriot, £47 9s. 9d. ; Sept. 12, Paid wages by Cash £9 3s. ; Sept. 14, Accepted Draft of J. Torrington at one month, £102 ; Received of J. Burton his acceptance at two months, £47 16s. ; Paid into Bank for discount J. Burton's and J. Fowler's Acceptances—Discount 14s., £182 16s. ; Sept. 19, Paid wages by Cash £9 3s. ; Sept. 24, Drew Cheque on Bank £75 ; Paid S. Thompson £67 10s. ; Sept. 26, Paid wages £9 3s. ; Paid into my Account at Bank by W. Herriot £47 8s. ; Sept. 28, J. Fowler's Acceptance returned by Bank dishonoured £135 ; Paid noting charges

on above, 1*s.* 6*d.* ; Sept. 30, Received of J. Fowler amount of dishonoured bill and charges, £135 1*s.* 6*d.* ; Goods on hand, £375.

(*College of Preceptors' Certificate Examination ; Christmas,* 1894.)

Ex. 6. (*a*) Explain the difference between a " Trial Ledger Balance "
and a " Balance Sheet," and state on which side the Debit and Credit
Accounts are respectively shown in the same. (*b*) Name the four books
that are offshoots of the Journal, and in each of which Personal and
Impersonal Accounts are respectively dealt with, stating at the same
time in each case which are Debits and which are Credits. Give the
rulings of these four books. (*c*) Jones pays me £50 ; state in which
books the entry appears, and where (on the Double Entry System
that ": every debit requires a credit " and *vice versa*) such entry is
shown as a Debit and where as a Credit. Similarly in dealing with a
Bill Receivable, as also with a Bill Payable, a personal account and
an impersonal account are in each case operated upon. State which
account is in each case affected, and on which side (debit or credit).
(*d*) Explain the meaning of the expression, " Marshalling the Assets
and Liabilities," in connection with a Balance Sheet, and show the
advantage thereof. (*e*) Give the ruling of a Cash Book where all
moneys received are at once banked, and every payment is made by a
cheque. In the ruling provide for ": Discounts and Allowances,"
and for elucidation's sake head the respective columns on both sides.

(*Institute of Bankers ; Preliminary, May* 1900.)

CHAPTER XII

Ex. 1. Pass the following transactions through the proper books
(including a Bills Receivable Book to be ruled up by yourself), and
make the complete entries which are necessary to comply with the
double-entry system. 1910. Oct. 1. Received from A. Bishop
& Co. their acceptance No. 1 drawn by me in my own favour, payable
two months from to-day, at 27, Cheapside, E.C., for £150 ; Oct. 4,
Received from Geo. Thomas a Bill of Exchange, No. 2, drawn by
myself on him in my own favour, payable ten days after date at 17,
Piccadilly, Manchester, dated Oct. 4, 1910, for £300 ; Oct. 6, Received
from R. Simpson Bill No. 3, drawn by me on him in my own favour,
payable three months after date at the Bank of England, London,
dated Sept. 20, 1910, for £175 ; Oct. 7, I discounted Bill No. 3 with
my bankers, being charged £2 3*s.* 9*d.* discount ; Oct. 14, Bill No. 2,
due to-day, was paid by me into my Bank, but was returned dishonoured, the Bank charging me 2*s.* for noting expenses.

Ex. 2. Pass the following transactions through my books, in double-
entry form, including a properly ruled Bills Payable Book. All bills
are made payable at my Bankers. The total of the Bills Payable Account
is to be posted in its proper place. 1910. Oct. 2, Accepted F. Williams'
draft two months from date in his own favour, dated Oct. 2, 1910
(Bill Payable No. 46), for £200 ; Oct. 3, H. Colmer drew on me, in his
own favour, at ten days after date, dated Oct. 3, 1910, for £250, and
I accepted the same (No. 47). Oct. 7, Accepted F. Martin & Son's
draft in their own favour, dated Oct. 6, 1910, payable one month after
date (No. 48), for £1000 ; Oct. 13, Bill Payable No. 47 was paid by the
Bank.

ANSWERS TO EXERCISES AT END OF CHAPTERS

1A (Q4). Total of invoice, £11 1s. 6d.
    (Q5). Total of each side of the account, £11 1s. 6d.
1D (Q5). Amount of cheque, £65 16s. 3d.
    (Q6). R. Jones owes £11 5s. 0d.
1E (Q4). £99 13s. 4d.
    (Q5). (a) May 7, 1910.
        (b) May 5, 1910.
    (Q6). (a) £3 13s. 10d.
        (b) £2 2s. 2d.
1H (Q3). Debit Balance, £225 9s. 0d.
2B. Cash Balance, £15 7s. 8d.
2C. Cash Balance, Feb. 28, 1910, £25 8s. 6d.
2E. Bank Balance, Feb. 28, 1910, £176 0s. 8d.
2D. Bank Balance, Feb. 28, 1910, £179 17s. 0d.
2F. Balances, Feb. 28, 1910, Cash, £15 2s. 9d. ; Bank, £486 18s. 3d.
2G. { Balances, Feb. 28, 1910, Cash, £21 1s. 11d. ; Bank, £230 3s. 8d.
    { Totals of Discount Columns, Dr., £7 3s. 8d. ; Cr., £5 12s. 3d.
2H. Balance of Cash in hand, Feb. 16, 1910, £14 9s. 2d.
3A (Q4). Total of purchases, £6 19s. 6d.
    (Q5). Total of returns, £1 6s. 1d.
3B. Total purchases, £13 8s. 0d.
3C. Total of the Purchases Book, £68 8s. 6d.
3D.   ,,   ,,   ,,   £81 2s. 6d.
3E.   ,,   ,,   ,,   £57 6s. 3d.
3F.   ,,   ,,   ,,   £224 10s. 10d.
3G. Total of Returns Outwards Book, £10 0s. 0d.
3H. Total of Purchases Returns Book, £8 13s. 6d.
4A (Q3). Total of Sales, £20 12s. 0d.
4B. Total of Sales Book, £76 17s. 0d.
4C.   ,,   ,,   £83 8s. 0d.
4D.   ,,   ,,   £60 12s. 6d.
4E.   ,,   ,,   £29 10s. 1d.
4F.   ,,   ,,   £175 12s. 9d.
4G. Total of Returns Inwards Book, £8 4s. 3d.
4H. Total of the Sales Returns Book, £41 0s. 9d.
5B. Debit Balance, £67 0s. 3d.
5E. Balances : Cash, Dr. £47 5s. 0d. ; Horses, Dr. £8 0s. 3d. ; Expenses, Dr. £3 4s. 3d ; C. Wilson, Cr. £33 0s. 0d.
5F. Balances : R. Bradbury, Cr. £14 2s. 6d. ; C. Wright, Cr. £212 10s. 0d. ; Expenses, Dr. £24 5s. 0d. ; Premises, Dr.

£1015 9s. 3d. ; Cash at Bank, £434 6s. 6d. ; Cash in hand, £24 0s. 0d. ; Purchases, Total, £414 2s. 6d.

5G (Q1). Capital Account, Cr. £242 12s. 2d.

(Q2).   „   „   Cr. £1866 16s. 1d.

6B. Journal Totals, £1586 15s. 0d.

6C. Starting Capital, £290 ; Total of transactions, £950.

6D. Journal Totals, £2211 5s. 7d.

6E.   „   „   £4368s. 6d.

6F.   „   „   £157 15s. 6d.

6G. Capital Account, Dr. £1567 10s. 9d.

6H.   „   „   Cr. £3736 4s. 10d.

7B (Q5). Capital, £1462.

7C. Cash Balance, Jan. 31, £3 12s. 4d. ; Bought Book, £70 17s. 3d. ; Sales Book, £13 8s. 6d.

7D. Balances, Jan. 7, 1910 : Bank, £1084 8s. 4d. ; Cash, £18 10s. 0d. ; Purchases, £1044 0s. 0d. ; Sales, £1009 15s. 0d. ; Returns Inwards, £21 7s. 6d.

7E (Q2). Cash Balance, Dec. 31, 1905, £241 0s. 0d.

7F. Balances, Jan. 30 : Cash, £10 19s. 11d. ; Bank, £120.

7G. Starting Capital, £1570 19s. 3d. ; Balances at June 30, 1910 : Bank, £918 17s. 1d. ; Cash, £5 15s. 10d. ; Purchases, £253 7s. 0d. ; Sales, £277 4s. 0d.

7H. Balances, March 31 : Bank, £186 15s. 0d. ; Cash, £155 14s. 0d. ; Purchases Book, £41 15s. 0d. ; Sales Book, £10 8s. 0d.

8B. Trial Balance Totals, £157 10s. 0d.

8C.   „   „   £2690 16s. 0d.

8D.   „   „   £7100 0s. 0d.

8E.   „   „   £52,531 13s. 11d. ; Capital, June 1, 1909, £4778 10s. 5d.

8F. Trial Balance Totals, £7197 10s. 0d.

8G.   „   „   £861 0s. 0d.

8H.   „   „   £734 5s. 3d.

9B. Gross Profit, £2073 5s. 8d.

9C.   „   „   £100 2s. 7d.

9D. Gross Loss, £58 14s. 10d.

9E. Gross Profit, £5362 9s. 9d.

9F.   „   „   £1606 9s. 8d.

9G.   „   „   £2367 19s. 7d.

9H.   „   „   £330 10s. 3d.

10B. Net Profit, £200 1s. 9d.

10C. Net Loss, £263 18s. 7d.

10D. Net Profit, £303 14s. 1d.

10E.   „   5s. 10d.

10F. Gross Profit, £2079 10s. 7d. ; Net Profit, £385 17s. 1d.

10G.   „   „   £910 4s. 9d. ;   „   £280 14s. 1d.

10H.   „   „   £757 1s. 5d. ; Net Loss, £301 6s. 10d.

11A (Q7). Balance Sheet totals, £185.

11B (5).   „   „   £3830.

11C. Capital, £2447 5s. 2d. ; Balance Sheet totals, £3945 8s. 2d

11D (1). Trial Balance totals, £2875 11s. 9d.

 (2). Gross Profit, £415 13s. 5d. ; Net Profit, £92 16s. 9d.

 (2). Capital, £893 13s. 3d.

11ᴇ. Gross Profit, £74 2s. 0d. ; Net Profit, £33 2s. 0d.; Final Capital, £1398 2s. 0d.
11ꜰ. Gross Profit, £84 2s. 0d. ; Net Profit, £30 2s. 0d. ; Final Capital, £1207 2s. 0d.
11ɢ (Q2) Credit balance of account, £184.
(Q3). Balance, £172 7s. 8d.
(Q5). Net Profit, £215.
11ʜ (Q3). Cash Balance, £76 10s. 0d.
(Q4). Debit Balance of account, £103.
(Q5). Net Profit, £311 ; Final Capital, £1511.
12ɢ. Total of Bills Receivable Book, £1250.
12ʜ. Total of Bills Payable Book, £950.

ANSWERS TO EXAMINATION PAPERS

U. ᴏꜰ O. Lᴏᴄᴀʟ Exᴀᴍ. March 1909 : Gross profit £10,505; net profit £6280 ; final capital £16,280.
July 1909 : Balances—cash £27 11s. ; bank £371 ; trial balance totals £1855 ; net profit £149 5s. ; final capital £1349 5s.
U. ᴏꜰ C. Lᴏᴄᴀʟ Exᴀᴍ. July 1909, I : Trial balance totals £1996 11s. 11d. ; net profit £122 9s. 7d. ; final capital £1309 18s. 5d. II : Profit £208 19s. 9d.
December 17, 1909, I : Trial balance totals £2671 6s. 5d. ; net loss £47 8s. 9d. ; final capital £1889 19s. 2d. II : Taplin's cheque £8 16s. 9d.
December 18, I : Trial Balance totals £1289 3s. 7d. ; net profit £33 16s. ; final capital £729 19s. 5d.
Cᴏʟʟᴇɢᴇ ᴏꜰ Pʀᴇᴄᴇᴘᴛᴏʀs. Midsummer 1909, I : Balances—cash £371 3s. 10d. ; discounts 3s. II : Net profit £33 9s. ; final capital £336 15s. 9d. III : £87 14s. 5d.
Christmas 1909 : (A) Gain on tea £66 10s. 10d. ; loss on coffee £24 3s. 4d. ; gain on consignment £27 11s. 8d. ; net profit £36 2s. 6d.
Rᴏʏᴀʟ S. ᴏꜰ A. Exᴀᴍ. Stage I, 1908 : (iv) Balances—cash £157 0s. 1d., bank £64 8s. 11d. ; (vi) Balances—cash £68 15s., bank £405.
Stage I, 1909 : (iii) Total of invoice 7s. 11¾d. ; (iv) balance due £22 8s. ; (vi) bank balance £134 16s. 4d.
Stage I, 1910 : (3) Balance due £163 7s. 6d. ; (5) bank balance £3370 11s. 6d.; (Ex.) balances—cash £2 1s. 2d., bank £179 12s. 3d.
Tʜᴇ L. C. ᴏꜰ C. Exᴀᴍ. Junr. 1909 : (2) Balances—cash £12 ; bank £693 15s. ; (3) trial balance totals £23,185 ; gross profit £3500, net profit £1015, initial capital £4185, final capital £4500.
Junr. 1910 : (1) Trial balance totals £4952, gross profit £270, net profit £165 5s., final capital £58 10s.
Mɪᴅ. Cᴏᴜɴᴛ. U. ᴏꜰ E. Iɴsᴛ. Elem. 1908 : (Part I) Trial balance totals £5154 3s. 6d., net profit £383 1s. 8d., final capital £3383 1s. 8d.
Elem. 1910 : Trial balance totals £1190 3s. 2d., net profit £11 15s. 5d., final capital £979 13s. 7d.
Prelim. 1910 : (Part I) Trial balance totals £754 3s. 3d.

C. C. OF W. R. OF YORKS. 1st stage 1909 : (4) Trial balance totals £380 5*s*. 11*d*. ; (5) balance due from Sharp £27 8*s*. 10*d*.

Tech. School Exam. 1910 : (1) Trial balance totals £150 18*s*. 8*d*., net loss £87 10*s*. 2*d*., final capital deficit £70 15*s*. 2*d*. ; (2) balances— cash £1 11*s*. 2*d*., bank £3 11*s*. 4*d*.

LANCS. AND CHES. INST. Junr. grade 1909 : (5) Gross profit 20%, net profit 6% ; (6) net proceeds £545 3*s*. 7*d*. ; (7) trial balance totals £1945 11*s*. 6*d*. ; (8) net loss £31 16*s*. 3*d*., final capital £894 13*s*. 9*d*.

Junr. grade 1910 : (2) The banker would reckon days, and the number would be the number of days in the quarter, say, 91 + 3 = 94 ; then amount of discount £2 1*s*. 3*d*. ; (4) cash payment is better than bill by £7 12*s*. 6*d*. ; (7) trial balance totals £910 1*s*. 8*d*. ; (8) net loss £22 10*s*. 7*d*., final capital £64 12*s*. 2*d*.

N.U.T. EXAM. Elem. 1909 : (2) Total of sales book £32 2*s*. ; (3) profit £1 15*s*. 6*d*. ; (Ex.) trial balance totals £1704 1*s*. 11*d*., net profit £44 9*s*. 9*d*., final capital £1048 5*s*. 9*d*.

Elem. 1910 : (2) Capital deficit £70 ; (3) Scott must pay £28 ; (Ex.) trial balance totals £1977 19*s*. 5*d*., net loss £90 5*s*., final capital £1154.

ANSWERS TO SUPPLEMENTARY EXERCISES

Chap. I : Ex. 1 (*b*) Total of invoice, £4 10*s*. 5*d*. ; (*c*) debit balance, 11*s*. 4*d*. Ex. 2 (*c*) £15 7*s*. 9½*d*., £16 4*s*. ; (*d*) £15 19*s*. 2½*d*. Ex. 3 (*a*) (i) 26th Nov., 1910 ; (ii) 24th Nov., 1910 ; (*c*) £496 9*s*. 10*d*., £496 12*s*. 1*d*. Ex. 4 (*c*) £1 5*s*., 17*s*. 6*d*. ; (*d*) 2*s*. 5*d*., 223$\frac{1}{13}$%, 1*s*. 11*d*. Ex. 5 (*a*) £30, debit side ; (*c*) Credit balance.

Chap. II : Ex. 1, Balance, first week, 7*s*. 9*d*. ; second week, 11*s*. 11*d*. Ex. 2, Balance, £14 10*s*. Ex. 3, Balance, £300 17*s*. 8*d*. Ex. 4, Balance, £157 1*s*. 2*d*. Ex. 5, Balance, cash £8 14*s*., bank £256 12*s*. 2*d*. Ex. 6, Balance, bank £315 18*s*. 3*d*., cash £6 14*s*. 1*d*. ; discounts, Dr. £2 16*s*. 10*d*., Cr. £17 19*s*. 10*d*. Ex. 7, Balance in hand £15 3*s*. 2*d*.

Chap. III : Ex. 1, Total, £3 17*s*. 3*d*. Ex. 2, Total, £21 9*s*. 2*d*. Ex. 3, Total, £140 14*s*. 6*d*. Ex. 4, Total, £185 6*s*. 6*d*. Ex. 5, Total, £111 6*s*. 7*d*. Ex. 6, Total, £5 3*s*. Ex. 7, Total, £8 17*s*. 7½*d*.

Chap. IV : Ex. 1 (*b*) 19*s*. 4*d*. ; (*d*) Total £6 18*s*. 6*d*. Ex. 2, Total £32 14*s*. 10*d*. Ex. 3, Total £105 19*s*. Ex. 4, £4 1*s*. 5*d*. Ex. 5, £72 3*s*. 10*d*. Ex. 6, £1 5*s*. Ex. 7, £1 5*s*. 5½*d*.

Chap. V : Ex. 1, Credit balance, £8 18*s*. Ex. 4, Cash Dr. balance, £9 7*s*. ; Dogs Dr. balance, £107 8*s*. ; J. Learoyd Cr. Balance, £21 8*s*. Expenses Dr. Balance, £7 5*s*. 9*d*. Ex. 5, Bank Dr. Balance, £241 19*s*. 4*d*.; Cash Dr. Balance, £23 0*s*. 10*d*. ; G. O. Smith Cr. Balance, £25 ; S. Bloomer Cr. Balance, £304 14*s*. 6*d*. ; Purchases Book Total £529 14*s*. 6*d*. Ex. 7, £2848 16*s*. 1*d*.

Chap. VI : Ex. 6, Capital, £1824 16*s*. 6*d*. Ex. 7, Capital Debit Balance, £1083 17*s*. 1*d*.

Chap. VII : Ex. 4, Total Sales Book, £966 10*s*. 4*d*. ; Purchases Book, £707 17*s*. 6*d*. Ex. 6, Total of Trial Balance, £13,675.

Chap. VIII : Ex. 2, Correct total of Trial Balance, £3930 15*s.* Ex.
3, Total of Trial Balance, £2270. Ex. 4, Total of Trial Balance,
£9857 17*s.* 10*d.* Capital, £6189 10*s.* 9*d.* Ex. 5, Total of Trial Balance,
£2701. Ex. 6, Total of Trial Balance, £1523 2*s.* 1*d.* Ex. 7, Total of
Trial Balance, £3065 12*s.* 1*d.*

Chap. IX : Ex. 1, Gross Profit, £1691 12*s.* 6*d.* Ex. 2, Gross Profit,
£1073 16*s.* 10*d.* Ex. 3, Gross Loss, £495 9*s.* 9*d.* Ex. 4, Gross Profit,
£3950 14*s.* 7*d.* Ex. 5, Gross Profit, £6781 4*s.* 4*d.* Ex. 6, Gross Loss,
£613 13*s.* Ex. 7, Gross Profit, £420 19*s.* 11*d.*

Chap. X : Ex. 1, Net Profit, £113 13*s.* 5*d.* Ex. 2, Net Loss,
£90 19*s.* Ex. 3, Net Profit, £543 4*s.* 1*d.* Ex. 4, Net Profit, £44 8*s.* 4*d.*
Ex. 5, Gross Profit, £3555 11*s.* 10*d.* ; Net Profit, £2004 1*s.* 9*d.* Ex. 6,
Gross Profit, £64 1*s.* 2*d.* ; Net Loss, £906 15*s.* 8*d.* Ex. 7, Gross Profit,
£1273 7*s.* 11*d.* ; Net Profit, £675 15*s.* 8*d.*

Chap. XI : Ex. 1, Capital Account, £1114 7*s.* 10*d.* Ex. 2, Gross
Profit, £1106 4*s.* ; Net Profit, £734 19*s.* 3*d.* Capital Account,
£2206 15*s.* 9*d.* Ex. 3, Gross Profit, £89 10*s.* ; Net Profit, £33 15*s.* ;
Final Capital, £2113 15*s.* Ex. 4, Net Profit, £119 9*s.* 5*d.* ; Final
Capital, £5239 10*s.* 2*d.* Ex. 5, Net Profit, £7 8*s.* 3*d.* ; Final Capital,
£964 13*s.* 9*d.*

MACDONALD & EVANS'S
COMMERCIAL TEXT-BOOKS
FOR EVENING CONTINUATION CLASSES

On the Requisition List of the L.C.C.

THE ELEMENTS OF COMMERCIAL LAW. With Brief Notes
on Scots Law. By H. W. Disney, B.A. Oxon., Barrister-at-Law, Lecturer at the London School of Economics, Member of the Faculty of Laws in the University of London. Crown 8vo. 220 pp. Price 2s. 6d.

This is a very clearly written text-book of moderate compass, eminently suitable for evening schools.

The Accountants' Magazine says: "The language is simple, the style lucid; yet withal it is written in a thoroughly scientific spirit."

The Law Student's Journal says: "The learned writer of this handbook makes it clear from his preface that the book is intended for commercial students. He has accordingly not burdened his text by citing authorities, and has as far as possible avoided legal technicalities. . . . Altogether it is a very excellent handbook."

A Teacher writes as follows: "Hitherto we have used Stevens' in this college, but I am adopting your book as its style and moderate compass is much more adapted to our requirements."

MARINE INSURANCE: Its Principles and Practice. By
Frederick Templeman, Adjuster of Claims to the Alliance Assurance Co. Limited. Second Edition. Crown 8vo. 244 pp. Price 3s. 6d.

This book is thoroughly practical from start to finish; and, considering its elementary character, exhaustive. A higher point of commendation is that it is thoroughly reliable. The basis of the work is a series of lectures delivered at the instance of the London Chamber of Commerce. The lectures have been carefully revised and expanded, and the text of the Marine Insurance Act, 1906, the Rules of Practice of the Average Adjusters, and the York-Antwerp Rules, have been added.

The Shipping Gazette says: "A highly valued work."

The Economist says: "Concise, clear, and interesting."

Fairplay says: "An excellent handbook."

MODERN COMMERCIAL CORRESPONDENCE. By John
King Grebby, Examiner in Handwriting and Commercial Correspondence to the Royal Society of Arts; Private Secretary to the late Sir Courtenay Boyle, K.C.B. Second Edition. Crown 8vo. 296 pp. Price 2s 6d.

This book is no mere hash-up of old matter, usually characteristic of books of the kind, but a fresh and very helpful handbook that should go far towards making the student a thoroughly able writer of commercial letters. It is in four sections, dealing with Handwriting, Spelling, Grammatical Rules, Punctuation, Paragraphing, Use of Capital Letters, Arrangement of Business Letters, Modes of Address, Telegrams, Indexing, etc., 300 model letters relating to different trades, a very full list of abbreviations used in Commerce, foreign words and phrases, and over 50 pages explanatory of Commercial Terms and Documents, with 20 commercial documents reproduced in facsimile. It is undoubtedly the best work of its kind published.

The Schoolmaster says: "A notable book, full of good points."

MODERN BUSINESS TRAINING AND THE METHODS AND
MACHINERY OF BUSINESS. By JOHN KING GREBBY, Author of
"Modern Commercial Correspondence." Crown 8vo. Two vols.:
Elementary and Advanced. Price 2s. net per vol., or 3s. 6d.
net complete. The complete book extends to 600 pp.

A thoroughly authoritative and exhaustive work. Some idea of its
scope may be gathered from the following list of topics dealt with.

Postal Information, Replying to Advertisements, the Letter Book,
Copying and Duplicating Processes, Filing Arrangements, Correspon-
dence, Telegraphing and Cabling, Invoicing, Rendering, Checking,
Paying and Receipting Accounts, Remittances, Trade Routes, Markets,
Sale of Goods, Carriage of Goods, Exporting, Importing, Cheques,
Bills of Exchange and Promissory Notes, etc.; Drawing, Accepting,
Discounting, Bills, etc.; the Banking Account, Savings Banks, the
Bank of England, Money, the Foreign Exchanges, Life, Fire, and
other kinds of Insurance; Marine Insurance, the Stock Exchange,
Partnerships, Joint Stock Companies, Bankruptcy. The book is full
of reproductions of actual commercial documents obtained from
business firms, and the technical parts of the book have all been
written under the supervision of experts.

For Intermediate and Advanced Students

BOOK-KEEPING AND ACCOUNTS. By L. CUTHBERT
CROPPER, F.C.A., Senior Examiner to the London Chamber of
Commerce, an Examiner to the Royal Society of Arts, and late
Lecturer to the Chartered Accountants' Students' Society of
London. Crown 8vo. 750 pp. Price 3s. 6d. net.

Recommended by the Institute of Bankers

This is an exhaustive and, as might be expected, a thoroughly
authoritative treatise covering the whole subject.

The Secretary says: "The result is a book that should be of lasting value, both to
Examinees and Teachers of Book-keeping."

The Incorporated Accountants' Journal says: "The first thing that strikes us about
this book is that it deals with the subject *as it is treated in actual practice* . . . Notwithstanding the many publications on Book-keeping now on the market, Mr. Cropper's
book, which extends to some 750 pp., must be regarded as an addition to accountancy
literature, possessing distinct value to the student."

The Accountant says: "It does not often happen that a practising accountant has
had the varied experience as examiner and tutor that Mr. Cropper has before publishing
his first book. It is only to be expected that the reader should profit from this delay, and
that will certainly be the case with those who acquire Mr. Cropper's book, for throughout
it bears the impress of experience. His readers will find themselves in safe hands, and can
rest assured that they will not learn from the work methods which presently they will
have to unlearn."

The Schoolmaster says: "It is, we say at once, one of the best, if not absolutely
the best, work on the subject we have seen. . . . We strongly commend it to the notice
of all—whether teachers or students."

The Accountants' Journal says: "It is perfectly true, and no more than just, to say
that this volume should be in the possession of all students."

The Book-keepers' Magazine says: "An extremely good and valuable book."

*The Publishers will send upon application a copy of the voluminous Index,
post free, to any teacher or student.*

ELEMENTARY BOOK-KEEPING: A Text-Book for Beginners.

By L. CUTHBERT CROPPER, F.C.A., etc., Author of " Book-keeping and Accounts." Crown 8vo. 280 pp. Price 2s. net.

The publishers have no hesitation in saying that so lucid and helpful an elementary text-book on this subject has not hitherto been written. It explains the subject not as it existed twenty years ago, but as it is exemplified in the practice of the present day. There is an abundance of exercises.

THE COMPLETE POCKET BOOK-KEEPING EXERCISE BOOK.

By J. LEHMANN REES, A.S.A.A., Incorporated Accountant. 8″ × 5¼″. Price 8d.

This MS. book is on entirely different lines to any existing book, and will be found to be "just what the students want." Each book consists of six sections of 24 pp., and each section forms a complete set books, ruled as in business practice.

AN ELEMENTARY MANUAL OF STATISTICS. By A. L.

BOWLEY, M.A., Trinity College, Cambridge, Guy Silver Medallist and Vice-President of the Royal Statistical Society, 1895; Newmarch Lecturer 1897 and 1898; Reader in Statistics in the University of London. Crown 8vo, cloth. Price 5s. net.

Mr. Bowley is one of the first statisticians of the day. His "Elements of Statistics," a book that has gone through several editions, is the standard work upon the subject. But the price is high and the knowledge presumed on the part of the reader is considerable, as the book is intended for the use of post-graduates. The present work provides an introduction to the study of Statistics adapted to the requirements of beginners.

The Lancet says : " Deals in masterly style with some of the more difficult problems that perplex the beginner."

A PLAIN GUIDE TO INVESTMENT AND FINANCE. By

T. E. YOUNG, B.A., F.R.A.S., Past President of the Institute of Actuaries, Past Chairman of the Life Offices Association, late Head Actuary of the Commercial Union Assurance Co. Secon Edition. Crown 8vo. 350 pp., cloth. Price 5s.

This work will prove invaluable to all teachers of the methods and machinery of business. It deals with Trade, Commerce and Industry—Markets generally and the Money Market in particular—Bank of England—Joint Stock Banks—Bills of Exchange—Foreign Exchanges—Bill Brokers—Stock Exchange—Brokers and Jobbers—Bulls and Bears—Sympathy of Markets—Causes of the Variations in the Prices of Securities—Effect of War on the Prices of Securities—Dear and Cheap Money—Condition of Trade in its Effect on the Prices of Securities and Consols—Accrued Interest as affecting the Cost of Securities—The Return derived from an Investment—Ex Dividend and Ex Interest, Cum Dividend and Cum Interest—Sinking Funds, Speculation and

Gambling—The Phase of Commercial Crises in the Course of Trade—
and the Succession of Sun Spots—Index Numbers, etc.

LANDLORD AND TENANT: their Rights and Duties, By

ALBERT E. HOGAN, LL.D., B A., London University Law Scholar,
Law Society's Scholar in International Law, Quain Essay Prizeman, Whittuck Essay Prizeman, etc.; Solicitor, Foolscap 8vo,
cloth. 160 pp. Price 1s. 6d. net ; limp cloth, 1s. net.

A practical handbook by an able practitioner, explaining in simple
and, as far as possible, non-technical language, the relationship of landlord and tenant. It covers every point likely to arise out of the
relationship, and will prove a most useful guide both to landlords and
tenants.

HOW TO MAKE AND PROVE A WILL. By ALBERT E. HOGAN,

LL.D., B.A., Solicitor, Author of "Landlord and Tenant." Fcap.
8vo. 160 pp. Price 1s. 6d. net; limp cloth, 1s. net.

A practical guide similar in character to that of "Landlord and
Tenant," explaining fully everything that Testators, Executors,
Trustees, and Beneficiaries require to know.

A PLAIN GUIDE TO INVESTMENT. By T. E. YOUNG, B.A.,

F.R.A.S., Past President Institute of Actuaries, late Head Actuary
of the Commercial Union Assurance Co. Ltd. Crown 8vo.
110 pp. Price 1s. 6d. net.

In this little book Mr. Young gives the investor the benefit of his
long actuarial experience. It should be the constant companion of all
who have money to invest, for, as the *Post Magazine*, the leading organ
of the Insurance World, says, "No other author is better equipped to
supply real and wide knowledge." Mr. Oscar Darton, F.C.A., writer of
the articles headed "Insurance and Thrift" in the *Daily News*, has
frequently recommended the book to readers of that journal.

MACDONALD & EVANS, 4 Adam Street, Adelphi, LONDON, W.C.